Symbols and Legends in Western Art

A Museum Guide

Symbols and Legends in Western Art

A Museum Guide

E. S. Whittlesey

Charles Scribner's Sons
New York

87-106

Printed in the United States of America
Library of Congress Catalog Card Number 71–162764
SBN 684–12583–8 (trade cloth)

Introduction

This handbook was put together primarily for the viewer of Western art in the museum and art gallery. Upbringing today generally places less emphasis on a knowledge of our Judeo-Christian Bible than formerly, and less time is given in education to the wealth of legends and myths of our Classical inheritance. Yet Western art, until recent years, has been largely concerned with representations of these very legends and the symbols springing from them, enlarged upon further by the Christian church. How often the spectator is at a loss to remember why St. Anthony Abbot is shown with a pig (if he ever knew), why Daniel was put in the lion's den, why Actaeon was turned into a stag, or why Apollo and Heracles fought over a tripod. If a picture or sculpture is looked at with some knowledge of its characters, story, and symbols, the viewer, as he pursues meaning, gives the art more than a cursory glance and enjoys not only the composition and color, but the subtleties of the artist's point of view and of the period in which he executed the work. Guidebooks rarely supply this much-needed, on-the-spot information, with the notable exception of the guidesheets supplied in each room of the National Gallery in Washington, D. C. This handbook is therefore for the layman who wishes to have with him a quick explanation, or refresher, of the subject matter that he is most likely to encounter. In the short summaries, nothing is described in depth and not every legend, person, or symbol is here; but I think reward will be found in the brief material, which combines story and fact and can be rapidly read in the presence of the artist's work.

Classical myths have been told by many writers in different forms; the Romans adopted the Greek legends and borrowed the Greek gods, identifying them with their own. The legends selected here are the most popular ones and the ones most likely to be seen. Where the original source is Greek, the material is generally placed under the Greek name, with the Roman name following. Therefore Roman and Renaissance art, usually shown under the Latin name, require a cross reference to obtain the complete story. The listing is alphabetical, mingling Classical and Biblical subjects together. The events in the life of Jesus Christ are all listed under his name, with the idea that they will be better understood, so grouped. The after-life events, miracles, and parables follow under this same heading. Representations of the Virgin Mary are treated in a similar manner. Asterisks are placed after every name that has a heading of its own, facilitating consultation of the many cross references for those who are interested in enlarging on the material. The art examples given at the end of the summaries are all works in American museums and galleries, the intention being to show the variety of media used for representing scenes, and, as much as possible, the distribution of art throughout the United States. An appendix is supplied which may be of help in identifying Classical art, so often unlabeled in foreign museums. This includes *Chariots—How Drawn, Murders and Sudden Deaths, Supernatural Beings and Monsters, Heroes in Single Combat,* and *Group Combats.* A serious student will, of course, look to the many excellent source books, among which are those listed in the bibliography used for this compilation. Much pleasure has been derived from sorting out the material here; I hope some of it will be shared by those thumbing through these pages.

E.S.W.

Museums Referred to in the Text

Art Institute of Chicago, Chicago, Illinois
Atlanta Art Association Galleries, Atlanta, Georgia
Birmingham Museum of Art, Birmingham, Alabama
Cleveland Museum of Art, Cleveland, Ohio
Clowes Fund Collection, Indianapolis, Indiana
Columbia Museum of Art, Columbia, South Carolina
Crocker Art Gallery, Sacramento, California
Denver Art Museum, Denver, Colorado
Detroit Institute of Arts, Detroit, Michigan
Fogg Art Museum, Cambridge, Massachusetts
Frick Collection, New York, New York
Isaac Delgado Museum of Art, New Orleans, Louisiana
Isabella Stewart Gardner Museum, Boston, Massachusetts
M.H. De Young Memorial Museum, San Francisco, California
Metropolitan Museum of Art with Cloisters Collection, New
  York, New York
Museum of Fine Arts, Boston, Massachusetts
Museum of Fine Arts of Houston, Texas
National Gallery of Art, Washington, D.C.
Philadelphia Museum of Art, Philadelphia, Pennsylvania
Philbrook Art Center, Tulsa, Oklahoma
Pierpont Morgan Library, New York, New York
Portland Art Museum, Portland, Oregon
Seattle Art Museum, Seattle, Washington
Toledo Museum of Art, Toledo, Ohio
University of Indiana, Bloomington, Indiana
University of Kansas, Lawrence, Kansas
Virginia Museum of Fine Arts, Charleston, Virginia
Walters Art Gallery, Baltimore, Maryland
William Rockhill Nelson Gallery of Art, Kansas City, Missouri
Worcester Museum of Art, Worcester, Massachusetts
Yale University Art Gallery, New Haven, Connecticut

Bibliography

Attwater, Donald, *The Penguin Dictionary of Saints*
Penguin Books, Middlesex, England, and Baltimore, Maryland, 1965

Avery, B. Catherine (editor), *New Century Classical Handbook*
Appleton-Century-Crofts, New York, 1962

Brewer's Dictionary of Phrase and Fable (Revised and Enlarged)
Harper and Bros., New York (no date given)

Buttrick, George Arthur, *Interpreters Dictionary of the Bible*
Abingdon Press, New York, 1962

Demetrakopoulos, George H., *Dictionary of Orthodox Theology*
Philosophical Library Inc., New York, 1964

Ferguson, George, *Signs and Symbols in Christian Art*
Oxford University Press, New York, 1954

Graves, Robert, *The Greek Myths*
Penguin Books, Baltimore, Maryland, 1955

Hervieux, Jacques, *The New Testament Apocrypha* (trans. Dom Wulstan Hibberd)
Hawthorn Books, Publishers, New York, 1960

Miller, M. S. & J. L., *Harper's Bible Dictionary*
Harper and Row, New York, 1952

Rachleff, Owen S., *Great Bible Stories and Master Paintings*
Abradale Press, New York, 1968

Reau, Louis, *Iconographie de L'Art Chretien*
Presses Universitaires de France, Paris, 1956

Seyffert, Oskar, *Dictionary of Classical Antiquities* (Revised and Edited by Henry Nettleship and J. E. Sandys, 1894)
Meridian Books, New York, 1956

Tarbell, F. B., *A History of Greek Art*
Macmillan Company, New York, 1905

Tatlock, Jessie, *Greek and Roman Mythology*
Appleton-Century-Crofts, New York, 1917

Williams, Albert N., *Key Words of the Bible*
Duell, Sloan and Pearce, New York, 1956

Symbols and Legends in Western Art

A Museum Guide

Aaron (ar'un)   In the Old Testament, the elder brother of Moses*, and his co-leader during the Exodus*. He was commended by God for his eloquence, and became the first head of the Hebrew priesthood. During the absence of Moses in the wilderness, he weakened, and driven on by the impatient Jews, he fashioned a false god of deliverance in the form of a golden calf, made from his followers' jewelry. When Moses descended from Mount Sinai, he found the people worshipping the calf. He was so enraged he broke the tablets of the Ten Commandments*, given to him by God. Then he burned the calf, ground it to powder, mixed it with water, and made the worshippers drink it. Aaron served the priesthood forty years, and was buried at an advanced age at Mt. Hor, during the trek to Canaan. Painting: *Worship of the Golden Calf*, Tintoretto, National Gallery, Washington.

Aaron's Rod   Each tribe of Israel had a rod. At the Lord's command, Moses ordered each of the twelve tribes of Israel to bring a rod to the Tabernacle*. When the rods were left in front of the ark*, Aaron's rod budded miraculously and bore almonds (Numbers 17:5-11). This was interpreted as evidence of God's choice of the one who should exercise priestly office. Aaron used his blessed rod in Egypt to effect plagues and again in crossing the Red Sea. When he came with Moses before the Pharaoh*, asking that the people of Israel be allowed to leave Egypt, Aaron threw his rod upon the ground and it turned into a serpent. The Pharaoh's magicians changed their staffs into serpents also, but Aaron's serpent ate all those of the magicians. Painting: *Moses before the Pharaoh*, Felix Chretien, Metropolitan, New York.

1

Abel (ā'bel) In the Old Testament, the second son of Adam*
and Eve*. He was the brother of Cain*, who slew him out of
jealousy because God favored Abel's gift of sheep over his own
gift of agricultural fruits. It is not clear whether Abel's gift of
blood was more acceptable because it symbolized the essence of
life, or because it was offered with more sincerity, but this first
"murder" probably epitomizes the struggle between cultivator
and herdsman in early society (Genesis 4:2-8). A stone capital
from the church of Moutiers-Saint Jean shows *Cain and Abel's
Sacrifices to the Lord*, Fogg Museum, Cambridge, Massachusetts.

Abigail (ab'i-gail) In the Old Testament, the wife of Nabal,
"the fool," a rich landowner of Maon. She saved her husband
from the hot-tempered young David*, who was angry with Nabal
for his refusal to pay tribute for the protection of his flocks. The
beautiful Abigail, accompanied by a convoy of asses, brought
food to David, as appeasement. When the apoplectic Nabal died
shortly afterward, David took Abigail for his wife (1 Samuel
25:2-42). Painting: *Abigail*, Rubens, Detroit Art Institute.

Abimelech (a-bim'e-lek) The king of Gerar, a Philistine* city-
state. He made covenants with Abraham* and his son Isaac*, and
had difficulty with their wives.

Abraham (ā'bra-ham) or Abram In the Old Testament, a
founder of the Hebrew people, in early life called Abram. He was
brought up under a polytheist religion, and had revealed to him
by God a concept of religion far ahead of his people and times,
establishing the basis of monotheism. As a young man, Abraham
married his half-sister Sara, later called Sarah*, and then moved
from Ur to Haran. He was driven by famine to Egypt and was
accompanied by his nephew Lot*. In Egypt he insisted that his
beautiful wife be known only as his sister, fearing if the Pharaoh
coveted her, her husband might be slain. The Pharaoh* took
Sarah into his house and treated Abraham well, but God, in
disapproval, sent a plague upon Egypt. When Sarah's marriage
status was discovered by the Pharaoh, he was disturbed and sent
Abraham and his family back to Canaan. (This incident is repeated again at the court of King Abimelech, both by Abraham
and his son Isaac*. Where Sarah was concerned, the Lord intervened by sending a dream to King Abimelech which told him that
Abraham was a prophet of God who would pray for him, and
Sarah was not touched.) Abraham settled in Mamre and Lot
moved to Sodom* where there was more room for his flocks.
When Lot was made a prisoner in the wars of the Sodom chieftains, Abraham rescued him. Sarah, who had always been barren,
gave her Egyptian maid Hagar* to Abraham for a wife, hoping to

*Early
years*

*Move to
Egypt and
Sarah's
marriage
position*

*Return to
Mamre*

claim a child of theirs as an heir. When Hagar bore Ishmael* to *Hagar's* Abraham, the child became a source of jealousy between the two *child* women, and Sarah dealt harshly with Hagar. Still the Lord blessed Abraham in all things, and one day the Lord appeared to him with two companions, usually represented as angels. A feast was *Visit of* prepared in Abraham's tent and the Lord disclosed that Sarah *angels* would bear a son for their old age. When his words were fulfilled and the child Isaac was born, the jealousy between Hagar and *Birth of* Sarah was renewed. Abraham then banished Hagar and the boy *Isaac* Ishmael, reassured by the knowledge that God had promised *Hagar* greatness to all his descendants. Now God decided to put *banished* Abraham's faith to a final test, and he asked him to sacrifice his son Isaac, as a burnt offering. Abraham prepared to carry out the command, saddled an ass, cut wood, took his knife, and went *Sacrifice* with Isaac to the place of sacrifice. The Lord, witnessing this *of Isaac* supreme gesture, sent his archangel Michael* with a ram for the burnt offering, in place of Isaac, and Abraham was blessed again. When Sarah died at the age of one hundred and twenty-seven, *Sarah's* Abraham bought a cave for her resting place at Machpelah. Isaac, *death* still living at home at the age of forty, was unmarried. So Abraham took his servant Eliezer aside and asked him to seek a wife for Isaac among their kinsfolk in the Mesopotamian country. Eliezer swore to do this by placing his hand under Abraham's thigh. The trip was successful and Rebekah* was found for Isaac. *A wife for* In the last years of his life, Abraham took another wife who bore *Isaac* him six children, but he left all that he had to Isaac. He was buried next to Sarah, by Isaac and Ishmael, at the age of one *Burial of* hundred and seventy-five, in the cave at Machpelah (Genesis *Abraham* 12:1—25:10). In art, Abraham is represented as a patriarch with a full beard, usually as an older man, sometimes carrying a knife, alluding to the sacrifice of Isaac. Painting: *Abraham Entertaining the Angels*, School of Messina, Denver Art Museum.

Absalom (ab'sal-om)   In the Old Testament, the third son of King David*, noted for his physical beauty, especially his abundant hair. When he murdered his half-brother Amnon for raping their sister Tamar, he was forced to flee from Jerusalem. Three years later, King David welcomed him back to the city, but Absalom stirred up a rebellion, which was ultimately fatal to himself. While trying to escape in battle, his long hair caught in the branches of a tree, and Joab*, commander in chief of his father's army, came upon him and killed him. King David lamented this son greatly, crying in his grief, "Would God I had died for thee, O Absalom, my son, my son!"

Acacia   In Christian iconography, a symbol of friendship and the immortality of the soul.

3

Achelous (ak-el-ō'us) In Greek legend, the river god who could assume the forms of a man with a bull's head, a speckled serpent, or a bull. Heracles* wrestled with him when they were both wooing Deianira*, and succeeded in vanquishing him in all three forms. One of his horns, broken off in battle, became the cornucopia*, or horn of plenty. Painting: *The Feast of Achelous*, Rubens, Metropolitan, New York.

Achilles (a-kil'ēz) In Greek legend, the greatest hero of the war against Troy, described in Homer's epic poem, The Iliad. He was a son of Peleus* and the goddess Thetis* and a descendant of the god Zeus* through his grandfather Aeacus*. His goddess mother, hearing a prophecy that her baby would die at Troy, endeavored to make him immortal by bathing him in the river Styx* (or by
Vulnerable burning away his mortality in fire), but she held him by the heel,
Heel and this spot remained vulnerable. His education was entrusted to the centaur Chiron*, from whom he learned the arts of hunting, music, and healing. When the Trojan war expedition was being
Disguise organized, Thetis quickly disguised Achilles as a girl and hid him
at Scyros among the daughters of King Lycomedes at Scyros. During his sojourn at the court he fell in love with the king's daughter Deidamia* and they had a son Neoptolemus*. But the wily Odysseus* was sent to find Achilles, and came to Scyros, disguised as a pedlar. He uncovered Achilles among the girls of the court when Achilles picked out a sword from his merchandise rather than feminine ornaments. Odysseus then persuaded Achilles to join the Greek forces. Achilles is represented as the swiftest, bravest, and handsomest of the Greeks, the mere sight of whom struck terror in the hearts of the enemy. He was also
Trojan War arrogant and relentless. In the last year of the siege of Troy, he quarreled with King Agamemnon* over the possession of the captive girl Briseis*, and refused to take further part in the war.
Deaths of When his great friend Patroclus* was killed, however, by the
Patroclus Trojan hero Hector*, he rushed to avenge the death, slew Hector,
and and shamefully dragged his body around the walls of Troy. When
Hector Hector's father, King Priam*, came to Achilles secretly at night to ransom his son's body with gifts, Achilles gallantly returned the
Priam's body, and granted eleven days' truce for the funeral games.
Visit Before Troy fell to the Greeks, Achilles was slain by Hector's brother Paris*, the abductor of Helen and the cause of the Trojan
Death war. The arrow directed by Paris struck Achilles on his vulnerable heel. There are many scenes of Achilles on Greek pottery. Painting: *Achilles at the Court of Scyros*, Nicolas Poussin, Museum of Fine Arts, Boston.

Actaeon (ak-tē'on or ak'teon) In Greek mythology, a huntsman who inadvertently surprised Artemis*, while she was bathing with her nymphs at a spring. Incensed by the intrusion, Artemis splashed water in his face and so transformed him into a stag. Actaeon fled, but his own hounds picked up the stag scent, chased, overtook him, and tore him to pieces. There is a Greek red-figured vase-painting (5th century B.C.), *Death of Actaeon*, by the Pan Painter, Museum of Fine Arts, Boston.

Adam   In the Old Testament, the first man, created in the image of God. He lived in the Garden of Eden*, and Eve* was created for him by God out of his rib, later to become the mother of his children Cain*, Abel*, and Seth. When Adam disobeyed God's command to refrain from eating the fruit of the tree of the knowledge of good and evil, he was expelled from the garden with Eve, and was compelled to till the ground from which he was taken (Genesis 1, 2). Painting: *Adam and Eve*, Jan van Scorel, Metropolitan, New York.

Admetus   See Alcestis.

Adonis (a-dō′nis or a-do′nis)   In Greek mythology, the son of the incestuous union of Myrrha* with her father Cinyrus. The discovery of this sin forced Myrrha to flee, and she was trans-

Venus and Adonis. Titian. The Metropolitan Museum of Art, the Jules S. Bache Collection.

formed into a myrrh tree. The tree split open for the birth of Adonis. He was brought up by nymphs and grew to be a man of surpassing beauty. Both the goddesses Aphrodite* and Persephone* vied for his love, but Aphrodite, with her magic girdle of love, monopolized most of his time. Adonis was a lover of the chase. When he was killed by a wild boar, Aphrodite was inconsolable and persuaded the god Zeus to arrange for him to live in the upperworld six months of the year. The red anemone is said to have sprung from his blood, the blossom flourishing briefly. The death and resurrection of Adonis, the Adonia, was celebrated in the ancient world in midsummer. The legend and cult is thought to have come from Asia Minor to Greece, typifying the withering of nature and its renewal. Painting: *Venus and Adonis*, Rubens, Metropolitan, New York.

Adoration of the Magi or Wise Men　See Jesus Christ—Life Events.

Adoration of the Shepherds　See Jesus Christ—Life Events.

Adrastus (a-dras'tus)　In Greek legend, a king of Argos, the only hero to survive the war of the Seven Against Thebes*. Adrastus escaped on the winged horse Arion, which had been given to him by Heracles*. Ten years later, Adrastus and the sons of the Seven, [called] the Epigoni*, fought a war to avenge their fathers. This time they took Thebes, but Aegialeus, son of Adrastus, was killed in the attack. Adrastus died of grief on the way home to Argos.

Aeacus (ē'a-kus)　A son of the god Zeus* by Aegina, on whose island of the same name he was king. When the island was beset by famine and plague, the inhabitants all died. Zeus, answering the prayers of Aeacus, transformed the ants on the island into citizens, thereafter known as Myrmidons (ants). Aeacus was known for his justice, and after his death, he was made a judge of the lower world. His sons, by Endeis, were Telamon and Peleus*, in turn, fathers of Ajax* and Achilles*.

Aeetes (ē-ē'tez)　In Greek mythology, the king of Aea in Colchis, brother of Circe*, Pasiphae*, and Perses, the father of Medea* and Apsyrtus. The Golden Fleece* was hidden in his kingdom (see Jason and Medea).

Aegaeon　See Briareus.

Aegeus (ē'jē-us or ē'joos)　In Greek mythology, king of Athens, best known as the devoted father of the famous hero Theseus*, who was his first-born, but illegitimate, son by Aethra of

Troezen. Aegeus did not see Theseus until, in young manhood, he came to his court, wearing the sandals and sword which Aegeus had left hidden as tokens for Theseus to find under a rock when he was grown. Aegeus was married at this time to the sorceress Medea*, and she had borne him another son Medeus. With the arrival of Theseus, unrecognized by his father, Medea realized he was a threat to her own son's succession, and tried to poison him with a cup of wine. Aegeus recognized Theseus by the sword and sandals just in time, and dashed the poisoned wine to the ground. Medea then fled mysteriously in a serpent-drawn chariot with Medeus. Every nine years King Aegeus was obliged to send fourteen Athenian maidens and youths as tribute to King Minos* of Crete, because Androgeus, son of Minos, had been ambushed and slain in Greece. These unfortunate young people were thrown to the Minotaur*, a monster, half-human, half-bull, which lived in a labyrinth* at the city of Knossos. Theseus, against his father's pleas, insisted on joining the expedition with the purpose of slaying the Minotaur. He promised his father that if he succeeded he would replace the ship's black sail of mourning with a white sail on the homeward voyage. This he forgot to do, and Aegeus, who was watching for the boat, hurled himself into the sea, which henceforth was called after him, the Aegean.

Aegis (ē'jis)   In Greek legend, the shield or breastplate of the god Zeus*; it was made by the god Hephaestus* and was covered with the hide of the goat Amalthea*, which had nursed the infant Zeus. It was often lent to the goddess Athena*, the daughter of Zeus, and is most frequently seen borne by her, its center decorated with the head of the snaky-locked Medusa*, which was given to Athena by Perseus*. In early legend, the aegis was a pelt that was shaken at the enemy to dazzle him. It was also occasionally worn by Apollo*, but in art it is usually seen on Athena.

Aegisthus (ē-jis'thus)   In Greek legend, the son of Thyestes* and Pelopia*, who was Thyestes' own daughter. Pelopia was ravished by her father at night, without her knowing who he was. Soon she married Atreus*, the brother of Thyestes, and when the illegitimate child Aegisthus was born, put him out to die. Atreus rescued him, however, and brought him up as his own son. Later, when Thyestes revealed that he was the actual father of Aegisthus, Pelopia killed herself with his sword. Aegisthus was persuaded by his father to kill Atreus, so that Thyestes might take the throne, but his cousin Agamemnon*, son of Atreus, forced Thyestes into exile. When Agamemnon went off to the Trojan war, Aegisthus became the paramour of Agamemnon's wife Clytemnestra*. He helped her kill Agamemnon upon his return from Troy, ten years later. He then ruled with Clytemnestra for seven years until Orestes*, son of Agamemnon and Clytemnestra, killed both Aegisthus and his mother, thus avenging his father's murder (see Atreus).

Aeneas (ē-nē′as) In classical mythology, the son of the goddess Aphrodite* and Anchises, king of Dardanus. According to Homer, Aeneas joined the Trojan cause in the ninth year of the war against the Greeks, because Achilles, at this time, made a raid on his cattle. Aeneas fought with great valor and skill, protected by the gods, since he was destined, after the sack of Troy, to found a new home for the Trojan race in Italy. When Troy fell, Aeneas escaped, carrying his old father Anchises on his shoulders from the burning flames of the city. Aided by the goddess Aphrodite, he fled with his family and a few followers, carrying the sacred images of Troy to Mt. Ida. From there he roamed many years, as described by the Roman poet Vergil in his epic, The Aeneid, and founded the colony the Romans claimed as their origin (see Dido). The Metropolitan, New York, has an enamel by the Master of the Aeneid, *Aeneas Sights Italy.*

Aeolus (ē′ō-lus) In Greek mythology, the guardian of the winds, entrusted with their control by the gods. The winds were kept on a small island, locked behind high cliffs, and were released through a hole that Aeolus had pierced with a spear. When he stopped up the hole, the winds were shut off. Aeolus gave Odysseus* a skin in which all the winds were confined on his homeward journey from Troy. This speeded his way to Ithaca, but as he approached its shores, his comrades unfortunately opened the bag, thinking it held treasure. The wind escaped, and they were blown out to sea again.

Aeschylus (525-456 B.C.) The first great writer of Greek tragic drama. He wrote approximately ninety plays, seven of which are now extant. Legend tells that he was killed when a tortoise was dropped by an eagle on his bald head.

Aesculapius (es-kū-lā′pi-us) See Asclepius.

Aethra (ēth′ra) In Greek legend, the daughter of King Pittheus of Troezen, and mother, by Aegeus*, of Theseus.

Agamemnon (a-ga-mem′non) In Greek legend, the king of Mycenae, son of Atreus*, brother of Menelaus*, husband of Clytemnestra*, and father of Orestes*, Electra*, Iphigenia*, and Chrysothemis*. After the murder of his father by his step-brother (and cousin) Aegisthus*, he came to the throne with the help of

Aeneas and his followers received by King Latinus as they seek land for their new city in Italy. Courtesy of the Newark Public Library.

Tyndareus, king of Sparta, and father of Clytemnestra, whom he married. When Paris*, son of King Priam* of Troy, abducted Helen*, the wife of his brother Menelaus, Agamemnon organized an expedition against Troy. Great storms arose as the Greek fleet assembled at Aulis, caused by Artemis*, because of the slaying of one of her sacred stags by Agamemnon. Under great pressure from the members of the expedition, Agamemnon followed the advice of the soothsayer Calchas and sacrificed his daughter Iphigenia to appease the goddess. The winds died instantly, and the fleet sailed to wage the war against Troy, which lasted ten years. When the city finally fell, Agamemnon returned home, bringing Priam's daughter Cassandra* as a hostage. Clytemnestra pretended to give Agamemnon a magnificent welcome, but as he stepped from his bath, she murdered him with the help of her lover Aegisthus, revenging the sacrifice of their daughter Iphigenia. Cassandra, potentially a rival wife, was also murdered (see Briseis).

St. Agatha   A 3rd-century Christian martyr, a girl of noble family, who was tortured during the Decian persecution* of 251 at Catania, Sicily. Legend tells that she was pursued by Quintian, a man of consular rank whom she rejected. He proceeded against her as a Christian, and tried, in vain, to have her corrupted. She was tortured in many ways. An earthquake saved her from fire, her breasts are said to have been cut off, and St. Peter is said to have appeared to her in a vision and healed her wounds. After her death, the volcano of Mt. Aetna erupted over Catania. The citizens advanced toward the lava carrying St. Agatha's veil on a spear. The lava flow was miraculously arrested, and many converts to Christianity were made. In art, she is usually shown carrying her breasts on a dish. The resemblance of breasts to bells led to the adoption of Agatha as patron of bell-founders; their resemblance to loaves of bread led to blessing bread on her feast day, February 5.

Aglaia (ā-glā'ia)   The youngest of the Greek Charites* or Graces. Some legends say she was the wife of the god Hephaestus*.

St. Agnes   A Christian martyr during the Diocletian persecution*. She was killed about 303 at the age of thirteen, having refused marriage in order that she might dedicate herself to God. She was placed naked in a house of prostitution by the father of her young suitor, but as she prayed, her hair grew and covered her body. She was tied to a stake and the fire went out; a soldier then drew his sword and stabbed her in the throat. She is the patron of young virgins and chastity. She is shown with a lamb* in art, because she declared herself to be the bride of Christ. She may be enveloped in her long hair. Feast day: January 21. St. Agnes is seen in a painting: *The Death of St. Claire*, the Master of Heiligenkreuz, National Gallery, Washington.

Agony in the Garden   See Jesus Christ—Life Events.

Ahab (ā′hab)   In the Old Testament, a king of Israel about 875 B.C. He married Jezebel, a princess of Sidon and a Baal (pagan god) worshipper. She converted Ahab to her less demanding religion, and tried to force the whole nation to conform. The prophet Elijah* foresaw the disintegration of Ahab and predicted his doom (1 Kings 17:1). Ahab was fatally wounded between the plates of his armor, standing in his chariot during the battle of Ramoth-gilead.

Ahasuerus (a-has-ū-ē′rus)   The Hebrew form of Xerxes, used in the Old Testament. He was the husband of Esther*.

Ajax (ā′jaks)   In Greek legend, son of Telamon of Salamis, a man of great height, who became king of Megara and who, next to Achilles*, was the most famous Greek fighter of the Trojan war. When he was born, Heracles* covered him with his lion skin, making the baby invulnerable except for his armpits and neck. When the Trojan hero Hector* challenged a Greek to engage in single combat to decide the outcome of the war, Ajax was the warrior to accept. The two men fought all day, neither gaining the advantage, and they were so impressed with each other's prowess, they exchanged gifts, Hector receiving Ajax's belt and A-jax Hector's sword. With Odysseus*, Ajax went to Scyros to fetch Achilles to the war. Ajax defended the fallen body of Patroclus*, and was the rescuer of the dead body of Achilles on the battle-field. When Achilles' armor was awarded to Odysseus instead of himself, Ajax went mad with jealousy. He slaughtered innocent cattle in his frenzy, and when he came to his senses, was so humiliated, he abandoned his devoted wife Tecmessa, his young son Eurysaces, and fell on the sword that Hector had given him. Out of his blood sprang the purple lily on whose petals are traced the first letter of his name, *A*. He was buried on Cape Rhoeteum, and Achilles' arms, lost at sea in a storm on their way back to Greece, were washed up onto his grave. Ajax and Hector are frequently illustrated in combat on Greek pottery.

Alb   In Christian ritual, a white robe symbolizing chastity and purity, sometimes with embroidery on it symbolizing the five wounds of Christ from the crucifixion*. It was the robe in which Christ was clothed by Herod's* soldiers when they mocked him in the praetorium, headquarters of the guards (Mark 15:16-17).

11

St. Alban Like· many other Christian saints, Alban is shown in art carrying his head in his hands to show that he was beheaded. He is venerated as the first martyr of Britain. A Roman-Britain, he gave shelter to a fleeing Christian during the Diocletian persecutions*, and was arrested and put to death himself. The Abbey of St. Alban rose on the site. Alban's attributes are a sword, crown, and cross. Martyred in 303, his feast day is June 22.

Alcestis (al-ses'tis) In Greek mythology, the daughter of Pelias and wife of Admetus. Admetus was promised by the goddess Artemis* that he would be spared death, if someone would die in his place when death came for him. At the appointed time, Alcestis devotedly gave herself in his stead. Heracles*, learning of her sacrifice, went to the underworld, wrestled with death, and restored her to Admetus.

Alcinous (al-sin'ō-us) In Homeric legend, the king of the Phaeacians and father of Nausicaa*. When Odysseus* landed on the king's shores, Alcinous wanted to keep him as a son-in-law, but did not hold him against his will. Instead, he sent him to Ithaca on one of his own ships, laden with many gifts.

Alcmene (alk-mē'nē) In Greek mythology, a grandchild of Perseus*, the wife of Amphitryon*, and the mother of Heracles*. While Amphitryon was away at war, avenging the deaths of her eight brothers, the god Zeus* visited her one night, disguised as her husband. In due time, she bore twins, one of which was Heracles, the son of Zeus, the other, Iphicles*, the son of Amphitryon. Alcmene learned from the seer Tiresias* that Heracles had been fathered by Zeus. Fearing the goddess Hera's* jealousy, she abandoned the child, but the goddess Athena* picked him up and persuaded Hera to nurse him. Heracles suckled with such force Hera plucked him violently from her breast, and milk spurted across the sky and became the milky way. Then Athena returned the child, now immortal, to Alcmene. Alcmene outlived Heracles and became the protectress of his children.

Alexander the Great (356-323 B.C.) The son of the Macedonian ruler Philip II and Princess Olympias, born at Pella. He was the conqueror of all the civilized world known to the Greeks in the 4th century B.C., one of the greatest generals of all time, and one of the most powerful personalities of antiquity. His conquests, with the spread of Hellenism, made profound changes in the history of the world. Alexander passed early into legend. His youthful prowess is told in the story of how he broke his father's unmountable horse Bucephalus*. He had observed that the horse was terrified of its own shadow. Alexander faced the horse into the sun, won its confidence, and then leaped on its back. From then on, the horse was his mount. Among his many spectacular feats he is said to have cut the Gordian Knot*. In art, he is shown on many coins as a handsome, clean-shaven young man with classic Greek features and waving hair. Painting: *The Triumph of Alexander*, Pinturicchio, Metropolitan, New York.

St. Alexis   A fifth-century saint, a hermit called "the man of God," a nameless man who lived by begging, and who shared the alms he received with other poor people. After his death in Mesopotamia, it was learned that he was the son of a Roman patrician, and it was said that he left a wealthy bride on his wedding day and had gone to live in poverty in Syria. One narrative claimed that he returned to his father's house seventeen years later and served him as an unrecognized servant. His legend was popular in the Middle Ages, and he became the patron of hermits. In art, he is represented with a staff, sometimes he lies extended on a mat with a letter in his hand, dying. Feast day: July 17.

Alfred the Great   A 9th-century king of Wessex, England, and leader of the opposition to the invading Danish armies. He was surprised and defeated at Chippenham in 878 and withdrew to Athelney, with the remains of his forces, to continue the resistance. Legend tells that he went into a cave for shelter, and broke a spider's web, which was stretched across the entrance. As he lay on the ground, much discouraged, he saw the spider reweaving all the damage his entrance had made. Spurred on by this example, he decided to renew his efforts. Another legend tells that when he reached Athelney he took refuge in a peasant's hut. The housewife, not recognizing him in his muddy attire, told him to watch her cakes baking in the fire. Alfred was so absorbed with his problems he let the cakes burn and got a good scolding from the housewife for being such a useless wretch. After Alfred's final victory, a monastery was built at Athelney to commemorate his resistance.

All Saints Day   A holiday in the Christian church, celebrated on November 1, on which all saints of the church are commemorated collectively.

All-Seeing Eye   The eye of God, shown by itself frequently in Greek Orthodox Byzantine mosaics.

Almond   A symbol of divine approval, in reference to the episode in the Old Testament when Aaron* was chosen as a priest of God. "And behold, the rod of Aaron . . . brought forth buds and bloomed blossoms, and yielded almonds." It is sometimes shown with the Virgin Mary* in allusion to Joseph's* almond rod which blossomed when he sought her hand in marriage (see Mandorla).

Alpha and Omega The first and last letters of the Greek alphabet. In Revelation (1:8), God says: "I am the Alpha and Omega, the beginning and the ending," symbolizing that He is eternal.

Alpheus (al-fē'us) In Greek legend, a river god, sometimes known as a hunter. He found Artemis* and her nymphs irresistible and tried to seize the goddess during her revels with her nymphs. Artemis daubed her face and those of her attendants with white clay, rendering herself indistinguishable from the others. On another occasion, Alpheus embraced the nymph Arethusa while she was bathing. Arethusa fled to Ortygia in Sicily, where Artemis turned her into a fountain. Alpheus pursued her under the sea, and rising into the fountain became one with her. The myth is derived from the fact that the Alpheus river flows underground for a space. Heracles*, for his 6th labor for Eurystheus, turned the course of the river Alpheus through the stables of Augeas in order to clean them. There is a 16th-century sculpture of *Alpheus and Arethusa* by Battista Lorenzi, Metropolitan, New York.

Alphaeus See Cleophas.

Althaea (al-thē'a) In Greek legend, the wife of Oeneus*, king of Calydon, and mother of Meleager*. At Meleager's birth, the Fates* prophesied that he would die when the brand of wood, then burning on the fire, was consumed. Althaea seized the brand and kept it aside for many years. Meleager was the leader for his father in the Calydonian boar hunt*. He awarded the boar's hide to the huntress Atalanta* for shooting the first arrow into the animal's side. When his uncles objected to this award a quarrel ensued, and Meleager slew them in sudden fury. Althaea, distraught by the death of her brothers, fetched the brand of wood and hurled it into the fire. In a few moments, it had burned away and, as foretold, Meleager died. Overcome by this violation of her maternal role, Althaea hanged herself.

Amalthea (a-mal-thē'a) In Greek mythology, a goat, or goat-nymph, which suckled the newborn god Zeus* during his upbringing by nymphs in a cave in Crete, while bees brought him honey. Zeus borrowed one of her horns, which resembled a cow's, and it became the famous horn of plenty*, which is always filled with whatever food or drink its owner may desire. When

Zeus became Lord of the Universe, he set Amalthea's image among the stars, as Capricorn. The Aegis* of Zeus and Athena* was also said to be covered with Amalthea's skin.

Amazons (am-a-zonz)   In Greek legend, a race of female warriors from the Caucasus mountains, who later moved to Scythia. They excluded men from their nation and were governed by a

Wounded Amazon. Roman copy of a Greek work, 440-430 B.C. The Metropolitan Museum of Art, gift of John D. Rockefeller, Jr.

queen. Girls had their right breasts cut off, that they might better draw a bow; male children were either killed or sent to their fathers for upbringing in a neighboring state. The Amazons spent their time hunting and fighting, and had many encounters with the Greeks. Bellerophon* attached them from the air on his winged horse. Heracles*, as his ninth labor, came to their land to fetch Queen Hippolyta's* girdle. Through misunderstanding, he killed and took many of them prisoners. Theseus* carried off Antiope* who was Hippolyta's sister, and she became the mother of his son Hippolytus*. The Amazons attacked Athens after this rape, but were defeated by the Greeks. Amazon Queen Penthesilea* was killed fighting for the Trojans against the Greeks. War between the Greeks and Amazons was often represented in Greek art. The Amazons were shown as martial maidens, often riding horses, usually in short tunics, the right arm bare, and armed with shields or spears. There is a Roman marble copy of a Greek statue (4th century B.C.) of a *Wounded Amazon*, Metropolitan, New York.

St. Ambrose Bishop of Milan, Italy, in the last half of the 4th century. He was a lawyer and governor, but when trying to settle a dispute over the election of a bishop, he himself was acclaimed for the office by the people of Milan. One legend says that a child's voice was heard in the crowd saying, "Ambrose is bishop." He unwillingly accepted the honor, but dealt well with many church problems. He was the first teacher in the West to make extensive use of hymns as a popular means of divine praise. His emblems are a beehive in allusion to the legend that a swarm of bees settled on his mouth when he was a baby in his cradle, indicating eloquence, and a lash to indicate the Arians (heretic Christians) he had expelled from Italy; also, a scroll of music. He is usually shown in art holding a book and is dressed as a bishop carrying a crosier (the bishop's staff) and wearing a miter (the bishop's crown). Feast day: December 7.

Ambrosia (am-brō′zia) Food of the Greek gods, which conferred immortality. It was accompanied by a drink called nectar.

Amor See Cupid.

Amphitrite (am-fi-tri′tē) In Greek mythology, a nereid, or sea nymph, who personified the sea, as wife of Poseiden*, and was identified with the Roman Salacia. To Poseiden she bore Triton*, Rhode, and Benthesicyme. She is represented with a net about her hair and with crab-claws on top of her head. She rides over the sea in a chariot made of shells, drawn by Tritons (figures that are human from the waist up and are fish or dolphins below).

Painting: *The Triumph of Neptune and Amphitrite*, Nicholas Poussin, Philadelphia Museum of Art.

Amphitryon (am-fit′rĭ-on)   In Greek legend, a descendant of Perseus*, married to Alcmene* daughter of Electryon of Mycenae. In a dispute over cattle he accidentally killed Electryon and was banished from Mycenae to Thebes. Alcmene refused to consummate their marriage until Amphitryon avenged the deaths of her eight brothers who had previously been killed by warring neighbors, the Taphians. While Amphitryon was away, the god Zeus* assumed the likeness of Amphitryon for the purpose of ravishing his wife. Amphitryon on his return learned of the visit from a seer. When twin sons were born, Heracles* and Iphicles*, Amphitryon accepted them both as his own According to one legend, he put two harmless snakes in their cribs. Heracles seized them both in his hands and strangled them with glee, while Iphicles screamed. From this test, Amphitryon knew which child was his own. Another legend says the goddess Hera*, jealous of the infidelity of Zeus, placed poisonous snakes in the crib, hoping to kill Heracles.

Ampula   The vessel that contains holy oil or consecrated wine, used in Christian services of baptism*, confirmation, extreme unction*, holy orders, and coronations.

Ananias (an-a-ni′us)   A member of the early Christian church who, with his wife Sapphira, held back part of a gift to the church and lied about it. The apostle Peter* asked him why he had conceived such a horrid act and why he had lied. Ananias was so upset he lay on the ground and died. When Peter questioned his wife later, she also fell dead at his feet (Acts 5:1-10).

Ananias   A Christian in the city of Damascus who helped restore Saul's (St. Paul's*) sight, and who afterward baptized him (Acts 9:10-18).

Anchises   See Aeneas.

Anchor   A symbol of the soul, of hope, adherence, and steadfastness; an attribute of the virtue* hope*. A anchor, with a cross, looking like an *f*, combined with the Greek letter *P* (rho), symbolizes hope. The anchor is also an attribute of St. Clement*, who was cast into the sea, bound to an anchor, and of St. Nicholas*, patron of seamen.

Anchorite   A solitary hermit. Anchorites fled to the desert to avoid religious persecution*.

St. Andrew   A Galilean fisherman of Bethsaida, brother to Simon called Peter (St. Peter*), a follower of John the Baptist*, described in the New Testament as the first "called" of the twelve disciples of Jesus* (John 1:35-41). He is said to have become a missionary in Asia Minor, Macedonia, and South Russia, but his martyrdom is said to have taken place in Patrae, Greece, in A.D. 70, where it is said he made so many converts the governor was afraid of a riot. In legend of the Middle Ages, he is said to have suffered many tortures and to have been crucified on an X-shaped cross, the cross saltire, or St. Andrew's cross. He is a patron saint of Russia and Scotland. In Christian art, he is shown as an old man with long white hair and beard, holding the gospel in his right hand and leaning on the X-shaped, cross saltire. Feast day: November 30.

Androcles   According to tradition, Androcles was a runaway slave, an early Christian who took refuge in a cave. A lion entered and, instead of tearing him to pieces, lifted up his paw so that Androcles might extract a vicious thorn. The slave subsequently was captured and doomed to fight with a lion in the Roman arena. By the grace of God, the same lion was let out against him, and recognizing his former benefactor, greeted him with affection and pleasure.

Andromache (an-drom′a-kē)   In Greek legend, the wife of Trojan Prince Hector*, and mother of Astyanax*. Her father and seven brothers were killed by Achilles* when he took Thebes. When the Trojan war was in its 10th year, she begged Hector to abandon the fight, and to live for her and their son. Hector foresaw his future death but he felt compelled to defend Troy, and was also killed by Achilles. After the fall of Troy, the boy Astyanax was taken from her arms and hurled to his death from the city towers. Andromache was awarded captive concubine to Neoptolemus*, the son of Achilles. He treated her kindly, and she bore him three sons. When Neoptolemus died, she was bequeathed to Helenus. Finally, at his death, she returned to Asia with her son Pergamus.

Andromeda (an-drom′e-da)   In Greek legend, a princess of Ethiopia, and daughter of King Cepheus and Queen Cassiopeia*. Cassiopeia angered the god Poseiden* by boasting that Andromeda was more beautiful than the nereids (sea nymphs)*. As punishment, Poseiden sent to prey upon the country a sea monster who, it was said, could only be appeased by the sacrifice of the king's daughter Andromeda. She was therefore chained to a cliff by the sea to wait for her death. Perseus* who was flying by on his winged sandals, after slaying Medusa*, discovered her

18

there. When the monster appeared Perseus slew him from the air and was awarded Andromeda as his bride. At the wedding feast, Phineas, a former suitor, burst into the ceremony and claimed the bride. When he attacked Perseus, Perseus, in self defense, exhibited the head of Medusa, and the suitor and his followers were all turned to stone. Andromeda bore Perseus seven children. At her death, the goddess Athena* placed her among the stars. A 16th-century bronze statuette: *Andromeda Chained to a Rock*; a marble sculpture: *Andromeda and the Monster*, Pierre Etienne Monnot, both at Metropolitan, New York.

Anemone (a-nem'o-nē) A symbol of the Greek Adonis*, since the flower was fabled to have sprung from his blood. In Christian iconography, it symbolizes sorrow and death, stemming from the fable of Adonis. It is shown in scenes of the crucifixion* with the Virgin Mary*, signifying her sorrow over the crucified Christ. The red spots on its petals symbolize the blood of Christ and legend adds that the anemone sprang up on Calvary* the eve of the crucifixion. Its triple leaf symbolizes the Trinity*.

Angel One of the types of spiritual attendants of God who conveyed the authority of the sender, as if he himself were present, serving both God and man. In the early 5th century, nine orders were given to angels: cherubim, seraphim, thrones, dominions, virtues, powers, principalities, archangels, angels. The "angel of the Lord" is the messenger of God, almost equivalent to the deity, yet distinct from him. The seven holy angels or archangels are: Michael*, Gabriel*, Raphael*, Uriel*, Chamuel, Jophiel, and Zadkiel. The first three are those frequently seen in art. The earliest known depiction of angels in art is on a Sumerian stele showing angels flying over the head of Ur-Nammu, ruler of Ur about 2300 B.C. Angels are a favorite subject in all art. There are two wooden, gilded angels (German), one with a lute and one with a rebec, Cloisters, Metropolitan, New York.

Anna In the New Testament, an ancient prophetess who hailed the baby Jesus when he was presented in the Temple by Mary* and Joseph*.

Annas See Jesus Christ—Life Events.

St. Anne or Anna The mother of the Virgin Mary* and wife of the shepherd Joachim*. She is not mentioned in the Bible but in the Apocryphal Gospel of St. Mary. Anne and Joachim were childless. When the devout Joachim brought offering to the Temple, the high priest refused it because Joachim had not fathered a child in Israel. Joachim left for the desert, and in the sheepfold he had a vision that his wife would bear a child. At the same time an angel visited Anne, foretelling a child that would be blessed throughout the world. (This divine intervention is a forerunner of the dogma of the Immaculate Conception.) When Joachim returned to Jerusalem, Anne stood at the Golden Gate to receive him, and she ran to him saying, "Now I know the Lord has greatly blessed me." St. Anne's cult is very old, and she has been especially popular since the Middle Ages. She is invoked by women in childbirth. Her feast day is July 26. In art, she is shown receiving the message from the angel, meeting Joachim at the Golden Gate; she is the center of scenes showing the birth of the Virgin; she is seen when the Virgin is presented as a young child in the Temple and is often shown teaching the Virgin to read. Most often she is seen in scenes of the Holy Family*, and often Mary, who is holding the Christ child, is placed on her knees. Her emblems are a green mantle and red dress, symbols of immortality and divine love. Painting: *St. Anne with the Virgin and Christ Child*, Hans Baldung Grien, National Gallery, Washington. A polychromed statue of *St. Anne* with a diminutive Virgin and child is at the Cloisters, Metropolitan, New York.

Annunciation   In the New Testament, the announcement of the angel Gabriel* to Mary* of Nazareth that she was to bear a son to whom God would give the throne of David (Luke 1:28-38). March 25 is observed as a festival in commemoration of the Annunciation, known as Lady Day. This scene has been shown hundreds of times in art. Example: Jan van Eyck, National Gallery, Washington.

St. Anselm (1034-1109)   An Italian churchman, made bishop of Canterbury, England, in 1093; a man of firm purpose during the conflicts of church and state during the reigns of William II and Henry I. Less a statesman than a man of holy life, he fell out with William II over the election of bishops. He left for Rome and did not return until Henry came to the throne. Anselm was an early proponent of the philosophical theory that what is known by faith is amenable to natural reason. "I do not understand in order to believe, but believe in order that I may understand," he wrote. In art his emblem is a ship, in allusion to his voyage to Rome and as a symbol of the church. Feast: April 2.

St. Anskar or Ansgor (801-865)   Anskar, born near Amiens, was called Apostle of the North, as he was the first missionary to Scandinavia. He was later consecrated archbishop of Hamburg, Germany. His emblem is a shield showing a figure in a woolen coat standing before mountains.

Antaeus (an-tē'us)   In Greek mythology, a gigantic wrestler, a son of Gaea* and the god Poseiden*, the earth and the sea. His strength was invincible as long as he touched the earth. He was finally vanquished by Heracles*, who lifted him into the air and crushed him.

Anteros (an'ter-os)   The brother of Eros* and son of the goddess Aphrodite* and the god Ares*. He is known as the god of unrequited love or sometimes as the god of mutual love. He is often shown, as Eros is, a nude child playing at the feet of Aphrodite and Ares.

St. Anthony Abbot   An Egyptian hermit of the 4th century, regarded as the father of Christian monasticism. He was born of wealthy parents but distributed all his goods to the poor and retired for most of his life to the desert. Here he struggled with many temptations of the flesh and these are often depicted in art. At the age of ninety, he heard a voice saying, "Paul the Hermit* is holier than thou, for he has served God in solitude for ninety years." Anthony went in search of Paul. He again met temptations, placed on his route by the Devil: a centaur, a satyr, and a nugget of gold; but he banished each with the sign of the cross. When he found Paul, he discovered a raven had been bringing him half a loaf of bread a day. Thereafter the raven brought a whole loaf. When Paul died, Anthony buried him with the help of two lions. Then he returned to his own abode until he died at the age of 105. In art he is represented in a monk's robe and on his left shoulder is the *T* for the Greek *Theos* (God). He often carries a crutch, signifying old age, and carries a bell, symbolizing his ability to dispel demons. A pig accompanies him, symbolizing his triumph over gluttony. Sometimes he is shown with a raven, sometimes there are flames under his feet representing the vanquished desires of the flesh. He is the patron of swineherds. Feast day: Jan. 7. Painting: *The Meeting of St. Anthony Abbot and St. Paul*, Sasetta, National Gallery, Washington. Painting: *The Temptation of St. Anthony*, Hieronymus Bosch, Metropolitan, New York.

St. Anthony of Padua (1195-1231)   Born in Lisbon, Portugal, Anthony joined St. Francis* and his order early in life and soon was renowned for his eloquent preaching. In a vision, he received the child Jesus* in his arms and is usually so represented in art. He is also shown with a kneeling ass. This refers to the legend that a heretic told Anthony he would not believe in Christianity until his ass kneeled before the church. A few days later, the ass met St. Anthony carrying the Eucharist* from the church, and the ass knelt before him. In art, Anthony usually wears the Franciscan robe. Attributes seen with him are the lily*, the flowered cross*, a fish*, a book*, and fire*. He is the patron of Padua. Feast day: June 13.

Antigone (an-tig′ō-nē)   In Greek legend, the daughter of Oedipus* by his mother Jocasta*. When Oedipus was banished in disgrace from Thebes, Antigone followed her unfortunate father, now pursued by the Furies*, and buried him, at last, with the aid of Theseus* at Colonus, in Attica. After her brothers Eteocles* and Polynices* slew each other in the war of the Seven Against Thebes*, her uncle Creon*, now regent of Thebes, forbade the burial of Polynices, saying that he had attacked his own city. Antigone, in spite of the command, performed the funeral service for her brother. When Creon learned of this act, he had Antigone buried alive.

Antilochus (an-til-ō-kus)   In Greek legend, a son of Nestor* who became a great fighter in the Trojan war* and a great friend of Achilles*. He was sent to tell Achilles of the death of his friend Patroclus*, and was buried in the same mound with the two warriors. Odysseus* saw the three men together in the underworld.

Antinous (an-tin′ō-us)   The favorite of the Emperor Hadrian (c. A.D. 110-130). His beauty was legendary, and when he was drowned in the Nile on a journey in Egypt, Hadrian mourned him greatly. He had him deified and founded the city of Antinoopolis in Egypt, as well as a cult in his honor. Coins were struck with the head of Antinous and many busts and statues were made showing him with heavy locks, melancholy eyes, and full breasts.

Antiope (an-tī-ō-pē)   In Greek mythology, an Amazon*, sister to Queen Hippolyta*. According to one legend, Theseus* abducted her and made her the mother of Hippolytus*. In the war that the Amazons waged against Athens, perhaps because of the rape of Antiope, she fought loyally at the side of Theseus against her own countrywomen and was killed in battle. Other accounts say that Theseus killed her when she tried to prevent his marriage to Phaedra*.

Antiope   In Greek mythology, the daughter of Nycteus of Thebes. She was seduced by the god Zeus* in the form of a satyr* and bore him twin sons. When her angered father died, her uncle Lycus took over and exposed the babies on Mt. Cithaeron, where they were found and brought up by shepherds. Antiope was treated cruelly by Lycus and his wife Dirce*. After years of persecution, she fled from them to Mt. Cithaeron. Dirce followed her and discovered she was in the hut of her sons, now grown to manhood but unknown to their mother. Dirce commanded them to kill Antiope, but a shepherd revealed Antiope's identity to the young men, and they threw Dirce, instead of their mother, onto the horns of a wild bull. Painting: *Antiope and Jupiter*, Pinturicchio, Metropolitan, New York.

St. Antipas   The first bishop of Pergamon in Asia Minor, called, by St. John*, "my faithful martyr" (Revelation 2:13). Tradition declares that he was roasted to death on a brazier in A.D. 90. His emblems are a head, wearing a miter, or bishop's hat, and an ox in the background, symbolizing patience and strength.

Antony, Marc (82-30 B.C.)   A Roman soldier and politician, one of the romantic figures of history, notorious from his youth for riotous living, but admired for his courage in war, even by his enemies. His career was filled with political intrigue, and he was one of the conspirators who assassinated Julius Caesar*. In 42 B.C., Antony met Cleopatra*, queen of Egypt. Their tragic love affair ended in their both committing suicide. (See Cleopatra)

Ape   In Christian iconography, a symbol of malice, cunning, lust, and the blind, slothful soul of man, sometimes representing Satan*. When portrayed in chains, the ape symbolizes sin conquered by virtue, and in this connection appears in scenes of the Visitation of the Magi*.

Aphrodite (a-frō-di′-tē) (Ro. Venus)   In Greek religion, the goddess of love, beauty, and irresistible generative powers of nature, one of the twelve Olympian deities. According to some legends, she was the daughter of the god Zeus* and Dione, but usually it is said she was born out of seafoam and was borne to land on a seashell, whence her epithet Anadyomene (risen from the sea). She was married to the lame god Hephaestus*, the god of fire and metal work, to whom she was notoriously unfaithful, particularly with the god Ares*. To Ares, she bore Eros*, god of love, and Anteros*, god of unrequited love. To the god Dionysus*, she bore Priapus*, the promoter of fertility in crops, cattle, and women, and to the mortal Anchises, she bore Aeneas*, the founder of Rome. As goddess of fertility, she is most closely connected with Adonis*. Aphrodite was an exacting goddess and, when angered, inflicted terrible punishments. At other times, she was most helpful, as with Theseus*, when she caused Ariadne* to fall in love with him, guiding him through the Cretan labyrinth*, or when she induced Medea's* passion for Jason* and her help to secure the Golden Fleece*. To Trojan Prince Paris*, who awarded her the "apple of discord*" when she competed with the goddesses Hera* and Athena* at the wedding of Peleus* and Thetis*, she promised Helen*, the beautiful wife of Greek Menelaus*, and then helped Paris to abduct her. This brought about the Trojan war*, during which time Aphrodite was consistently against the Greeks. Aphrodite was identified with the Oriental goddess Astarte (Ishtar)*, and there is reason to believe that her worship was imported into Greece from the Orient. The myrtle, rose, poppy, and apple were sacred to her, as were the dove, sparrow, swan, swallow, hare, goat, and ram. Incense and flowers were offered to her in sacrifice. The Romans claimed Aphrodite as their ancestress through Aeneas and worshipped her as Venus. She is represented in art as a young and very beautiful woman, nude or lightly clad. Roman marble copy of a Greek work (300 B.C.): *Aphrodite with a Dolphin*; also, bronze statuette (4th century B.C.); both Metropolitan, New York.

Apocalypse   A type of ancient Hebrew and Christian prophetic literature, exemplified by the Biblical book of Revelation. The Four Horsemen of the Apocalypse are allegorical figures (Revelation 6:1-8). The rider on the white horse has many interpretations; one is that he represents Christ. The rider on the red horse is war, on the black horse famine, and on the pale horse death.

Apocrypha   Fifteen books written during the last two centuries before Christ and first century of the Christian era. They are: 1 & 2 Esdras, Tobit, Judith, Esther (additions), Wisdom of Solomon, Ecclesiasticus, Baruch, Letter of Jeremiah, Prayer of Azariah and Song of Three Young Men, Susanna, Bel and the Dragon, Prayer of Manasseh, and 1 & 2 Maccabees. Roman Catholics accept all these books, except 1 & 2 Esdras and Prayer of Manasseh, as authoritative scripture, part of the Holy Bible. Protestants regard them all as apocryphal, and in their versions of the Bible, include them in an appendix, if at all.

Apollo or **Phoebus Apollo (a-pol'ō)**   "Lord of the silver bow," one of the twelve great Olympian gods in Greek religion. He is god of light, music, poetry, dance, prophecy, healing, and pastoral pursuits. In classic times he was also the god of plastic arts and science, the god of intellect, and the enemy of barbarism. Originally a god of shepherds and beekeepers, he would send pestilence and wolves against the flocks. He was identified with Helius*, the sun god. Legend tells that he and his twin sister the goddess Artemis* were born to Leto* and the god Zeus* on the island of Delos, which became one of his principal shrines. Delphi was his greatest shrine, and here he was a god of prophecy speaking through the oracle. One of the legends of

Delphi tells of his slaying of the Pythian dragon, which guarded Delphi's spring. He had many loves, not all successful. When he pursued the nymph Daphne* she fled, and her father, a river god, saved her by turning her into a laurel tree. Apollo made the laurel his own sacred tree. Another love was Coronis*, who was unfaithful to him. A white raven brought Apollo the news; he turned its feathers black for tattling and went to Coronis and caused her death. As she lay on the burning pyre, he commanded the god Hermes* to snatch the unborn child from her womb and sent it to Chiron*, the centaur, to rear. This son was Asclepius* who became such a successful healer he raised men from the dead. Once Apollo found some of his cattle missing from their pasture. By his powers of divination, he knew it was his baby brother Hermes. He went to his cradle in the cave on Cyllene and accused him of the theft. Hermes protested innocence, but Apollo carried him off to his father Zeus for judgement. Hermes played his newly invented lyre and so charmed Apollo that he exchanged the cattle for the lyre. The attributes of Apollo were the lyre, the bow, and the tripod*. Sacred to him were the laurel and palm trees, the wolf, deer, swan, hawk, raven, snake, mouse, and grasshopper. The Apollo cult was adopted by the Romans, who worshipped him primarily as a god of healing. In art, Apollo is shown as a beautiful young man, usually nude or lightly draped. He is characterized with arrows, the lyre, the oracular tripod of Delphi, the serpent, the dolphin, and sometimes a shepherd's crook. There is a 16th-century Italian bronze statuette of *Apollo*, (Venetian school), at the Metropolitan, New York; also, a scene of *Apollo Fighting with Heracles for the Tripod of Delphi*, on a 6th-century B.C. Greek vase (amphora), by the Andokides painter. (See Delphi)

St. Apollonia (a-pol-lōn′ĭ-a) A third-century Alexandrian Christian who, as deaconess of the church, refused to worship pagan gods. When she made the sign of the cross before idols, they broke into thousands of pieces. For this her teeth were pulled out with pincers, and she was cast upon a burning pyre. Her attributes are the palm of martyrdom and pincers holding teeth. She is the patron of dentists. Feast: February 9. Painting: *Apollonia*, Piero della Francesca, National Gallery, Washington.

Apostate   One who renounces his faith.

Apostles   The term applied to the twelve, intimate disciples of Jesus who were to become his witnesses before mankind, the number twelve corresponding to the twelve tribes of Israel. They are often symbolized as a group, sometimes as twelve doves, as twelve sheep, or twelve men with twelve sheep. An apostle's qualifications included his ability to give firsthand testimony that he had "seen the lord." Traditionally, the twelve disciples include Judas*, not Matthias*, and the twelve apostles include Matthias and not Judas. St. Paul* is always classed as an apostle, as are sometimes a few others. The symbols of the twelve, with Matthias and Paul, are:

Andrew—an X-shaped cross (saltire cross) on which he was crucified.

Bartholomew—three flaying knives with which he was flayed alive.

James the Great—a scallop shell, a pilgrim's staff, and gourd bottle, as patron saint of pilgrims.

James the Less—a fuller's pole (fulling is a cloth-processing) with which he was hit on the head, and a saw because he was cut in two.

John—a cup with a winged serpent flying out of it, alluding to the fact that he escaped from being poisoned.

Judas Iscariot—(a disciple, not an apostle) a bag because he kept the money for the disciples; a rope because he hanged himself.

Jude—a club with which he was martyred, and a ship because he travelled far.

Matthew—a hatchet (halberd) or axe because he was slain with one, and a purse because he had been a tax collector.

Matthias—an axe because he was stoned and then beheaded, and an open Bible for his missionary work.

Paul—a sword because his death penalty, as a Roman citizen, was a sword; also the symbol of his militant spirit for the church.

Peter—a bunch of keys, or crossed keys, which Jesus gave him as the "keys to the kingdom of heaven"; a cock because he denied Jesus when the cock crowed (Matthew 26-75).

Philip—a long staff surmounted by a cross because he died tied to a tall pillar; also a cross with loaves of bread because he was concerned about bread for the multitudes (John 6:5-6).

Simon—a saw with which he was martyred and a book with a fish on it, indicating that he became a great fisher of men through the gospel.

Thomas—a lance with which he was pierced to death in India, and a carpenter's square because he built a church there.

Apple   An attribute of the Greek goddess Aphrodite*. Aphrodite was awarded the Apple of Discord* by Trojan Paris*. An apple bough is an attribute of Nemesis*, the goddess of the inevitable. This apple bough is the passport to Elysium* (the heaven of the Greek underworld). When seen in the hand of Adam* or Eve*, it symbolizes sin, illustrating the first sin of man. When shown in the hand of the Christ* child (the new Adam), or in the hand of the Virgin Mary* (as the new Eve), it is the fruit of salvation. Three apples are an attribute of St. Dorothea*, sometimes in a basket, in reference to the miraculous appearance of apples at her execution.

Apple of Discord   In Greek mythology, a golden apple inscribed with the words, "For the fairest." It was thrown among the guests at the wedding of Peleus* and Thetis*, which the twelve Olympian gods* attended. Eris*, the goddess of discord, had not been invited, and it was she who threw the apple into the assembly of the gods. Hera*, Athena*, and Aphrodite* each put in claims for it. The decision was submitted to Paris*, the son of King Priam* of Troy. To influence his decision, Hera offered him an empire and riches; Athena offered glory in war; Aphrodite offered Helen*, the fairest woman in the world, who was already the wife of Menelaus* of Greece. Paris decided in favor of Aphrodite. The abduction of Helen by Paris led to the Trojan war*. Painting: *The Judgement of Paris*, Lucas Cranach, the elder, Metropolitan, New York.

Apples of the Hesperides (hes-per'i-dēz)   In Greek mythology, Gaea* (earth) presented the goddess Hera* with a tree that bore golden apples for a wedding present. The tree was planted in the far west and was guarded by the Hesperides*, who were daughters of Atlas*.

Arachne (a-rak'nē)   In Greek legend, a maiden so skilled in the art of spinning and weaving she challenged the goddess Athena* to a trial of skill. One story says she wove so delicately, no flaw could be found in her work, and the goddess in a frenzy of jealousy destroyed it. Another says that Athena surpassed her with ease. In either case, Arachne is said to have hanged herself in despair, and Athena furthered the revenge by changing her into a spider, condemned to hang on a thread and spin eternally.

Arcas (ar'kas)   See Callisto.

Archangels   The chief angels of God, differing from other angels only in importance. The four mentioned in the New Testament are Michael*, Gabriel*, Raphael*, and Uriel*. In Hebrew tradition, seven archangels sustain the throne of God. In Christian tradition, they are heavenly messengers, guides, and protectors of the church militant. They are often shown in Christian art, always as beautiful young men with wings.

Areopagite (ar-ē-op'a-jīt) The title applied to St. Dionysius*, a convert of St. Paul at Athens (Acts 17:34). Tradition makes him a martyr and the first bishop of Athens. He appears to have been a member of the council of the Areopagus (supreme court of Athens).

Ares (air'ēz) (Ro. Mars) In Greek mythology, the god of war, one of the twelve great Olympian gods, a son of the god and goddess, Zeus* and Hera*. He was a lover of the goddess Aphrodite*, who was the wife of the god Hephaestus*, but by Aphrodite, Ares was the father of Eros* and Anteros*. Hephaestus is said to have trapped Ares and Aphrodite in their lovemaking under a large, invisible net, thereby greatly embarrassing them. Ares was also the father of many other children, among them Harmonia* and Hippolyta* and Pentheshea*, Amazon queens. He was given the attributes of courage, endurance, and cleverness in battle. In art, he is represented as a muscular, handsome man, often bearded, wearing armor. Sometimes he carries a spear or blazing torch, and wears only a helmet as armor. He is often shown in the company of Aphrodite with their son Eros and sometimes Anteros. Sacred to him are the vulture, dog, and boar. He favored the Trojans in the Trojan war*, sometimes interfering unfairly on their behalf. Painting: *Mars and Venus*, Veronese, Metropolitan, New York.

Arethusa (ar-e-thū'za) See Alpheus.

Argonauts (ar'gō-nauts) In Greek legend, the heroes and demi-gods who sailed with Jason* on the ship *Argo* to fetch the Golden Fleece* from Colchis. Among them were Orpheus*, Heracles*, Castor* and Polydeuces*, Peleus*, Meleager*, and the huntress Atalanta*. There is a cassone (chest) panel with scenes from *The Story of the Argonauts* by a follower of Pesselino, Metropolitan, New York.

Argus (ar'gus) According to Greek legend, the fabulous creature with a hundred eyes whom the goddess Hera* set to watch over Io*, after she had been turned into a heifer by the god Zeus*, to save her from the jealousy of his wife. The god Hermes* rescued Io from Argus by entertaining him with songs and stories until his hundred eyes fell asleep. Then he cut off his head. Hera placed the eyes in the tail of her favorite bird which

28

was sacred to her, the peacock. There is a painting on a red-figured Greek vase (5th century B.C.): *Hermes About to Slay Argus*, Museum of Fine Arts, Boston.

Ariadne (ar-ē-ad'nē)   In Greek mythology, the daughter of Cretan King Minos* and his wife Pasiphae*. When Theseus* came to Crete, as one of the fourteen youths and maidens who were sent as tribute from Greece every nine years to be thrown to the Minotaur*, Ariadne fell in love with him. With her aid, Theseus killed the Minotaur, and it was said that it was she who gave him the ball of string that enabled him to find his way out of the labyrinth* where the Minotaur was kept. Ariadne then led Theseus and his companions to their Greek ships, and they escaped, taking her with them. Theseus deserted her on the island of Naxos, however, where she had fallen asleep. The god Dionysus* found her there, fell in love with her, and married her. The god Zeus* gave her immortality and set her bridal crown among the stars (Corona Borealis). In Italy, as the wife of Bacchus* who was identified with the wine god Liber*, Ariadne was worshipped as the wine goddess Liberia*. A Roman marble sarcophagus (coffin) of A.D. 2nd century has a scene: *Ariadne Giving Theseus the Thread*, Metropolitan, New York.

Arian Heresy   See St. Hilary and St. Athansius.

Ark of the Covenant   The chest containing two stone tablets given to Moses* by the Lord, inscribed with the Ten Command-ments*. It was kept in the holiest part of the ancient Jewish tabernacle (Exodus 25:16).

Ark of Noah   In the Old Testament, the three-story houseboat, which the Lord instructed Noah* to build for his family and every living thing of flesh (two of every sort, male and female), in which they lived until the one-hundred-and-fifty-day flood, loosened upon them, was over (Genesis 6:15-19). The building of the ark is often represented in art. Painting: *Animals Entering the Ark*, Edward Hicks, Philadelphia Museum of Art.

Armageddon   In the Old Testament, the name given in the Apocalypse to the site of the last, great, symbolic battlefield where the final contest between forces of good and evil is ulti-mately to take place (Revelation 16:16).

Armor   A symbol of chivalry and a protection against evil. St. George*, and usually St. Joan*, are represented in art wearing armor and carrying a sword. Armor with a cross on a coat of mail is frequently worn by the archangel Michael*. St. William* of Aquitaine is shown as a mailed soldier.

29

Arrows   Arrows with a quiver are an attribute of Artemis*, goddess of the hunt, and of Eros*, the gold-winged god of sexual passion, who used his arrows to set hearts on fire. The huntress Atalanta* carried arrows and was the first to bring down the Calydonian Boar*. The Amazons* carry arrows and quiver. The arrows of Heracles* were poisoned with the blood of the Hydra*, which he killed as his second labor. In Christian iconography, the arrow indicates dedication to the service of God. Arrows are the emblem of St. Sebastian*, whose body was pierced with many arrows, and St. Ursula*, who was also tortured with many arrows. Flaming arrows, piercing the heart, represent St. Theresa*. Three arrows are an emblem of St. Bartholomew* and St. Edmund*; one arrow, an emblem of St. Giles*.

Artemis (ar'te-mis) (Ro. Diana)   In Greek mythology, one of the twelve Olympian gods. Daughter of the god Zeus* and Leto*, she was a huntress who resisted all lovers. She is sometimes called Delia, Cynthia, or Phoebe. Primarily she was the guardian, as well as the huntress, of wild animals; complementary to the light god Apollo*, her twin brother, she was goddess of the moon and the night. She was also the protectress of youth, particularly maidens, but she had a revengeful nature, if crossed. When Actaeon* discovered her bathing in a pool with her maidens, she turned him into a stag, and his own dogs destroyed him. She loosed a wild boar on the lands of Oeneus* because he failed to sacrifice to her. This was the boar of the Calydonian hunt*. When Agamemnon* killed a stag that was sacred to her, he was forced to appease her by sacrificing his daughter Iphigenia* on the altar. She killed all of Niobe's* twelve children with the help of Apollo in order to avenge an insult to their mother Leto. Like Apollo, she was probably born on Delos, a little before him, but some legends say she was born on the island of Ortygia, and then helped her mother across the water to give birth to Apollo. Her attendants were all virgins; those who forgot their vows of chastity were punished. In Asia Minor, notably Ephesus, she was worshipped, not as a virgin, but as the Great Mother, equated with Astarte, and as such, depicted in art with many breasts. Worship of Artemis was widespread in the Mediterranean and she was combined with various earth and nature goddesses as well as those of the night. Her attributes were the bow and quiver, torch, javelin, and crescent. In classic art, she is represented as a young woman, usually in a short tunic, generally bearing a bow and quiver and wearing sandals. Often she is accompanied by a dog or doe; sometimes she rides a chariot drawn by hinds. There is a red-figured Greek vase painting (5th century B.C.), *Artemis with her Bow and Arrow*, by the Pan Painter, Museum of Fine Arts, Boston.

King Arthur   See Knights of the Round Table.

Arthurian Legend   A series of romances relating to the exploits of King Arthur and his knights. They were originally Breton romances, amplified in Wales and adopted at the court of the Plantagenets as the foundation of chivalry. The English *Morte d'Arthur* of Sir Thomas Malory was perhaps translated from an early compilation of Hélie de Borron. The stories of Arthur, Guinevere, Merlin, Launcelot, Tristan, Galahad*, Percival, Yseult, Sir Gawain, and the Holy Grail* are the principal romances (see Knights of the Round Table). Fourteenth-century tapestry, *Nine Heroes* showing King Arthur on His Throne, Cloisters, Metropolitan, New York.

Asaph (a-saf)   In the Old Testament, a cymbal-playing Levite who was appointed the leader of David's choir; possibly author of certain psalms (1 Chronicles 16:4-6).

Ascension of Christ   In the New Testament, Christ's final post-Resurrection manifestation to his followers (Acts 1:1-11). Having told the disciples that the Holy Ghost* would come upon them and that they would be witnesses to him to the uttermost parts of the earth, "he was taken up; and a cloud received him out of their sight." Ascension Day is commemorated by many churches, forty days after Easter (see Jesus Christ—After-Life Events). Like all events to do with Christ, the scene is frequently shown in art.

Asclepius or Asklepius (as-kle'pi-us) (Ro. Aesculapius)   In Greek mythology, a son of Coronis* and the god Apollo*, reared by the wise centaur Chiron*, who taught him the art of healing. Aided also by his father Apollo, he became a skilled surgeon and prescriber of drugs. The goddess Athena* gave him drops of Medusa's* blood to use for their medicinal properties. There were temples and shrines to Asclepius throughout the Grecian world. His most famous shrines were at Epidaurus in Greece, at Pergamon in Asia Minor, at Tricca in Thessaly, and on the island of Cos. Serpents, which annually renew their skins, were sacred to him and connected with the art of healing. In art, he is always shown with a serpent; often it is climbing around his staff. The cock was commonly sacrificed to him (see Caduceus and Apollo).

Ashes   In Christian religion, a symbol of penitence. In the Christian church, consecrated ashes from the previous Palm Sunday are placed on the forehead the first day of Lent, known as Ash Wednesday. Ashes may also represent death. The phrase, "Ashes to ashes, dust to dust," is used in the English burial services.

Ash Tree In Greek mythology, the seasonal disguise for Nemesis*.

Aspen Legend relates that when the aspen tree was chosen for the cross of Christ, its leaves trembled with shame and have trembled ever since.

Asperges or Aspergillum The bush or sponge on a handle with which holy water is sprinkled on the altar and on the congregation during the Roman Catholic mass. It is supposed to drive away evil spirits and is an attribute of saints who are known for exorcising devils, notably Sts. Benedict* and Anthony Abbot*. It is also an attribute of Martha of Bethany*.

Asphodel In Greek religion, the asphodel fields were the meadows of the dead, its pale blossoms symbolizing the dead. It was an attribute of Dionysus*, referring to his descent into Hades* to fetch his mother Semele* from the fields.

Ass In Christian religion, a symbol of the humblest of creatures. Its presence, with the ox, in the Nativity* scenes refers to, "the ox knoweth its owner, and the ass his master's crib" (Isaiah 1:3). The Virgin Mary rides an ass in scenes of the flight into Egypt*. Jesus, as was foretold, rides an ass for his entrance into Jerusalem*. The ass is often shown with St. Anthony of Padua*, sometimes with St. Jerome*. In the Old Testament, Abigail* has a convoy of asses.

Ass's Ears In Greek mythology, King Minos* was given ass's ears, as a punishment.

Assumption of the Virgin The name given for the ascension of the Virgin Mary into heaven, after her falling asleep (Dormition, as it is called in Orthodox theology). Painting: *The Assumption of the Virgin*, Paolo di Giovanni Fei, National Gallery, Washington.

Asteria (as-tē′ri-a) In Greek mythology, a sister of Leto*. When she was pursued by the god Zeus*, she turned herself into a quail and was then transformed into the tiny island of Ortygia. (In some legends, Ortygia was changed into the island of Delos.) Here Leto, fleeing from the goddess Hera's* jealousy, found a welcome refuge where she could bear Artemis*.

Astyanax (as-tī′a-naks) In Greek legend, the son of Trojan Prince Hector* and his wife Andromache*. At the fall of Troy, Odysseus* advised Agamemnon* to kill Astyanax, lest he grow up to avenge his father's death. He was taken from his mother's arms and hurled to his death from the walls of Troy. The scene is frequently shown on Greek pottery.

Atalanta   In Greek legend, the huntress who joined the Calydonian Boar hunt*. Her father, Iasius of Arcadia, was anxious for her to marry, but Atalanta had been warned against marriage by the oracle at Delphi*. Finally she agreed on the condition that any suitor asking for her hand must run against her in a foot race. If she beat him, he would die; if he won, she would marry him. Hippomenes defeated her with the help of Aphrodite*, the goddess of love, by dropping three golden apples during the contest, which Atalanta turned aside each time to catch. The two young people, happy in each other, forgot to sacrifice to Aphrodite. She then caused them to violate the temple of Cybele*, who avenged the insult by turning them into lions, yolking them to her chariot (see Meleager). Painting: *Atalanta with Meleager*, Rubens, Metropolitan, New York.

St. Athanasius (295-373)   A patriarch of Alexandria, Egypt, called the father of orthodoxy. He was a defender of Catholicism against Arianism, a doctrine teaching that Jesus Christ was neither eternal nor equal with God. His attributes are two Doric columns with an open Bible between them. Feast: May 2.

St. Athanasius the Athonite (920-1003)   Born in Trebizond, Athanasius became abbot of Mt. Athos in Greece where he was the builder and founder of communal monasteries. He was killed by a falling cupola when inspecting the rebuilding of a church.

Athena or **Pallas Athena (a-thē′na)** (Ro. Minerva)   In Greek mythology, one of the twelve Olympian gods*, fabled to have sprung fully armed from the head of Zeus*. She is the goddess of eternal virginity and presided essentially over the whole moral and intellectual life of the Greeks. From her were derived all the creations of wisdom and understanding, every art and science, whether for war or peace. Inventions of every kind were ascribed to her: the plough, the oxen's yoke, horse training, household arts, construction, healing, and music. Above all, she gave Attica the treasured olive tree. According to legend, Poseiden* and Athena contended for control of the Athenian citadel. Poseiden struck the rock of the Acropolis with his trident and a fountain of sea water gushed forth. Athena struck the rock and an olive tree sprang up. The gods decided that Athena's gift was the more beneficial. Athena then took the city and gave it her name. She was also a contender with the goddesses Hera* and Aphrodite* for the Apple of Discord*, a prize of beauty. When Paris*, son of

King Priam* of Troy, awarded the prize to Aphrodite, Athena became an implacable enemy of Paris and during the Trojan war was always on the side of the Greeks. Odysseus* was one of her favorites and she is said to have inspired his stratagem of the Trojan Horse*. After the war, she helped him to reach his own shores and there she assisted him and his son Telemachus* in the slaying of the reveling suitors who were molesting his wife Penelope*. Athena helped Cadmus* to found Thebes, and Perseus* to cut off Medusa's* head. She gave drops of Medusa's blood to Asclepius* for healing purposes. Later she placed the head of Medusa with its snaky locks on her Aegis* or shield. She aided Heracles* with his labors; she was a friend to Jason* and supplied the prow for the ship *Argo* in which the Argonauts* sailed to obtain the Golden Fleece*. She taught Bellerophon* how to subdue the winged horse Pegasus*. Athena was worshipped throughout Greece. Her greatest temple was the Parthenon, built on the Acropolis of Athens. Here she was protectress and defender, as well as the personification of victory. Her chief festival, annually celebrated at Athens, was the Panathenaea*, which originated as a harvest festival. The sea eagle, cock, serpent, and olive tree were sacred to her, but above all, she was identified with the owl, symbol of wisdom. In art, Athena is usually represented as an imposing figure. She wears a helmet, as goddess of war, the Aegis covers her breast or serves as a shield with Medusa's head on it. The resistless spear is in her hand or occasionally the thunderbolt of Zeus. As goddess of peace and the useful arts, she is shown without her helmet, holding a distaff. As Athena Nike (victory), she is shown holding the figure of victory in her outstretched hand. Bronze statuette (5th century B.C.): *Athena Helmeted and Carrying an Owl*, Metropolitan, New York.

Atlas In Greek mythology, one of the Titans*, a son of Iapetus, brother of Prometheus*, Epimetheus*, and father of the Pleiades*, the Hyades, and the Hesperides*. As the leader of the Titans in their war against the Olympian gods, he was condemned by Zeus* to stand at the western end of the earth, upholding the sky on his shoulders and hands. When Heracles*, as one of his labors for Eurystheus*, sought Hera's golden apples from the garden guarded by the Hesperides, he persuaded the slow-witted Atlas to pick the apples for him while he, in exchange, took over the burden of holding up the heavens. When Atlas returned with the apples, Heracles asked him to hold up the heavens again for a moment while he padded his shoulders. Atlas obligingly complied and Heracles walked quickly off with the apples. When Perseus* visited Atlas, after slaying the Gorgon Medusa*, he asked for refreshment. Atlas refused, so Perseus displayed the head of

Medusa and turned him to stone. This bulk of stone is now the Atlas mountains in Africa. Engraving: *A tlas*, after Abraham van Diepenbeck from Michel de Marolle's Tableaux du Temple des Muses, Metropolitan, New York.

Atonement The doctrine that Christ, through his death upon the cross and his many sufferings, atoned, or paid for the sins of man, something which man had not the ability to do by his own resources; a dogma of faith (see Jesus Christ).

Atreus (ā'trē-us) In Greek legend, a king of Mycenae. He was the son of Pelops* and Hippodamia*, and brother of Thyestes*. Since Pelops had refused to honor his promise to the charioteer who had helped him to win the hand of Hippodamia, he and his family were cursed. Atreus brought an even greater curse upon himself and his family, the result of many struggles between himself and his brother Thyestes for the throne of Mycenae. The two brothers first murdered their stepbrother and were banished from the kingdom by Pelops. Atreus then got possession of Mycenae from Eurystheus*. He had been given a golden lamb by the god Hermes which he claimed gave the possessor royal authority and which he had killed, stuffed, and kept in his possession. Thyestes then seduced Aërope, who was the wife of Atreus and the mother of his children Agamemnon*, Menelaus*, and Anaxibia. With the help of Aërope, Thyestes obtained the golden lamb and thus took over the kingdom. Atreus took revenge by killing the sons of Thyestes whom he then served up to the unsuspecting father at a family feast. When Atreus revealed to Thyestes that he had eaten the flesh of his own children, Thyestes laid a curse on the House of Atreus and went into exile. Aegisthus*, son of Thyestes by Pelopia, later killed Atreus at his father's command. Thyestes and Aegisthus seized the throne of Mycenae, once more, and banished Agamemnon and Menelaus, the sons of Atreus.

Augeas (o'jē-as or o-jē'as) In Greek mythology, king of Elis and one of the Argonauts*. He was the owner of three thousand prize oxen, which were kept in a stable that had not been cleaned for thirty years. As one of the labors for Eurystheus*, Heracles* was commanded to clean the Augean stables in one day. Augeas agreed to pay Heracles one-tenth of his cattle, if he succeeded. Heracles cleverly diverted the rivers Alpheus and Peneus from their regular courses and made them flow through the stable. When Augeas refused to honor his agreement to pay in cattle, claiming the job had been done for Eurystheus anyway, Heracles gathered a force around him and killed Augeas, making Phyleus, who had supported his cause, ruler in place of his father Augeas.

Augurs (o'gers)   The Roman priests who foretold events by interpreting omens or auguries.

St. Augustine of Canterbury (died about 605)   An Italian missionary, called the Apostle of the English. He was a Roman Benedictine monk who was sent at the head of forty monks to England in 596, by Pope Gregory the Great, to preach the gospel to the heathen. He was to become the first archbishop of Canterbury. When he saw the fair-haired English children in the marketplace, he said, "These are not Angles (English) but angels." Feast day: May 28.

St. Augustine of Hippo (354-430)   Bishop of Hippo, North Africa, for thirty-four years, and one of the four Latin Church Fathers. He was a native of Algeria, brought up by a Christian mother, but not baptized into the church until the age of thirty-three. As a student at Carthage, he had lived with a young woman for fourteen years to whom he was devoted and by whom he had a cherished son. His decision between marriage and wealth or religious vows was made after agonizing conflict in a garden in Rome, when he was reading the epistles of St. Paul*. He became one of the greatest bishops in the Christian church, leading his clergy under strict rule, and looking after the needs of the church and the poor. He is the great founder of Christian theology, and his influence on Christianity is second only to St. Paul. His *Confessions* is considered a classic work of Christian mysticism. One event in his life, frequently represented in art, is the story of St. Augustine observing a small boy trying to empty the ocean into a hole in the sand. Augustine is said to have told him that the task was impossible. The child replied that it was no more difficult than for Augustine to explain the mysteries upon which he meditated. Augustine is usually shown dressed as a bishop, holding a book or a pen. His attribute is a flaming heart, pierced by arrows. Feast day: August 28. Portrait: *St. Augustine*, Taddeo di Bartolo, Delgado Museum of Art, New Orleans.

Augustus (see Octavius Augustus)   An honorary title given in the year 27 B.C. to Octavius, the founder of the Roman Empire. It was not a hereditary title, but was taken by succeeding emperors at the insistence of the senate, gradually becoming an official title.

Aureole   An elongated nimbus*, a symbol of divinity, used only in surrounding the entire body of Christ*, the Virgin Mary*, God the Father*, or the Trinity* (see mandorla). It may be white, gold, blue, or multicolored (see Glory and Halo).

Aurora (a-rō′ra) In Roman mythology, the goddess of the dawn. She drove out of the ocean in a chariot, her rosy fingers spreading dew (see the Greek Eos).

Autolycus (o-tol′i-kus) In Greek mythology, a son of the god Hermes* and Chione. He was a famous robber and, from the god Hermes, possessed the power of making himself, and the things that he took, invisible. He was the thief who stole the cattle of Eurytus, of Oechalia, and after changing their color, sold them to Heracles*. He was the grandfather of Odysseus*, and it was while Odysseus, still a boy, was visiting him, that he received a scar on his leg from the gash of a boar's teeth. The old nurse of Odysseus recognized him by this scar, as she was washing his feet, when he returned to Ithaca, disguised as a beggar, after the Trojan war*.

Axe In Christian iconography, the axe is a symbol of destruction. It is an emblem of Joseph of Nazareth*, who was a carpenter, and of Sts. Matthew* and Matthias*, both of whom were beheaded with an axe. It is also an emblem of John the Baptist*. In the Gospel of Matthew (3:10), John preached, ". . . every tree which bringeth not forth good fruit is hewn down." When an axe is shown in art imbedded in a tree, it symbolizes the cutting down of that which does not bear God's fruit.

B

Baal (bā'al) The name used throughout the Old Testament for the local fertility divinities of Canaan. They were fought against for three centuries by the Hebrew prophets who saw the orgiastic worship as backsliding. The real advent of Baal worship in the nation occurred when King Ahab* (875-854 B.C.) married Jezebel*, a princess of Tyre who was a confirmed Baal worshipper. The prophet Elijah* brought Ahab and Jezebel ultimately to their deaths.

Babel (bā'bel) The Hebrew name in the Old Testament for Babylon, the polyglot city in the plain of Shinar (Genesis 10:10). The name "Babel" became synonymous with the confusion of tongues such as characterized Babylon (Genesis 11:4-9). The tower of Babel, completed under Nebuchadnezzar*, was a seven-story ziggurat made of sun-dried bricks. Each of the lower stories formed a platform on which the next one was built.

Babylon The capital of the Babylonian Empire, famous for its "hanging gardens" on the roof of Nebuchadnezzar's palace. These gardens were considered one of the Seven Wonders of the Ancient World*. Babylon was at its peak in the 6th century B.C. under Hammurabi.

Bacchanalias (bak-a-nal'yas) These were triennial Roman, orgiastic night festivals, derived from the Greek Dionysia. They were characterized by drunkenness, debauchery, and licentiousness. Originally they were quite different, important for their connection with choragic, literary contests, from which originated both tragic and comic drama and for which most of the Greek masterpieces were written.

Bacchants and Bacchantes or **Bacchae**   The priests and priestesses of Bacchus.

Bacchus (bak'us)   The name adopted by the Romans for the Greek Dionysus*. He was the god of the vine, personifying its cultivation and preparation as well as the bad qualities of wine. Bacchus is represented in Roman art as a beautiful youth with flowing curls, fileted with ivy, often wearing a panther skin, while holding grapes in an outstretched hand. His chariot is drawn by panthers. Painting: *Infant Bacchus with Nymphs*, Nicholas Poussin, Fogg Art Museum, Cambridge, Mass. A 16th-century Italian bronze statuette, Metropolitan, New York. (See Dionysus.)

Balaam (bā'la-am)   In the Old Testament, a Midian magician. The king of Moab tried to bribe Balaam to lay a curse on the Israelites, who were approaching his land on their trek across Canaan. The Lord intervened, telling Balaam to refuse to make the curse, but to make a journey to Moab's kingdom. Balaam saddled his ass and rode off, but suddenly the ass was stopped in its tracks by an invisible angel of the Lord, standing before them with a sword. Balaam, unaware of the angel's presence, beat the ass until it cried out, "What have I done to thee?" The angel then revealed himself and told the terrified Balaam to continue his journey. Balaam came to King Moab's court, and seven altars were built for sacrifice to Moab's god, but when Balaam opened his mouth to speak, he could only bless the people of Israel and prophesy a great future for them. (Numbers 22:4—24:9)

Baldachino or **Baldachin (bal'da-kin-ō)**   The dias, or canopy, under which the Holy Sacrament* is carried in Roman Catholic processions. It is also the canopy above the altar. The name comes from the Italian *Baldacco*, meaning Bagdad, the place from which the cloth first came.

Bag for Money   In Christian iconography, an attribute of Judas Iscariot*, because he was the disciple of Jesus* who managed the money of the group.

Balls   In mythology, the ball is an attribute of the Greek goddess Tyche* and the Roman goddess Fortuna*, the juggler's of fortune. A ball of thread was given by Ariadne* to Theseus*, with which to find his way out of the labyrinth*, in Crete. In Christian iconography, three balls are an attribute of St. Nicholas of Bari*, symbolizing the dowries that he gave to three, marriageable daughters of an impoverished count.

Banner   In Christian iconography, a banner with a red cross symbolizes victory, usually on a white ground. It is frequently shown to depict the conversion of St. Constantine* to Christianity, and is also carried by St. George of Cappadocia* and St. Ursula*. A banner carried by the Lamb of God* symbolizes victory over death. Christ* carries the Banner of Victory, after rising from his tomb, and in scenes of his Descent into Hell (see Jesus Christ—Apparitions). John the Baptist* carries a banner, either with a cross, or with the words *Ecce Agnus Dei* (Behold the Lamb of God) written on it. Military saints carry banners, such as St. James the Great*, the military patron saint of Spain.

Baptism   In the New Testament, this rite was characteristic of the ministry of John the Baptist* (see Mark 1:4), and it was imposed upon converts of the Christian church from the beginning. Jesus*, in submitting himself to John's ritual, was consecrated to bestow baptism but refrained from personally administering the ceremony. Baptism was not specifically included in the instructions of Jesus to his disciples. The rite is nowhere described in detail, but immersion was commonly used (Mark 1:10), and is so shown in art. The use of water in religious ceremonies is found in the Eleusinian Mysteries* in Greece, in Babylonian ritual, and in Jewish ordinances (see Jesus Christ—Life Events). Painting: *The Baptism of Christ*, Master of the Life of John the Baptist, National Gallery, Washington.

Barabbas (bar-ab'bas)   The notable prisoner released in place of Jesus by Pontius Pilate*, in response to the clamor of the mob who were incited by Christ's priestly accusers (Matthew 27:15-26). This act of clemency was a Roman concession to Jewish unrest at Passover*.

St. Barbara   A maiden of great beauty, born in Heliopolis, Egypt, whose father shut her up in a tower to discourage suitors. When he discovered she was converted to Christianity, he tried to kill her, but she was miraculously saved and carried beyond his reach. The authorities tried subjecting her to torture but without avail, whereupon her father tried to strike off her head. Straightaway a lightning flash laid him dead at her feet. Because of this punishment, Barbara is the patron of the artillery and gunsmiths, and is invoked against lightning. Her emblem is a tower, usually with three windows, indicating that her soul received light from the Father, Son, and Holy Ghost. Sometimes she carries the sacramental cup and wafer in reference to her dying request that all who honored her martyrdom would receive the grace of the sacrament. Feast: December 4. Gothic-Renaissance stone sculpture: *St. Barbara with a Tower*, Metropolitan, New York.

St. Barnabas   First-century Cypriot missionary, martyred at the port of Salamis in Cyprus. Known as a prophet, teacher, and apostle, he was a compatriot of St. Mark*, his relative, and of St. John*. He is shown in art with the Gospel, a stone*, and a pilgrim's staff. Feast: June 11.

Bartholomew (bar-thol'u-mū)   One of the twelve disciples of Jesus*, known also by his given name Nathaniel. He was present in the select company that went fishing after the crucifixion (see Jesus Christ—Apparitions). Tradition says he traveled as far as India, but he was flayed alive in Armenia in A.D. 44. His symbol is a butcher's knife with which he was martyred and he is also shown with human skin over one arm to indicate the flaying of his body. Feast: August 24. Painting: *St. Bartholomew*, Pietro Perugino, Birmingham Art Museum, Alabama.

St. Basil (bā'zil) (330-379)   Known as the Great. Bishop of Caesarea, in Cappadocia, he was one of the Four Fathers of the Greek church, and a strong defender of orthodoxy against the Arian heresy (heretic Christians) in the Byzantine church. He was born into an old Christian family of wealth and distinction, whose remarkable religious history includes six saints. He was educated in Constantinople and Athens where he formed a great friendship with St. Gregory*, and for a time settled as a monk with St. Gregory at Annesi in Northeast Asia Minor. Later, at Caesarea, he founded the first recorded hospice for travellers, built dwelling houses, a church, and a hospital for the sick, all on such a scale he made a new town. Once when Basil was holding mass in the Cathedral of Caesarea, Emperor Valentius entered with gifts and attended the service. He was so overcome watching the devotion of Basil, he fainted. Once Basil saved a young widow from a prefect who threatened to kidnap her. The prefect summoned Basil to court. A large, protesting crowd gathered who so terrified the prefect he appealed to Basil. With one gesture Basil dismissed the crowd and the official escaped. Basil was headstrong, and often tactless, which lost him the friendship of St. Gregory, but he was much lamented at his death. He wrote many doctrinal works including the Eucharist liturgy that bears his name. His symbol is an outstretched hand or arm with a dove perched on it. Feast: June 14.

Basilisk   A medieval animal, half-cock, half-snake, which was the symbol of the devil.

Bathsheba (bath-shē'ba)   In the Old Testament, the wife of Uriah, the Hittite. She was coveted by Kind David*, who beheld her bathing from the roof of his palace in Jerusalem. David sent for her and seduced her while her husband was away fighting against the Ammonites. Bathsheba conceived and sent word to David that she was with child. David then ordered Uriah into the forefront of the battle where he was killed, and when the mourning had passed he took Bathsheba for his wife (2 Samuel 11). The Lord was displeased and this first child of Bathsheba's died, but the second, Solomon*, survived. When David was an old man, Bathsheba extracted the promise from him that Solomon would succeed him as king. Painting: *The Toilet of Bathsheba*, Rembrandt, Metropolitan, New York.

Baucis (baw'sis)   See Philemon.

Bears   In Greek mythology, bears were sacred to the goddess Artemis*. She is said to have transformed herself into a bear when the god Zeus* tried to seduce her. One of her maidens, Callisto*, and Callisto's son, Arcas*, were changed into bears by Artemis or Zeus. In the Old Testament, the bear is a symbol of cruelty and evil, identified with the kingdom of Persia, which was finally destroyed by God. Legend says that bears are born formless and are given shape by their mothers. The bear in this context became a symbol of the reformation of infidels by Christians. A bear is an attribute of St. Euphemia*.

Beatitudes (bē-at'i-tūds)   In the New Testament, the eight blessings pronounced by Jesus* at the opening of the Sermon on the Mount* (Matthew 5:3-11). The moral ideals include: the poor in spirit, those tested by sorrow, the lowly, those who hunger for righteousness, the merciful, the pure in heart, and the peace seekers. It is generally held that these are the qualities of character that Jesus expected of his followers.

Bee   In ancient religion, the bee was sacred to the goddess Artemis*, in her role of orgiastic nymph. The honeycomb is sacred to the goddess Demeter*, as a symbol of productivity. The goddess Cybele* is worshipped as a queen bee. Romans considered a flight of bees a bad omen. In Christian religion, the bee is a symbol of the zealous and industrious Christian. Its honey is a symbol of sweetness and eloquence, of Christ, and the virtue of the Virgin Mary*. A beehive is a symbol of the unified Christian community and an expression of honeyed words. As such, it is an attribute of Sts. Bernard of Clairvaux*, Ambrose*, and John Chrysostom*.

Bel and the Dragon   This story is told in the Apocrypha* of the Old Testament. During the reign of King Cyrus of Persia, the Babylonians worshipped an idol called Bel, which was fed daily by the priests. The prophet Daniel* refused to worship it, telling the king it was not a living god. He proved this by secretly scattering ashes one evening on the temple floor. The following morning the footprints of the priests were found in the ashes, showing that they, and not Bel, had consumed the food. The angry king had the priests slain, but then claimed that the "living god" was a great dragon, which was also worshipped by the Babylonians. Daniel declared that he would kill it without weapons. He took pitch, fat, and hair, and stuffed them into the dragon's mouth until it burst. The Babylonians were indignant and persuaded King Cyrus that he must throw Daniel into the lion's den, and here he stayed for six days. But the Lord was mindful of Daniel, and a prophet named Habbacuc was picked up by the hair on his head and flown miraculously by angels at night to bring him food. On the seventh day, the king came to the den to bewail Daniel, but he found him quite alive. Then Cyrus cried, "Great art thou, O Lord of Daniel." And he cast into the den those who had wished to destroy Daniel, and these same were devoured in a moment before his eyes.

Bell   In Christian religion, the bell is the sounding of the word of God. It is carried by saints as an exorciser of demons. The sanctus bell, used during Holy Communion service, announces the coming of Christ. Bells are used in church towers to summon the faithful. It is an attribute of St. Anthony Abbot*.

Bellerophon (be-ler'ō-fon)   In Greek legend, a son of Glaucus* and grandson of Sisyphus*. He left Corinth as a youth after accidentally killing his brother, and sought refuge with Proetus, king of Tiryns. Anteia (or Antia), the wife of Proetus, fell in love with Bellerophon and made advances to him. When she was rejected, she reported to her husband that Bellerophon had tried to dishonor her. Proetus decided to destroy Bellerophon and sent him to his father-in-law Iobates, king of Lycia, with a letter recounting the insult to Anteia and asking that the bearer be put to death. Iobates, unwilling to perform this act in his own kingdom, sent Bellerophon to perform the impossible task of killing the Chimaera*, a fire-breathing monster with a lion's head, *Chimaera* the body of a goat, and a serpent's tail. The goddess Athena* came to Bellerophon's aid, and gave him a golden bridle with which to capture the winged horse Pegasus*, advising him to catch Pegasus *Pegasus* when he was off-guard, drinking at the spring of Pirene in Corinth. Bellerophon followed the directions, leaped on the horse's back, befriended him, and flew off to the Chimaera. Avoiding the flames from his position in the air, he was able to kill the monster. Iobates tried Bellerophon with other perilous adventures but when he always returned triumphant, he was forced to make him his heir and gave him his daughter in marriage. Grown prosperous and proud, Bellerophon attempted to fly to Mt. Olympus* (the home of the gods), on Pegasus. Zeus sent a gadfly to sting the horse, and Bellerophon was thrown down, lamed and blinded. He spent his last days in miserable wandering. There is a painting on a Greek vase (7th century B.C.): *Bellerophon*, Museum of Fine Arts, Boston.

Belshazzar (bel-shaz'er)   In the Old Testament, the son of Nebuchadnezzar*, and the last king of Babylon. At a tremendous feast of oriental splendor given by Belshazzar to a thousand noblemen, handwriting mysteriously appeared on the wall: "Mene, mene, tekel, upharsin." The astrologers could not explain the words, so the prophet Daniel* was sent for, and he interpreted the words as a prophecy of doom. That night Belshazzar's kingdom fell to Cyrus II, the founder of the Persian Empire (Daniel 5).

St. Benedict (died around 547)   Born near Spoleto into a wealthy Italian family, the well educated Benedict became a hermit at an early age and founded an order of monks, which he finally established about 530 in an old pagan spot at Monte Cassino. The product of Benedict's personal experience appears in the seventy-three chapters of the Rule of Benedict. The monks, when not engaged in divine office, were ordered to study, teach, or engage in manual labor. Legend says that when Benedict was still young, he retired from Rome to a cave where he was assailed by thoughts of a beautiful, female acquaintance. He conquered temptation by rolling in brambles outside the cave, which promptly turned into roses. Once, in his monastery, Brother Placidus went to fetch water and fell into the river. St. Benedict learned of the accident by revelation and sent Brother Maurus to help. The brother walked over the water as though it were land, seized brother Placidus by the hair, and saved his life. Benedict's sister, St. Scholastica*, founded a similar order for nuns. When Scholastica died, Benedict is said to have seen her soul ascending to heaven in the form of a dove. In art, Benedict is shown in the Benedictine robe (black and white), either with a white dove, in reference to his sister Scholastica, or a blackbird, in reference to his temptations by the devil. Sometimes he carries an asperges*, as a symbol of warding off the devil. Painting: *St. Benedict Orders St. Maurus to Rescue St. Placidus*, Fra Filippo Lippi, National Gallery, Washington.

Benediction   The blessing in the Roman Catholic and Protestant church is made with an open hand, the thumb touching the palm. In the Orthodox church, the index finger is stretched out straight and the middle finger is slightly bent, thus forming the letters *IC*, which are the first letters of the words Jesus Christ; the thumb is stretched out and the fourth finger is bent, the two fingers forming the letter X. The little finger is slightly bent, forming the letter C. Letters X and C form the first and last letters of the word Christ in Greek. The gesture of blessing is the sign of the cross and its mysterious powers, and is so used by priests and laymen alike (see Sign of the Cross).

Benjamin   In the Old Testament, the younger son of Jacob* and Rachel*, who died giving him birth. He was a full brother to Joseph*, who was sold into slavery by his ten half-brothers when Benjamin was still a small child. Benjamin became the pet of the family, and after Joseph's disappearance, his father was unwilling to part with him. Joseph had risen through sheer ability to the post of governor for the Pharaoh* of Egypt, and was administrator during the famine years that struck the Middle East. When his half-brothers came down to Egypt to buy corn, Joseph, unrecognized, demanded that Benjamin should accompany them on their next trip. The needy brothers went home and their father was forced to let Benjamin accompany them back to Egypt. When they arrived, Joseph gave a feast for his brethren, and it was to Benjamin that he gave a portion that was "five times as large as any of theirs." Then he concealed a silver cup in Benjamin's sack, so that when the brothers left the city, he could call them back, accusing them of theft. In the midst of the drama, he revealed himself to the bewildered men. Joseph also gave to Benjamin three hundred pieces of silver and five changes of clothing (Genesis 42 and 45). Benjamin became the founder of one of the twelve tribes of Israel.

Berenice II (be-re-nī'sē)   Queen of Egypt in the third century B.C., the daughter of King Magas of Cyrene. After her father's death, she did away with her mother and an unwanted suitor, in order that she might marry Ptolemy III. She was a great beauty and vowed to sacrifice her hair to the gods if Ptolemy should return home, the vanquisher of Asia. She suspended her hair from the temple of Arsinoë at Zephyrium, but it was stolen on the first night. The Samian astrologer, Conon, reported that the winds had wafted the hair to heaven where it still forms the seven stars near the tail of Leo, called "Coma Berenices". The story is often shown in art. (The apostle Paul* appeared in Caesarea in A.D. 1st century before another Berenice who was the daughter of Herod Agrippa I.)

St. Bernard of Clairvaux (1091-1153)   Bernard was the abbot of the Cistercian monastery, which he founded at Clairvaux, France, in 1115, and remained there all his life, despite the efforts of the church to move him to higher posts. A holy life, unusual eloquence, and a reputation for miraculous cures made Bernard renowned. He became the most powerful influence in all Western Europe, and it was he who led the long struggle to seat Pope Innocent II. He procured the condemnation of Abelard, he preached the second crusade, and he stopped a wave of pogroms in 1146. In 1174, he was canonized (declared a saint). His symbol is a white shield with three miters on a round base. In art, he is usually shown with the white robe of the Cistercian order, with a book or pen in his hand, as a Doctor of the Church. Sometimes he is shown with a demon in chains, representing his attack on heresy*, and with three miters, representing the three bishoprics he refused. Sometimes he is seen with a beehive in token of his eloquence. Feast day: August 20. St. Bernard is shown in the Agnolo Gaddi Triptych: *Madonna Enthroned*, National Gallery, Washington.

St. Bernard of Menthon (932-1008)   This Bernard was a Savoyard churchman and the founder of the Alpine hospices of St. Bernard. From the beginning, his Augustinian canons succored pilgrims crossing the Alpine passes. For the purpose of finding those lost in the snows, the St. Bernard, a large mountaineering dog, was bred. Feast: May 28.

St. Bernardino of Siena (1380-1444)   Bernardino was born of a good family in Siena, and early pledged himself to a life of asceticism. In 1400, a terrible plague broke out and he devoted himself to the stricken. Following this experience, he became a Franciscan friar and soon made a name as a travelling preacher throughout Italy. He became influential in public and religious affairs, but insisted on leading the life of a missionary. While preaching he used the Greek letters *IHS*, symbolizing the name of Jesus* (Latin: *Jesus Hominum Salvator*, "Jesus Saviour of Men"). Pope Martin brought him to trial for this "heresy," but he was acquitted, and this led to further display of the holy name. In art, Bernardino is represented as a Franciscan, holding a tablet or disk inscribed with *IHS*. Sometimes he is shown with three miters, symbolic, as with St. Bernard, of the bishoprics he refused. Feast day: May 20. Painting: *St. Bernardino of Siena*, Vicenzo Foppa, National Gallery, Washington.

Bethany   See Jesus Christ—Life Events—Supper at Bethany.

Bethlehem   In the New Testament, the birthplace of Jesus* and one of the great shrines of the world. It is placed on a hill and looks across the Dead Sea and beyond. In the Old Testament, it was the birthplace of Benjamin*, the scene of the Book of Ruth*, the home of King David*, and, as foretold by the prophets, the city in which the Messiah would be born.

Birds In Christian religion, birds symbolize winged souls, the spiritual life.

Biretta In the Christian church, an ecclesiastical hat, square with three or four ridges on top and a pompon on its center; black for priests, purple for bishops, and red for cardinals.

Biton See Cleobis.

Blackbird In Christian religion, a symbol of sin and temptation of the flesh. It is often seen with the praying St. Benedict*, symbolizing the devil, whom Benedict vanquished with the sign of the cross (see Raven).

St. Blaise An Armenian physician who became bishop of Sebastea, Armenia. Moved by divine inspiration, he retired to a cave in the wilds where he befriended the animals. He was found by some huntsmen of the emperor, suspected, and sentenced to torture. His flesh was torn with iron combs, and he was thrown into a lake. Miraculously, his wounds were healed, and he walked upon the water preaching to the multitudes. He was recaptured and beheaded. In art, he is shown with a white beard, dressed as a bishop. His emblems are the iron comb of his martyrdom and a candle, in reference to his last wish for the healing of the sick. Sometimes there are two crossed candles. His blessing is asked for the afflictions of the throat. He is a patron of wild animals. Feast day: February 3. A 15th-century painting: *St. Blaise*, Crocker Art Gallery, Sacramento, Calif.

Blessing of Children See Jesus Christ—Life Events.

Blood In Christian belief, a symbol of life, and the blood shed by Christ* on the cross to redeem mankind from sin. At the Last Supper (see Jesus Christ—Life Events), Christ gave the disciples wine from his cup saying, "Drink. . . . For this is my blood of the new testament" (Matthew 26:27-28).

Blue The color blue symbolizes truth in Christian art and is worn by Jesus* and the Virgin Mary*.

Boar In Greek mythology, the boar is an attribute of the god Ares*. Disguised as a boar, Mars gored Adonis* to death. The Calydonian Boar* was sent by the goddess Artemis* to ravage the land of Oeneus*. Heracles* killed the Erymanthean boar as his third labor for Eurystheus*.

Boat and River Attributes of St. Julian*.

Boaz   See Ruth.

Boil on Thigh   An attribute of St. Roch*, symbolizing the plague.

St. Bonaventura (1221-1274)   An Italian bishop and theologian, born in Tuscany, he studied in Paris and then joined the Franciscan order. In 1257, he was chosen minister-general and officiated in the office with such zeal he is regarded as the greatest friar minor after St. Francis of Assisi himself. Legend says his name was bestowed upon him when he was taken as an ailing child to St. Francis. When he recovered, Francis exclaimed, *"O buona ventura!"* ("Oh good fortune"). Bonaventura was simple and unassuming. A story is told that when the ambassadors of the pope came to present him with his cardinal's hat, he told them to hang it nearby on a tree; he was washing his dinner plate, and his hands were wet and greasy. In art, he is frequently painted with his cardinal's hat hanging beside him or at his feet. Sometimes he is shown with an angel bringing him a sacramental wafer in reference to the legend that he was too humble to go to the altar to receive the Holy Sacrament*. He may carry a chalice (communion cup) or a cross, and is usually beardless, dressed as a friar in Franciscan robes, or as a cardinal. Feast day: July 14.

Book   A book in Christian art is a symbol of the Bible (Scriptures), often shown in the hands of the Evangelists*. In the hands of St. Stephen*, it represents the Old Testament. It is carried by the archangel Uriel* as interpreter of judgements. In the hands of saints, it represents learning; it is frequently seen with the founders of monastic orders, the founders of the church, and in the hands of missionary saints. It is shown with St. Anne*, the mother of the Virgin Mary*, in reference to the Psalm 139:16 ". . . in thy book all my members were written." A book on which the alpha* and omega* are written refers to Christ. A book with a fish on it is an attribute of St. Simon* who was a fishmonger (see Scroll).

Boreas (bor'ē-us)   In Greek mythology, the god of the north wind. He was the son of Astraeus, a Titan*, and Eos*, the morning; he lived in a cave on Mt. Haemus, in Thrace. He stole his wife Orithyia in a gust of wind, while she was playing. A stormy character, he was often used by the gods to torment those who were under their displeasure. Hera* asked him to shipwreck Heracles* on the island of Cos. Instructed by an oracle during the Persian war, the Athenians sacrificed to him, and he routed the Persian fleet lying off Euboea with a violent storm. Boreas is identified with the Roman god Aquilo. Small bronze statue: *Boreas Carrying off Orithyia*, Fogg Art Museum, Cambridge, Mass.

Bow In Greek religion, Apollo* is lord of the silver bow. He first used it against the python at Delphi*. His sister Artemis* as goddess of the moon and the hunt, is goddess of the silver bow. Brazen bows were carried by the Amazons*. Eros* is seen with bow and arrows. In Christian iconography, the bow symbolizes war and worldly power.

Box of Ointment An attribute of Mary Magdalene*, referring to the pound of ointment with which she anointed the feet of Jesus (John 12:3), and to the spices she brought to anoint the body of Christ* at the tomb. It is also an attribute of the physician saints Cosmos* and Damian*.

Boys Three small boys are an attribute of St. Nicholas*.

Bramble A symbol of the purity of the Virgin Mary*, who experienced divine love without knowledge of lust.

Bread In the Old Testament, bread is a symbol of God's providence. In the New Testament, it symbolizes the staff of life and the body of Christ* (Luke 22:19). A loaf of bread is an attribute of St. Dominic*, who obtained it by divine intervention for his monastery. Three loaves of bread are an attribute of St. Mary of Egypt*, who went to live in the desert with only three loaves of bread. A raven carrying a loaf of bread is an attribute of St. Paul the Hermit*. Loaves of bread with a cross are an attribute of St. Philip*, because he participated in Christ's miracle of the Loaves and Fishes.

Breasts An attribute of St. Agatha*, usually shown on a platter, who had her breasts torn off by shears during her martyrdom.

Briareus (brī-ar'e-us) In Greek mythology, a sea giant who possessed a hundred arms and some say fifty hands. He was the offspring of Uranus* (heaven) and Gaea* (earth), and was one of the race of Titans* (giants), who fought against the Olympians*. Homer says the gods called him Briareus but men called him Aegaeon (Iliad 1-403). When the sleeping Zeus* was put into chains, or a net with a thousand knots, by Athena*, Hera*, and Poseidon*, the sea goddess Thetis* summoned Briareus to free him.

Bridle and Yoke   In Greek mythology, these are attributes of Nemesis* as symbols of control.

Briseis (brī-sē'is)   In Homer's Iliad, a daughter of Briseus, who was a captive spoil of the great warrior Achilles* during the Trojan war*. She was much loved by Achilles and when she was taken away from him by King Agamemnon* of Mycenae, the leader of the expedition, Achilles sulked in his tent, refused to go into battle, and the Greeks lost ground daily. Patroclus,* the great friend of Achilles, went to the field in his stead and was slain. Then Achilles sprang into action, avenged the death of Patroclus by slaying Trojan Prince Hector*, and soon after Troy fell to the Greeks.

St. Bruno (1033-1101)   Born at Cologne of noble birth, he was the founder of the severe order of Carthusian monks who combine solitary and communal living. The order started with six companions at Grande Chartreuse, near Grenoble, France, and the name in England, "charterhouse," is used in all the English monasteries. Pope Urban II summoned Bruno to Rome as an adviser, but allowed him to found another Chartreuse monastery near Rome in Calabria. Feast day: October 6.

Bucephalus (bū-se'fa-lus)   The favorite horse of Alexander the Great*. The story of how he was tamed by young Alexander is famous. He was a horse of speed and fire, and Alexander was devoted to him. He lived until the age of thirty and was buried in India at the site of Bucephalia, signs of which still exist near the town of Jhelum in Pakistan.

Bull   In Greek mythology, the god Zeus*, disguised as a bull, abducted Europa*. The Cretan bull* was captured by Heracles* as his seventh labor. The god Dionysus* was symbolically killed and devoured as a bull in midsummer festivals. Black bulls were sacrificed to the god Poseiden*. The Minotaur* had a bull's head and a human body. Oceanus* sometimes wears bull's horns on his head. In Christian religion, the bull is an attribute of St. Sylvester* because he restored a bull to life as proof that Christ was the God of Life. A brass bull is an attribute of St. Eustace*, who was incarcerated inside one with his family. A winged bull or ox is an emblem of St. Luke* the Evangelist.

Bulrushes (papyrus)   In the Old Testament, bulrushes are most famous for concealing the baby Moses*. The Pharaoh (ruler) of Egypt, fearing the growing power and number of Hebrews who had immigrated to Egypt, put out a decree that all male Hebrew babies should be killed. The baby Moses was hidden in bulrushes by the river and by this ruse his death was circumvented.

Burning Bush   In the Old Testament, this bush is the one in which Moses* saw the Angel of the Lord, and from which God's voice called out to him, telling him he must lead the Hebrews out of Egypt (Exodus 3:2-3). The miracle was not that it seemed to burn, but that it was not consumed.

Butterfly or Butterfly Wings   In Greek symbology, the butterfly is the personification of Psyche*. In Christian interpretation, it is a symbol of resurrection and eternal life.

C

Cadmus In Greek legend, the son of the king of Phoenicia. His sister Europa* was carried off by the god Zeus* in the form of a bull. Cadmus was sent with his brothers to look for her, threatened with exile if they returned without her. Their mother accompanied them, but died on the journey when they came to Thrace. Cadmus continued to Delphi* to seek advice from the oracle. He was told to abandon the search for Europa, to follow a cow, and to found a city on the spot where she lay down. The cow met him in Phocis, led him to Boetia, and then lay on the ground. Cadmus prepared to sacrifice her to the goddess Athena*, and sent his followers to get water for the ceremony. When they came to a spring, a dragon appeared and destroyed all the companions. Cadmus promptly slew the dragon, and at Athena's command, took its teeth and sowed them in the ground. A host of armed men sprang up who attacked and killed each other until only five of them remained. These five helped Cadmus to build the city of Thebes, and were the ancestors of its citizens. Cadmus married Harmonia*, daughter of the god Ares* and the goddess Aphrodite*, who bore him five children. Misfortune followed the family of Cadmus and his descendants because of the slaying of the dragon and because of the wedding gifts given to Harmonia. In his old age, Cadmus and Harmonia were turned into serpents by Zeus and carried to Elysium, in the underworld.

Caduceus (ka-dū′sē-us) In Greek legend, the rod carried by the god Hermes*, entwined with serpents and sometimes winged. Known as the caduceus, it was a symbol of peace and prosperity and became a symbol of commerce, Hermes being the god of commerce. It was the emblem also of the physician Asclepius*, and is the emblem of physicians today. The rod represents power;

the serpents, wisdom: and the wings, diligence and activity. The caduceus is also carried by the goddess-messenger Iris* and by Eirene*, the goddess of peace.

Caesar (sē'zar), Caius Julius (100-44 B.C.)   A Roman statesman and general, no less famous as an orator and writer. Endowed with extraordinary natural gifts, he received his education under the supervision of his mother Aurelia, and early established himself in the first ranks. His two great works have survived, the *History of the Gallic War* and the *History of the Civil War.* These describe his great military prowess, gift of strategy, and the taking over of the Roman Republic. His political success was due in great part to public popularity, but he had many powerful enemies and was brutally murdered entering the senate. The public reaction was so great, Caesar was instantly deified by the senate, and it became the custom to offer sacrifices at the base of the column raised to him in the Forum.

Cain   In the Old Testament, the eldest son of Adam* and Eve*, brother of Abel* and a tiller of the soil, while Abel was a shepherd. Cain and Abel made sacrifices to the Lord on separate altars, and God favored Abel's sacrifice over Cain's. In jealousy, Cain killed Abel and became a fugitive. When the Lord observed this murder he asked Cain, "Where is thy brother Abel?" Cain answered, "I know not. Am I my brother's keeper?" Then the Lord cursed Cain (Genesis 4:1-16). Painting: *Eve with Cain and Abel*, Bacchiacca II, Philadelphia Museum of Art.

Caiphas (kā'ya-fas)   See Jesus Christ—Life Events—Trial before High Priest.

Calling of Fishermen   See Jesus Christ—Life Events.

Calliope (kal-ī'ō-pē)   In Greek mythology, the chief of the nine muses*, the patron of epic poetry and eloquence. She was the mother of Orpheus* by the god Apollo*. In a dispute between the goddess Aphrodite* and the goddess Persephone* for the possession of Adonis* as a lover, Calliope decided that his year should be divided in three; one third to be spent with Aphrodite, one third with Persephone, and a third by himself. Her emblems are a stylus (writing instrument) and wax tablets.

Callisto (kal-is'tō)   In Greek mythology, a beautiful nymph and a companion of Artemis*, who attracted the attention of the god Zeus* and bore him a son Arcas. In order to put an end to this infatuation, his jealous wife, the goddess Hera*, turned the nymph into a bear. The unhappy Callisto fled through the forest, living a life of terror. Years later, her son Arcas came upon her while hunting and was about to shoot her, when Zeus rescued them both and placed them in the sky as constellations. Hera then persuaded the god Poseiden* to forbid them to bathe in the sea, and for this reason they never sink below the horizon, but revolve in the sky as the Great and Little Bears. Engraving: *Callisto and Her Son*, follower of Hendrik Goltzius, Metropolitan, New York.

Calvary (kal'vu-rē) Latin for the Hebrew word Golgotha, meaning skull. In the New Testament, this is the place where Jesus* was crucified outside the walls of Jerusalem. It is mentioned as Calvary in the Bible just once (Luke 23:33), elsewhere as Golgotha. According to tradition, the identification of the site was made by St. Helena* early in the 4th century when she found the supposed relic of the cross. The spot is now occupied by the Church of the Holy Sepulchre (see Jesus Christ—Life Events).

Calydonian Boar or Hunt In Greek legend, a huge boar was sent by the goddess Artemis* to ravage the land of Calydon in Aetolia, because King Oeneus* had forgotten to sacrifice to the goddess. A band of heroes joined Meleager*, the son of Oeneus and the leader of the hunt; among whom were Jason*, Castor* and Polydeuces*, Theseus*, Perseus*, Nestor*, and the huntress Atalanta*. The boar was wounded by Atalanta and killed by Meleager. Fresco transferred to canvas, *The Calydonian Boar Hunt*, Pinturicchio, Metropolitan, New York.

Calypso (kal-ip'sō) In Greek mythology, the queen of the island of Ogygia, on which Odysseus* was wrecked. She kept him with her for eight years, promising eternal youth and immortality if he would remain with her. The goddess Athena* intervened and persuaded the god Zeus* to send his messenger, the god Hermes*, to Calypso with instructions to provide Odysseus with a raft and all that was necessary to continue his homeward journey to Ithaca and his wife Penelope*.

Camenae (ka-mē'nē) Four maidens, identified by the Romans with the Greek muses*.

Cana, Marriage at See Jesus Christ—Miracles.

Canephorus (kan-ef'or-us) A sculptured figure of a youth or maiden bearing a basket on his head. In ancient Greece, the canephori bore the sacred things necessary for the feasts of the gods.

Cap   An egg-shaped cap with a star is an attribute of the Dioscuri*. A pointed cap (Phrygian cap) is often seen on Odysseus*.

Cardinal's Hat   A red hat with a broad brim and a low crown, decorated with two cords and fifteen tassels. St. Jerome* is often shown with this hat in Renaissance painting, although the hat was unknown in his time; also St. Bonaventura*.

Carnation   In Christian iconography, a symbol of commitment; betrothal.

Carpenter's Square or Rule   An attribute of St. Thomas*, as a builder, and of Joseph of Nazareth*, as a carpenter.

Caryatid (kar-i-at'id)   A sculptured female figure, serving as an ornamental support in place of a column or pilaster. In Greek mythology, there was a Laconian maiden loved by the god Dionysus*. When she died suddenly at Caryae, she was changed into a walnut tree. The goddess Artemis* brought the news to the Laconians, and *caryatis* (of the walnut-tree) became one of her epithets. It was at Caryae that a temple was built to Artemis in which female statues acted as columns. (The most famous caryatids are those of the Erectheum Temple on the Acropolis in Athens, Greece.)

Cassandra (ka-san'dra)   In Greek legend, the fairest of the twelve daughters of King Priam* and Queen Hecuba* of Troy. She learned the art of prophecy from the god Apollo*, but when she would not accept him as her lover, he turned her gift into a curse. She was considered mad and her prophecies were never believed. She predicted the fall of Troy when her brother Paris* set off for Greece to abduct Helen*, the wife of Menelaus*. She foresaw the conspiracy of the Trojan Horse*, and even tried to set fire to the horse when it was brought inside the city walls but was restrained by her countrymen. At the fall of Troy, Cassandra was violated by Ajax*, the lesser, but she went as captive concubine to Agamemnon* who took her back to Mycenae with him. Here she was killed by Agamemnon's wife Clytemnestra* shortly after Clytemnestra had murdered her husband with the aid of her paramour Aegisthus*. A painting on a red-figured, Greek vase (5th century B.C.): *Ajax Seizing Cassandra*, Metropolitan, New York.

Cassiopea (kas-i-ō-pē'a)   In Greek mythology, the wife of Cepheus, king in Ethiopia, and mother of Andromeda*. This boastful woman, comparing her mortal daughter's beauty to the

Nereid* nymphs, incurred the wrath of the god of the sea Poseiden*, and in consequence brought destruction to her country and suffering to her daughter. Her own death was caused by the sight of the head of Medusa* at Andromeda's wedding. Poseiden set her image among the stars, but in such a way as to humiliate her. At certain times of the year, she appears, hanging in the heavens, upside down. The chief stars of the constellation form the outline of a woman in a chair, holding her hands out in supplication.

Castle   See Tower.

Castor and Pollux (the Roman names for the Dioscuri*)   In Roman mythology, as in Greek mythology, Castor and Pollux are the devoted twin sons of Leda*. Castor was mortal, the son of Leda's husband Tyndareus. Pollux was immortal, born with his famous sister Helen* from an egg which his mother produced after she had been seduced by the god Jupiter* in the form of a swan. (One legend recounts that Leda produced two eggs from one of which sprang Castor and Clytemnestra*, from the other sprang Helen and Pollux.) As young men, they rescued their sister Helen from the Attic fortress of Aphidnae where she had been carried off by Theseus*. They took part in the expedition of the Argonauts* and were members of the Calydonian Boar Hunt*. Later they quarreled with their cousins, Idas and Lynceus, in one story, over cattle. In another legend, they raped their cousins Phoebe and Helaira who were betrothed to sons of Aphareus. In either event, the mortal Castor was killed, and the disconsolate Pollux asked Jupiter to give the twin brother his own immortality. Jupiter decreed that they might share their lives, spending alternate days on Mt. Olympus* (the home of the gods) and the underworld. As tribute to their devotion to each other, he placed their images among the constellations, known as the Gemini (twins). Together they were patrons of sailors to whom they appear as the phenomenon of corposant, a ball of fire which is sometimes seen playing around the masts of ships in a storm, promising good weather beyond the bad. This phenomenon is also called St. Elmo's* fire in Christian legend.

St. Catherine of Alexandria (or Katherine)   Legend says that Catherine was a virgin of royal descent who, in the 4th century, publicly confessed to Christian faith at a sacrificial feast, sponsored by the Roman Emperor Maximus. Confronted by fifty philosophers, she demolished their arguments, and they were burned alive for failing to answer her. When she refused to marry the emperor and deny her faith, she was beaten and imprisoned. In her cell, she was fed by a dove and Christ* visited her in a vision. An attempt was made to break her will on a spiked wheel (the Catherine wheel), but it fell to pieces and she was not hurt. This constancy brought about the conversion of two hundred soldiers who were straightway beheaded. Finally Catherine herself was beheaded and from her veins flowed milk instead of blood. Her body was carried by angels to Mt. Sinai, where she has a shrine. Legend also tells that before she was baptized she had a dream in which the Virgin asked the Christ child to take Catherine as a servant. The child turned his head away, saying she was not beautiful. Catherine pondered the dream and found no peace until she was baptized. Then Christ appeared to her again and took her as his celestial spouse, placing a ring on her finger which she discovered on her hand when she awoke. Feast day: November 25. In art, Catherine is frequently shown with the Christ child placing the ring on her finger. She usually wears a crown to signify royalty. She is shown with her attribute, the spiked wheel, with a book indicating her learning, with the palm of victory and the sword of martyrdom. Painting: *The Mystic Marriage of St. Catherine*, Antonio di Correggio, National Gallery, Washington.

St. Catherine of Siena (1347-80) An Italian mystic, a member of the third order of Dominicans, who by spiritual authority alone became a powerful diplomat, frequently writing letters and influencing the actions of those in power; unquestionably one of the great figures of the Middle Ages. She was the youngest of a large family, a lively girl, but while still young was found praying with a white dove on her head. She became a sister of the Dominican order and spent much time in prayer, experiencing many raptures, culminating in the pain of the stigmata (the bodily marks of wounds, suffered by Christ on the cross), and is usually so presented in art. She wears the Dominican robes and sometimes holds a cross surmounted by a heart in reference to the legend that Christ, in a vision, replaced her heart with his own. The *Dialogue of St. Catherine* is a work much used in devotional literature. Feast day: April 30. Painting: *The Miraculous Communion of St. Catherine of Siena*, Giovanni di Paolo di Grazia, Metropolitan, New York.

Cauldron of Oil An attribute of St. John the Evangelist*, who was miraculously saved when hurled into boiling oil.

St. Cecelia or Cicely According to legend, Cecelia was a wealthy, Roman Christian who was betrothed to a young pagan named Valerian. After their marriage, she begged him to respect her vow of chastity and persuaded him to accept baptism. His brother likewise became a Christian, and they undertook to

57

preach the gospel. The governor of Rome had the brothers arrested and executed. Cecelia was brought before the governor, and when she refused to perform an act of idolatry, he sentenced her to be stifled in her bath. The steam failed to suffocate her, so an executioner was sent to behead her. He struck three ineffectual blows, and she lingered for three days during which time she distributed her wealth to the poor. Cecelia was also a beautiful singer, the "inventor of the organ," and a writer of hymns, hence patroness of music. According to one legend, an angel fell in love with her for her musical skill. Her husband saw the heavenly visitant who gave them both a crown of martyrdom, which he brought from Paradise. Feast day: November 22. In art, Cecelia is usually shown playing a musical instrument or singing. Her attribute is frequently an organ or harp. She also has a crown of red and white roses. Sometimes she is shown with three wounds on her neck (see Crown of Roses).

Cecrops (sē'krops)   In Greek mythology, the first king of Athens. He was half-serpent and half-man, the serpent being an ancient symbol of the life-giving earth. He introduced the elements of civilization, establishing monogomy and the first principles of law and religion. When the goddess Athena* and the god Poseiden* vied with each other for the control of Athens, Cecrops, according to one legend, awarded the city to Athena for the gift of the olive tree; another says the gods made the decision during the reign of Cecrops.

Cedar   A symbol of Christian incorruptibility.

St. Celestine V (1215-1296)   Celestine, born Pietro Murrone, was elected pope in his old age in 1294, and was then promptly used as a political tool. From his youth, he had been an ascetic, dwelling in the mountains of the Abruzzi. Feeling his inadequacy as pope, he resigned, but his successor, afraid of reprisal, shut him up in a castle until his death. During his years in the mountains, he had gradually collected around him a number of young monks, later called Celestines, who were part of a great visionary movement popularizing ascetic practices. Feast day: May 19.

Censer (sen'ser)   A metal vessel in which incense is burned during Christian church services. It is a symbol of prayer wafting to God. It has four or five chains on which hang small bells, representing the twelve apostles*.

Centaurs (sen'tors)   In Greek mythology, the descendants of Ixion* and Nephele, conceived as half-men and half-horse, of wild nature. They are said to have dwelt in ancient Thessaly, a myth probably derived from the expert horsemanship of the original inhabitants. They were followers of the god Dionysus* and of the god of love Eros*. Some centaurs, like the famous Chiron*, were kindly teachers of men. In a famous legend, the centaurs were invited to the marriage feast of Hippodamia* and Pirithous*, the king of the Lapithae*. The centaurs, unused to strong wine, became intoxicated and attacked the women, particularly the bride. A fierce battle ensued in which the Lapithae, aided by guests such as Nestor* and Theseus*, drove off the centaurs. This wedding battle is frequently shown in art. The centaurs had another inebriated battle with Heracles* in a cave near Mt. Pholoë, in which Heracles slew many of them and drove off the rest. In later times, when associated with the god Dionysus, they moved peacefully in his train of satyrs*, nymphs, and Bacchantes*, drawing the chariot with him and his wife Ariadne*. Sometimes women and children are represented in the form of centaurs. In Christian religion, the centaur symbolizes savage passions, adultery, heresy, and man divided against himself. A centaur is said to have acted as a guide to Anthony Abbot* in the desert. Painting: *St. Anthony Abbot with Centaur*, Sassetta, National Gallery, Washington.

Cephalus (sef-a-lus) In Greek legend, [the] son of the god Hermes* and Herse*, the husband of Procris, whom he loved deeply. Unfortunately each was suspicious of the other's fidelity, and this ate into their love. When the goddess of dawn, Eos*, fell in love with Cephalus, she disguised him as an unknown, handsome youth, and in this semblance, caused him to woo Procris. This deceit made Procris waver and Cephalus felt betrayed. Procris, feeling rejected, left for Crete to serve the goddess Artemis*. When she returned with a dog and a swift spear that never missed its aim, Cephalus did not recognize her and offered her his love, if she would only part with the dog and spear. They were reunited, however, but one day when Cephalus was searching for Procris, she crept through the bushes to ascertain whether he was out walking with a rival. Cephalus, hearing a noise and seeing the bushes move, thought it was a wild beast, and hurling his javelin in her direction, killed her. The unhappy man could not forgive himself and one day leaped into the sea. Murals: *Cephalus and Procris*, Bernardino Luini, National Gallery, Washington.

Cerberus (ser'ber-us) In Greek mythology, the three-headed dog with a serpent's tail and a mane of serpents' heads, the offspring of Typhon and Echidna. He guarded the gate of Hades* in the underworld, and the honey which the Greeks buried with their dead, was intended to quiet him. Orpheus*, Aeneas*, and

Odysseus* successfully passed Cerberus on visits to Hades. The last labor of Heracles* for Eurystheus* was to bring Cerberus from below to the upper world. This he did by grasping Cerberus around the neck, and disregarding the snake bites, he choked him until he yielded. When Cerberus saw the light of day, foam gushed from his mouth and from this foam sprang the poisonous plant, aconite. Attic plate (6th century) with painting: *Heracles Seizing Cerberus in the Presence of Hermes*, Museum of Fine Arts, Boston.

Cercopes (ser-kō'pez)   In Greek legend, a race of gnomes, or apes, who attacked Heracles* as he slept, and stole his weapons. When Heracles awoke, he picked them up and put them in his lion skin. He took them to Queen Omphale*, whom he was serving to expiate his impulsive and unwarranted murder of Iphitus, in a fit of madness.

Ceres (sē'rēz)   An Italian goddess of grain and the harvest, identified by the Romans with the Greek Demeter*. Her cult was one of the early ones, known as Cerealis. When the Romans took over the legend of the rape of Proserpina* by King Pluto*, the inconsolable Ceres is said to have hidden in a cave in Sicily. Famine followed. Ceres was therefore depicted in Sicily as a mourning figure in black, holding a pigeon in one hand and a dolphin in the other. Her worship was connected with the earth-goddess Tellus Mater*, and involved not only fertility rites, but rites for the dead. In the Italian countryside, Ceres was offered a sow before the beginning of harvest, and the first cuttings of the corn were dedicated to her. Painting: *The Triumph of Ceres*, Soldari, Museum of Art, University of Kansas. (See Demeter.)

Cerynean Hind (ser-i-nē'an)   In Greek mythology, a fabled creature with golden horns and bronze hoofs, sacred to the goddess Artemis*, and swift as the wind. It was captured by Heracles* as the fourth of his labors for Eurystheus*. Legend says he pursued it through Arcadia and finally transfixed its forefeet with one arrow before carrying it back to Eurystheus.

Chains   In Greek legend, Prometheus* is bound in chains. In Christian symbology, chains are an emblem of the Passion*, referring to the flagellation of Christ (see Jesus Christ—Life Events). It is also an attribute of St. Leonard*, who visited the prisoners of King Clovis.

Chalice   A cup used in Christian liturgy for the consecrated wine of Holy Communion*, usually covered with a veil, referring to the Last Supper* (see Jesus Christ—Life Events). A chalice with a snake is a symbol of redemption and an attribute of St. John the Evangelist*. A chalice with a cross symbolizes Jesus' agony in the Garden of Gethsemane* (see Jesus Christ—Life Events), and is also carried by St. Thomas Aquinas* because of the nature of his writings. The chalice is an attribute of St. Bonaventura*.

Charites (kar'i-tēz)   In Greek mythology, the name for the three graces: Aglaia* (brilliance), Euphrosyne* (joy), and Thalia* (bloom of life)*, goddesses who personified everything that lends beauty and charm. They were associated with the muses* and dwelt with them on Mt. Olympus*. In art, they are shown as beautiful, young women, often holding hands, sometimes in the company of the goddess Aphrodite*, the god Eros*, and the god Dionysus*. The inspiration of the graces was believed to be as necessary for the arts as it was for the enjoyment of life.

Charity   English word for the Greek *agape*, or supreme love (see Virtues).

St. Charity   See St. Faith.

Charlemagne (shar'lu-mine) (742-814)   Son of the Frankish king, Pepin the Short, who became the sole king of the Franks in 771. Early in his reign, he supported Pope Adrian I, and received the title of patrician of the Romans. After capturing Pavia, he took over the Lombard throne; in 778, he invaded Spain and was repulsed at Saragossa by the Moors, but kept Navarre, Pamplona, and Barcelona. His greatest wars were with the Saxons, whom he finally conquered in 804. When Pope Leo III was threatened with deposition, Charlemagne came to his aid, and by refusing to recognize Irene as empress of the East, was himself crowned Emperor. Charlemagne was a great organizer. He systematized his government, extending control into distant lands; he was preoccupied with welfare, and instrumental in settling theological controversies. His court at Aachen was an intellectual center where he initiated the preservation of Classical literature, and he established schools for all classes of people throughout the empire. Although he kept several wives and concubines, he was beatified after his death. His achievements led to magnificent, romantic legends in which he was characterized as a bearded, patriarchal figure, surrounded by twelve peers, the champion of Christendom. His role is vividly described in the epic poem, *The Song of Roland.*

Charon (kā'ron)   In Greek mythology, the ferryman of Hades* who bore the newly dead across the river Styx to the underworld.

In Greece, the coin placed in a dead man's mouth was said to be Charon's fee for the ferry ride to the Elysian Fields*. In art he is usually represented as a brutal, avaricious, old man. The Etruscans show him frequently on tombs as an old man with tusks.

Chariot Chariots are driven by many Greek gods and heroes (see Chariots—How Drawn, in Appendix). In the Old Testament, the prophet Elijah* rides up to heaven, at his death, in a fiery chariot.

Charybdis (ka-rib′dis) In Greek mythology, a greedy monster whom the god Zeus* hurled, with a thunderbolt, into the straits of Messina, opposite the treacherous rock Scylla*, causing a dangerous whirlpool. In Homeric legend, she is said to gulp in the waters and spew them out again three times a day, endangering those who try to navigate past the spot.

Cherries In Christian iconography, a symbol of sweet character and good works.

Cherub (*plural*, cherubim) (cher′ub; cher′a-bim or cher′yoo-bim) A kind of angel. In the Old Testament cherubim are symbolic, mythological creatures guarding the tree of life in the Garden of Eden* (Genesis 3:24). In the Hebrew Temple, they were protectors of sacred objects, probably thought of as composite creations, like the Assyrian winged creatures with lions' bodies and human faces. In Jewish tradition, they were beautiful, young men. Later, Christian art made plump children of them. Like the seraphim, they are said to be in the very presence of God.

Chestnut In Christian iconography, a symbol of chastity and triumph over the temptations of the flesh, because it lies in its husk, unharmed by its surrounding thorns.

Child Jesus on a Book or Carried in the Arms of a Saint Attribute of St. Anthony of Padua*. A child or young man carried as a dead corpse is shown with St. Zenobius*.

Chimaera (kī-mē′ra) In Greek mythology, a fire-breathing monster of divine origin that had the body of a goat or lion, the head of a lion, and the tail of a serpent. It lived in Lycia, and was slain by Bellerophon*. Sometimes it is described as having three heads, one a serpent, one a goat, and one a lion. A 7th-century vase painting: *The Chimaera*, Museum of Fine Arts, Boston.

Chiron (kī'ron) In Greek mythology, the wise, just centaur*, renowned for his powers of healing, prophecy, music, and hunting. He was the famous teacher of Achilles*, Asclepius*, Jason*, and many other heroes. Unlike his wild, unruly brother centaurs, he befriended many men. Peleus* and the goddess Thetis*, parents of Achilles, were married in his cave. Heracles*, while pursuing the wild centaurs, accidentally inflicted an incurable wound in the leg of Chiron with one of his poisoned arrows. Chiron suffered great pain from which he could not be relieved, since, as the son of the Titan Cronus*, he was immortal. He finally escaped the pain by giving his immortality to Prometheus* and this enabled him to go to Hades* (the underworld) in Prometheus' stead. The god Zeus* placed Chiron in the heavens as Sagittarius, the archer.

Chloe (klō'ē) See Daphnis.

Christ See Jesus.

St. Christopher Christopher, whose date is unknown, is the patron of travel, and is said to have been martyred in Asia Minor. Legend relates that Christopher was a ferryman of great stature who carried travellers on his shoulders across a rushing stream. One rainy night a child asked to be carried over. During the crossing the waters rose, and the child became heavier with each step, until Christopher was afraid. "Child," he cried, when he reached the far shore, "thou hast put me to great peril. I might bear no greater burden." The child replied, "Marvel not, for thou hast borne the whole world upon thee and its sins likewise. I am the Christ." St. Christopher, meaning Christ bearer, is usually represented in art as a huge man with the Holy Child on his shoulders, leaning on a staff as he crosses the swollen stream. It is said that after carrying the child across the water, he planted his palm staff in the ground and it took root and bore fruit. Fresco: *St. Christopher*, Domenico Ghirlandaio, Metropolitan, New York.

Chrysothemis (kri-soth'e-mus) A daughter of Agamemnon* and Clytemnestra*, the sister of Electra*, Iphigenia*, and Orestes*; a timid girl who accepted the fate of the House of Atreus* with resignation.

Church Model on a Saint's Hand In Christian iconography, this symbolizes a founder of the church. St. Helena* is shown with the model of a church, representing the Holy Sepulchre*.

Circe (ser'sē) In Greek legend, a daughter of Helius* and Persa, and sister of Aeetes and Pasiphae*. She was a noted sorceress, learned in the use of herbs and charms, and noted for her cruel transformations. When Jason* and her niece Medea* visited her on their way home from Colchis, she purified them of the murder of Medea's brother Apsyrtus, sprinkling pig's blood on their hands, but her kind acts were rare. When Glaucus refused her love, preferring Scylla*, Circe turned her into a horrid monster. The companions of Odysseus*, on the homeward journey from Troy, were enticed into her palace where she turned them all into swine. Odysseus was able to rescue his friends and resist her sorcery by means of a magic herb, given to him by the god Hermes*. Odysseus and his men lingered many months on Circe's island, reveling in her hospitality. She bore him three sons, one of whom, Telegonus, grew up to kill Odysseus unintentionally. Odysseus and his men finally set sail for Tartarus in the underworld, having been given full directions by Circe as to how he might learn about his future from the dead seer Tiresias*. Telemachus*, the son of Odysseus by Penelope*, is said to have married Circe after his father's death. Painting: *Circe*, Bartolommeo Guidobono, Metropolitan, New York.

Circle In Christian iconography, the circle is a symbol of eternity and the everlasting God. A circle in a triangle symbolizes eternity and the Trinity*. Three circles intertwined symbolize equality, unity, and the co-eternal nature of the Trinity (see Halo).

Circumcision A custom observed by the Jews as a sign of the covenant between God and Abraham* of the Old Testament. According to Jewish law, a male child must be circumcised and given his name on the eighth day after his birth.

St. Clare of Assisi (1194-1253) Clare was the founder of the order of Poor Ladies. She came of a noble family, and although she refused two marriages, she did not decide to become a nun until she met St. Francis* at the age of eighteen. Francis put her in the care of Benedictine nuns, where she was later joined by her sister St. Agnes and her widowed mother. She was established by St. Francis in a community house in Assisi, and from Pope Innocent obtained the privilege of poverty in 1215. *The Little Flowers of St. Francis* relates that Clare was desirous of sharing a meal with Francis. When he granted her request, she came with one of the sisters to Santa Maria degle Angelioni, the church where she had taken her vows. The monks joined the nuns and they sat on the ground to eat, as was the Franciscan custom, while Francis began to speak in praise of the Lord. His eloquence was so extraordinary, the people of Assisi saw the church from afar as though it were on fire. When they hastened to put out the flames, they found Francis and Clare and the companions absorbed in contemplation. The spiritual food was so nourishing, the repast on the ground had not been eaten. St. Clare outlived St. Francis by twenty-seven years. In art, she is shown carrying a monstrance*, a receptacle for consecrated bread in reference to the legend that she saved her convent from invading Saracens by placing the monstrance at the door. Feast day: August 12. Painting: *St. Claire*, Lippo Memni, Metropolitan, New York.

Claudia Quinta   See Vestal Virgins.

Cleansing of the Temple   See Jesus Christ—Life Events.

St. Clement   The patron of tanners, being himself a tanner. He was converted to Christianity by St. Paul*, and became bishop of Rome. He was the first Christian writer to use the phoenix* as an allegory of the Resurrection (see Jesus Christ—After-Life Events). His authority is shown in his epistle to the Corinthians in which he bids the church to cease its quarreling. Legend says that he was martyred in the Crimea where he had been sentenced to hard labor by the Emperor Trajan for refusing to deny Christianity. He and his converts suffered here for lack of water. Clement prayed and a lamb appeared. He struck the spot where the lamb had stood with an axe, and a stream of water gushed forth. His oppressors lashed him to an anchor and threw him into the sea (about A.D. 100). Some legends say the waters receded, and his body was found inside a temple. In art, Clement is shown with an anchor around his neck, or with the emblem. Feast day: November 23. Painting: *The Trinity Appearing to St. Clement*, from the workshop of Tiepolo, Metropolitan, New York.

Cleobis and Biton (klē'ō-bis and bī'ton)   In Greek legend, the sons of Cydippe, a priestess of the goddess Hera* at Argos. During a festival, the priestess had to ride to the temple in a chariot, and as the oxen were not at hand, Cleobis and Biton dragged the chariot many miles for her. At the end of the journey, Cydippe prayed to Hera that her sons might receive the greatest blessing as a reward for their filial piety. Hera sent them immediate, painless death.

Cleophas (klē'ō-pas)   In the New Testament, the husband of Mary*, the mother of James the Less*, one of the Marys who stood at the foot of the cross of Christ (Matthew 27:56). Cleophas is also known as the father of James, by the Greek form of the name, Alphaeus.

Cleopatra (klē-ō-pa'tra) (69-30 B.C.)   The last Macedonian queen of Egypt, one of the great romantic heroines of all time. At seventeen, as was the family custom, she was married to her younger brother Ptolemy XII. In 48 B.C., she was put off the throne but was reinstated by Julius Caesar*, who was captivated by her charms. She lived with Caesar in Rome from 46-44 and bore him a son, known as Caesarion, who was later put to death by Octavius Augustus*. After Caesar's murder, Cleopatra returned to Egypt, hoping to re-establish the power of the Egyptian throne. In 42, Marc Antony* fell under her spell and repudiated his wife Octavia, the sister of Octavius, for her sake. Marc Antony was defeated at Actium, fighting against Octavius, and committed suicide. Cleopatra then killed herself by means of the bite of an asp. She had three children by Antony. Besides her extraordinary charm, she possessed a fine mind and could converse in seven languages.

Clio (klī'ō)   In Greek mythology, the muse of history, one of the nine daughters of the god Zeus* and the Titaness* Mnemosyne* (memory). In art, she is shown with a scroll in her hand, and sometimes a trumpet of fame.

Cloak   When a cloak is shown, divided in half by a sword, it is an attribute of St. Martin* who halved his cloak in winter and gave one piece to a beggar.

Clover   Like all trefoils, clover is a symbol of the Trinity*. The shamrock or Irish clover symbolizes the evangelizing of Ireland by St. Patrick*, and is Ireland's emblem.

Clovis (clō'vis)   See St. Remy.

Club   In Roman mythology, the club is an attribute of Heracles* and sometimes of the hero Theseus*. Periphetes, the giant robber of the Argolid, carried the huge iron club which Theseus seized from him, and after battering him to death, made it his own. It is an attribute of the hunter Orion* and is shown with Giants*. It is also seen with the muse Melpomene*, as an attribute of violent tragedy. In Christian iconography, it is a symbol of the betrayal of Christ (see Jesus Christ—Life Events). It is an attribute of James*, the brother of Jesus, and of Jude*, because of their martyrdoms. It is also seen in the hand of the virtue, Fortitude (see Virtues).

Clytemnestra (klī-tem-nes'tra)   In Greek legend, the daughter of Spartan King Tyndareus and Leda; sister to Helen*, Castor*, and Polydeuces*. Her first husband, Tantalus, and their baby were killed by King Agamemnon* of Mycenae, who then forced her to marry him. She bore him three daughters, Electra*, Iphigenia*, and Chrysothemis*, and a son, Orestes*. At the beginning of the

Trojan war, when the Greek ships were massed and ready to sail for Troy, the ships were becalmed. Agamemnon was informed by the seer Calchas that the goddess Artemis* was angry with him for killing one of her sacred stags. He deceitfully sent to Clytemnestra for their daughter Iphigenia, pretending she was to be a bride for the hero Achilles*, and then sacrificed her on the altar of Artemis. Artemis was appeased, the winds appeared, but Clytemnestra had lost a second child. While Agamemnon was away at the war, Clytemnestra, stung by the wrongs she had suffered, betrayed her husband and took his cousin Aegisthus* as a lover. When Agamemnon returned, ten years after his departure, Clytemnestra pretended to receive him royally, but with Aegisthus, brought about his murder while he was in his bath. For the next seven years, Clytemnestra and Aegisthus ruled in Mycenae. In the eighth year, Orestes, grown to manhood, returned home, and with the encouragement of his sister Electra, avenged his father's death by killing his mother and the throne usurper, Aegisthus.

Clytie (klī′tē) In Greek mythology, an ocean nymph so enamoured of the sun god Apollo*, she watched his course each day across the sky. The gods, pitying her unrewarded love, turned her into a sunflower, or heliotrope, whose face follows the sun, on its daily course, unwavering in devotion.

Cnossus See Knossos.

Cock In Greek mythology, Demeter* and her daughter Persephone* claimed the cock, as goddesses of fertility and the rising spring. It was an attribute of the goddess of war, Athena*, as cocks are always ready to fight. As a bird of sacrifice for healing purposes, it is an attribute of Asclepius*, the god of medicine. In Christian iconography, it is an attribute of St. Peter*, because the cock crew after Peter had thrice denied Jesus; a symbol therefore of the Passion* (see Jesus Christ—Life Events—Denial of Peter).

Cockle Shell See Scallop Shell.

Colossus of Rhodes (ko-los′us of rōdz) A large, bronze statue of the sun god Helius, completed about 280 B.C., which stood next to the harbor on the island of Rhodes. According to the ancients, it was one of the Seven Wonders of the World*. It stood a hundred feet high and is said to have been designed by the Rhodian sculptor Chares of Lindus. Legend says that it was built from the abandoned bronze weapons and armor, left by the soldiers of King Demetrius I of Macedon, when he was defeated in his siege of Rhodes in 304 B.C. The 16th-century story that the Colossus was built striding the harbor is false. In 244 B.C., it was toppled by an earthquake, and for many centuries the bronze fragments lay on the shore.

Columbine   In Christian iconography, the columbine is a symbol of the Holy Ghost*. In art, the Holy Ghost is represented in the form of a dove. The Latin *Columbinus* means dove-like. The flowers are supposed to look like doves.

Comb   In Christian iconography, a square, carding comb is an attribute of St. Blaise* whose flesh was torn with such a comb during his martyrdom.

Commandments   The Ten Commandments*, given by God to Moses* on Mt. Sinai. In the Christian church they are often called the Decalogue, meaning "ten words." In the New Testament, Christ summed up the Decalogue with the two commandments of love. "Thou shalt love the Lord thy God, with all thy heart, with all thy mind, with all thy soul and with all thy strength: and thou shalt love thy neighbor as thyself."

Comus (kō′mus)   In Roman mythology, the god of mirth, represented as a winged youth, bearing a torch and a drinking cup. Like satyrs*, he was a lover of song, dance, and wine, and a follower of Bacchus*.

St. Constantine   The Roman Emperor who stopped the persecutions* against Christians in 313, with the Edict of Milan. During a great battle against Maxentius, his Western rival, Constantine had a vision of Christ bearing a banner on which was written, "*In hoc signo vinces* (By this sign thou shalt conquer)." The battle ended victoriously, Constantine embraced the Christian faith and used the words as his motto. He moved the capital of the empire to Byzantium, which was renamed Constantinople in his honor. According to tradition, he was baptized on his death bed in 337. Constantine was made a saint in the Orthodox church for his help to Christianity. His mother was St. Helena* who found the True Cross about 325. Constantine's feast day is celebrated with his mother's on August 18.

Cord   Worn by monks in allusion to Christ's flagellation. It symbolizes chastity.

Core or Kore (kō′re)   Another Greek name for Persephone*, the daughter of the goddess Demeter*. The name means maiden.

Corinthian Order (ko-rin'thi-an)   In architecture, this is the most ornate of the Classical orders and the most slender in its proportions. The capital is shaped like a bell, adorned with rows of acanthus leaves. Legend says that the evolution of the capital by Callimachus, in the 5th century B.C., came from a calthus (woman's basket) placed on a maiden's tomb which was covered with a tile about which the leaves of the acanthus grew.

Corn   In Ancient Greece, a symbol of productivity and fruitfulness, an attribute of the goddess Demeter*, her daughter Persephone*, and also of the Roman goddess Fides*, personification of honor.

Cornelia (kor-nēl'ya)   A Roman matron of the 2nd century B.C., the daughter of Scipio Africanus, the wife of Tiberian Semperonius Gracchus, and the mother of the Gracchi. After her husband's death, she refused to remarry, and devoted herself to her children's education, instilling in them a sense of civic duty and a desire for glory. It is said that a wealthy matron of Rome boasted about her jewels. Cornelia turned to her and pointed to her sons saying, "These are my jewels."

Cornucopia or Horn (kor-nū-kō'pi-a) (Latin, *cornu copiae*)   The horn of plenty which, in Greek mythology, was the horn from the goat Amalthea* with which the baby god Zeus* was fed. The Romans said it was the horn of the river god Achelous*, who turned into a bull to fight Hercules* and lost a horn in the struggle. Legend held that the horn was always full of whatever food or drink one desired. It was an attribute of the god Hades and his wife Persephone*, as givers of the fruits of the earth's wealth; an attribute of Tyche* and Fortuna who as goddesses of fortune, heap gifts from a horn of plenty: an attribute of Eirene*, as goddess of wealth, and of Themis*, as the goddess of hospitality.

Coronis (kor-ō'nis)   In Greek legend, the mother of Asclepius*, who was killed by the god Apollo* when he learned she had been unfaithful to him. See Apollo.

Corposant (cor'pō-sant) or St. Elmo's Fire.   The ball of fire which is sometimes seen playing around the mast of ships during a storm, indicating a change of weather.

Corpus Christi   A festival of the Christian church, kept on Thursday after Trinity Sunday (the eighth Sunday after Easter), in honor of the Blessed Sacrament. The festival was instituted by

Pope Urban IV in 1264. Corpus Christi is especially a flowery feast, and in many countries the procession is held out of doors with great pageantry. It was the regular time for religious dramas by the medieval guilds. The plays of England's York, Coventry, and Chester are extant.

St. Cosmos and St. Damian (cos'mos & dā'mi·an) Fourth century martyrs who were physicians who took no fee. By tradition they were Arabian twins, and as patrons of Florence, they appear frequently in Florentine art, dressed alike. One legend of their practice of medicine tells of a man whose leg was eaten away by a canker. While he was sleeping, Cosmos and Damian appeared with their knives and salves. Where shall we get the flesh to replace this bad flesh? they asked themselves. Damian remembered an Ethiopian who had been buried in the cemetery the same day, so he went and cut off the Ethiopian's leg. Together, he and Cosmos amputated the sick man's leg and fastened on the other in its place. When the man awoke, he felt no pain and thought he was someone else. When he had collected his senses, he fell out of bed for joy. People who went to the Ethiopian's tomb found the body had a leg missing and a white leg lay nearby. During the persecution* of Christians under Diocletian*, Cosmos and Damian were cast into the sea, but rescued by an angel. They were next thrown into a fire, but the flames did not touch them. They were bound to a cross and stoned, but the stones rebounded to kill those who had hurled them. Finally they were beheaded. In art, they are always shown together in the long red gown and cap of physicians, holding a box of ointment and a surgical instrument, or a mortar and pestle. They are patrons of physicians and apothecaries and were also adopted as patron saints of the Italian Medici family. Feast day: September 27. Painting: *St. Cosmos and St. Damian*, Fra Angelico, National Gallery, Washington.

Cow In Greek mythology, the cow is sacred to the goddess Demeter*, as a symbol of productivity. The cow was sacrificed to the goddess Hera*.

Crane The crane, because of fable, has become a symbol of vigilance and loyalty. Legend recounts that cranes form a circle around their king at night, holding a stone in one foot while standing on the other. Should a crane fall asleep, the stone would fall and arouse him to renew his watch.

Creation In the Old Testament, the Creation is the act whereby God, in six days, brought into existence the heavens, the earth, their luminaries, life-forms, and elements (Genesis 1, 2). On the first day, God separated light from darkness. On the second and third days, he divided the waters, creating heaven and earth. The fourth day, he created the sun, the moon, and the stars. The fifth day, he gave life to birds and sea creatures, and on the sixth day, he created animals and man himself. The seventh day he blessed and sanctified as a day of rest. The oldest Biblical account is Psalm 104, influenced by the Hymn to the Sun of Egypt's monotheistic ruler, Akhenaton (1370-1353 B.C.). Latin Bible woodcuts: *The Six Days of Creation*, Rare Books Department, New York Public Library.

Creon (crē'on)   In Greek legend, the brother of Jocasta*. He became regent of Thebes after the banishment of Oedipus*, who was his brother-in-law. Creon helped Eteocles*, one of the sons of Oedipus, to take the kingdom away from his brother Polynices*. When the brothers killed each other in the battle of the Seven Against Thebes*, Creon buried Eteocles with honor but refused to allow proper burial for Polynices, on the grounds that he had attacked his own city. Antigone*, sister of both men, took it upon herself to perform the funeral rites denied to Polynices. For this religious act, Creon had Antigone buried alive.

Crescent   In Greek religion, the crescent is an attribute of Artemis* as goddess of the moon, often shown in the crescent of stag horns. In Christian religion, the crescent is an attribute of the Virgin Mary. A crescent in a circle symbolizes the Kingdom of Heaven.

Cressida (kres'i-da)   Daughter of the priest Calchas and the beloved of Troilus*.

Cretan or Marathonian Bull (krē'tan, mar·a thon'i-an)   In Greek mythology, a magnificent bull, given to King Minos* of Crete by the god Poseiden*. Minos so admired its beauty he did not sacrifice it to the god, as he had promised to do. In punishment, Poseiden caused Pasiphae*, the wife of Minos, to fall in love with the bull, and by him to mother the Minotaur*, a monster with the head of a bull and the body of a man. Heracles* captured the bull as his seventh labor for Eurystheus*, and swam it back to Greece. There it was let loose at Marathon, terrifying the populace. Known now as the Marathon Bull, it was at last slain by Theseus*. A 5th-century Greek vase painting: *Theseus and the Marathonian Bull*, Metropolitan, New York.

St. Crispin   A shoemaker, and therefore patron saint of that craft. Legend says that two brothers, Crispin and Crespian, born in Rome, went to Soissons, France, in 303 to propagate the

Christian faith, maintaining themselves as cobblers. St. Crispin's day: October 25. St. Crispin's emblem is a shoe.

Croesus (krē′sus)   A king of Lydia, son of Alyattes, who ruled from 560-540 B.C. He continued his father's policy of conquering the Greek Ionian cities of Asia Minor, but he was friendly to the Greeks and is supposed to have given refuge to Solon*. He had the reputation for enormous wealth. After twenty years' reign, he was defeated in battle at his capital Sardis by Cyrus the Great* of Persia. Legend tells that he was placed on a pyre to be burned alive, but when he called on the god Apollo* to save him, a cloudburst fell, extinguishing the fire. Cyrus, astounded by this miracle, had Croesus brought to his side while the Persians went about the business of plundering the city. Croesus asked Cyrus what his soldiers were doing. "Plundering your city," Cyrus replied. Croesus corrected him. "Plundering your city," he said. The self-evident answer impressed Cyrus so much, he kept Croesus by him from then on, bestowing marks of favor upon him.

Cronus (krō′nus)   In Greek legend, the youngest of the Titans*, son of Gaea* (earth) and Uranus* (heaven). Cronus was lord of the universe before the era of the Olympian gods. He led the Titans in the revolt against Uranus, emasculating his father with a sickle, and his reign was so peaceful it was known as the Golden Age. He married his sister Rhea* and fathered the great gods Poseiden*, Demeter*, Hera*, and Hades*, whom he swallowed at birth lest they dethrone him. When the god Zeus* was born, Rhea hid him, presenting Cronus with a stone, wrapped in a blanket, to swallow instead. When Zeus grew to manhood, he gave Cronus a potion that caused him to disgorge his brothers and sisters. Zeus then led them all in a victorious war against Cronus, and sent him away to rule over Elysium* in the underworld. In works of art, Cronus is represented as an old man with a mantle. He holds a sickle in his hand, in reference to the emasculation of Uranus. He is identified with Roman Saturn*.

Crosier or **Crozier (krō′zher)**   A bishop's or abbot's staff, which, originally, may have been a walking staff or shepherd's crook. St. Zeno* carries a crosier with a fish.

Cross   The Latin cross is the most commonly used form of the cross. It has a longer upright than crossbar and symbolizes the Passion* of Christ, since tradition says Christ was crucified on a Latin cross. The Greek cross has four equal arms, and is used to suggest the Church of Christ. The diagonal cross, or cross saltire, is the cross of St. Andrew, who is said to have been crucified on that cross. The T or Tau, Egyptian cross, is known as the Old Testament cross, and is an attribute of St. Philip* and St. Anthony*, both martyred on this cross. A double-barred cross is used by patriarchs and archbishops. A triple-barred cross is used by the pope. See also St. Margaret, St. Bonaventura, St. Albans, and St. Louis of France.

Cross with bread loaves is an attribute of St. Philip.

Cross and Chalice (cup) are a symbol of the Agony in the Garden* (see Jesus Christ—Life Events).

Cross and crown are a symbol for the reward of the faithful in after-life. When shown on a clerical robe, it is an attribute of St. Augustine*.

Cross entwined with flowers is an attribute of St. Anthony of Padua*.

Cross surmounted by a lily or heart is an attribute of St. Catherine of Siena*.

Cross with hammer and nails (the "True Cross") is an attribute of St. Helena*, because of her alleged discovery of Christ's cross, early in the fourth century.

Cross on a staff is an attribute of St. Philip*.

Crown   Crowns are worn in Christian art by royalty who were saints and by the Virgin Mary*, as queen of heaven. A crown on a martyr indicates victory over sin and death. A triple crown is an attribute of St. Elizabeth* of Hungary, symbolizing her royal birth, her royal marriage, and royal status in heaven.

Crown of Roses   An attribute of St. Cecelia*, in reference to the legend that an angel placed a crown of roses on her head.

Crown of Thorns and Nails   An emblem of Christ's Passion* and crucifixion* (see Jesus Christ—Life Events). It is an attribute of St. Catherine of Siena* because of her wounds of the stigmata and an attribute of St. Louis of France*, and St. William of Norwich*.

Crow   In Greek religion the crow is sacred to the god Apollo*. The crow's feathers were originally white but were turned black by Apollo when it told tales about Coronis*. It was an attribute of the goddess Athena*, as the one who inspires oracles and presides over the arts. In Christian iconography, two crows are an attribute of St. Vincent* whose relics, according to legend, were brought to Lisbon, Portugal, accompanied by two crows (see Raven).

Crucifix   In Christian iconography, the crucifix represents Christ* on the cross. A crucifix between the antlers of a stag is a representation of a legend told of Saints Eustace* and Hubert*.

Crucifixion of Jesus   The execution of Jesus was precipitated by the political pressure exerted on the Roman authorities by the Hebrew priesthood and the judicial court. It followed immediately after the sentence had been pronounced by the procurator of Judea, Pontius Pilate*. The instrument of execution was a cross, a custom for impaling criminals which had been in use for many centuries (see Jesus Christ—Life Events). Painting: *Christ on the Cross with the Virgin and St. John*, Rogier Van Der Weyden, Philadelphia Museum of Art.

Crutch   In Christian art, a crutch represents great age and is an attribute of St. Anthony Abbot*. A bell is sometimes attached to the crutch, as a symbol of his power to exorcise evil.

Cuckoo   In Greek mythology, the cuckoo is sacred to the goddess Hera*, as the messenger of spring. The god Zeus* seduced Hera, when he wooed her, transforming himself into a cuckoo.

Cumaean Sibyl   See Golden Bough and Sibylline Books.

Cup   In Greek mythology, the cup is an attribute of the god Dionysus*, as the bringer of wine; also of the Roman god of mirth, Comus*, and of Vesta*. In Christian iconography, the cup is a symbol of Christ's agony in the Garden of Gethsemane*. "O my Father, if it be possible, let this cup pass from me" (Matthew 26:39). (See Jesus Christ—Life Events—Garden of Gethsemane; see goblet).

Cup and Wafer   These are the sacramental symbols of the Eucharist*, or Holy Communion (see Jesus Christ—Life Events—Last Supper). The cup and wafer are sometimes carried by St. Barbara*.

Cupid (kū′pid)   The Roman name for the Greek Eros*, sometimes called Amor. He was the god of love, the son of the goddess Venus* and the god Mars*. When Cupid shot his arrow, no man or god was safe from passion. He is usually represented in art as a beautiful winged youth or boy, sometimes blindfolded, carrying arrows and a bow, often in the company of his mother and also Mars. Cupid and Psyche* is a famous, ancient legend, an allegory representing the progress of the soul to perfection. Cupid loved the beautiful, mortal Psyche, and secreted her in a palace where he visited her in the dark, at night. He prevented her from seeing him by forbidding her to use lights. Psyche's jealous and curious sisters urged her to find out whether he was a monster, so she disobeyed Cupid's orders and brought a lamp into the room while he was sleeping. As she looked at the handsome youth with joy, some oil from the lamp fell on him. He awoke and immediately spread his wings and flew away, reproaching her for her disobedience. Psyche wandered for many months searching for her beloved, and suffered many hardships. She even became the slave of Venus who imposed heartless tasks on her and treated her cruelly. Finally the god Jupiter* gave her immortality and reunited her with Cupid forever. (See Eros.)

Cybele (sib'e-le) In Phrygian and Lydian religion, the great mother of the gods, identified with the Greek Rhea*. She rode in a chariot drawn by lions, attended by Corybantes (dancing priests) and Dactyls (dwarfs and music makers). Her love for Atys, the Phrygian Adonis*, was celebrated in a spring festival of orgiastic fertility rites. When her worship was imported into Greece in the 6th century B.C., she was identified with the goddess Demeter*, as well as Rhea. Her cult moved to Rome during the 3rd century B.C. and was established in a temple on the Palatine Hill. The oak, pine, and lion were sacred to her. Her other attributes were the drum, cymbals, flute, and horn. In art, she is usually represented enthroned between lions (see Atalanta), wearing a tower-like crown on her head and carrying the ritual drum or cymbal. Statuette: *Cybele Seated on a Lion Throne*, Roman copy of 4th-century work, Metropolitan, New York; painting: *The Triumph of Cybele*, Pinturicchio, also Metropolitan.

Cyclamen In Christian art, the red center of the cyclamen symbolizes the bleeding sorrow of Mary*, at the death of her son Jesus*.

Cyclops (sī-klops) In Greek mythology, three one-eyed giants, sons of Uranus* (heaven) and Gaea* (earth). They were great builders, said to have erected the walls of Mycenae and Tiryns, and as mastersmiths for the god Hephaestus*, legend said they had forged the thunderbolts of the god Zeus*. They helped Zeus and the other Olympian gods defeat Cronus*, before dividing up his universe. The descendants of the Cyclops went to Sicily where Odysseus*, on his way home from the Trojan war, encountered one of them, Polyphemus*. Aeneas* also landed on the island, but left hurriedly when he learned on whose land he was ashore.

The god Apollo* slew the Cyclops to avenge the death of his son Asclepius*, who had been killed by one of the thunderbolts of Zeus.

Cymbal (sim'bl)   In Classical mythology, the cymbal is an attribute of Cybele*, the Lydian and Phrygian great mother goddess. It is also carried by the Maenads*, who were followers of the god Dionysus* and, like Cybele, played on it during orgiastic festivals. The cymbal is made of metal and is shaped like a concave plate. Usually two are held and struck together.

Cypress (sī'prus)   In Greek religion, the cypress is sacred to the god of the underworld, Hades*, as a symbol of death. In Christian religion, it is also a symbol of death, as the tree never springs up again when it is cut down.

Cyrus (sī'rus) the Great   Cyrus was the founder of the Persian Empire. His father was the Persian Cambyses, his mother the daughter of King Astyages of the Medes. In legend, Astyages is said to have ordered the death of Cyrus at his birth, because of a dream that the child would usurp his throne. Cyrus was saved, and brought up by a shepherd. At the age of ten, he was already playing the king with his companions, and his true identity was discovered by Astyages. The wise men of the court suggested to Astyages that his dream had been fulfilled in the games of the boy and he was not to be feared. Cyrus succeeded to the Persian throne in 559 B.C. He then led a revolt against the Medes and defeated the armies of Astyages, thus taking over the throne. Next followed the defeat of Lydian Croesus* and Babylonia's King Belshazzar* in 539. Cyrus was known for his clemency to subdued peoples. He allowed the captured Jews to rebuild the Temple in Jerusalem (II Chronicles 36:22) and they wrote of Cyrus as "God's shepherd."

D

Daedalus (dē′da-lus)   A legendary Greek sculptor, builder, and mastersmith, said to have been instructed by the goddess Athena*. Various improvements in architecture were attributed to him, and he was supposed to be the inventor of the axe, awl, and level. He was banished from Athens, accused of the murder of his nephew, who was becoming a gifted rival, and escaped to Crete. Here he built the famous labyrinth* with a thousand turnings for King Minos*, in which the Minotaur* could be confined, the monster offspring of Pasiphae*, the wife of Minos and the Cretan Bull*. Daedalus and his son Icarus* were confined in the labyrinth for a time because Daedalus had given Ariadne* the clue whereby she guided Theseus* from the maze. Daedalus escaped with Icarus by constructing wings of wax, and they flew off into the sky. Young Icarus soared too near the sun, and as the wax melted, he fell into the sea and was drowned. Daedalus recovered the body and buried it on the island of Icaria. Then he flew on to Sicily and settled in the realm of King Cocalus. Minos pursued him from Crete, but King Cocalus refused to surrender the gifted man. In his last years, Daedalus moved to Sardinia. In ancient times, many archaic works were believed to be his work.

Daemon (day′mon or dē′mon)   In Greek mythology, a supernatural agent holding a middle place between gods and men; hence a guiding spirit (see demons, devils).

Dagger   In Christian art, a dagger is an attribute of St. Lucy*, who was stabbed.

Daisy   In Christian art, a symbol of the Christ Child's innocence. It is often shown in a conventionalized form.

St. Damasus I (303-384)   A Spaniard who became Pope from 366 until his death. He is remembered for his efforts to memorialize the early martyrs with inscriptions on their tombs and for his restoration of the catacombs. Feast day: December 11.

Damian   See Cosmos.

Damon and Pythias (dā′mon & pith′i-as) (4th century B.C.)   These two inseparable friends were said to be Pythagorean philosophers. Pythias plotted against the Sicilian tyrant of Syracuse, Dionysius, and was condemned to death. He obtained leave to go home to arrange his affairs, after Damon offered to place himself in the tyrant's hands as a substitute. This offer included execution in his stead, should Pythias not return. Dionysius was so struck by this friendship of honor, he pardoned them both.

Danae (dan′ā-ē)   In Greek legend, the daughter of Acrisius, king of Argo. When it was prophesied that the son of Danae would cause his death, Acrisius imprisoned her in a bronze tower, but his precaution was in vain. The god Zeus* came to her in the form of a shower of gold, and she bore him a son, whom she called Perseus*. Acrisius refused to believe that this was a child of Zeus, and shut Danae and the boy in a chest, which he cast into the sea. The chest floated safely to the island of Seriphus, where it was found by Dictys, a fisherman. He sheltered Danae and Perseus until the child grew to manhood. Polydectes, brother of Dictys and king of the island, fell in love with Danae. In order to rid himself of Perseus, he sent him to fetch the head of Medusa*. Danae went into hiding to avoid the king's harassing attentions. When the successful Perseus returned and learned of his mother's situation, he punished the king and his people by exhibiting the head of Medusa where they were banqueting, and they were all turned to stone.

Danaidae (da-nā′i-dē)   In Greek mythology, the fifty daughters of Danaus, ruler of Libya. His brother Aegyptus wished the girls to marry his fifty sons, thereby consolidating the family power. But Danaus, warned by an oracle that he would die at the hands of a son-in-law, fled with his daughters to the Peloponnesus in Greece where he made himself king of Argos. The sons of Aegyptus pursued their female cousins to Argos and besieged the city. Danaus then yielded to their demands, telling each bride to murder her husband on their wedding night. All obeyed but Hypermnestra who, divinely inspired, spared her husband Lynceus (legend says that he killed his father-in-law later in life).

His descendants were the Danai, another name for the Greeks. The Danaidae sisters buried their husbands' heads at Lerna and the bodies below the walls of Argos. They were punished for the murders in Hades (the underworld), and had to draw water everlastingly in sieves from a deep well.

Dance of Death   An allegorical representation of death as a skeleton or corpse, leading all sorts and conditions of men in a dance to the grave. It originated as a morality play in Germany in the 14th century and quickly spread to France and England, surviving later by means of pictorial art. The most famous representation is a series of woodcuts by Hans Holbein, painted in 1538.

Dandelion   In Christian iconography, the dandelion, as a bitter herb, is a symbol of the Passion* of Christ and is shown at the crucifixion* (see Jesus Christ—Life Events); also, sometimes with the Madonna* and Child.

Daniel   A book in the Old Testament relates the visions and life of Daniel, a prophet of the 6th century B.C. He spent his career at the court of Mesopotamian rulers, where he was called Belteshazzer (bel'tēsh-a-zar). He ably interpreted the dreams of Nebuchadnezzar*, the first of which was a dream of a great beast of gold, silver, brass, iron, and clay, whose image was broken asunder by a great stone. Daniel's interpretation was that the beast represented Nebuchadnezzar's power and the gradual disintegration of the kingdoms coming after him (Daniel 2). The second dream, Daniel said, foretold Nebuchadnezzar's future madness (Daniel 4). As Daniel rose in favor and power, his friends Shadrach, Meshach, and Abednego were placed in positions of authority in Babylon. Being Jews, they would not worship Nebuchadnezzar's golden image, and were cast into a fiery furnace. Miraculously they were not consumed by the flames. Nebuchadnezzar, recognizing the power of their protective god, promoted them to higher positions (see Three Holy Children). During Belshazzar's* reign, Daniel interpreted the mysterious writing that appeared on the walls of his banquet hall (Daniel 5). Darius, who was the next ruler, made Daniel overseer of the whole realm. The jealous princes of the realm tricked Darius into signing a religious decree which Daniel, as a Jew, could not obey. Darius was therefore forced to send him to the lion's den. Once again the god of the Jews saved a worshipper, and Darius was "exceeding glad" to find that after seven days of exposure to the lions, Daniel was still alive (see also Bel and the Dragon). Daniel had four apocalyptic visions through which he was supposed to have revealed the course of history from 601 to 164 B.C. They

Nebuchad-nezzar's dream

Apocalyptic visions

are often shown in art. The visions showed four great beasts: the first, a lion with eagle's wings and a man's face (representing Babylon), the second, a bear with three ribs in its mouth (representing Media), the third figure, a leopard with a fowl's wings and four heads (representing Persia), and the fourth figure, one with great iron teeth and ten horns (representing Greece), with a further horn, out of which sprang the eyes and mouth of a man (representing Antiochus Epiphines) plus an ancient man in a white garment, sitting on a throne of fire (representing the end of an age). The Book of Daniel was probably written in the 2nd century B.C., a forerunner to the Revelation of St. John* in the New Testament. Susanna and the Elders* is a part of Daniel; appearing in the Apocrypha*.

Dante, Alighieri (1265-1321)   The Italian poet who is the author of the narrative poem, *The Divine Comedy*. It is divided into three parts and describes the journey of the poet (symbolizing the soul of man) through Hell and Purgatory, accompanied by Virgil*, and through Paradise, accompanied by his ideal woman and love, Beatrice (symbolizing heavenly love), and for whom, after her death, the poem was written. Scenes from the poem are often seen in art. Allegorical portrait: *Dante*, 16th-century Florentine School, National Gallery, Washington.

Daphne (daf'nē)   In Greek mythology, the daughter of the river god Peneus. She was a huntress, and like the virgin goddess Artemis*, rejected all suitors. When the god Apollo* fell in love with her and showed his affection, she fled in terror, and as she approached the river Peneus, she prayed to her father to save her. Apollo was about to clasp her in his arms when her father transformed her into a laurel tree. Embracing the trunk, Apollo declared its leaves would always be green. Thenceforth he bound his head with laurel leaves, and the laurel wreath became the prize for the victors in the Pythian Games at Delphi*, and symbol of victory. Painting: *Daphne Pursued by Apollo*, Giovanni Tiepolo, National Gallery, Washington.

Daphnis (daf'nis)   In Greek legend, a son of the god Hermes* and a Sicilian maiden. Daphnis was brought up by shepherds, and the god Pan* taught him to play the flute, while the muses* endowed him with a love of poetry. He fell in love with a nymph called Nomia, to whom he swore fidelity, but when a rival made him drunk, he was unfaithful to her and she blinded him. Daphnis mourned the loss of his sight in song, and thus pastoral melody was born. Hermes took pity on him, and transformed him into a spring called Daphnis near his home in Sicily where sacrifices were offered to him.

Daphnis and Chloe (klō´ē) A Greek pastoral romance, attributed to the sophist Longus (3rd century B.C.). It recounts the loves and pastoral life of a shepherd's foster son called Daphnis (laurel-like) with a goatherd's foster daughter called Chloe (blooming). Both were supposed to be of divine parentage. After many vicissitudes, they are united and their noble birth acknowledged.

Darius I, the Great (dar-rī´us) King of Persia from about 558-486 B.C. Legend relates that after the death of his predecessor Cambyses, seven Persian princes banded together, stormed the palace and killed an impostor who had seized the throne. They decided to choose the next king from among themselves, the arrangement being that the choice would go to the one whose horse neighed first when they met the next day. Prince Darius was determined to win. He spoke to his groom who arranged to bring a mare to the meeting just as Darius, riding a stallion, arrived at the scene. His horse neighed first, a flash of lightning followed, and the six other nobles sprang from their horses and knelt before him. Darius put down revolts throughout Persia, extended and brought order to the Empire, continuing the policy of Cyrus to support the Jewish state. He set up an administrative system of satraps, which in turn were checked by other officials, all responsible to the king alone. The system was so efficient it outlasted the Achaemenid Empire into the reign of Alexander the Great*. He was the ancient king who built a canal from the Nile to Suez. His greatest difficulties lay with the rebel Greek Ionian cities. When trying to punish the Athenians, and Eretrians who had aided in the insurrection, he was defeated at Marathon in 490 B.C., one of the decisive battles of history. Before he could put his forces in motion again, he died and was succeeded by his son Xerxes*.

Darkness In art, it manifests spiritual darkness, the devil* being the prince of darkness.

David In the Old Testament (I, II Samuel, I Kings), the second Hebrew king (1000-961 B.C.), the successor of Saul. David was the youngest son of Jesse*, a Bethlehemite, a shepherd of beautiful countenance who was chosen by the Lord, through the ministry of Samuel*, to succeed Saul. Samuel rejected Jesse's other sons, and anointed David with his horn of oil in the midst *Samuel* of his brethren. David first won a place at Saul's court by playing *anoints* his harp to ease Saul's spirit. Then he killed the giant Philistine *David* Goliath* in single combat, felling him to the ground with one stone from his slingshot, which sank into the giant's head. David *David kills* brought the head to Saul, and as he stood before him, Saul's son *Goliath*

Saul's
court

Marriage

Escape

Life of
Fugitive

Abigail

King David

Psalms

Jonathan* was stirred, and the soul of Jonathan was knit with the soul of David, loving him as his own soul. David married Saul's daughter Michal, and triumphed with Saul in the wars against the Philistines. The women came out of the cities dancing and singing, "Saul hath slain his thousands and David his ten thousands," and Saul was set against David. He tried to smite him with a javelin and David was forced to flee. Michal let him out through the window of their house; she put a pillow of goat's hair in his bed and pretended he was sick. David hid in the fields, and Jonathan, by a signal of three flying arrows, warned him he must flee. The two men parted in tears, swearing kindness to each other's houses. From then until Saul's death, David lived a wanderer's life, gathering personal power with a small band of followers, while Saul continued to pursue him. When he protected Nabal's shepherds, he and his men were refused sustenance, and David was very angry. Nabal's wife Abigail* quickly made amends. She gathered up a quantity of food, rode out with a convoy of asses to David, and made peace with her offering. Nabal died soon afterward, and David took Abigail for his wife. Although Saul never found David, David discovered Saul asleep and offguard three times. Each time he could have killed Saul but spared him as "the anointed king of God," although he knew Saul would always be treacherous. Finally, when Saul and his sons were killed fighting the Philistines, David, lamenting their deaths, was made king. He recaptured the ark from the house of a Levite, returned to Jerusalem in triumph, sacrificed oxen, and danced before the Lord. David was powerful and subdued many enemies, changing the rude confederation of Jewish tribes into a settled, national state. By moving the capital from Hebron to Jerusalem, he made the city the eternal city of the Jews. Bathsheba* became his queen, and bore him his successor Solomon*. His son Absalom* plotted his death, but David mourned him deeply when he was killed. David was a great poet as well as a national hero, and about seventy psalms of the Bible are undoubtedly his. His descendants, known as the House of David, retained the kingdom of Jerusalem until 586 B.C. When the messianic hope appeared in Israel, it centered in this house, and according to the gospels, Jesus was of the royal seed. Painting: *David with the Head of Goliath*, Andrea del Castagno, National Gallery, Washington.

St. David   A 6th-century patron saint of Wales, and the first abbot of Menavia. Legend relates that he was the son of Prince Cereticu, but he was brought up as a priest and became an ascetic on the Isle of Wight. He established a strict rule, was a zealous missionary, founded twelve monasteries, and went on pilgrimage to Jerusalem. One legend says that the priest who baptized David was blind, but David splashed some baptismal water in his eyes and immediately he could see again. Once when he was speaking to thousands of people in an open field, he could not be heard, so the field behind him rose up into a hill and the crowd could hear: also, it is said a white dove appeared on his shoulder. David is said to have lived on leeks and water, and was traditionally known as "the waterman." His emblems are a dove and leeks, which are also the Welsh, national emblem. Feast day: March 1.

Dawn In Christian art the dawn is a symbol of the advent of Christ and of eternal salvation through the shedding of his blood for mankind. Christ sometimes wears rose color in scenes of the resurrection* (see Jesus Christ—Life Events).

Day of Judgement or **Doomsday** In the Bible, this is the time when sin will be followed by penalty, and goodness by a promised reward. The belief is taught from the beginning of the Bible, illustrating the law that "what a man sows, that shall he reap" (Galatians 6:7). The New Testament doctrine predicts that the world will come to an end, the dead will be raised up in general resurrection, and Jesus will come in glory to judge the living and the dead; sinners will be cast into hell and the righteous will live in heaven forever (Matthew 24:3-25; Luke 21:5-23).

Deborah (deb'ora) In the Old Testament, a judge of Israel, the only woman to hold that office. Under her guidance, the army leader Sisara was conquered, and Israel was delivered from the tyranny of King Jabin. The triumphant song of Deborah (Judges 5) is one of the finest poems in the Bible (see Jael).

Decalogue Another name for the Ten Commandments, meaning "ten words."

Decapolis Deaf Mute See Jesus Christ—Miracles.

Deer In Greek religion, the doe and stag are sacred to Artemis*, as goddess of the hunt and protector of wild animals. The doe is frequently seen with her in art. In Christian art, a deer seen with its head in a man's lap, refers to St. Giles*. A stag with a crucifix between its antlers refers to St. Eustace* or St. Hubert*.

Deianira (dē-ya-nī'ra) or **Dejanira (dē-jan-i'ra)** In Greek legend, the daughter of Oeneus* and Althaea*, and sister to Meleager*. After the death of her brother, Heracles* made a journey to the underworld to fetch Cerberus*, the watchdog who guarded the entrance. Here he met the brave shade of Meleager, and promised him that he would wed Deianira on his return to earth. Heracles kept the promise, after overcoming Deianira's unwelcome suitor, the river god Achelous*, and Deianira bore him five children. Once when she was journeying across a river with Heracles, the centaur Nessus* offered to carry her over on his back. In so doing he attempted to seduce her, and Heracles shot him with a poisoned arrow. Before he died, Nessus secretly told Deianira to preserve some of his blood as a love charm which she might need, if the affections of Heracles ever strayed. Later Heracles went off to battle, and after an absence of fifteen months sent home a captive concubine. Deianira thought maybe the moment to use the love charm had come. She rubbed it on a robe, summoned a herald, and sent it off to Heracles. Noticing a bit of wool smoldering on the ground with which she had anointed the robe, she hastily tried to recall the herald, but it was too late. Heracles received the robe and put it on. Soon his body was burning with the poison of the arrow with which he had killed Nessus. Deianira hanged herself in despair. Painting: *The Rape of Deianira*, Antonio Pollaiuolo, Yale University Art Gallery, New Haven Conn.

Deidamia (dē-i-da-mē'a)   In Greek legend, a daughter of king Lycomedes of Scyros. When Achilles* was disguised as a girl and hidden at the court of her father in an attempt to keep him from going to his death at Troy, he seduced Deidamia and she became the mother of Neoptolemus*. When Neoptolemus grew up, he left his sorrowing mother for the war also, but unlike his father he was not killed there. One legend says he gave Deidamia in marriage to Helenus, a son of King Priam of Troy*, at the end of the Trojan war.

Delilah (dē-lī'la)   In the Old Testament, a Philistine woman who was the paramour of Samson*. She inveigled from him the secret of his strength and betrayed him to the Philistine lords, who then blinded and imprisoned him in Gaza (Judges 16).

Delos   A small island of the Cyclades in the Aegean sea, fabled to have been the birthplace of Apollo*; in some legends, of Artemis* also. Sometimes Delos is identified with the island of Ortygia (see Leto).

Delphi (del'fi)   The seat of the Delphic Oracle, the most powerful of the oracles in ancient Greece, located in Phocis, near the foot of the south slope of Mt. Parnassus. It was looked upon by the ancients of the world as the navel of the earth, symbolized by the great stone Omphalos*. The oracle gave answers to all questions, public, private, political, social, and religious. It was the preeminent shrine of the god Apollo*, but in winter when Apollo was absent with the Hyperboreans (a happy people said to dwell in perpetual sunshine), Delphi was sacred to the god Dionysus*. According to Homer, Apollo took forcible possession of the oracle soon after his birth, slaying with his first arrow the serpent Python, a son of Gaea* (earth) who guarded the spot, (hence Apollo's epithet, Pythian). Apollo had to flee and atone for this murder by performing menial duties for eight years before he could return to Delphi. The penance and purification of Apollo were commemorated every eight years in a sacred drama at Delphi, with Apollo represented by a boy with two living parents. The oracle proper was a cleft in the ground in the innermost sanctuary, from which rose cold vapors, and these had the power to induce ecstacy. The oracles were spoken by a prophetess, seated on a golden tripod, who was called the Pythia. The prophecies were interpreted by a priest, in verse, to the questioner. Persons seeking the help of the oracle brought rich gifts, and the shrine grew very wealthy. Heracles* sought information from the oracle, and was denied an answer by the priestess because of his impiety. Heracles, enraged, attempted to seize the golden tripod* of the priestess, threatening to set up his own oracle. Apollo hastened to protect the shrine, and the two struggled openly until the god Zeus* parted them with a thunderbolt. The priestess then gave Heracles an answer and the sanctuary remained in Apollo's possession. The repute of the oracle dwindled in Roman times and was finally silenced in A.D. 4th century by the Christian Emperor Theodosius II, and in its last years its treasures were looted and placed elsewhere. Painting on a 6th-century red-figured vase *Heracles Seizing the Delphic Tripod*, signed by Andokides, Metropolitan, New York.

Deluge   In the Old Testament, the deluge is the overwhelming flood that covered the earth, and destroyed every living thing except the family of Noah* and the creatures in his ark (Genesis 6-8).

Demeter (de-mē'ter) (Ro. Ceres)   In Greek mythology, one of the twelve great Olympian deities*, a daughter of Cronus* and Rhea*. She was the Mother Earth, the giver of the earth's fruits and flowers, and the benefactress of the civilization based on agriculture. The Eleusinian Mysteries*, established by herself, were among the holiest rites celebrated by the Greeks. She was the mother of the god Plutus* (wealth) by Iaison, a Titan*, and the mother of Persephone*, or Kore, by her brother, the god Zeus*. The rape of Persephone by the god of the underworld Hades is the center of her legend, and worship of Demeter, with Persephone, symbolizes the death and rebirth of the nourishing produce of the earth. When Hades* had carried off Persephone,

Search for Persephone

85

Demeter was brokenhearted, and wandered over the earth for nine days, searching everywhere for her. On the tenth day, she learned the truth from the all-seeing sun god Helius*. Furious with Zeus for permitting this act of violence, she abandoned Mt. Olympus*, and traversed the land of men in the form of an old woman. When she arrived at Eleusis, she was kindly received by King Celeus and Queen Metanira, and found comfort in tending their newly born son Demophon. One night as she was trying to immortalize the child by holding it in the fire, she was surprised and forced to reveal her deity. She commanded King Celeus to raise a temple in her honor, and instructed him and his sons in the mystery rites, while she gave herself up to grief. In her despair, she made the earth barren and mankind was threatened with famine and destruction. Zeus sent his winged-footed messenger, the goddess Iris*, to persuade her to return to Olympus. Demeter ignored her because Zeus had ignored the abduction of Persephone. In the end, Zeus sent the god Hermes* to Hades, ordering Persephone's return to her mother. Since Persephone had eaten four pomegranate seeds in the underworld, she was allowed to spend only eight months of the year in the upperworld. Demeter returned to Olympus, leaving the gift of corn and her holy mysteries with King Celeus at Eleusis in grateful remembrance. She sent the son of Celeus, Triptolemus*, around the world to impart the knowledge of agriculture, carried in her chariot which was drawn by serpents. The honeycomb, fruit, the cow, and the sow were offered to her as emblems of productivity. Her attrib-

Attributes utes are poppies, symbolizing sleep and death, and ears of wheat or corn. She is sometimes shown in art with a basket of fruit and a little pig, or with a torch or serpent, the serpent in the shedding of its skin symbolizing renewal of life. In art, Demeter is shown as a mature woman, always clothed, and often in the company of Persephone. Sometimes Dionysus* is shown with her, to whom she was joined in his role as god of wine.

Demon in Chains   In Christian art, this combination is a symbol of the defeat of heresy*. It is an attribute of St. Bernard of Clairvaux*.

Denial of Peter   See Jesus Christ—Life Events.

St. Denis or Dionysius of Paris   Popularly regarded as the patron saint of France, Denis is fabled to have been a Roman missionary who penetrated far into Gaul from 250 until he was beheaded in 272. The legend places his martyrization on the hill now called Montmartre, "Martyr's Hill." He is one of the martyrs who are supposed to have carried their severed heads to their burial places, in this case the site of the church of St. Denis. Feast day: October 9.

Deposition or Descent from the Cross   The scene, shown in Christian art, of taking the body of Jesus* from the cross, after the crucifixion*, by Joseph of Arimathea*, a disciple of Jesus (see Jesus Christ—After-Life Events).

Descent into Hell   See Jesus Christ—After-Life in Christian Belief.

Deucalion (dū-kā′lē-on)   In Greek mythology, a son of Prometheus*, and father of Hellen, the eponymous ancestor of the Hellenes, or Greeks. He and his wife Pyrrha* (pi′ra) were the only survivors of the great flood. An oracle told them to cast behind them the bones of their great mother, which they concluded meant the stones of the earth. They followed the directions, and the stones became human beings and repeopled the world. Engraving: *Deucalian and Pyrra*, after Hendrik Goltzius (illustration for Ovid's Metamorphoses), Metropolitan, New York.

Devils   Devils are evil angels, in contrast to good angels remaining faithful to God, and are found throughout the Bible. Their main function is to seek the perversion and downfall of man through temptation to evil.

Dia   See Hebe.

Diana (dī′ana)   An ancient Italian divinity, the goddess of the moon, protectress of women, and later identified with the Greek goddesses Artemis* and Selene*. Like Artemis, she was the goddess of the chase and woods, the protectress of chastity and the patroness of childbirth. She was called Luna, as goddess of the moon; Hecate*, as an infernal deity, invoked in magic rites; and Diana, as goddess of the hunt. Her famous shrine was at Aricia, near Lake Nemi, and was frequented by women who worshipped her here as the Great Mother, related to fertility rites. Her temple in the Aventine at Rome honored the virgin goddess of the Greeks. She is represented in art as a young woman, frequently attired, like Artemis, for the chase, and often accompanied by Hippolytus*, who, having built a temple to her at Troezen and devoted himself to her worship, was transported after his death to live in her sacred grove at Aricia. Painting: *Sacrifice to Diana*, Eustache Le Sueur, Museum of Fine Arts, Boston. (See Artemis.)

Diana of Ephesus.   See Ephesian Artemis.

Dice   In Christian art, a symbol of the Passion* (see Jesus Christ), referring to the soldiers who cast lots for the clothing of Jesus at the scene of the crucifixion*.

Dido (dī′dō)   In Roman legend the Princess Elissa, daughter of the king of Tyre, whose husband, Sychaeus, was murdered for his wealth by her brother Pygmalion*. Elissa fled to North Africa, where natives allowed her to purchase as much land as a bull's hide could encompass. By cutting the hide into narrow strips, a fabulous amount of land was encompassed. On this land, she founded Carthage, and became the city's queen. The Roman writer Virgil, in his epic tale, the Aeneid, gives Elissa the name of Dido. The story tells how Aeneas* was driven in a storm to her shores, and how the goddess Venus* made her fall passionately in love with him. After a year's stay, Aeneas was forced, under divine command, to leave her. Dido, in despair, hurled herself upon a sword, cursing the Trojans and praying that her people and theirs would always be enemies. Later, when Aeneas visited the underworld, he saw the shadow of Dido in the region of those who had died of an unhappy love, but when he called out to her, she turned her back on him. Dido is the Phoenician name for Astarte (Artemis), goddess of the moon and protectress of the citadel of Carthage.

Dike   See Horae.

Dikir (Greek for two candles)   A double-branched candle stick which the bishop uses with the trikir (three-branched holder) to bestow blessings on the faithful, symbolizing the two natures of Christ, the human and divine. Trikir (Greek for three candles) symbolizes the three persons of the Holy Trinity*.

Diogenes (dī-oj′e-nēz)   A cynic Greek philosopher, famous for his eccentricities, who lived in Athens in the 4th century B.C. He believed that the virtuous life is the simple life, and dramatically disregarded conventions, taking up his abode in a tub. He is said to have thrown away his last utensil, a cup, when he saw a peasant drinking out of his hands. Alexander the Great* so admired him, he is quoted as saying, "If I were not Alexander, I would wish to be Diogenes." His daylight search with a lantern for an "honest man" was probably the most striking expression of his contempt for his generation. Painting: *Alexander and Diogenes*, Gaspard Crayer, Metropolitan, New York.

Diomedes (dī-ō-mē′dēz)   In Greek legend, king of Argos, and one of the Epigoni* who successfully attacked Thebes to avenge the deaths of their fathers. He was also a hero during the siege of Troy, and among the Greeks, second only to Achilles* in bravery. As a favorite of the goddess Athena*, he vanquished all mortals, among them Aeneas*, and wounded even the god and goddess Ares* and Aphrodite*. Once in fierce combat, he came face to face with Glaucus*. As the encounter started, the two men discovered that their grandfathers had been friends. Putting down their weapons, they swore friendship and exchanged armor, Glaucus giving his golden suit for the bronze one of Diomedes. When it was learned that Troy could not be taken without the arrows of Heracles*, which were in the possession of Philoctetes* at Lemnos, Diomedes went with Odysseus* to fetch them. From Lemnos, they continued to Scyros and persuaded Neoptolemus*, the son of Achilles, to join the Greeks at Troy. As a last mission, he and Odysseus stole the Palladium* of Troy, by using an underground passage leading to the citadel of the city. He was one of those to enter Troy in the wooden horse* and one of the few who had a prosperous voyage home. There is a scene of Diomedes carrying the Palladium from Troy, on a 4th-century Argos coin, Museum of Fine Arts, Boston.

Dionysius (di-ōn-i′shi-us), The Areopagite (ar-ē-op′a-gīte) A 1st-century saint who was an Athenian, converted to Christianity by St. Paul* (Acts 17:34). Tradition made him a martyr and the first bishop of Athens.

Dionysus (di-ō-nī′sus) (Ro. Bacchus) In Greek mythology, the god of fertility and wine, the patron of choral song and drama, and the youngest of the Olympian gods. He was born at Thebes, the son of the god Zeus*, and the mortal Semele*, the only god to have a mortal parent. Semele was unhappily destroyed by the lightning of Zeus, and the child was born at six months. Zeus rescued the baby, and sewed him into his thigh until his birth time was ripe, and then gave him over to the god Hermes* and the nymphs to raise, Silenus* becoming his tutor. Dionysus grew up into a girlish-looking young man, and wandered through the world planting the vine and spreading his worship among men with his wine-flushed train of maenads*, satyrs*, woodland nymphs, and Silenus. For his ceremonies, he wore a faun or panther skin about his body, and a band of ivy or vine leaves in his hair. He carried a reed, tipped with a pine cone, for his staff, known as the thyrsus. Whoever welcomed Dionysus received the gift of wine, those who resisted or criticized him were often treated cruelly. (Where serious religious ritual existed, the dissolute worship of Dionysus was unwelcome). His cult passed to the islands, in particular to Naxos where Dionysus found and wed Ariadne*. One fable relates that Dionysus fell in with pirates who put him on their ship in chains. His fetters fell off, the sails became wreathed in vines, the god changed into a lion, and the seamen, throwing themselves madly into the sea, were turned into dolphins. Dionysus, like Persephone*, belongs to the world below as well as to the world above, representing the death of vegetation until it rises from the dead to new life, a symbol of immortality. The rites, expressing grief and joy at the death and reappearance of the god, were wild even to savagery, performed by women known as maenads, thyiades, and bacchae. These rites seem to have been unknown in Attica where Dionysus was worshipped at the Eleusinian mysteries with Persephone and Demeter under the name of Iacchus, as a brother or bridegroom of Persephone or Demeter. In works of art, he is sometimes represented as an ancient, bearded man, sometimes as a youth of feminine lines, generally naked or with a panther skin over his shoulder, his long hair restrained by a crown of vines. He is either reposing or leaning idly back with grapes, a cup, or the thyrsus in his hand. Often he is in the company of fauns, satyrs, the muses*, or Eros*, the god of love. Sometimes he is represented in the form of a mask, and in this guise is the god of theatre. Sacred to him were the vine, ivy, rose, panther, lion, goat, lynx, ox, and dolphin. Painting: *Zeus Drawing Dionysus from his Thigh in the Presence of Hermes*, on a red-figured greek vase (5th century B.C.), Museum of Fine Arts, Boston.

Dioscuri (dĭ-os-ku'rĭ)   In Greek mythology, the twin brothers Castor and Polydeuces are known as the Dioscuri, respectively the horse tamer and master boxer. They are sons of Leda* and the brothers of Helen* and Clytemnestra*. The generally accepted account is that Tyndareus* was the father of Castor and Clytemnestra, while Polydeuces and Helen were the children of the god Zeus*. In any event, they were so manly they were known as the Dioscure, or striplings of Zeus. They were patron gods of war-like youth, protecting gods in the rites of hospitality, protectors of mariners, their benevolent presence being seen in the flame that appears at the mast during storms (see corposant). Their attribute is an egg-shaped cap with a star. Sometimes they are represented in art with their horses Xanthus* and Cyllaros.

Dirce (der'sē)   In Greek mythology, the wife of Lycus. She was put to death by the two sons of Antiope* in revenge for her ill treatment of their mother, and was bound to the horns of a bull and dragged to death. The body of Dirce was thrown into a well on Mt. Cithaeron, near Thebes, and thereafter was known as the fountain of Dirce.

Dis   See Pluto.

Discord   See Apple of Discord.

Distaff   In Greek religion, an attribute of the goddess Athena*, as goddess of the useful arts.

Dives (dī'vēz)   A name commonly applied to the unnamed man of wealth in the parable of the Beggar Lazarus (see Jesus Christ—Parables).

Divine Comedy   See Dante.

Dog   A symbol of fidelity. In Greek religion, the dog is an attribute of the god Ares*, as a companion in combat. The dog Cerberus* is the guardian of the underworld for the god Hades*. Sea dogs are associated with Poseiden*, god of the sea. His wife Amphitrite* transformed Scylla* into a monster whose waist was girded by dogs' heads. The hunting dogs of Actaeon* tore him apart. Pandareus stole the golden dog, made by the god Hephaestus* for the god Zeus. In the Old Testament, Tobias* is accompanied on his travels by a dog. In Christian legend, a dog brings bread to St. Roch*. A dog carrying a flaming torch in his mouth is an attribute of St. Dominic*, symbol of his spreading of the gospel. Black and white dogs also symbolize the black and white robes of the Dominican friars.

Dolphin   In Greek mythology, the dolphin is sacred to Poseiden*, as god of the sea. The god Apollo* changed himself into a dolphin, so that he might lure Cretan sailors to Delphi* to act as priests. It is an attribute of the god Dionysus*, because he dwelt with the nereid Thetis* in the sea, and of Aphrodite*, because she was born from seafoam and is goddess of the deep sea. In Christian art, the dolphin symbolizes resurrection and salvation. When it is shown with an anchor or boat, it symbolizes the Christian travelling to salvation. Sometimes the dolphin carries the souls of the dead to the world beyond. It also frequently represents the whale in the story of Jonah* and his resurrection.

St. Dominic (1170-1221)   Dominic was born into a Spanish family of the nobility. He was educated at the University of Valencia, and then decided to renounce all worldly honors and entered the church in 1206. He became a great preacher, called the "Inquisitor-General" by Pope Innocent III for his zealous missions against heretics, and used his vehemence against the anti-clerical sects in France, as he established his headquarters at Toulouse. Here, the idea of a highly trained group of preachers, bound by vows of poverty, began to take shape. In a few years, the black-and-white-robed friars penetrated into every corner of Europe. Dominic always gave importance to the help of women in his work, and one of his undertakings was to establish nuns at San Sisto in Rome. He penetrated England by sending thirteen of his "Black Friars" to Oxford. In France, they were known as

"Jacobins," because their mother establishment was on the rue St. Jacques. In art, he is usually represented in the robes of his order with a rosary, for it was he who instituted the devotion of the rosary. He has a sparrow at his side, symbolizing the devil who appeared to him in this form, and a star on his head, in reference to the star said to have appeared on his forehead when he was baptized. A dog carrying a flaming torch in its mouth is frequently shown by him, referring to the story that his mother during her pregnancy dreamed that she had given birth to a dog carrying a flaming torch which lighted the world. When he is seen with a loaf of bread, it refers to the legend that one morning there was nothing to eat in the monastery, but Dominic ordered the monks to assemble at table. While they were reciting prayers, two angels appeared and gave each monk a loaf of bread. Another attribute is the lily of purity. Feast day: August 4.

Doomsday   See Day of Judgement.

St. Donatus   One colorful saint of this name was said to have been of noble birth, educated, and brought up a Christian with his foster brother Julian who then became emperor in 355. In time, Emperor Julian renounced his faith, and persecuted Christians. Donatus fled to Arezzo, and was later made its bishop. Legends attribute miracles to him. One story tells of a tax collector whose wife buried his collections while he was away on a journey. The woman died before he returned and the tax collector was accused of theft. He appealed to Donatus, who went to the tomb of the wife and asked her to reveal the hiding place. A voice answered from the tomb, and the money was found. Once when Donatus was holding mass, hooligans came into the church and broke the Communion cup. Donatus put the cup together perfectly, and the rowdies were converted to Christianity. In art, he is shown in bishop's robes, often holding the Communion cup. The story of the tax collector is also frequently depicted.

Dormition of the Virgin Mary   The name given to the falling asleep, or death, of the Virgin Mother. In the Roman church, it is a dogma of faith; in the Orthodox church, a pious belief that when Mary died, her body was taken to heaven (see Assumption).

St. Dorothea   A Christian virgin of Cappadocia, Asia Minor, noted for her beauty, who was martyred in Diocletian's reign about 303. Two apostate (guilty of loss of faith) women were sent to pervert her, but Dorothea reconverted them, and was thereupon sentenced to be beheaded. As she was being led to execution, an officer mocked her and asked her to send him flowers from Paradise. Immediately after the execution, a young angel appeared to him with a basket of apples and roses saying, "From Dorothea in Paradise." The officer became a Christian and was also martyred. In art, Dorothea is shown with roses in her hand or on her head, or with an attending angel holding a basket of apples and roses. Sometimes she is seen offering a basket of fruit and roses to the Virgin* and Child. She may also be seen tied to a stake with a burning torch on one side. Feast day: February 6.

Doubting Thomas   See St. Thomas.

Dove   In Greek religion, the dove is sacred to the goddess Aphrodite*. The turtle dove is an attribute of Fides*, the Roman personification of fidelity. It is one of the most ancient symbols of peace and purity. In the Old Testament, Noah* sends a dove out of the ark to see if the water has receded, and it brings back an olive branch. The offering for the purification of a newborn child, under the laws of Moses, was a dove. In Christian symbology, the dove seen alone represents the Holy Ghost*, and is always shown in representations of the Trinity*. When seven doves are shown, they represent the seven gifts of God's grace (Isaiah 11:1-2). Twelve doves sometimes symbolize the twelve apostles* of Jesus. The dove is shown with St. Catherine of Siena*, referring to the dove seen on her head when she was praying as a child; with St. Gregory*, referring to the legend that the Holy Ghost* came to him to dictate his writings in the form of a dove. It is also an attribute of St. Basil*, St. David*, and St. Eulalia.

Dragon   In Christian iconography, the dragon is a symbol of the devil, or evil. It is an attribute of Sts. George*, Martha* of Bethany, and Margaret*, all of whom fought and vanquished a dragon. Christ*, the Virgin Mary*, and the archangel Michael* are shown trampling a dragon under their feet, as victors over the power of darkness. The dragon also appears with the apostle Philip* and with St. Sylvester* (see Serpent).

Drum   An attribute of the goddess Cybele* and the maenads*, which they played upon during their orgiastic festivals (see Cymbal).

St. Dunstan (909-988)   Dunstan was born in Glastonbury ten years after the death of King Alfred*, and was attracted to the priesthood because of a dangerous illness. About 943, he began to restore monastic life to England and founded many abbeys, adopting the Rule of St. Benedict*, and integrating the monasteries into the life of the people. In 959, he was made bishop of Canterbury. As well as his sacred ministry, he was credited with dexterity as a metal worker. He was a skillful scribe and draughtsman; he played the harp and loved to teach the choir boys of the cathedral. In art, he is represented in pontifical robes, carrying a pair of pincers or tongs in his right hand, referring to the legend that on one occasion he seized the devil by the nose with a pair of red hot tongs, and refused to release him until he promised never to tempt him again. St. Dunstan was also noted for his skill at shoeing horses. One day the devil asked him to shoe his single hoof. Dunstan, knowing who his customer was, tied him tightly to the wall, and as he proceeded with the job, put the devil to so much pain he roared for mercy. Dunstan consented to release him on condition that he never enter a place where a horseshoe was displayed; hence the tradition that a horseshoe over a doorway is a protection. St. Dunstan is the patron of goldsmiths. Feast day: May 19.

Crozier, decorated with a scene of St. Michael Slaying the Dragon, 13th century. French Limoges, enamel on copper.

E

Eagle In Greek religion, the eagle was sacred to the god Zeus*. In some accounts, Zeus abducted Ganymede*, in the form of an eagle. The sea eagle was an attribute of the goddess Athena*. In Christian religion, the eagle is the symbol of the highest inspiration, and as such, the attribute of St. John the Evangelist* (see Ezekiel 1:1-10). It is also a symbol of resurrection, based on the belief that by flying close to the sun and then plunging into water, the eagle renews its youth and its plumage. In art, it is used on the baptismal font as a symbol of new life. When represented as a bird of prey, it symbolizes evil.

Ear In Christian art, the ear is a symbol of Christ's betrayal, because the disciple Peter cut off the ear of one of the high priest's servants (see Jesus Christ—Life Events—Betrayal).

Ecce Homo Latin for the words "Behold the man," spoken by Pontius Pilate*, the governor of Judea, when he handed Jesus over to the soldiers for crucifixion (see Jesus Christ—Life Events—Crowning with Thorns).

Echo (ek'ō) In Greek mythology, a mountain nymph, who by her chatter, distracted the goddess Hera*, and prevented her from discovering her husband, the god Zeus*, cavorting with the nymphs. Hera punished Echo for siding with Zeus, by taking away her power of speech, leaving her the ability to speak only the last words spoken to her. Echo fell in love with a beautiful youth named Narcissus. He rejected her, and she pined so much for his love, she dwindled away into nothing but her own voice.

Eden (ē'den) See Garden of Eden.

95

St. Edmund (841-869)   At fifteen years of age, Edmund is said to have been chosen king of the East Angles (English). He was a devout Christian and, during a pagan invasion, he refused to give up his faith and share his kingdom with the heathen invaders. He was tied to a tree, shot with arrows until his body was like a thistle, and then his head was cut off. He was soon revered as a martyr, and his body was enshrined at Bury St. Edmunds, where a great abbey was founded in 1020. His emblem is three arrows. Feast day: November 28.

Edward the Confessor (1004-1066)   King of England, the son of Athelred, and for a time patron of England, later supplanted by St. George*. Edward was a principal benefactor of Westminster Abbey in London. He governed well, but had much political difficulty in his own kingdom, and as time went on, took less interest in the realm and more in religion. His piety bestowed upon him the name "confessor," as one who bears witness to Christ by his life. Legend tells that once Edward was passing through a village where a church was being consecrated to St. John the Evangelist*. He stopped and was asked for alms by an old man. Edward had nothing with him so he gave him his ring. Some years later two pilgrims lost their way in the Holy Land. An old man appeared to them and said, "I am John the Evangelist. Give this ring back to your king and tell him that within a year he shall rejoice with me in heaven." The pilgrims fell asleep, and when they awoke they found themselves back in England, on the downs. They hastened with the ring to the king. Six months later, Edward died. He was canonized in the twelfth century. His emblem is a finger ring. Feast day: October 13.

St. Edward the Martyr (962-978)   Edward was the son of King Edgar of England by his first wife, and succeeded his father at the age of thirteen. Despite opposition of some of the noblemen, Edward was crowned, but could not control the kingdom. Legend says he was on his way to visit his half-brother Ethelred, when he was attacked by Ethelred's retainers and murdered at the instigation of his stepmother, who wanted the throne for her own son. Soon supernatural manifestations were alleged to support the charge. Edward's body was taken to the nunnery at Shaftesbury. Miracles occurred there, and Edward came to be venerated as a saint and martyr by the populace. Feast day: March 18.

Egg   In Greek mythological legend, Leda* was seduced by the god Zeus*, in the form of a swan and produced the egg that gave birth to Helen* and Polydeuces*. Some legends say Nemesis* was visited by Zeus as a swan, and she produced and gave the egg to Leda. In Christian iconography, the egg symbolizes chastity and purity, derived from the purity of a chicken born out of an egg.

Eight   The figure 8 in Christian iconography is a symbol of rejuvenation, purification, and eternity. It also symbolizes the resurrection*, for Christ rose from his tomb on the eighth day after his entry into Jerusalem* (see Jesus Christ—Life Events).

Eirene or Irene (ī-rē-nē)   In Greek mythology, the goddess of peace, identified with the Roman Pax*. She was one of the Horae*, and was worshipped as goddess of wealth. In art, she is often shown as a young woman with the infant Plutus* in her arms. Her attributes are the cornucopia (horn of plenty)*, the olive branch, the caduceus* of Hermes*, and ears of corn.

Electra (ē-lek′tra)   In Greek legend, the daughter of King Agamemnon* of Mycenae and his queen Clytemnestra*, and a sister of Iphigenia*, Chrysothemis*, and Orestes*. When Agamemnon returned victoriously from the Trojan war, and was murdered by his wife Clytemnestra and her lover Aegisthus*, Electra secretly saved Orestes from a possible murder by Aegisthus and sent him away to Phocis. Electra remained in Mycenae, in virtual slavery to her mother and Aegisthus, for the next eight years. Then Orestes returned to Mycenae, with his friend Pylades*, and was reunited with her. Electra, burning with revenge, encouraged and supported Orestes in the murder of their mother and Aegisthus. Electra ultimately married Pylades, and bore him two sons.

Eleusinian Mysteries (el-ū-sin′i-an)   These were the principal religious mysteries of ancient Greece, held at Eleusis, about fourteen miles west of Athens. The mysteries dealt with the legends of the goddess Demeter* and her daughter Persephone* or Kore; also the god Dionysus*, known in this fertility cult as Iacchus. There were Greater and Lesser Eleusinia; the former lasted nine days and was celebrated between harvest and seed time, the latter in early spring. The events celebrated the descent of Persephone into the world below, and her return to light and her mother. The rites included processions, sea bathing, sacrifices and libations, fasts, torch ceremonies, and religious dramas. At first, initiation into the mysteries was limited to Greeks, but later Romans were admitted to the privileges of membership. The symbolic representation excited and strengthened faith in the continuance of life and the rewards and punishments after death. The ancient writers speak of the revelations as having beneficial influence on morality, and there are suggestions that the errors of polytheism and the unity of the Godhead comprised the famous secret of the mysteries. Eleusinian mysteries maintained their position for a long time, continuing in existance until the end of A.D. fourth century, when they were abolished by the Roman emperor Theodosius II.

St. Eligius   See St. Eloi.

Elijah (ē-lī′ja)   An outstanding Hebrew prophet in the Old Testament, who lived about 875 B.C. He is first heard of when he confronts King Ahab* with a prophecy of draught to last until "Israel forsake her evil ways." Elijah's mission was to destroy the worship of foreign gods and to restore justice. His fanatical zeal brought about at least a temporary banishment of idolatry. He was a rugged man, able to dwell in caves and resist the elements to perform extraordinary feats. His story is colored with many incidents. He survived a famine because the Lord guided him to a brook and sent ravens to feed him bread and flesh morning and evening; he miraculously created food for a poor widow from a handful of meal and a little oil, which lasted for days; he raised the widow's son from the dead by stretching himself out three times upon the boy, placing his eyes, mouth, and hands on those of the boy. He was fed twice by an angel in the wilderness, which enabled him to traverse the desert without food for forty days to Mt. Horeb where he heard the voice of the Lord as "a still small voice," and following the word of the Lord, he transferred his spiritual leadership to the youthful Elisha*, making known his invitation to the young man by throwing his mantle over him. Twice he summoned fire from heaven to consume the soldiers of Samaria, that they might know that he was a prophet of the Lord. Finally he departed from earth in a chariot of fire, witnessed by his successor Elisha. In art, Elijah is represented as an outdoor man of unconventional appearance and dress, often wearing a leather belt around his hips. Painting: *Elijah Taken Up in a Chariot of Fire*, Battista Piazetta and Francesco Polazzo, National Gallery, Washington.

Miracles in his life

Elisha chosen as his successor

Fiery chariot

St. Elisabeth or Elizabeth   In the New Testament, a kinswoman of the Virgin Mary* and mother of John the Baptist*. John was born to her late in life, as a consequence of the prayers of her husband, the priest Zacharias*, and to whom the angel Gabriel* appeared in the Temple with the blessed news. The emotional reaction of Zacharias to this unbelievable announcement produced temporary speechlessness, which lasted until the day of the baby's circumcision. When the Virgin knew that she also was miraculously with child (see Annunciation), she came to visit Elisabeth for three months. The encounter of the two women upon her arrival is frequently portrayed in art and is known as "The Visitation" of the Virgin (Luke 1:39-55). The great passage in the Bible is known as "The Magnificat" and has often been put to music. Elisabeth is also often shown in scenes of the Christ child with her young son John. Feast day: November 5. Painting: *The Visitation with Two Saints*, by Piero di Cosimo, National Gallery, Washington. (See also Elizabeth)

Elisha (el-ī'sha)   In the Old Testament, a 9th-century B.C. prophet who was selected by Elijah* to follow in his footsteps. *Initiation as prophet* Elisha was ploughing the fertile land of his father's estate with oxen, when the elder prophet cast his mantle of succession upon him. Elisha understood the invitation implied in the ritual, sacrificed the team of oxen at a farewell feast, kissed his parents goodbye, and became the lowly helper of Elijah. Where Elijah had been aggressive, Elisha gained his objectives through diplomacy, and his wisdom and counsel gained him great popularity. Most of his miracles show a kindly nature, several of them similar to those *Miracles* of Elijah. He produced a supply of oil for the empty jars of a poor widow, with which to pay her debts—by divine means; he raised a young Shunamite boy from the dead, after a fatal sunstroke, by lying on him as Elijah had done; he cured the Syrian captain Naaman of leprosy by seven mud baths in the Jordan river; and he created food for the multitudes from a few loaves of bread, ears of corn, and fruit, as Christ was later to do. He took an active part in political affairs, frequently warning the imperilled King Joab of Israel, in time for him to escape. His services to Israel were on such a spiritual plane, he dared to diagnose the illness of the Syrian king as fatal. King Joab paid a visit to Elisha on his deathbed, and wept over his face. Elisha told the king to *Death* take his bow and arrows and shoot one eastward out of the window. This arrow, he prophesied, was the arrow of deliverance from the oppression of Syria. In contrast to Elijah, Elisha was bald, wore conventional clothes, and carried a walking stick. His tastes were cultivated. He responded to court music, and his house in Samaria was in comfortable surroundings. Like Moses and Elijah, he supported Israel through an era of religious crisis and progress.

St. Elizabeth of Hungary   Patron saint of queens, being herself a queen, the wife of King Louis II of Thuringia, Germany. She was widowed while very young, and was turned out of the castle at Wartburg, by her brother-in-law, leaving her three small children in his care. A few months later, she renounced the world and found refuge in Marburg, where she joined the order of St. Francis. She put herself under the direction of her confessor, Master Conrad of Marburg, and this austere man separated her from her children, but her spirit was not broken. Her sweet disposition and kind care of the needy won her the devotion of all Thuringia, care which even included fishing to find food for the poor. Her health failed early and she died when she was in her late twenties. In art, she is portrayed with a triple crown, as queen by birth, queen by marriage, and queen through her glorification in heaven. She usually carries roses because of the legend that her husband disapproved of giving bread to the poor. One day he halted her on her rounds, and the bread she was carrying miraculously turned to roses. Elizabeth is enshrined in a church in Marburg. Feast day: November 19. Painting: *St. Elizabeth of Hungary*, Lippo Vanni, Nelson Gallery of Art, Kansas City, Missouri. (See also Elisabeth)

St. Elmo   See St. Erasmus.

St. Eloi or **Eloy** (el'loy) or **Eligius**   A 6th-century Frankish bishop of Noyon, patron saint of artists and smiths, because he was a famous worker in gold and silver, and was also said to be a blacksmith. Once he had difficulty in shoeing a devilish horse, but a young man, who may have been Christ, successfully helped him. The horse was tied up, the leg was detached so that St. Eloi could shoe him comfortably, and when the operation was over, the leg was put back on the horse. The scene is frequently shown in art, St. Eloi holding a detached hoof or leg. Feast day: December 1. A limestone French-Gothic statuette: *St. Eloi With a Horse's Leg and Anvil*, Metropolitan, New York.

Elysian or **Elysium Fields** (ili'zhun or ili'zhium)   In Greek mythology, this is the abode of the blessed, the otherworld for heroes favored by the gods, who are carried there without passing through Hades*. Homer (8th century B.C.) describes Elysium as a lovely meadow at the western extremity of the world, on the banks of the river Oceanus*. Here a life of perfect happiness is lived in a faultless climate, where fruit is produced three times a year. In later times, Elysium is part of the underworld, the pleasant section of the righteous dead.

Emmanuel (ē-man'u-el)   In the Old Testament, Isaiah foretold the coming of the Messiah Emmanuel (also written Immanuel), of the House of David (Isaiah 7:14). Jesus* fulfilled the conditions stated in the prophecy and chose the Messiah's way for his entry into Jerusalem* (John 12:14). See Jesus Christ—Life Events.

Emmaus (em-ā'us)   A place outside Jerusalem, to which Cleophas and another disciple were going when they met the risen Christ walking in the same direction on the first Easter afternoon (Luke 24:13-32). Unrecognized by the two men, Christ joined them on the seven-mile journey, and did not reveal his identity until they broke bread together in a village home. Several sites claim to be the original Emmaus, each a long round-trip from Jerusalem (see Jesus Christ—After-Life Events—Apparitions). Painting: *Christ at Emmaus*, Diego Velazquez, Metropolitan, New York.

Endymion (endim'i-on)   In Greek mythology, a beautiful youth, sometimes said to be a king, sometimes a shepherd, who,

Endymion and Selene, Roman Sarcophagus, 3rd century, A.D. Rogers Fund, The Metropolitan Museum of Art.

as he slept on Mt. Latimus, so moved the cold heart of the moon goddess Selene*, she came down and kissed him and lay at his side. He woke to find her gone, but the dreams that she gave him were such that he begged the god Zeus* to give him eternal slumber and undying youth. Another legend says that Selene bound him by enchantment, so that she might visit him nightly. Selene was supposed to be the mother of fifty daughters by Endymion. Painting: *Endymion and Selene*, Nicholas Poussin, Detroit Institute of Art.

Entombment of Christ   See Jesus Christ—After-Life Events.

Entry into Jerusalem of Christ   See Jesus Christ—Life Events.

Eos (ē'os)   In Greek mythology, the personification of the dawn, goddess daughter of the Titans Hyperion* and Theia, sister of Helius*, the sun, and Selene*, the moon. Her husband was

Astreaus, and their children were the winds, Zephyrus (west), Boreas* (north), Nortus (south), and Eurus (east); also all the stars, among them Hesperus, the evening star, and Heosphorus, the morning star. Her hair was beautiful, her arms and fingers rosy, and her wings white. She rises early from her couch on the Eastern Ocean in a saffron-colored mantle, riding on a golden chariot drawn by white horses, proclaiming for her brother Helius the arrival of the day. She is represented, in art, riding her chariot or hovering in the sky, moving with her torch before the god Ares*, whom she is said to have seduced, or sprinkling dew from a vase over the earth. Eos is supposed to have had many mortal lovers. When the blind Orion* came to the east, she fell in love with him, and persuaded Helius to touch his lids with his rays and restore his sight. She also loved Cephalus* and upset his life with his wife Procris. She stole Ganymede* for the god Zeus* to be his cup-bearer, and she carried off Tithonous and by him bore Memnon, who joined the Trojans in their war against Greece. When Memnon was killed, Eos withdrew her light, and darkness covered the earth, but the Horae* brought her to Zeus and he insisted that she continue her course. From then on, Eos wept dew every morning in lament for Memnon. Eos is identified with the Roman goddess Aurora*. Painting: *Eos and Tithonous*, on a red-figured Greek vase (5th century B.C.), Museum of Fine Arts, Boston.

Ephebus (e-fē′bus)   In Greek antiquity, the Athenian name for a youth over sixteen years of age. Upon completing his sixteenth year, a festival was held at which the ephebus made a drink-offering to Heracles*, and entertained his friends with wine. For the next two years his education, moral, physical, and military, was taken over by the state, and conducted with rigid discipline, preparing him to understand and perform the duties of citizenship. After an examination, the ephebi were entered on the list of their tribe, presented to the people assembled in a theater, armed with a spear and shield, and taken to the sanctuary of Agraulos at the foot of the citadel, where they bound themselves by solemn oath to serve and defend their country. In Greek art the name is applied to any youth, particularly if he is bearing arms.

Ephesian Artemis or Diana of the Ephesians   This Artemis is an ancient, Asiatic divinity whose worship was adopted by the Ionian Greeks in Asia Minor. She was a personification of the fruitfulness of nature, and was quite distinct from the Greek Artemis*, although incorporated with her by the Ephesians because of some resemblance of her attributes. She is shown in art wearing a flat-topped, high crown; she has many breasts from her neck to her waist, and her lower body is tightly sheathed and decorated with symbolic figures. The temple of Artemis at Ephesus, one of the twelve Ionian cities, was famous as a sanctuary, and was known as one of the Seven Wonders of the Ancient World*. It was burned in the 4th century B.C., and subsequently rebuilt. Finally, in A.D. 262, it was sacked by the Goths.

Ephod (ē'fod)   An apron-like garment held in at the waist by a girdle of many colors, which was worn by the high priests of Israel under the breast plate. It was sometimes used for divination (Exodus 28:4-8).

Epigoni (ē-pig'ō-nī)   The word means "after-born," and in Greek legend the name was given to the descendants of the Seven Against Thebes*, who ten years after the disastrous rout, joined once more against Thebes. Unlike their fathers, they started with the happiest promise of victory from the oracle at Thebes, provided Alcmaeon* commanded the expedition. Alcmaeon accepted the leadership, and Thebes was conquered and destroyed. The best fruits of their victory were dutifully sent to the god Apollo at Delphi. This successful expedition took place in the 14th century B.C., before that of the Argonauts* and before the Trojan war*.

Epimetheus (ep-i-mē'thē-us)   In Greek mythology, the brother of Prometheus*, the name meaning "after-thought." Epimetheus is said to have created the animals, giving them all the best means of protection, while Prometheus came to man's rescue by giving him the ability to stand up. Prometheus also stole fire from heaven for man's use. The god Zeus* took revenge, and counterbalanced the gift by ordering the god Hephaestus* to create the maiden Pandora*. All the gods of Olympus endowed Pandora with talents, including a crafty mind. She was taken to Epimetheus as a present by the god Hermes*, bearing with her a jar as her dowry. In spite of the warnings of Prometheus to refuse any gift from Zeus, Epimetheus was quickly ensnared by Pandora's charms, and married her. Pandora, anxious to see the dowry she had brought with her, opened the jar. Out flew evil, trouble, and disease, hitherto unknown to man. Only Hope remained, because Pandora clapped back the lid of the jar before she could escape.

Epiphany (e-pi'fan-ē)   This day falls on the 6th of January, and is known also as the Twelfth Night after Christmas. In Christian religion, it is the feast which commemorates the visit of the Magi* (known also as Three Wise Men or Kings) to Bethlehem to visit the Christ child, manifesting him as king of the Gentiles (Matthew

2). It also commemorates the baptism of Jesus (Mark 1) in the Jordon river, manifesting Jesus as the son of God. This manifestation took place as Jesus emerged from the water, and the voice of God was heard saying, "This is my Beloved Son in whom I am well pleased." It also commemorates the miracle at Cana (John 2), manifesting Christ's power to perform miracles (see Jesus Christ—Miracles). Painting: *The Epiphany*, from the workshop of Giotto, Metropolitan, New York.

Eponymoi (e-pon′i-mē)   These were the ancient Greek heroes who gave their names to the ten tribes of Clisthenes. Their statues were placed in the Agora (market place) of Athens, and public notices were posted near them.

St. Erasmus or Elmo   A bishop in Syria, Asia Minor, who was persecuted under Diocletian, and martyred about 303. Legend recounts that he was put to death by having his intestines wound out of his body onto a windlass or capstan, and he is honored, therefore, as a patron of sailors. The name, "St. Elmo's Fire" (see Castor and Pollux), which is given to electrical discharges during a storm and sometimes seen at the masthead of ships, refers to him. These lights were taken as a sign of protection and a change of weather. In art, his emblem is a windlass. Feast day: June 2.

Erato (er′a-tō)   In Greek mythology, the daughter of Zeus* and Mnemosyne*, the goddess of memory. She was the muse of lyric and amorous poetry, and in art, is usually represented as a beautiful maiden with a lyre, often in the company of her eight sister muses. Fresco transferred to canvas: *Erato*, Guilio Romano, Metropolitan, New York.

Erebus (er′ē-bus)   In Greek mythology, the son of Chaos and the brother of Nyx* (night), Aether (air), and Hemera (day). He was the father of the Fates* by his sister Nyx, and evils such as death, doom, misery, and deceit, as well as of slumber and dreams. He was darkness personified and his name was given to the underground cavern through which the shades walked on their way to Hades* (underworld).

Erinyes or Eumenides (Ro. Furiae or Dirae)   In Greek mythology, the female deities, older than the Olympian gods, who were daughters of Gaea (earth) and lived in Erebus in the underworld. They are usually represented as three hideous maidens with snakes in their hair, sometimes dogs' heads, with scourges in their hands. They pursued criminals, drove them mad, and tormented them in Hades* (underworld). When Orestes* avenged his father's murder, by killing his mother Clytemnestra*, he was pursued by the Erinyes until a trial was held on the Areopagus (supreme court) of Athens. The goddess Athena*, goddess of order and wisdom, came to the defense of Orestes, and persuaded the bitter Erinyes to change their character and take residence in a grotto on the Acropolis. Here they were honored by the Athenians as the "Solemn Ones." Their name Eumenides (the kindly) implies that through the destruction of evil, well-being is achieved.

Eris (er'is) In Greek mythology, a daughter of Nyx*, the goddess of night, or of the god and goddess Zeus* and Hera*, and a twin of the god of war, Ares*. She is the goddess of discord and is famous for throwing the Apple of Discord* among the guests at the wedding feast of Peleus* and Thetis*. The Romans identified her with Discordia.

Ermine In Christian iconography, a symbol of chastity and purity because of its white fur, associated with the motto, "Better death than dishonor." It is also connected with the conception of Christ, since legend relates it conceived through the ear, which parallels the belief that Mary*, the mother of Christ, conceived by the Word of God, that is, through the ear (see Immaculate Conception).

Eros (er'os or ē'ros) (Ro. Cupid) In Greek mythology, Eros is the god of love in all its manifestations: physical passion, romantic love, sportive and friendly love, love-making and flirtation. In an old legend, he is the offspring of Chaos, personifying creative power, harmony, and devoted friendship. In late legend, he is the youngest of the gods, son of Aphrodite*, goddess of love and the god Ares*, or sometimes said to be the son of the god Hermes* or the god Zeus*. He is represented as a beautiful, winged boy or youth, carrying a bow and arrows, or as a mischievous irresponsible child who shoots his arrows at random without regard for those whose hearts he wantonly sets on fire. The Olympian gods had not the smallest compunction about employing him to further their own ends. He is sometimes represented with his brother Anteros*. In later times, the Romans identified Eros with Cupid, or Amor. He is often shown in art in the company of Aphrodite, surrounded by many cherubic boys. Painting: *Sleeping Eros*, Caravaggio, Indiana Museum of Art, Bloomington. (See Cupid)

Erymanthian Boar (er-i-man'the-an) In Greek legend, a savage boar that ravaged the slopes of Mt. Erymanthus. One of the labors of Heracles* was to bring it alive to Eurystheus*. He accomplished this by driving it into a snow drift where it was helpless, and thus captured and carried it back across his shoulders to Mycenae. When he appeared with the animal, Eurystheus was terrified and hid in a large pithos (storage jar). The scene is frequently shown in Greek art.

Esau (ē′saw) In the Old Testament, a son of Isaac* and Rebekah*, the twin of Jacob* and the firstborn. Esau was a hunting man, ruddy and hairy, and the favorite of his father. Once, when he had been hunting, he came near to starving. He appealed to Jacob for food, and Jacob gave him a mess of pottage (lentils) on condition that he cede him the birthright and blessing, which was due to him from his father as the eldest son. When Isaac was an old man, Jacob cemented this trick. With the help of his mother, he covered his arms with a goat skin so that his blind, old father would think he was the hairy Esau. The old man was deceived and blessed Jacob, giving him authority over his brother and all the tribe. Esau was violently angry, but was compelled to seek his living away from home and settled near Mt. Seir. Later in life, he and Jacob were reconciled, as Jacob was passing through East Palestine. The two brothers symbolize the supremacy of the younger land of Canaan over the older Edomite country; hence the allusion, "the elder shall serve the younger" (Genesis 25:23).

Esther (e′stur) In the Old Testament, the beautiful Jewish heroine of the book that bears her name, who through the efforts of her cousin and adopted father Mordecai*, was selected by Persian King Ahasuerus to be his queen. Esther remained faithful to Mordecai and her Jewish people. When the vizier Haman hatched a plot, not only to destroy the Jews but to hang the faithful Mordecai, Esther, as the adored queen of Ahasuerus, put on her best apparel and went into the king's inner court. Although this was not customary, she found favor in the king's sight and he held out his golden sceptre to her, asking what she desired. Esther asked that he and Haman attend a banquet she was preparing. That night the king had a dream, which reminded him of Mordecai's services to him, and with Esther's maneuvering at the banquet, she cleverly induced the king to expose Haman, who was then hanged in Mordecai's stead. The Jewish feast of Purim commemorates these events. Painting: *Esther before Ahasuerus*, Artemesia Gentileschi, Metropolitan, New York.

Eteocles (ē-tē′ō-klēz) In Greek legend, a son of Oedipus* and Jocasta*, and the brother of Polynices*. Legend recounts that when Oedipus* learned that he had fathered children by his own mother, he blinded himself in horror, whereupon his sons Eteocles and Polynices banished him from the kingdom. Oedipus then laid a curse on his sons; that they should divide their inheritance by the sword. The brothers agreed between themselves to rule the kingdom by turns, but Eteocles, who had the first term as the eldest, refused to give up the throne at the allotted time. He banished Polynices*, who fled to Argos, and with the aid of Adrastus*, led the ill-fated expedition of the Seven Against Thebes*. During the battle, the brothers met to decide who should have the kingdom, and fighting it out in single combat, killed each other. Creon*, uncle of the brothers, succeeded to the throne. He gave Eteocles a funeral with full honors, but had the body of Polynices flung to the birds, saying he had attacked his own city (see Antigone).

Ethon (ē′thon)   In Greek mythology, the eagle or vulture that gnawed the liver of Prometheus*.

Eucharist (ū′kar-ist)   In the Christian church, the Eucharist is another name for Holy Communion. It means a "thanksgiving," for the sacrament, as well as a sacrifice. To take the Eucharist is to "come in union" with Christ and with other fellow-Christians. In receiving the bread and wine, the body and blood of Christ are received.

St. Eugenia (ūjēn′ia)   There are no dates for this saint, but there is evidence that she was martyred at Rome in early Christianity and that she was buried in the cemetery of Apronian on the Via Latina. A legend arose about her saying she had put on male dress and become abbot of a monastery in Egypt. She was accused of misconduct, but cleared herself by declaring her sex. She left then for Rome where she was beheaded for being a Christian. Her story was a popular one and spread all over the Christian world, gathering legends as it traveled. Feast day: December 10.

Eumaeus (ū-mē′us)   The slave and swineherd of Odysseus*, with whom he found refuge upon his return to Ithaca.

Eumenides (ū-men′i-dēz)   In Greek mythology, another name for the Erinyes*, meaning the good-tempered ones, because the punishment of evil secures the well-being of the good, and thus the Erinyes prove themselves to be benevolent.

Euphemia (ū-fē′mia)   A virgin martyr persecuted under Diocletian, who met her death at Chalcedon about 307. Many churches were dedicated to her, and legends arose. One recounts that she was thrown to wild beasts in the arena. A bear or a lion came gently to her and spared her. She is shown with one of these animals in art.

Euphrosyne (ū-fros'i-nē) In Greek mythology, one of the charites*, or graces; she was the goddess symbolizing joy.

Europa (u-rō'pa) In Greek mythology, a Phoenician princess, the daughter of Agenor, and sister of Cadmus*. The god Zeus* became enamored of her, and sent the god Hermes* to lure her to the seashore, while she was playing with her maidens. Zeus then appeared to her in the form of a white bull with golden horns, and rubbing against her, enticed her to ride on his back. Suddenly he plunged into the sea with Europa still on his back, and carried her off to Crete. When Zeus left Europa, she married King Asterius of Crete who adopted her sons, by Zeus, as his heirs. Europa was worshipped in Crete as "Hellotis" and a festival was held in her honor, the Hellotia. Painting: *The Rape of Europa*, Titian, Gardner Museum, Boston.

The Rape of Europa. Titian. The Isabella Stewart Gardner Museum.

Euryclea (ū-rē′clē-a)   In Greek legend, the nurse of Odysseus*, who brought up his son Telemachus*. When Odysseus returned home, disguised as a beggar, after twenty years' absence, she recognized him by a scar on his leg, while bathing his feet. A sign from Odysseus kept her from revealing his identity, but afterward she was the first to tell Penelope*, the wife of Odysseus, that her husband had returned and that he had slain her unwanted suitors.

Eurydice (ū-rid′i-sē)   In Greek mythology, the beloved wife of the poet Orpheus*. Aristaeus, who was a noted beekeeper, tried to seduce her, and as she fled from him, she stepped on a snake and died of its bite. As punishment, all the bees of Aristaeus died. Orpheus, who was overcome with grief at the loss of his wife, descended to Hades* (underworld) with the god Hermes* in an effort to bring Eurydice back to earth. He so moved Queen Persephone* by the music of his song, she permitted him to take Eurydice with him, on condition that Orpheus lead the way and not look back at her until they reached the daylight. Orpheus led her through the realm of the dead, and they almost reached safety. Then his impatience led him to glance back, and Eurydice's shade was snatched away from him forever. One legend says that he was ultimately reunited with her in Hades, where they could be seen strolling together in the Elysian Fields.* Marble group: *Orpheus and Eurydice*, Auguste Rodin, Metropolitan, New York.

Eurynome (ū-rin′ō-mē)   In Greek mythology, the mother by the god Zeus* of the three charites*, or graces. Legend says that she helped Thetis* save the god Hephaestus*, when his mother, the goddess Hera*, hurled him out of heaven.

Eurystheus (ū-ris′thē-us)   In Greek legend, king of Mycenae, who was a grandson of Perseus*, through his father Sthenelous. Legend says that through the cunning of the goddess Hera*, the birth of Heracles* was delayed so that Eurystheus would be the first child born to the house of Perseus, hence, ruler over its descendants. This was to come about because the god Zeus*, knowing that he had fathered a descendant of Perseus through Alcmene* and knowing that the birth was imminent, vowed that the first child born to a descendant of Perseus would reign over Argos. Hera's trick made Heracles a subject of Eurystheus, but she agreed that after Heracles performed whatever twelve labors Eurystheus should demand of him, Zeus could make Heracles immortal. Heracles carried out the twelve labors for Eurystheus, but Eurystheus was always in terror of him, and banished him from Argos when the labors were ended, claiming he was a threat to the throne. Next he pursued the children of Heracles, afraid also that they might unseat him. In attempting to force their expulsion from Attica, he was slain in battle by Hyllus*, a son of Heracles. Eurystheus is frequently shown in Greek art, hiding in panic in an enormous pithos (storage jar), while Heracles stands before it brandishing the Erymanthean boar, which he caught and brought back alive to Argos. (See Heracles)

St. Eustace   A Christian martyr who died about 118. Legend relates that he was an officer under the emperor Trajan. While he was out hunting one day near Tivoli, he was converted to Christianity by a vision of a white stag, bearing a luminous crucifix between its antlers. After this conversion, he refused to join in worshipping pagan gods, and was roasted to death with his wife and sons, inside a huge, brass bull. The episode of the stag is a favorite in art. Eustace is usually shown as a knight with his horse and hounds. Sometimes he is shown with a brazen bull, as a symbol of his martyrdom. He is the patron of huntsmen. Feast day: September 20. The story of the stag and the crucifix is also told about St. Hubert*.

St. Eustochium   See St. Paula.

Euterpe (ū-ter′pē)   In Greek mythology, one of the nine muses, daughters of the god Zeus* and Mnemosyne* (memory). She is the muse of music, simple Dionysiac music rather than that of the god Apollo*. She is the inventor of joy and pleasure, and patroness of flute players. She is usually represented in art as a young woman with a lute in her hand, or with various musical instruments around her. Fresco transferred to canvas: *Euterpe*, Giulio Romano, Metropolitan, New York.

Evangelists   Authors of the four canonical Gospels of the New Testament, written in the first Christian century, were called Evangelists, meaning "messengers of good tidings." Their individual symbols, based upon imagery of Ezekiel* (Old Testament) and Revelation (New Testament), found their way early into Christian art. They are usually represented as follows:

> *Matthew* is shown with a pen in his hand and a scroll before him, looking over his left shoulder at an angel. Matthew represents man, the mystery of the incarnation, and the virtue of reason. His symbol is a winged man or man's face.

> *Mark* is seated writing, and by his side lies a couchant, winged lion. The lion is his symbol, representing the mystery of the resurrection and the virtue of courage.

> *Luke* is shown with a pen, looking in deep thought over a scroll, and near him is an ox or bull, chewing its cud. He is also

frequently shown painting a picture, since tradition says he painted the portrait of the Virgin Mary. His symbol is the winged bull or ox, meaning sacrificial passion and the virtue of renunciation.

John is shown as a young man of great delicacy, with an eagle in the background. The eagle is his symbol, meaning ascension and the expectancy of immortality and sublimity.

Eve   In the Old Testament, Eve is the first woman, fashioned by God from Adam's rib, bone of his bone and flesh of his flesh, called Woman by Adam*, because she was taken out of Man. They lived together in the Garden of Eden*, naked and unashamed, with everything needed to enjoy life. Eve was beguiled, however, by a serpent, who told her her eyes would be opened, if she ate of the fruit of the tree of the knowledge of good and evil. God had forbidden the eating of this fruit on penalty of death. When Eve ate the fruit and gave some to Adam, she precipitated their expulsion from the Garden of Eden. (Genesis 2:21-3:24) After this tragedy, "the mother of all living," bore Cain*, Abel*, and Seth. The subordinate position of woman may be based on the primacy of Adam. Painting: *The Creation of Eve*, Fra Bartolommeo della Porta, Seattle Art Museum.

Exaltation of the Cross   A feast held in the Roman Catholic church on September 14 (Holy Cross Day), in commemoration of the victory over the Persians in 627 when Heraclius recovered and restored to Calvary the cross that had been carried away by Khosroes, Sassanian king from 590 to 628.

Exodus   The sacred book of the Old Testament, which relates the departure of the Israelites from Egypt, under the guidance of Moses*, about 1250 B.C. The migration, during a forty-year period, included a trek across the wilderness and mountains, and a prolonged residence at the oasis of Kadesh.

Extreme Unction   The Sacrament of Holy Unction, which comes from the Latin *in extremis*, meaning, "near the end," and which involves anointing, is given in the Roman Catholic church by a priest to the dying. The custom is based on James 5:14: "Is any sick among you? let him call for the elders of the church; and let them pray over him, anointing him with oil in the name of the Lord."

Eye   In Christian iconography, the eye is a symbol of the "all-seeing" ever-present God. When it is surrounded by a triangle, it symbolizes the Trinity*. A pair of eyes, sometimes on a platter,

111

sometimes held in the hand, is an attribute of St. Lucy* who tore them from her head.

Ezekiel (ēzēk'yel) Ezekiel is the third book of the Major Prophets, and describes the prophetic career of Ezekiel in the 6th century B.C. The central point of the work is the fall of Jerusalem in 586 B.C. Aroused at first by extraordinary visions whose imagery was borrowed later by the Evangelist*, Ezekiel's life was then guided by continuous communications from God, which he followed with ardor, ending with a vision of the ideal Temple. Famous passages from Ezekiel include the sword of God's wrath (21), the greatness of Tyre (26 through 28), the lament over Egypt (31 and 32), and the field of dry bones (37). The imagery, borrowed by the Evangelist, he described as follows: I saw in the heavens four creatures, each with wings, and the one had the face of a man, the second the face of a lion, the third an ox, and the fourth in the likeness of an eagle. Painting: *The Nativity with Prophets Ezekiel and Isaiah*, Duccio di Buoninsegna, National Gallery, Washington.

Face of a Man   See Evangelists—Matthew.

St. Faith   A legendary saint, represented as a sister of saints Hope and Charity, all said to be the children of St. Sophia. The story says they were all martyred in Rome under the emperor Hadrian in A.D. second century. Feast day: August 1.

Falcon   In Christian iconography, the domesticated falcon symbolizes the pagan converted to Christianity, or one who is holy. The wild falcon symbolizes evil. The domestic falcon is sometimes seen with the Magi*.

Fall of Man   In the Old Testament, the description given to the degeneracy of the human race in consequence of the disobedience of Adam* in the Garden of Eden* (Genesis 3). Painting: *Fall of Man*, Albrecht Altdorfer, National Gallery, Washington.

Fates, Fata, or Parcae   In Roman mythology, the three goddesses of destiny who foretold the course of every human life. They were Clotho, who held the spindle or distaff; Lachesis, who spun the thread of life; and Antropas, who cut the thread with shears when life ended. They became identified with the Greek Moerae, who functioned at every birth, determining and predicting destinies.

Faunus and Fauns   Faunus was an Italian deity of the forest, a creature like a satyr, half-man, half-goat, later identified with the Greek god Pan*. Faunus was supposed to reveal the future in dreams. Like Pan, he was accompanied by small fauns, merry, capricious beings who caused nightmares. Originally fauns were

113

shown as human with short goat-tails, small horns, and pointed ears. Later, when identified with Pan, the hind legs of a goat were added. Two festivals called Faunalia were celebrated in honor of Faunus, which were accompanied by libations of milk and wine, sacrifice of goats, and the performance of games. (See Pan.)

Feast of the Gods   According to a story of the author Ovid (43 B.C.-A.D. 17), the Olympic gods held a bacchanalian feast at which the god Priapus* lost his heart to the nymph Lotis. As she was lying asleep in the grass, Priapus stole up to embrace her but the raucous braying of an ass betrayed him. The nymph sprang up in terror amidst the laughter of the gods. Painting: *Feast of the Gods*, Giovanni Bellini, National Gallery, Washington.

Feather   In Christian iconography, a peacock feather is an attribute of St. Barbara*, in reference to Heliopolis, the city where she was born.

Fetters or Chains   In Christian iconography, an attribute of St. Leonard*, who was instrumental in obtaining the release of prisoners. It also refers to the flagellation of Christ* (see Jesus Christ—Life Events).

Fides (fi'dāz)   The Roman personification of the goddess of faith, or fidelity. She is usually represented as a matron wearing a wreath of olive or laurel leaves, carrying ears of corn or a basket of fruit. In the sacrificial ceremonies to Fides, the right hand was bound with a white cloth to indicate that honor dwelt in the right hand.

Fig Tree   In Greek mythology, the fig tree is an attribute of the goddess Demeter*, because she gave the fig tree to Attica, in Greece. In Christian iconography, the fig is a symbol of fruitfulness and good works, but is also a symbol of lust, because Adam* and Eve* covered their naked bodies with fig leaves in the Garden of Eden*.

Finger Across the Lips   This gesture is an allusion to St. Benedict's* rule of silence.

Fir Tree   In Christian religion, a symbol of patience and of those whose virtue raises them above common desire.

Fish   In the Old Testament, Tobias* restored the eyesight of his father with the gall of a fish, hence the fish is his attribute and that of the archangel Raphael*, who helped him. In Christian iconography, the fish is used as a symbol of Jesus Christ since the five Greek letters spelling fish, IXθUS, are the initials for "Jesus Christ, God's Son, Saviour." It is an attribute of Sts. Peter*, Simon*, and Zeno*, all of whom were fishermen, and of St. Anthony of Padua*, who preached to the fish. Fishes and loaves of bread in a basket are an attribute of St. Philip*, because he distributed this food to the multitudes for Jesus (see Jesus Christ—Miracles—Loaves and Fishes). In Greek religion the fish is an attribute of the god of the sea Poseiden*, particularly the tunny fish.

Five   In Christian iconography the number five is symbolic of the five wounds Christ received on the cross (see Jesus Christ—Life Events—Crucifixion).

Flag   See Banner.

Flagellants   The term is applied to the groups of Christians who practiced public flagellation (whipping or flogging) as a penance. The practice supposedly grew out of floggings administered to erring monks, though flagellation, as a form of religious expression, is an ancient usage. The movement appeared in Europe in the twelfth century, and is still practiced in moderation in some monastic orders today (see Jesus Christ—Life Events—Flagellation of Christ).

Flames   In Christian art, flames symbolize religious zeal and the persecution of martyrs; as such they are an attribute of St. Anthony Abbot* and St. Agnes*. They are an attribute of St. Anthony of Padua* as the patron saint and protector against fire. A burning tunic is shown on St. Laurence*, in reference to his martyrdom on a gridiron. Flames may indicate tortures in hell. If they are shown on the heads of the apostles in scenes of the Pentecost*, they indicate the presence of the Holy Ghost*.

Fleur De Lys   In Christian religion, the fleur de lys symbolizes the Trinity*. It is also an emblem of the Virgin Mary* as queen of heaven. It is particularly the emblem of French royalty, and is the attribute of St. Louis of France* and St. Louis of Toulouse*, having been chosen by King Clovis originally, as the emblem of his purification through baptism. It is also the emblem of the city of Florence, Italy.

Flight into Egypt   See Jesus Christ—Life Events.

Flood   In Greek mythology, the flood was the means that the god Zeus* employed to destroy the wicked men of the Iron Age. Deucalian* and his wife Pyrrha* were spared to create a new race of men. (Some accounts say Megarus, a son of Zeus, was warned by cranes and fled to Mt. Gerania where he was changed by nymphs into a beetle and so flew to Mt. Parnassus.) The flood is identified with the deluge story of the Old Testament (Genesis 6:7-22). When God became aware of man's wickedness on earth, he decided to wash the earth and destroy the race, with the exception of Noah*, whom he commissioned to build an ark (houseboat). Noah's family, and a male and female of every species of animal, bird, and insect, entered the ark and were preserved from the destruction of the deluge. When the flood finally abated, the ark rested on Mt. Ararat (Genesis 8:4), and life on earth began all over again.

Flora   A Roman goddess, originally a Sabine deity, the patron of flowers and spring, also regarded as the goddess of the flower of youth and its pleasures. Her festival, the Floralia, was celebrated at the end of April with games, mummery, and the usual, licentious behavior accompanying fertility festivals. In works of art, she is represented as a blooming maiden decked with flowers. She was identified with the Greek Chloris*.

St. Florian   The warrior-saint and patron of Poland, also patron of mercers (textile merchants), having been of their craft himself. He was also prayed to as a protector against fire, because he miraculously extinguished the flames of a burning city by throwing a single bucket of water on it. He was martyred in 230, drowned with a stone about his neck. His cult was introduced into Poland in 1183. In art, he is sometimes shown with flowers in reference to his name. Painting: *St. Florian*, Francesco del Cossa, National Gallery, Washington.

Flowers   An attribute of the Greek goddess Chloris*, the Roman goddess Flora*, both patrons of flowers, and the Christian St. Florian.

Flute   In Greek mythology, the flute is an attribute of the god Dionysus and his followers, the maenads*, who play the flute in his festivals. It belongs to Euterpe*, as the muse of music, and to Cybele*, as the mother of the arts in Asia Minor.

Fly   In Christian iconography, the fly is a bearer of evil and pestilence. It is sometimes shown with the goldfinch, a protector against the plague. When shown with the Madonna* and Child, they represent sin and redemption.

Fons (fonz)   In Roman mythology, Fons is the god of springs.

At the time of his festival in October, the Fontanalia, fountains and springs were decorated with wreaths, and garlands were thrown in the water as offerings.

Foot   In Christian iconography, the foot is a symbol of humility and service, because Jesus* washed the feet of the disciples at the Last Supper* (John 13:5). The feet of Jesus were also washed with the tears of an unknown woman (Luke 7:38). See Jesus Christ—Life Events—Supper at the House of Simon.

Fortuna (for-tūn′a)   In Roman mythology, the goddess of fortune and good luck, corresponding to the Greek Tyche*. She was worshipped in Rome in many aspects, among them as goddess of women, of newly wedded girls, and of virility in men. In art she is generally represented carrying a cornucopia as the bestower of blessings. She is shown with a rudder, as the pilot of destiny, and with wings, wheel, and ball, as emblems of chance, the turning of the year, and the juggler of fortune.

Forty   This number is a number of trial. In the Old Testament, the Israelites were forty years in the wilderness. Moses* was forty days on Mt. Sinai. In the New Testament, Christ* was also forty days in the wilderness. In the Christian church, the fast of Lent begins forty days before Easter, on Ash Wednesday.

Forty Martyrs   These martyrs were soldiers of several nationalities, who were stationed at Sebastea in Armenia (now Sivas, Turkey), and formed one of the most celebrated groups of early martyrs. In 320, the emperor Licinious suddenly commanded all Christians in the East to repudiate their faith. Forty soldiers of the twelfth legion refused, and when persuasion failed, they were stripped naked and placed on a frozen pond while fires and hot baths were kept going within eyesight. Those who did not die overnight from exposure were killed the next day. Their bodies were burned, and charred bits were preserved as precious relics of the martyrs. A Greek text of this story has been preserved, written by Meletius, one of the martyrs.

Fountain   In Christian iconography, the fountain is an attribute of the Virgin Mary*, based on Psalm 36:9, "For with thee is the fountain of life." It is an attribute of St. Clement*, who miraculously found water in the desert, and of St. Ansanus, as a symbol of baptism.

Four   In Christian religion, the number four is a symbol for the four Evangelists.

Fox   In Christian iconography, the fox is a symbol of cunning and the devil.

St. Francis of Assisi (1181-1226)   The founder of the Franciscan monks and one of the greatest Christian saints. He was the son of a wealthy merchant, and spent a carefree youth, until he was steadied by the experience of sickness and civil warfare. One day he met a poor man and was so filled with compassion, he gave him his own fine clothes. He went to the church of San Dominiano to pray, and heard the voice of Christ urging him to repair "my falling house." Full of zeal, he sold some of his father's goods, but was brought to court by his father, who repaid his son's rebellious spirit by disinheriting him. In 1206, Francis went to Rome, wed to what he called the "Lady Poverty," and with eleven other companions soon became roving preachers of Christ, exemplifying humility, simplicity, lowliness, and evangelical freedom. Their headquarters were at Assisi in the Portiuncola chapel, and recruits poured in. In 1212, he founded the first community of Poor Ladies with St. Clare*. In 1224, while praying on Mt. della Verne in the Apennines, there appeared on the body of St. Francis scars corresponding to the five wounds of the crucified Christ (the phenomenon called "stigmatization"), from which he suffered for the rest of his life. He is said to have appeared to his followers as an apparition with arms outstretched on the cross, and in the form of a dazzling light above a chariot of fire. He is a favorite subject in art and wears the brown robes of his order. He is often surrounded by wild animals and birds in the woods, to whom he is said to have preached. Another favorite subject is the story of his taming the ferocious wolf of Gubbio, who devoured men as well as animals. St. Francis talked earnestly to the wolf, and made peace between him and the townsfolk. Another dramatic scene is that of the newly committed young Francis who stripped himself of his clothes and handed them back to his father as a symbol of irrevocable renunciation. He is sometimes shown curing lepers; or at the moment when his prayer for water was answered by the appearance of a spring. He is most often represented in prayer, miraculously receiving the stigmata, symbolically embracing the Lady Poverty, or receiving the Christ Child from the arms of the Virgin Mary*. His attributes include the skull, symbol of the penitent saint, the lily and lamb, symbols of purity, and the wolf. Feast day: October 4. Painting: *St. Francis Receiving the Stigmata*, Jan van Eyck, Philadelphia Museum of Art.

Frankincense (frank'in-sens)   Its literal meaning is true or pure incense. It is a fragrant gum-resin from the genus Boswellia, abundant in Somalia and South Arabia. The ceremonial use of

Saint Francis in Ecstasy. Giovanni Bellini. Courtesy of the Frick Collection.

frankincense was practiced by the Egyptians, Persians, Babylonians, Hebrews, Greeks, and Romans, and is currently an important ingredient of incense used liturgically. During Roman times, frankincense was burned in the funeral pyre, possibly to disguise the odor of burning bodies. In the New Testament, it is offered to the infant Christ by one of the Wise Men (Magi*) Balthazar in token of divinity. Since frankincense was in limited supply and expensive, it ranked with gold as a suitable gift for the child (see Jesus Christ—Life Events—Adoration of the Magi).

Frog   In Christian art, the frog is a symbol of repulsive sin, sometimes of worldly pleasures, sometimes of heretics*.

Fruit   In Greek mythology, fruit is a symbol of productivity for the goddess Demeter*, and for the Roman Fides*, the goddess of faith. Fruit, in Christian religion, symbolizes the twelve fruits of the spirit: peace, love, joy, faith, gentleness, goodness, patience, modesty, meekness, chastity, temperance, and longsuffering. Fruit in a basket is an attribute of St. Dorothea* in reference to the miraculous appearance of fruit and flowers after her execution.

Furiae (fū′ri-ē) or Furies   The furies are a Roman adaptation of the Greek Erinyes*. They are generally represented as torturing the guilty in the world below, but are also sometimes shown driving men to madness on earth.

119

G

Gabriel (gā′bri-el) The name means "God is my strength." Gabriel is an archangel of Hebrew mythology, the guardian of the heavenly treasury, and the guardian of church entrances, prohibiting the entrance of demons. He is an angel of redemption, above all the messenger of annunciations. In the Old Testament, it is Gabriel who announces to Daniel* the return of the Jews from captivity (Daniel 9:21-27). He predicts the birth of Samson* (Judges 13), he shows young Joseph* the way to his brethren (Genesis 37:15-18), he appears as the destroyer of the hosts of Sennacherib* (2 Kings 19:35), and he is said, in the Koran of the Mohammedans, to have borne Mohammed to heaven. In the New Testament, he announced to Zacharias* and Elisabeth* the coming of a son (John the Baptist*), he is the angel of the Annunciation*, heralding to the Virgin Mary* the birth of Jesus (Luke 1:28-38). In this annunciation, Gabriel usually bears a lily as a sign of purity, or an olive branch signifying peace, the sceptre in his hand symbolizes a herald of God. Sometimes he has a scroll on which is inscribed *Ave Maria, Gratia Plena* (Hail Mary, full of grace). He may be richly robed with large multicolored wings, his hand outstretched in benediction. Painting: *The Archangel Gabriel*, Masolino da Panicale, National Gallery, Washington.

Gaea (jē′a) or Gaia or Ge In Greek mythology, the goddess of the earth. According to the Greek writer Hesiod (8th century B.C.), she sprang from Chaos and was the mother of Uranus* (sky) and Pontus (sea), the mountains and many terrible beings. Her cults were numerous and in Homeric legend, she is invoked with the god Zeus* as a witness to oaths, and is worshipped with the sacrifice of a black lamb. The earliest oracles at Delphi* were hers, as was the first oracle at Olympia*. The corresponding Roman goddess was Tellus.

Sir Galahad (gal'a-had)   The noblest and purest of the knights of the Round Table, the son of Elaine and Launcelot*. At the festival of the Round Table, the initiated sat as apostle knights with the Holy Grail in the center, leaving one seat vacant which was reserved for one called Galahad. If any man tried to sit in the place of Galahad, the earth swallowed him up. The seat which symbolized that which the Lord had occupied, was therefore called the Siege Perilous. The Holy Grail disappeared when men became sinful, and the honor of England was dependent on its recovery. Only the pure Sir Galahad, who was brought to the knights at the appointed time by a mysterious man dressed in white, succeeded in the quest (see Arthurian Legend). Mural paintings: *The Quest of the Holy Grail*, Edwin Austin Abbey, Main Public Library, Boston.

Galatea (gal-a-tē'a)   In Greek legend, the name given to the maiden who was sculpted by Pygmalion*.

Galilee   In the Bible, the name given to the north section of Palestine, west of the Jordan. (see Jesus Christ—Life Events). The sea of Galilee is in the same section, an integral part of the Jordan River waterway.

Ganymede (gan'i-mēd)   In Greek mythology, a beautiful Trojan youth who was carried away to Mt. Olympus*, the home of the gods, to be the cupbearer of the god Zeus*, and become an immortal. In late legends, he is carried away by Zeus himself in the form of an eagle, or by the goddess of dawn, Eos*. To console and repay Tros, the father of Ganymede, Zeus gave him four immortal horses for his chariot. (Troy and the region around Troy, known as The Troad, were named for Tros.) Ganymede supplanted Hebe* as cupbearer, which annoyed the goddess Hera*, and added to her dislike of the Trojans. Ganymede was regarded also as the genius of the waters of the Nile. He is represented in the heavens as the constellation Aquarius. Painting: *Ganymede with a Hoop and a Cock*, on a red-figured Greek wine jug, (5th century B.C.), attributed to the Pan Painter, Metropolitan, New York.

Garden of Eden   In the Old Testament, the extremely fertile first home of man, often called an earthly paradise. God established the garden with its trees of knowledge and life as a dwelling place for Adam* and Eve*, the first man and woman, and here they lived naked and unashamed, until Eve was beguiled by a

121

serpent into eating the forbidden fruit of the tree of the knowledge of good and evil; and knowing now that they were naked, they covered themselves with fig leaves. When the Lord discovered that the serpent had persuaded Eve to pluck the fruit, he cursed it, making it an enemy of man, and turning Adam and Eve out of the Garden of Eden for disobeying him, he cursed them both, committing the lives of men and women to sorrow, suffering, and toil. Eden has been located variously over the Old World, especially in Lower Mesopotamia. Painting: *The Fall of Man*, Albrecht Altdorfer, National Gallery, Washington.

Garden Enclosed   In Christian iconography, the garden enclosed is a symbol of the Immaculate Conception*, borrowed from the Song of Solomon in the Old Testament, "A garden inclosed is my sister, my spouse, a spring shut up, a fountain sealed" (4:12).

Garden of Gethsemane   See Jesus Christ—Life Events.

Gate   In Christian art, the gate of departure from this world and the entrance into Paradise are frequently shown. A gate is also a motif in representations of Christ's descent into hell* (see Jesus Christ—After-Life in Christian Belief), and is used to divide the righteous and the doomed in scenes of the Last Judgement*.

Genesis   The first book of the Bible, known in Hebrew as *bereshith* (in the beginning), which is the book's first word. It contains: the origin of the world and man, the creation*, Adam* and his descendants, Noah* and his sons, Abraham* and Isaac*, and Joseph* and Jacob*.

Genevieve (je-na-vēv′) (422-512)   The patroness of the city of Paris, born at Nanterre, a religious from childhood who took the veil at fifteen. She devoted herself to charitable works and prayer, and her prayers were considered influential in averting a threatened attack on Paris by Attila, the Hun. When the Franks blockaded Paris, she led a convoy bringing food to the starving, and she persuaded King Clovis to liberate captives of war. In art, she is represented with the keys of Paris, the devil at her side, blowing out her candle while an angel relights it. She is also shown restoring sight to her blind mother and guarding her father's sheep. Feast day: January 3.

Genius   The name given to the lesser divinities (good or bad) by the ancients, to whose charge are committed the destinies of individual human beings.

Gentiles   The word means peoples or nations. In Jewish thought Gentiles included all non-Hebrews. There were far more Gentiles than Jews in the early Christian church, and the decision not to make them subscribe to the Law of Moses was fundamental to the spread of the Gospel of Jesus*.

St. George of Cappadocia The patron saint of the kingdom of England, of the Italian cities Venice and Ferrara, of soldiers, boyscouts, and numerous churches throughout the world. Legend

St. George and the Dragon. Raphael. National Gallery of Art, The Mellon Collection.

says he was brought up a Christian by his parents in the third or fourth century and suffered martyrdom at Diapolis, in Palestine. The most popular story of St. George is a medieval one, representing him as a knight from Cappadocia, who at Silene in Lybia rescued a princess from a dragon to which she had been offered in sacrifice, since the dragon was infesting the country. Making the sign of the cross, St. George engaged the dragon in combat and pinned him to the ground with his lance, running him through with his sword. The legend represents the triumph of right over wickedness. In art, this warrior saint is represented as a young knight, clad in shining armor emblazoned with a red cross. (His flag is a red cross on a white field.) Often mounted on a charger, he transfixes the dragon. When he is shown alone as a saint, he holds a shield, a lance, or a sword. Feast day: April 23.

St. Gerasimus (jer-az′i-mus)   A 5th-century abbot, born in Lycia, Asia Minor, who left home to settle as a monk near the Dead Sea. About 455, he built a communal monastery near Jericho to train aspirants for the solitary way of life. A 5th-century book, written by John Moschus, recounts the story of St. Gerasimus, and says he once drew a thorn from a lion's paw; he then trained the grateful animal, which he named Jordon, to fetch and carry for the monks. When Gerasimus died in 475, the disconsolate lion lay down on his master's grave to join him in death. The lion is his emblem. Feast day: March 5.

St. Gertrude   A 7th-century abbess who founded hospices for pilgrims, and so is saint of travellers. Christian legend recounts that she harbored souls on the first night of their three-day journey to heaven. She is also protectress against rats and mice, and is sometimes represented in art surrounded by them, either running by her distaff as she spins, or running up her pastoral staff. She died at the monastery of Nivelles in 659, when she was about thirty. Feast day: March 17.

Geryon (jē′ri-on or ger′i-on) or Geryones   In Greek mythology, a monster with three heads, three bodies, and three sets of wings, who dwelt on the island of Erythea. He possessed a herd of cattle, said to eat human flesh, which was guarded by his shepherd and two-headed dog Orthus. The tenth labor of Heracles* was to carry away the cattle, which he successfully accomplished by killing the shepherd, the dog, and Geryon himself.

Gethsemane, Garden of   In the New Testament, a place frequented by Jesus* on the Mount of Olives*, identified as a garden near the brook Cedron (John 18:1). Jesus went to this garden with his disciples Peter*, James*, and John*, praying in anguish, before his midnight arrest took place. The location of the sight is believed by many to have been located by St. Helena* in A.D. 326 (see Jesus Christ—Life Events—Garden of Gethsemane). Painting: *The Agony in the Garden,* on a predella by Benvenuto di Giovanni, National Gallery, Washington.

Giants or Gigantes   In Greek mythology, an earth-born race, sprung from the blood of Uranus* (heaven), when he was emasculated by his son Cronus*. The Giants, not to be confused with the Titans*, waged a fierce war against the Olympic gods, but were put down with the aid of Heracles*, whom the gods called to their assistance, a prophecy having warned them that they would be unable to destroy the Giants without the aid of a mortal who wore a lion's skin. In early works of art the Giants are represented in human form, armed with spears, sometimes harness. Later they wear animal skins, have wild hair and beards, and carry clubs; sometimes they are given serpent's bodies and powerful wings.

Gideon (gid′ē-on)   In the Old Testament, an unassuming Israelite whom the Lord called upon to overthrow the idol worship of Baal, and to destroy the Midianites. Gideon, seeking a sign from God, laid fleece on the open ground for two nights. On the first morning the fleece was wet and the ground dry; on the second morning the fleece was dry and the ground wet. Gideon considered these omens favorable signs from God, and was persuaded that he could go into battle. With only 300 Israelites, he overcame the Midian oppressors in a night attack. He then refused to take the throne, and returned to private life.

St. Giles (jīlz)   Very little is known about this Christian saint, other than that he was a hermit living at Saint-Gilles, near Arles, France. According to legend, he had a pet hind which was hunted one day by the Visigothic king Wamba. The hunting party shot an arrow into the bushes, and when they came into a clearing they found Giles wounded by the arrow; the hind was in his arms and the hounds were standing motionless before him. As Giles refused treatment for his wound, preferring mortification of the flesh, he remained a cripple for life, and therefore became the patron saint of cripples. His emblems are an arrow and a hind. Feast day: September 1.

Girdle   In Christian religion, the girdle is a symbol of chastity and obedience. It is a part of the habit of monks. The Virgin Mary* is seen holding a girdle as she leans down from heaven, in scenes with St. Thomas*.

Glaucus (glaw'kus)   In Greek legend, the son of Sisyphus and father of Bellerophon*. Glaucus refused to let his mares breed, believing they would be better race horses. This so infuriated the goddess of love Aphrodite* she drove the mares mad, and at the funeral games of Pelias*, they overthrew his chariot. Glaucus was hurled to the ground, the mares tore him to pieces and devoured his flesh.

Glaucus   In Greek legend the grandson of Bellerophon*, the commander of the Lycians who were allies of Troy in the Trojan war*. He was connected by ties of family friendship with his Greek enemy Diomedes*. When the two met in battle, they not only refrained from fighting but exchanged armor in token of amity. As the armor of Glaucus was of gold and that of Diomedes of brass, it was an exchange of mutual admiration and cordiality.

Globe   In Christian symbology, the globe represents sovereignty and power. It is the particular attribute of God, the Father*.

Glory or Gloria   In Christian art, the glory, or gloria, is the name given to the light which is shown surrounding both the head and body of God the Father* and Christ* his son. Light around the body is known as the aureole* and is similar to the glory, but is not as luminous around the head. Light around the head only is known as the nimbus*, or halo*.

Goat   In Greek mythology, the goat is sacred to the god Dionysus*, associated with wine. It was an animal of sacrifice for Dionysus, and was killed and devoured in midsummer festivals. In early legend, Dionysus was temporarily transformed into a goat as a child, to protect him from Hera's* jealousy. As a baby the god Zeus* was fed on the milk of the goat Amalthea*, and the Aegis* was said to be made out of its skin. The goatskin was an attribute of Roman Juno* when she was worshipped as a saviour of warriors. In Syria, the goat was an emblem of the love goddess Aphrodite, as part of the seasonal, sacrificial year. In Christian religion, the goat is a symbol of the damned in scenes of the Last Judgement* (the second coming of Christ) when the sheep (the believers) will be separated from the goats (the unbelieving) (Matthew 25:31-46).

Goblet or Glass   In Christian iconography, a broken goblet is an attribute of St. Donatus*, who miraculously mended a broken communion cup. St. Benedict* is also said to have performed this miracle as a child, and sometimes carries it. Both St. John* the Evangelist and St. Benedict are shown with a goblet from which a serpent is escaping. This refers to attempted poisoning from which each escaped when the poison left the glass in the form of a serpent (see Cup).

God the Father　In early Christian art representation of God was considered a sacrilege (see Ten Commandments). First his hand emerging from a cloud was depicted, then gradually the whole figure was portrayed. Before the Renaissance the figure of God represented the Trinity* (God the Father, God the Son, and God the Holy Ghost). In art, God the Father is shown as a man of older years and frequently with a triangular halo*. Sometimes he holds a globe, symbol of sovereignty, sometimes a book; he may be dressed as a pope.

God the Son　As the Son of God, Christ appears seated on the right hand of the Father, the judge of the living and the dead. He is usually shown as younger than the Father. He may be represented as a lamb, in reference to the words of John the Baptist*, "Behold the lamb of God, which taketh away the sin of the world." He may be represented as a lion* or, in early Christian art, as a fish*.

God the Holy Ghost　A white dove usually represents the Holy Ghost, but a human form is sometimes seen in representations of the Trinity*, similar to God the Father and God the Son, or younger. In paintings of the Pentecost*, the Holy Ghost appears as rays of light or flames.

Gods: Greek-Roman	Gods: Roman-Greek
Aphrodite—Venus	Amor—Eros
Apollo—Apollo	Apollo—Apollo
Ares—Mars	Bacchus—Dionysus
Artemis—Diana	Ceres—Demeter
Athena—Minerva	Cupid—Eros
Charites—Graces	Diana—Artemis
Demeter—Ceres	Dis—Hades
Dionysus—Bacchus	Fates—Moerae
Eros—Cupid—Amor	Faunus—Pan
Hades (Pluto)—Dis	Graces—Charites
Hebe—Dia	Iris—Iris
Hephaestus—Vulcan	Iuventus—Hebe
Hera—Juno	Juno—Hera
Hermes—Mercury	Jupiter—Zeus
Hestia—Vesta	Mars—Ares
Iris—Iris	Mercury—Hermes
Moerae—Fates	Minerva—Athena
Pan—Faunus	Neptune—Poseiden

Gods: Greek-Roman	Gods: Roman-Greek
Persephone—Proserpina	Pluto—Hades
Pluto (Hades)—Dis	Proserpina—Persephone
Poseiden—Neptune	Venus—Aphrodite
Zeus—Jupiter	Vesta—Hestia
	Vulcan—Hephaestus

Golden Apples of the Hesperides   See Apples of the Hesperides.

Golden Bough   In Greek mythology, this was mistletoe, which was sacred to Persephone*, the queen of the underworld. The Cumaean Sibyl* told Aeneas* he must find the Golden Bough if he wished to visit the underworld, for with its possession, the ferryman Charon* would allow him to cross the river Styx*.

Golden Calf   In the Old Testament, the wandering tribes of Israel were impatient with the leadership of Moses*, and asked his brother Aaron* to make a god for them. During the absence of Moses on Mt. Sinai, Aaron collected the golden ornaments of his followers and with them fashioned a calf for which he built an altar and prepared a feast of consecration (Exodus 32). Painting: *Worship of the Golden Calf*, Jacopo Tintoretto, National Gallery, Washington.

Golden Fleece   In Greek legend, a famine once raged in the land of King Athamus of Orchomenus. His wife Ino persuaded Athamus that his son Phrixus* (her stepson) was the cause. The innocent Phrixus was about to be sacrificed to the gods, when the messenger god Hermes* sent a golden-fleeced, winged ram to the altar. Phrixus jumped on its back and escaped on it with his sister Helle, flying over the sea. As they were passing over the straits which separated Thrace from Asia Minor, Helle fell off, and the sea here has borne her name ever since, The Hellespont. Phrixus flew on to Colchis, and sacrificed the ram to the god Zeus*. He placed the skin under the protection of King Aeëtes, who hung it on a sacred oak where it was guarded by a dragon. Jason* organized his expedition of the Argonauts* to bring the fleece back to Greece, and successfully stole it with the aid of Medea*, daughter of King Aeëtes.

Goldfinch   In medieval times, the goldfinch was a savior bird, a protective symbol against the plague. In Christian iconography, it is a symbol of the Passion* (see Jesus Christ—Life Events); an eater of thorns, it thus relates to Christ's crown of thorns. When it is shown in scenes of the Christ Child, it symbolizes the closeness of his incarnation* and resurrection*.

Golgotha (gol'goth-a)   In the New Testament, the place outside of Jerusalem where Christ was crucified (see Jesus Christ—Life Events). The word is Aramaic and means "place of the skull." Tradition said that Adam's* head was found there. Calvary is another name for Golgotha.

Goliath (go-li'ath)   In the Old Testament, the nine-foot Philistine giant of Gath, who was slain by the stripling David*, with a small stone hurled from a sling (1 Samuel 17:23-54). This was one of the first exploits of the future king, and encouraged timid Israelites to go after the Philistines*. David placed Goliath's sword in the sanctuary of Nob..

Good Samaritan   See—Jesus Christ—Parables.

Goose   In Greek religion, the goose is sacred to the goddess Hera*, as a symbol of fecundity, since the goose is a prolific bird. In Christian iconography, the goose is an attribute of St. Martin*, whose presence was betrayed by a goose.

Gordian Knot   In Greek legend, a knot tied by Gordius when he was chosen king of Phrygia, Asia Minor, which connected the pole and the yoke of the ox cart, in which he was riding. It was so intricate it could not be untied. The oracle of the temple, in which the cart was preserved, declared that whoever should untie it would become master of Asia. Alexander the Great* solved the difficulty by cutting the knot with his sword, and the oracle was fulfilled.

Gorgons (gor'gonz)   In classical mythology, the gorgons were three maidens who were turned into horrible monsters with serpents on their heads, instead of hair. Sometimes they are portrayed with wings and claws. They lived in the Western Ocean and their faces were so terrifying that anyone who looked at them was instantly turned to stone. Medusa* was the only mortal one, and when she was slain by Perseus*, her head was placed on the shield carried by the goddess Athena*. Marble statue: *Perseus with the Head of Medusa*, Antonio Canova, Metropolitan, New York.

Goshen (gō'shun)   In the Old Testament, the section of northeast Egypt where the seventy hungry members of Jacob's family settled at the request of Pharaoh's prime minister Joseph*, who was Jacob's son.

Gospel   This word is from an Anglo-Saxon compound word, "god-spell," employed to describe collectively the life of Christ as narrated by the Evangelists in the New Testament, signifying the message of redemption set forth in those books. It is a term used for the entire Christian system of religion. The first four books of the New Testament, known as the Gospels, are ascribed to Matthew*, Mark*, Luke*, and John*.

Gourd In Christian tradition, pilgrims used a gourd for a flask. It is an attribute of St. James the Great*, because of the many pilgrimages made to his shrine at Santiago del Compostella in Spain. It is also an attribute of the archangel Gabriel* when he is shown as a traveller. It is sometimes seen with Christ on his trip to Emmaus* (see Jesus Christ—After Life Events). It has come to symbolize the Resurrection*, derived from the story, in the Old Testament, of the traveller Jonah*. When shown with an apple, symbol of evil, the gourd, symbol of resurrection, is the antidote.

Graces In Roman mythology, the Graces are the three goddesses, known as the Gratiae. They bestowed beauty and charm, and were the embodiment of both. In Greek mythology, they are known as the Charites*, and are daughters of the god Zeus*. Painting: *Venus Adorned by the Graces*, Annibali Carracci, National Gallery, Washington. (see Charites)

Graeae (grē´ē) The Gorgons'* sentinels. There were three of them—Dino, Enyo and Pephredo. They are depicted as having only one eye and one tooth among them.

Grail, the Holy The cup or chalice traditionally used by Christ at the Last Supper (see Jesus Christ—Life Events), around which a vast medieval legend and allegory arose. One account says Joseph of Arimathea* preserved the Grail, with some of Christ's blood, received into it at the Crucifixion. He brought it to England where it disappeared. Another account says it was brought by him, or by angels, to a group of knights who guarded it on a mountain top. If anyone approached it who was not entirely pure, it disappeared. Legend continued that the honor of England depended on its recovery. The quest of the Grail is the theme of the Arthurian tales about the Knights of the Round Table (see Galahad). Mural paintings: *The Holy Grail*, Edwin Austin Abbey, Boston Public Library.

Grain In Christian iconography, grain is a symbol of bread, the body of Christ, in the service of the Eucharist* or Holy Communion.

Grapes In Greek and Roman religion, grapes are attributes of Dionysus* as god of wine. Grape leaves are also an attribute. In

Christian iconography, they symbolize the blood of Christ*, and like grain and bread, wine is a part of the service of the Eucharist*.

Grasshopper　In Christian art, the grasshopper is seen with the Christ Child, symbolizing the conversion of pagan nations to Christianity. This is because God, in the Old Testament, sent plagues of locusts, or grasshoppers, to the unbelieving Pharaoh* of the Egyptians, when he would not let the Hebrews depart from Egypt (see Moses).

Great Mother　In ancient mythologies, the Great Mother is the goddess of birth and fertility. She is an almost universal concept, found in religious cults throughout the world.

St. Gregory　Pope Gregory I, known as the Great, who succeeded to the papacy in 590, was one of the four Latin Fathers of the Church. He was a Roman, born of noble parentage, but cared little for wealth, and after the death of his father, he converted his palace into a monastery of the Benedictine order. His breadth of activity was remarkable. Among his efforts he worked to abolish slavery. He established the rule of celibacy for the clergy, and made the arrangements of music known as the Gregorian chants. He sent St. Augustine* with forty other monks to Christianize England. In art, Gregory is shown wearing a pope's tiara (triple crown), and holds the crosier (bishop's staff) with the double cross. Sometimes he carries a small model of a church, signifying his work in establishing the foundations of the church. His attribute is a dove, referring to the legend that the Holy Ghost came to him in the form of a dove, to dictate the words of his writings. Feast day: March 12.

Gridiron　In Christian iconography, an attribute of St. Laurence*, who was roasted on one, when martyrized for distributing the wealth of the church to the poor.

Griffin　A mythical monster, fabled to be the offspring of the lion and eagle, usually shown with the head, wings, and feet of an eagle, and the body of a lion. In early myth, this creature was sacred to the sun, and kept guard over hidden treasures. In Greek mythology, griffins were sometimes called "hounds of heaven." Their duty was to guard the gold in the region of the Hyperboreans (a land of perpetual sunshine), which the one-eyed people of Scythia tried to steal from them. The chariot of Nemesis*, goddess of law and justice, was drawn by griffins. In Christian iconography, the griffin sometimes represents the savior, as a symbol of power, but because of its fierce qualities, it may also represent those who persecute Christians. It is applicable to all heroic commanders, as an emblem of valor and magnanimity, combining, as it does, the noble eagle and lion. It is a frequent motif in medieval art, as well as in early Greek sculpture.

Grill   In Christian iconography, an attribute of St. Vincent*, in reference to his martyrdom.

Guarded Tomb   See Jesus Christ—After-Life Events.

Gyges (gǐ'jēz)   A king of Lydia, Asia Minor, in the 7th century B.C. He founded a new dynasty, warred against Asurbanipal of Assyria, and is memorable for his ring and his prodigious wealth. According to the writer Plato (4th century B.C.), Gyges descended into a chasm of earth, where he found a brazen horse. Opening the side of the horse, he found the carcass of a man, from whose finger he drew a brazen ring which rendered him invisible. Wearing this ring, Gyges killed the ruling king and became king of Lydia in his place. According to the earlier historian Herodotus (5th century B.C.), Gyges was the trusted aid of Candaules, king of Lydia. Candaules was bewitched by his wife's beauty, so much so that he insisted Gyges should see her naked in order that he confirm the lavish praise. The strategy was for Gyges to hide in the bedroom while the queen disrobed, slipping out afterward. Gyges was horrified by this unlawful suggestion, but was unable to avoid the king's command and finally consented. All went as planned; the queen disrobed and went to bed, but she had noticed Gyges out of the corner of her eye. The next day she sent for him and said, "There are two courses open to you after this unlawful act. Kill Candaules and seize the throne with me as your wife, or die now on the spot." Gyges tried to remain loyal to the king, but the queen gave no leeway, so he made his choice to live. Following the queen's instructions, he slew Candaules in his sleep, usurped the throne, and married the queen. Painting: *Candaules and Gyges*, Jean Leon Gerorne, Ponce Museum, San Juan, Puerto Rico.

Hades or Pluto (hā'dēz or ploo'tō) (Ro. Pluto or Dis)   In Greek
mythology, the son of Cronus* and Rhea*, one of the twelve
Olympic gods who, at the division of the universe, received
dominion of the lower world. Here with his abducted queen,
Persephone*, he held sway over the ghosts of the dead. He is the
enemy of all life, but as the giver of earth's food and treasures, he
was known by his cult name Pluto (wealth), and is therefore
associated with Plutus*, god of wealth. Hades, like his brothers
and sisters, was swallowed by Cronus* when he was born, and
disgorged when his brother Zeus came to their rescue. In the war
that followed, the Cyclopes* gave him a cap of invisibility;
with it he stole the weapons of Cronus. The most celebrated
myth concerning Hades is the abduction of Persephone*. In
works of art, he is represented as a man of authority with a
scepter or a staff. Sometimes he is accompanied by Persephone,
or the dog Cerberus* who guarded his gates to the underworld.
The cypress and Narcissus are sacred to him; the helmet of
invisibility was the symbol of his empire. When he appears as
Pluto, he holds a cornucopia* or a two-pronged pickaxe.

Hades   In Greek mythology, the realm of the dead is also called
Hades and was said to be located in the west. Here the righteous
dwelt among sweet blossoms in the Elysian Fields*, while the
wicked lived among various torments in Tartarus, a deep and
sunless abyss. Hades was surrounded by five rivers, and the
ferryman Charon* carried the souls of the buried dead into Hades
across the river Styx*. The three-headed dog Cerberus* guarded
the gates, and kept the dead from escaping to the upper world. In
Biblical thought, Hades is also known as an abode of the dead,
identifying with the Greek word for Hell. It is the lowest of the

three-story conception of the universe, with earth and heaven above it.

Hagar (hā′gar)   In the Old Testament, the Egyptian handmaiden of Sarah*, wife of Abraham*; mother of Abraham's son Ishmael.

Hair   In Christian iconography, loose-flowing hair is a symbol of penitence, derived from the episode in the New Testament in which a woman wiped her tears from Christ's feet with her hair (Luke 7:37-38) (see Jesus Christ—Parables—Debtors). In art, flowing hair is often seen covering the body of Mary Magdalene*, who is associated with the story above. It is also seen thus on St. Agnes*, whose hair grew to cover her body when she was stripped of her clothes in a house of prostitution.

Halberd or **Axe**   In Christian iconography, an attribute of St. Jude*, who was killed with one.

Halo (hā′lō) (also called nimbus)   A symbolic ring of light shown in Christian art around the heads of divine or sacred persons. The triangular halo, referring to the Trinity*, is seen with God the Father*. The circular halo, within which is a cross, is seen with Christ, referring to his crucifixion. A simple circle is seen with saints; a square halo is given to living donors who are included in religious works of art; allegorical persons are sometimes shown with hexagonal halos. Nimbus is the Latin word for cloud, and sometimes three rays of light flow out from the head forming a halo, which symbolizes the Trinity*.

Hamadryad   In Greek myth, a wood nymph, supposed to live and die with the tree to which she was attached, sharing its joys, sorrows, and wounds.

Hammer   In Greek mythology, the hammer is an attribute of Hephaestus* as god of smiths. In Christian religion, hammer and nails are an attribute of St. Helena*, referring to her excavations to find Christ's crucifixion cross. A hammer is an attribute of Joseph of Nazareth*, in reference to his trade of carpenter; also of St. William of Norwich*, as a symbol of his murder, and of the Passion*, since Christ was nailed with a hammer to the cross.

Hands   In Christian art, the hand of the Lord is shown issuing from clouds, sometimes holding bolts and rays, symbolizing the power of the Almighty. When the thumb and first two fingers are extended upward, the gesture symbolizes the Trinity*. The hand turned outward represents the blessing of God; reaching down, it represents the Father Creator offering help. A hand closed over straws symbolizes the casting of lots for Christ's robe. A hand pouring money from one hand to the other, or holding a money bag, is an allusion to Christ's betrayal by Judas* (see Jesus Christ—Life Events—Betrayal). Hands over a basin refer to Pontius Pilate*, who washed his hands of the responsibility of Christ's crucifixion*. An outstretched hand with a dove on it is an attribute of St. Basil*.

Hanging Gardens of Babylon   The famous, terraced gardens built by Nebuchadnezzar to gratify his Median wife, who was weary of the flat plains of Babylon and longed for the hills of her childhood. The ancients considered them one of the Seven Wonders of the Ancient World*.

Hannah   The favorite wife of Elkanah of Mt. Ephraim, and the devout mother of the prophet Samuel*, who was born after years of sterility. Hannah had vowed before the priest Eli, that she would consecrate a son to the Lord, if he would favor her with a child. When the Lord remembered her and she did conceive, Hannah expressed her gratitude by returning the little boy to the Temple in the service of Yahweh (God), at the age of three (1 Samuel 1:1-28).

Hare   In Greek mythology, the hare is an attribute of the goddess Aphrodite*, as a symbol of fecundity. In Christian religion, it is a symbol of lust because of its fecundity. A white hare, shown with the Virgin Mary*, indicates triumph over lust.

Harmonia (har-mō′ni-a)   In Greek mythology, the daughter of the god Ares* and the goddess Aphrodite*, and wife of Cadmus* of Thebes. At her wedding, all the gods presented her with magnificent gifts. Among them were a necklace and a robe, the workmanship of the god Hephaestus*, which brought strife and bloodshed to anyone who possessed them, thus playing a part in the war of the Seven Against Thebes* and the Epigoni*. The gifts were finally brought to the sanctuary of the god Apollo* at Delphi, where they ceased to give trouble. Some legends say Harmonia and Cadmus in their later years were turned into serpents by the god Zeus*, and sent to the Elysian Fields*. Painting: *Harmonia and Cadmus*, on a red-figured Attic bowl (5th century B.C.), Metropolitan, New York.

Harp   In the Old Testament, the harp is the instrument of David*, who sang before King Saul* to drive out the evil spirit in him (1 Samuel 16:23). It is a symbol of all music in honor of God, shown often with angels. It is sometimes shown as an attribute of St. Cecelia*, the patroness of music.

Harpies (har′pēz) In Greek mythology, winged monsters, ravenous and filthy, having the head and body of a woman and the feet and wings of a bird of prey, sometimes confused with Sirens*. They were vindictive agents for the gods, and dealt with criminals and the dead. They also personified whirlwinds and storms.

Hat In Greek mythology, a flat, broad-brimmed round hat is an attribute shown in art on the god Hermes*. See Cardinal's hat.

Hatchet In Christian symbology, an attribute of John the Baptist*, referring to his preaching. It is an attribute of Joseph of Nazareth*, referring to his trade as a carpenter. Sometimes it is an emblem of destruction. The axe and halberd are interchangeable with the hatchet.

Hawk The hawk is sacred to Apollo*, as a symbol of divination.

Head A severed head in the hands of a lightly clad young man is usually a representation of the Old Testament story of David* with the large head of Goliath*. A severed head in the hands of a woman usually is illustrative of the Old Testament story of Judith*, who struck off the head of Holofernes. A severed head on a platter illustrates the New Testament story of the severance of John the Baptist's* head, which was performed at the request of Herod's stepdaughter Salome*. A severed head on a Bible is an attribute of St. Denis* of Paris, who is fabled to have carried his severed head to his place of burial. Saints who have been executed often carry their heads in their hands (see St. Albans and St. Winifred).

Heart In Christian art, the heart is a symbol of love and piety. A flaming heart indicates religious fervor. An arrow piercing the heart indicates repentance. Both are attributes of St. Augustine*. The heart is an emblem of St. Bernardine of Siena*, and, when seen with a cross, is an attribute of St. Catherine of Siena*, referring to the story that Christ, in a vision, replaced her heart with his own.

Heaven As described in the Old Testament, heaven was the upper region of the universe, a great concave, "firmament," a part of the Hebrew, three-story conception of heaven, earth and hell. In the New Testament, heaven is spiritualized and is known as the "Kingdom of Heaven," the place where the Christian will find eternal happiness, seeing God face to face.

Hebe (hē′bē) In Greek mythology, the goddess of eternal youth and spring, a daughter of the god Zeus* and his spouse the goddess Hera*. Until superseded by Ganymede*, she was the cupbearer of the gods of Olympus*. The power of rejuvenation was attributed to her. After the death and deification of Heracles*, she became his wife, and was worshipped with him under the name of Dia, rites celebrated with much merriment. Fresco transferred to canvas: *The Wedding of Hebe and Heracles*, Giulio Romano, Metropolitan, New York.

Hecate (hek′a-tē) In Greek mythology, a triple goddess, a personification of divine power, invoked at all sacrifices, conceived as a goddess of the night, the earth, and the lower world. As the last, she was associated with dead souls and witchcraft, and was portrayed as flying through the night, invisible, accompanied by ghostly hounds. She was also the goddess of the crossroads, identified with the Roman Trivia. In art, she is shown with triple bodies, standing back to back. Her attributes were keys, daggers, torches, snakes, and hounds, which were sacred to her.

Hecatomb (hek′a-tōm) In ancient Greece, the word for the slaughtering of a hundred oxen at a time, as an offering to the gods. Later, the term was applied to any great sacrifice.

Hector The Trojan hero of Homer's Iliad*, the eldest son of King Priam* and Queen Hecuba*, the husband of Andromache*, father of Astyanax*, and brother of Paris*, whose abduction of Helen* precipitated the Trojan war. Hector was the leader of the Trojan warriors, and one of the noblest characters of Greek literature, honorable, handsome, skillful at arms, an affectionate son, tender husband and father, a mature man who fought for his city against hopeless odds, knowing, although he was a favorite of the god Apollo*, that he was doomed to die. In an effort to end the war, he challenged the Greeks to send a champion against him in single combat. Ajax* accepted the offer and they fought all day, neither able to vanquish the other. At the end of the combat, they expressed admiration for each other by exchanging gifts. Hector presented Ajax with a sword, and Ajax gave Hector a belt. As the war continued, Andromache begged him to give up the war for her sake and that of their young son Astyanax, but Hector tenderly convinced her that he must continue to fight in order to carry out his destiny. When he killed Patroclus*, the friend of Achilles*, he was revengefully killed by that Greek hero, who lashed the body to his chariot and dragged it thrice around the walls of Troy. The body, protected by the gods, was recovered by King Priam, who went secretly to the tent of Achilles and begged with tears for its return. Achilles consented and all Troy mourned at the funeral honors, including Helen to whom he had always showed kindness. Hector was still worshipped in Troy at the time of the Roman Empire, even after the state had recognized Christianity. Scene: *Andromache Begging Hector to Refrain from War*, on a Franco-Flemish tapestry, Metropolitan, New York.

Hecuba (hek'ū-ba)   The second wife of King Priam* of Troy, to whom she bore 19 of his 50 sons, and 12 daughters. The most famous of these were Hector*, Paris*, and Cassandra*. Before Paris was born she dreamed, symbolically, of the doom the child was about to bring about, and at his birth he was given to shepherds to kill. Instead he was raised by them and the omen was fulfilled. During the Trojan war, which was brought about by the abduction of Helen* by Paris, Hecuba saw Hector killed before her eyes. In the sack of Troy her husband and son Politus were slain by Neoptolemus*. She herself was taken slave by Odysseus*, and the body of her son Polydorus, who had been slain by Polymnestor*, was washed ashore and brought to her. In sudden fury, Hecuba blinded Polymnestor and killed his two sons. She was afterward transformed into a dog, and threw herself into the sea.

Helen (of Troy)   In Greek legend, the divinely beautiful daughter of the god Zeus*, and of either Nemesis* or Leda*, whom Zeus is said to have seduced in the form of a swan. The most common legend is that Leda was the lady, and that Helen was born of this union in an egg with her brother Polydeuces*. Her other brother was Castor* and her sister was Clytemnestra*, both fathered by Leda's husband Tyndareus. At the age of twelve, Helen was already a beauty, and was kidnapped by King Theseus* of Athens and placed in a fortress at Aphidnae, from which she was rescued by her brothers and brought back to Sparta. She was wooed by many rich and powerful suitors and finally gave her hand to Menelaus*, king of Sparta, to whom she bore one child, Hermione*. The gods then took over with elaborate plans. Aphrodite had promised Trojan Prince Paris* the fairest woman in the world because he had awarded her the Apple of Discord*. During an absence of Menelaus in Crete, Paris carried Helen off to Troy. This was the origin of the ten-year Trojan war. Despite the consequences, Helen was loved for her beauty by the Trojans, and they refused to restore her to her husband. As the war progressed, Helen lamented her behavior, but was unable to return to her home, husband, and child. Legend says she bore Paris several children but they all died in infancy. After the death of Paris, though briefly wed to Deiphobus, she betrayed the Trojans into

138

the hands of Menelaus. Reunited with her husband, they took eight years getting home to Sparta, appearing throughout the rest of their lives to live in happiness and harmony. There are many versions and additions to Helen's life but the Trojan episode is the main one. Painting: *The Recovery of Helen,* on a black-figured Greek vase (6th century B.C.); also painting, *The Rape of Helen,* attributed to Cariani; both Metropolitan, New York.

St. Helena   The mother of the Roman Emperor, Constantine the Great*. Helena was converted to Christianity when her son had a vision of Christ, which brought him victory in battle. In 325, at the age of eighty, she had a number of churches built, and then made a religious pilgrimage to the Holy City of Jerusalem. According to tradition, she decided excavations should be made on the Mount of Calvary*, with the hope of finding the cross of Christ's crucifixion (see Jesus Christ-Life Events). Three crosses were discovered, and an inscription, "Jesus of Nazareth, King of the Jews," purported to be the one Pontius Pilate* had ordered to be placed upon the cross of Jesus (John 19:19). Helena was determined to ascertain which was the authentic cross. A sick man was brought to the scene and placed on each one of them. As he touched the "True Cross," he recovered completely. (This scene is sometimes called "The Invention of the Cross.") Helena is also said to have unearthed some of the nails of the cross which, when exposed, were "shining as gold." Likewise, she identified the site of the Holy Sepulchre*, and the site of the Garden of Gethsemane*. In art, she is represented in royal robes with the imperial crown of an empress. She carries either a model of the Holy Sepulchre in her hands or a cross and a hammer and nails. Helena died about 328; her feast day is August 18. Painting: *The Finding of the True Cross,* Sebastiano Ricci, National Gallery, Washington.

Heliotrope   See Clytie.

Helius or Helios (hēl'i-us) (Ro. Sol)   In Greek mythology, Helius is the sun god (called Hyperion by Homer), the brother of the dawn goddess Eos* and the moon goddess Selene*. He was the father of Phaeton* by Clymene, and father to Circe*, Pasiphae*, and Aeetes* by Persa. He is also the god of flocks, because of his own sacred flocks in Sicily. He is represented as a strong, beautiful youth with waving locks and a crown of rays, and drives a four-horse chariot. Each morning he rises from the ocean in the east and drives his steeds across the vault of heaven in his luminous chariot, descending at the day's end into the western sea. While sleeping he is carried in a golden boat, made by the smith god Hephaestus*, on the outer edge of the earth, back to the east for the next day's journey. Helius is the all-seer and revealer of what is done on earth. Rhodes was his particular island, and the famous statue of him, The Colossus of Rhodes, was built there in his honor. In later times the god Apollo* was confused with Helius.

Hell In Biblical thought, hell is the place and state of eternal punishment, demanded by God's justice as the lot of the damned; the result of sin which follows the soul into the next life. In the New Testament, it is often spoken of figuratively, as "lake of fire," and "where the worm does not die." In art, it is shown as a place with suffering figures.

Hellas The name given to Greece by the ancient Greeks from the peoples called Hellenes. The name Graecia came later from the Romans.

Helle See Golden Fleece

Hellespont (hel'es-pont) This is the strait between Thrace and Asia Minor, so called because Helle turned giddy and fell into it, when journeying through the air with her brother Phrixus* on the golden-fleeced Ram to escape from the cruelty of their step-mother Ino. It is the name also for the Dardanelles, celebrated in the legend of Hero* and Leander.

Helmet In Greek mythology, the helmet is an attribute of Ares* and of Athena, as god and goddess of war. The helmet of invisibility was an attribute of the god Hades*. Roman Juno also claims the helmet as a goddess of war. The oval helmet or cap, crowned with a star, is an emblem of the Dioscuri*.

Hephaestus (he-fes'tus) (Ro. Vulcan) In Greek mythology, Hephaestus is the god of fire and the arts of using fire. He was the son of the goddess* Hera and either the god Zeus* or Ares*. He was born ugly and lame, or made lame by Hera, who was ashamed of him and threw him out of Olympus* into the sea, where he remained for nine years under the protection of Thetis* and the nereids*. Here he fashioned works of art, among them a *Net to catch Hera* throne with an invisible net, which he sent to his mother on Mt. Olympus. When she sat in it, she was caught so fast no one could extricate her until Dionysus*, the god of wine, made Hephaestus so drunk he could bring him back to the heights again. He was the *Net to catch Ares and Aphrodite* husband of the beautiful goddess Aphrodite*, an unwilling wife who preferred the handsome god of war Ares*. When Helius the sun god reported her affair with Ares to Hephaestus, he fashioned a delicate net over his marriage bed in which they were caught,

140

and from which they could not escape. Hephaestus called all the gods to witness and laugh at the dishonor, but after releasing the culprits, all went as before, and Aphrodite followed her own pleasures. Besides making palaces of brass for the Olympian gods, Hephaestus created all the masterpieces used by them and by heroes. The aegis* of Zeus, the arms of Achilles*, the scepter of Agamemnon*, the fire-eating, bronze-hoofed bulls of Aeëtes*, Ariadne's* crown, and the breastplate of Heracles*. His artistic genius made him a special friend of the goddess Athena*. He was much worshipped in Athens at the Academy by the smelters, and at the Hephaestia festival, a torchrace was run in his honor. In art, he is shown as a vigorous man wearing a beard, equipped with a smithy's hammer and tongs, his left leg shortened to show his lameness. Painting: *The Return of Hephaestus to Olympus*, by the painter Lydis, on a 6th-century B.C. black-figured Greek vase, Metropolitan, New York.

Masterpieces

Hera (hē′ra) (Ro. Juno)   In Greek mythology, queen of the twelve Olympian gods, the eldest daughter of Rhea* and Cronus*, and the lawful wife of the great god Zeus*. Like her brothers and sisters, she was swallowed at birth by her father Cronus and rescued by Zeus. Her love was won in a stealthy manner by Zeus who disguised himself as a cuckoo. She was the mother of Hebe* by Zeus and of Hephaestus* by Zeus or the god Ares*. In early mythology, Hera symbolized the feminine aspects of natural forces, sharing with Zeus the phenomena of the atmosphere. The union of sun and rain symbolized their loving union; the conflict of winds, a matrimonial quarrel, usually attributed to the jealousy of Hera who, as goddess of women and childbirth, was regarded as the stern protectress of honorable marriage. Although the marriage of Zeus and Hera was the only proper one on Mt. Olympus*, it was an exceedingly stormy one. The continuous interest of Zeus in other women was a constant source of anger to Hera. Whenever possible, she punished the objects of his love, even when those pursued had submitted reluctantly to his advances, and she was as ungenerous to the children of these unions as she was to the parents. The two most tormented persons were Heracles*, whom she tricked at birth out of his kingship and racked all his life, and the Trojans, since she never forgave Trojan Paris* for awarding the Apple of Discord* to the goddess Aphrodite*, instead of herself. Hera was worshipped throughout the Greek world, and many places claimed to be her birthplace; others claimed the scene of her marriage, which was celebrated in the spring. Her most famous temples were the Heraeum at Nemea in the Argolid, the great temple on the island of Samos, and her ancient temple at Olympia. In works of art, she is represented as a large, majestic woman, fully clad in flowing draperies. She wears a crown or a diadem on her head, and often holds a scepter. Her attributes are the crow, the cuckoo, as messenger of spring, the peacock, because she set the one hundred eyes of the all-seeing Argus* in its tail, and the pomegranate, symbol of fruitfulness. Hecatombs* were offered to her in sacrifice as they were to Zeus.

Heracles (her'a-klēz) (Ro. Hercules)   One of the oldest and most illustrious heroes in Greek mythology, around whom is woven the richest fables. His deeds were famous for their courage and strength, and his sufferings, chiefly the result of the goddess Hera's* antagonism, were endured with fortitude. The god Zeus* *Parentage* fathered the hero, and chose for his mother the chaste mortal Alcmene*, a granddaughter of Perseus*, appearing to her in the form of her husband Amphitryon* of Tiryns. On the day upon which Heracles was about to be born, Zeus announced to the gods that the first descendant of Perseus*, born on that day, would rule over the Persidae. As usual, Hera was jealous of a child born of the infidelity of her husband Zeus, and cleverly delayed *Birth* the birth of Heracles by summoning the birth goddess Ilythia. Ilythia sat outside Alcmene's door with knees closed and hands clenched and thus delayed the birth until Eurystheus*, grandson of Perseus through his father Sthenelous, was born first. This robbed Heracles of his kingdom, and made him the subject of Eurystheus. Under pressure from Zeus, Hera then allowed that Heracles would become immortal, provided he first perform any labors demanded of him by Eurystheus. After this, she sent two *Snakes in* snakes to the cradle of the baby Heracles, where he was lying *cradle* with his mortal twin brother Iphicles*, the son of Amphitryon. Heracles joyfully strangled them with his hands, already manifesting his gigantic strength. He was raised by his foster father Amphitryon, and educated by renowned persons. His early physical prowess and his help to King Creon of Thebes won him *Marriage* Creon's daughter Megara in marriage, and they had three children. *to Megara* Now, as arranged by Hera, Eurystheus summoned Heracles to perform certain labors for him. Heracles deemed this service *Madness* unworthy of him, and he fell into a fit of madness and killed his children. When cured of this madness, the Delphic oracle ordered him to start the labors, and thus achieve immortality. The labors were a frequent subject of Greek art. Statuette: Heracles, Greek (5th century B.C.), Museum of Fine Arts, Boston. He was an equally popular subject in Roman art. The twelve famous labors follow:

The First Labor was to slay the Nemean Lion. Heracles drove it into a cavern, and strangled it with his arms. He then skinned it and used the pelt ever after as his cloak.

Heracles, presenting the Erymanthian boar to the terrified Eurystheus, hiding in a pithos. Greek 6th century B.C. The Metropolitan Museum of Art, Rogers Fund.

The Second Labor was to kill the many-headed Lernaean Hydra. As soon as one of its heads was cut off, two others grew in its place. Heracles summoned his charioteer Iolaus*, and as he cut off each head, Iolaus seared the stump with pitch. Heracles dipped his arrows in the blood of the Hydra, making them deadly and carried these arrows with him ever after. Eurystheus refused to recognize this labor because assistance had been given to him by Iolaus.

The Third Labor was to take the pestilent Erymanthian Boar alive. Heracles chased it north into a snow drift, caught it in a noose, and carried it on his shoulders to Mycenae. The sight of the beast threw Eurystheus into such a state of panic, he hid in a huge storage jar (pithos), and forbade Heracles to show his achievements within the city in the future.

The Fourth Labor was to catch the golden-horned Cerynean Hind alive, since it was sacred to the goddess Artemis*. Heracles pursued her for a year. Finally, as she was drinking at the river Ladon, he transfixed her forefeet with one perfect arrow shot from his bow and caught her.

The Fifth Labor was to drive off the bronze-beaked, arrow-feathered birds that were infesting the Stymphalian marsh. The goddess Athena* gave Heracles a bronze rattle, which he shook so violently the birds rose in startled flight and Heracles was able to hit many of them with arrows. The rest fled to the Black Sea, where they were later encountered by the Argonauts*.

The Sixth Labor was to clean in one day the dung of three thousand cattle from the filthy stables of King Augeas* of Elis. Heracles arranged with Augeas to complete the job by nightfall in return for one-tenth of his cattle. He then diverted the rivers Peneus and Alpheus from their regular courses, and sent them through the stables, cleaning the place by evening. When Augeas refused to honor his side of the bargain, Heracles killed him, and put his son Phyleus on the throne in his place.

The Seventh Labor was to bring back alive the mad Cretan Bull, a gift of the god Poseiden*, which was now ravaging the land of King Minos*. Heracles subdued the bull by himself, crossed the sea to Greece on the bull's back, threw him over his shoulders, and took him to Mycenae, where the fearful Eurystheus let him loose. The bull wandered through the Peloponnesus, infesting the countryside until he was killed, at length, by Theseus*.

The Eighth Labor was to kill the man-eating mares, which were fed with strangers by King Diomedes of Thrace. After a

Heracles roping the Cretan Bull. Greek, 6th century, B.C. The Metropolitan Museum of Art, Rogers Fund.

severe struggle, Heracles overcame the king, threw his body to the mares, and having thus tamed them, drove them over the mountains, harnessed to his chariot. When they arrived at Mycenae, Eurystheus consecrated the mares to the goddess Hera*, and then set them free. Ultimately they were torn to pieces by wild beasts on Mt. Olympus*.

The Ninth Labor was to bring home the girdle of the Amazon* Queen Hippolyta* for Admete, the daughter of Eurystheus. When Heracles came to her shores, he found the queen ready to give up the girdle of her own accord. But trouble-making Hera* spread a rumor among the Amazons that their queen was in danger. They marched against Heracles, and he, thinking he had been tricked, slew Hippolyta, took the girdle, and carried off her sister Antiope* as captive. The girdle went to Admete, and Antiope was presented to Theseus*, who made her his wife.

The Tenth Labor was to fetch the red cattle of Geryon*, a giant with three bodies and mighty wings, who dwelt in the far west on the borders of the Ocean stream. The cattle were guarded by a shepherd and his two-headed dog Orthrus*. Heracles travelled through Europe to Libya, and as he passed the boundary of both continents, he set up on either side of the straits (Gibraltar) the two promontories known as the Pillars of Hercules. Oppressed by the rays of the sun, Heracles aimed his bow at Helius*, the sun god, who, marvelling at his courage, gave him a golden bowl in which to cross the ocean. When he came to the western border he slew the shepherd, the dog, and Geryon, took the cattle, and returned with them to Eurystheus.

The Eleventh Labor was to find the Golden Apples of the Hesperides*, given to the goddess Hera* as a wedding present. They were guarded by a 100-headed dragon and the daughters of Atlas*, called the Hesperides*. Heracles was ignorant of their whereabouts, and therefore seized Nereus*, the god of the sea, and compelled him to give him directions. Then he travelled over land and sea until he came to the Caucasus where he found Prometheus*, chained to a crag while vultures gnawed his liver. Heracles killed the vultures and freed Prometheus, who was then able to take over the centaur Chiron's* immortality. Acting on instructions from Prometheus, Heracles approached the Titan Atlas*, who was holding up the heavens on his shoulders. Heracles offered to take over the heavens, if Atlas would fetch the apples from the garden. Atlas hesitated, fearing the dragon, whereupon Heracles sent an arrow over the wall and killed it. While he then shouldered the heavens, Atlas fetched the apples and then offered to take them to Eurystheus, since Heracles had been so kind as to take on his burden. Heracles agreed, but asked Atlas to relieve him a moment while he adjusted a cushion on his head. Atlas took back the heavens, and Heracles hurried off with the apples. These he gave to Eurystheus, but the goddess Athena* soon returned them to the garden, as the fruit was sacred.

The Twelfth Labor was to fetch the dog Cerberus* from the underworld. After having purified himself at Eleusis in ceremonies initiated for him as a foreigner (thereafter known as the Lesser Mysteries), Heracles was conducted by the god Hermes* and the goddess Athena* to Hades* through an opening in Laconia. He then terrified the ferryman Charon* into carrying him across the river Styx*. Among the shades in the underworld, that of Meleager* spoke to him, and Heracles promised him that he would marry his sister Deianira* on his return to earth. He found Theseus* immobilized on a chair of forgetfulness, and set him free. Then with Queen Persephone's* help, he induced King Hades* to allow him to take Cerberus with him, on the condition that he manage it without weapons. Heracles grasped the dog around the neck and choked him until he submitted. Accompanied by Theseus, he then carried Cerberus to Eurystheus and returned him back to Hades again.

The labors of Heracles for Eurystheus were now over, but his life continued with many adventures. He had established the Olympic games next to the Alpheus river, dedicating them to Zeus, right after his seventh labor. He paced out the stadium himself, and won all the contests in the first games. The gods awarded him all kinds of weapons, but Heracles preferred his own club, bow, and arrows. Between his ninth and tenth labors, he had joined Jason* on the Argonaut expedition for a short time. Now again he suffered from madness and killed his friend Iphitus. He returned to the Oracle at Delphi to learn how he could be cured. The priestess refused to answer him, whereupon Heracles seized her sacred Tripod*, threatening to start his own oracle. Apollo rushed to the scene, Heracles attacked the god, Zeus hurled a thunderbolt between them, and the priestess gave Heracles instructions. During the battle of the gods against the Giants*, the goddess Athena* hastily sought the assistance of Heracles, when the oracle disclosed that only a mortal, wearing a lion's skin, could defeat them. Finally Heracles kept his promise made to Meleager* during his twelfth labor, and married his sister Deianira*, who bore him five children. Inadvertently Deianira killed Heracles

Olympic Games

Madness

Fight with Apollo over Delphic Tripod

Marriage to Deianira

147

by sending him a poisoned robe which burned his flesh. Apollo had a great funeral pyre built for him. The flames had barely started when a cloud descended from heaven with thunder and lightning, and the son of Zeus was carried to Mt. Olympus, where he was welcomed as one of the immortals. Hera was reconciled to him, and he was wedded to her daughter Hebe*, the goddess of youth and spring. Heracles was worshipped throughout the Mediterranean world. Every town wanted to be connected with the great hero, which probably accounts for his many exploits. In art, he is represented as the ideal of manly strength with muscular limbs, a curling beard, a short neck, and a head often small in proportion to his limbs. He generally wears the lion skin and carries his club, sometimes a bow and arrows. He is most frequently shown performing his twelve labors. At the Metropolitan, New York, there are many scenes painted on Greek vases of his exploits, among them: a 5th-century red-figured vase, *The Infant Heracles Strangling the Serpents;* a 6th-century black-figured vase, *Heracles Bringing the Erymanthian Boar to the Frightened Eurystheus;* a black-figured scene, about 500 B.C., *Heracles Overpowering the Cretan Bull;* and a 6th-century black-figured vase, *The Contest of Heracles and Apollo for the Delphic Tripod.* Also, there is a fresco transferred to canvas: *The Wedding of Hercules and Hebe,* Giulio Romano. (see Omphale)

Hercules　　See Heracles.

Heresy　　A heresy applies to those who, of their own will, choose doctrines contrary to those commonly held by their church, considered a grievous sin.

Heretic　　One who believes or professes heresy.

Hermes (her'mēz) (Ro. Mercury)　　In Greek mythology, one of the twelve Olympian gods; their messenger, the god of flocks, of commerce, wealth, inventions, craft in oratory, and bringer of dreams. He was the one who led the dead to the underworld. His *Birth and first day inventions* mother was Maia, the daughter of Atlas* and his father the great god Zeus*. He was born in the morning in Arcadia, and immediately after his birth gave proof of his versatility. By midday, he had invented the lyre from the shell of a tortoise and seven sheep-gut strings; in the afternoon, he stole fifty head of cattle from his brother, the god Apollo*, which he hid so skillfully in a cave they could not be found. After sacrificing several of the cattle, on a fire which he lit by the invention of rubbing sticks together, he crept stealthily back into his cradle. Apollo divined the mischief maker and took him to Zeus, who ordered him to return the cattle, but Hermes so charmed Apollo by playing his new lyre to him, Apollo exchanged it for the cattle. Hermes became the protector of wayfarers, and at crossroads, heaps of stones were raised in his honor, known as Hermae. As the guide of both the living and the dead, he acted as an intermediary between the two worlds. As messenger of the gods, he performed many errands, mostly beneficial. Sacrifices were offered to him in the event of death, and Hermae were also placed on graves, later to become gravestones. In early art, he is represented with a beard, but later he is shown in diversified ways: as a shepherd with a sheep from his flock; as a mischievous little thief; as the god of wealth with a purse in his hand, at times with a lyre. He is usually represented as a graceful youth, with a staff entwined by snakes, called the caduceus, his emblem as messenger of the gods. On his head is a round, flat hat, and winged sandals on his feet. Sometimes the hat and the caduceus are also winged. Greek marble relief (4th-century B.C.): *Hermes with Three Nymphs and Achelous*, Metropolitan, New York.

Hero (hē′ro)   In Greek legend, a priestess of Aphrodite*, who lived at Sestos on the Hellespont. She was loved by Leander, who swam across the Hellespont every night from Abydos to see her in her solitary tower, to which he was guided by its light. One night the light was extinguished, Leander was lost in the waves, and washed up on the shore beneath the tower the next day. Hero, heartbroken, hurled herself from the tower, and drowned in the same sea. A scene: *Hero and Leander*, on a Maiolica 16th-century Italian plate, Metropolitan, New York.

Herod the Great (her′ud)   Herod was the ruler in Palestine at the time of the birth of Jesus; the man who ordered the "massacre of the innocents*," in his effort to do away with the baby Jesus who, he had heard, might be a possible rival (Matthew 2:16).

Herod Antipas   The son of Herod the Great, and the "tetrarch" of Galilee and Perea from 4 B.C. to A.D. 39, at which time he was deposed and banished to Gaul. He had the power of the king, but forfeited his prestige among Jews when he illegally married his niece Herodias*, the former wife of his half-brother Herod, an outrage which led to the beheading of John the Baptist. It was Herod Antipas whose curiosity led him to gladly question Jesus, when the prisoner was sent to him from Pilate. Jesus answered him nothing, so Herod allowed him to be mocked and sent him back to Pilate in a gorgeous robe (Luke 23:7-11).

Herodias (her-ōd′i-as)   The granddaughter of Herod the Great, who first married her uncle Herod, son of Herod the Great, and then divorced him to marry her uncle Antipas. When her daughter Salome* danced before this husband and gained the promise for anything she asked, Herodias instructed her to demand the head of John the Baptist* (Matthew 14:1-12).

Herse (her'sē) In Greek mythology, the daughter of Cecrops*, king of Athens, who was fabled to have been half-man and half-serpent. The god Hermes* fell in love with Herse, and appealed to her sister Agraulos to help him in his pursuit, but the jealous Agraulos refused, so he turned her to stone. Herse bore Hermes, Cephalus* and Ceryx, who became the first herald of the Eleusinian mysteries. Herse and her mother and sisters were given a chest to guard, by the goddess Athena*. Curiosity overcame them, and when they opened it and saw a child, half-snake and half-man, they all went mad, and jumped off the Acropolis of Athens. Athena was so shocked by the news, she dropped a colossal stone she was carrying for the walls of the Acropolis, which became Mount Lycabettos of Athens.

Hesperides (hes-per'i-dēz) The three daughters of Atlas*, who guarded the Golden Apples of the Hesperides* which the goddess Hera* had received as a wedding present. The daughters were assisted by a dragon whom Heracles* slew, before he carried off the apples to Eurystheus*, as his eleventh labor.

Hesperus (hes'per-us) (Ro. Vesper) The name given to the planet Venus, when it is the evening star.

Hestia (hes'ti-a) (Ro. Vesta) In Greek myth, one of the twelve Olympian gods, the daughter of Rhea* and Cronus*. She was the goddess of the hearth and household, who never left Olympus*. When she was pursued by both the god Apollo* and the god Poseiden*, she took an oath of chastity. As a result, the great god Zeus* granted her the honor of being worshipped at the beginning and end of every sacrifice and every festival entertainment. Her hearth was the center of cities, states, and colonies, in all of which she received sacrifices as their protectress. In art, she is represented as grave, gentle, fully clothed in simple drapery, and with unadorned hair. Her attribute is a scepter.

St. Hilarion (hi-lar'i-on) A hermit born near Gaza, about 291, who is the first-recorded solitary in Palestine. He lived for 50 years in a mud brick shelter, eating only figs and vegetables, working with his hands to support himself. By his example, he converted many to Christianity, and many miracles were attributed to him; the most notable was the one which enabled the charioteer Italicus to win a race, bringing Christianity close to his backers. In 360, he was so besieged by visitors he left for Egypt, but was arrested by Julian the Apostate, Emperor of Rome's Empire. He fled to the Libyan desert, and then to Sicily, where he collected and sold firewood, then went on to Yugoslavia, and finally to Cyprus, where he died at the age of eighty in 371. Feast day: October 21.

St. Hilary of Poitiers   Bishop of Poitiers in the 4th century who was the most outstanding opponent of Arianism in the West. (The doctrine of Arius is that Jesus, though divine, is not the equal of God the Father, but the best of God's creation). Hilary came from a well-to-do family, was early converted to Christianity, and elected bishop in 353, at the age of thirty-five, while his wife was still living. In 356, he was banished to Phrygia, Asia Minor, by the emperor, Constantine II. The highly cultivated man made a deep study of Greek theology while he was there. In 360, the Arians sent him back to Gaul because he was a "mischief maker" and a nuisance. He wrote many theological works, and composed poetry and hymns for the teaching of Christianity. Their metrical form was an influence on the hymn's development.

Hind   In Greek mythology, the hind is sacred to the goddess Artemis*, as the goddess of the chase. The fourth labor of the hero Heracles* was to fetch the Cerynean Hind for Eurystheus (see Stag).

Hippodameia   See Briseis.

Hippodamia (hi-pod-a-mi'a)   In Greek legend, the daughter of King Oenomaus* of Elis, who, because the oracle at Delphi had declared he would die at the hands of one of his daughter's children, refused to allow her to marry. To rid himself of the aspirants, Oenomaus asked her suitors to race against him from Olympia to the Isthmus of Corinth. After giving the contestant a head start, Oenomaus overtook him, and hurled a spear into his back. When Pelops* came as a suitor, Hippodamia fell in love with him, so she bribed her father's charioteer to remove the nails from the axle of her father's chariot. Pelops also spoke to the charioteer and, during the race, Oenomaus fell forward and was tangled in the reins, enabling Pelops to win. Hippodamia bore Pelops many children, among them Atreus* and Thyestes*. She established games in honor of the goddess Hera*, but her life was marred because she was implicated with her sons Atreus and Thyestes in the murder of a bastard son of Pelops. She escaped to Argolis, where she killed herself, one of the many catastrophies of the House of Pelops.

Hippodamia   The wife of Pirithous (see Lapithae).

Hippolyta (hi-pol′i-ta)   In Greek legend, queen of the Amazons*. She was daughter of the god Ares* and Otrera. She owned a beautiful girdle, given to her by her father. Heracles* went to fetch this girdle, as his ninth labor for Eurystheus*. Hippolyta was willing to give it to him, but her Amazon followers prepared to attack Heracles and he, thinking there was foul play, slew Hippolyta in the ensuing battle and took the girdle.

Hippolytus (hi-pol′i-tus)   In Greek legend, the son of King Theseus* and the Amazon Antiope*. After Antiope's death, Theseus married Phaedra*, and she fell madly in love with Hippolytus when he grew up to be a handsome, young man. As Hippolytus spurned the love of his stepmother, she slandered him to Theseus. Theseus then begged the god Poseiden* to avenge him, and banished this son from Athens. Hippolytus in fury at the injustice, leaped in his chariot and drove madly along the shore. Suddenly his horses were frightened by a great bull, sent forth in a wave from the sea, and he was thrown from his chariot and killed. Phaedra, conscious of the wrong she had done, killed herself, and Theseus learned too late that Hippolytus was innocent. In Roman times, Hippolytus was said to have been restored to life by the great physician Asclepius*, for the pleasure of the goddess Artemis*, of whom he had been a faithful worshipper during his lifetime. Artemis loved him as a huntsman, and took him to live in her sacred grove in Aricia, Italy, where he was worshipped under the name of Viribius. Brown ink wash: *The Death of Hippolytus*, Nicholas Poussin, Morgan Library, New York.

Hippomenes (hi-pom′e-nēz)   See Atalanta.

Hog   A Christian emblem of sensuality and gluttony, often shown with St. Anthony Abbot*, who struggled with and overcame these temptations (see Pig).

Holly or Ilex   In Christian symbology, holly is regarded as an emblem of Christ's crown of thorns (see Jesus Christ—Life Events), because of its prickly leaves. It is also a symbol of the Passion*, because legend said it was the only tree which did not splinter under the axe, permitting itself to be used for the cross.

Holofernes (holō-fur′nēz)   In the Apocryphal book Judith*, Holofernes is the general of Nebuchadnezzar, sent to invade Palestine. He was beheaded by Judith, to save her city Bethulia.

Holy Cross or True Cross   See St. Helena.

The Holy Family. El Greco. Courtesy of the Cleveland Museum of Art.

Holy Family   This is the title given in art to representations of
the infant Jesus*, his mother Mary*, her husband Joseph*, her
mother Anne*, and Elisabeth*, the cousin of Mary, with her
young son John*, later to become John the Baptist. Not all of
these figures are always present in pictures of the "Holy Family,"
but they are all considered members.

Holy Ghost In Christian theology, the third person of the Trinity*, the divine spirit represented in art as a dove, shafts of light, or flames (see God the Holy Ghost). In Greek Orthodox theology, known as Holy Spirit.

Holy Land The name given to Palestine by Christians, because it was the site of Christ's birth, preaching, and death.

Holy Sepulcher The church in Jerusalem whose site is supposed to be that of Christ's tomb. It is said to have been discovered by St. Helena* in the fourth century.

Holy Trinity In Christian theology, this is the descriptive name given to the three persons in God, the Father, the Son, and the Holy Ghost, or Holy Spirit. The three are one and one is three; all are equal and eternal. Orthodox theology says the Father is Unbegotten, the son Begotten and the Holy Ghost proceeds from the Father. In art, when the idea of oneness is being stressed, one figure or three identical figures may be used. If they are differentiated by individual attributes, God the Father is seen as an old man with a white beard, his Son is younger, bears the cross or is nailed to it, and the Holy Ghost is shown in the form of a dove. Sometimes there are three people of differing ages to represent the Trinity. Painting, Tintoretto, Columbia Museum of Art, South Carolina.

Honeycomb See Bee.

Hope In Greek legend, the only element left in the dowry box of Pandora*. In Christian thought, one of the three theological virtues, the others being faith and charity. It is the virtue by which one comes to trust in the eternal life. Hope is also a legendary saint (see St. Faith).

Horae (hō′rē) In Greek mythology, daughters of the god Zeus* and Themis*. They were named Eunomia (good order), Dike (justice), and Eirene* (peace), and as handmaidens of Zeus, were entrusted with guarding the gates of heaven, or Mt. Olympus*, of controlling the weather, and the supervision of the bloom and decay of changing seasons. They are also the guardians of social and political order, especially Dike, who presides over legal justice at the side of Zeus. The dance of the Horae was a symbolized representation of the seasons.

Horn In Biblical times, horns were a symbol of strength. When worn on a man's brow they indicated that God had granted prosperity and power to the individual. Moses* is sometimes

154

represented with this attribute (see Psalm 89:17 and 89:24). They are frequently shown on kings and deities of the Middle East. Sometimes hair was dressed to represent horns. In prophetic writings, horned beasts signified kings and kingdoms. There were horn-like projections at the four corners of the Hebrew tabernacle*. They were sacred, and therefore offered sanctuary to criminals who clung to them. Rams' horns were used as military bugles in battle. In Christian art, horns became an attribute of the devil (see also Cornucopia and Horn of Plenty).

Horse In Greek symbology, the horse was an attribute sacred to the god Poseiden*, who brought the horse out of a rock with one blow of his trident*. Poseiden instituted horseracing at the Isthmeian Games, near Corinth. Legend says he also seduced the goddess Demeter* in the form of a stallion. Horses were first used as cavalry by armed Amazons*. Pegasus* was the winged horse caught by Bellerophon*. Black horses were driven by the god Hades* in his chariot. White horses drew the chariot of the sun god Helius*, and were driven for one disastrous day by his son Phaeton*. In Christian symbology, the horse is an emblem of lust, derived from the book of Jeremiah 5:8, "They were as fed horses in the morning: every one neighed after his neighbor's wife." St. George* is usually portrayed mounted on an armored horse, as is St. James the Great* (Santiago) in Spain (see Apocalypse). (See Chariots—How Drawn, in Appendix.)

Host In the Christian mass of the Eucharist*, the host is the flat, round piece of unleavened bread, which is consecrated by the priest. When it is shown in art with the chalice*, it symbolizes Christ's sacrifice on the cross.

Hourglass In Christian iconography, a symbol of the brevity of life. It is an attribute of Time*.

St. Hubert An active missionary in the forest of Ardenne, in the 8th century, where idolatry had not entirely disappeared. He became the bishop of Tongres-Maestricht, but in 726 he met with an accident while fishing in a boat in the Meuse River. It caused him much suffering, and he died fifteen months later. He came to be regarded as a patron of hunters and trappers in the Ardenne, and this led to attributing to him the legend of St. Eustace*: conversion to Christianity upon finding a stag in the woods, which had a crucifix between its antlers. The stag has become his emblem, in consequence, and in art he is shown in scenes before a stag in the woods, similar to those of St. Eustace. Burgundian relief: *St. Hubert with the Stag*, Metropolitan, New York.

Hyacinthus (hi-a-sin'thus)   According to Greek myth, the beautiful son of King Amyclas of Sparta. He was beloved by both the god Apollo* and Zephyr*, the west wind, and they became rivals for his affections. Once when Apollo was teaching Hyacinthus to throw the discus, the jealous Zephyr drove Apollo's discus with such force against the boy's head, it killed him. From his blood, Apollo caused the hyacinth to spring, and the petals are thought to be marked with the word AI, meaning woe.

Hydra (hi'dra)   A nine-headed monster in the marshes of the Argolid, which was killed by Heracles*, as his second labor for Eurystheus*.

Hylas (hi'las)   In Greek legend, a young attendant and much-loved companion of Heracles*, on the Argonaut* expedition. When the Argonauts landed at Mysia, the fountain nymph Dryope fell in love with Hylas. She dragged him into a spring to live with her forever, and Heracles, in trying to find the boy, was left behind when the Argonauts set sail again.

Hyllus (hi'lus)   In Greek legend, the son of Deianira* and Heracles*, who was with his father during the last funeral rites at the burning pyre on Mt. Oeta.

Hymen (hi'men)   In early Greek mythology, a marriage song. Later personified as a god of marriage, he was represented as a beautiful youth, carrying a bridal torch.

Hyperion (hi-pir'i-on)   In Greek mythology, a Titan*, a son of Gaea* (earth) and Uranus* (sky), the father of Helius*, Selene*, and Eos*, the sun, moon, and dawn respectively. The name is sometimes given to the sun itself, instead of Helius.

Hypermnestra   See Danaidae.

Hypnos (hip'nos)   In Greek mythology, the god of sleep, identified with the Roman Somnus. He is the son of Nyx* (night) and brother of Thanatos* (death). In art, he is frequently represented with wings, accompanying Thanatos. His sons were the dream bearers Morpheus*, Icelus, and Phantasos. Painting: *Morpheus*, Jean Honore Fragonard, Cleveland Museum of Art.

Iacchus (ī'a-kus)   In Greek mythology, the name under which Dionysus*, the god of wine, was honored with the goddesses Demeter* and her daughter Persephone* at the Eleusinian Mysteries*. He is possibly a personification of the ritual cry of Dionysus, sounding like Bacchus. Sometimes he is called Phrygian Bacchus, but in this role, as a son of Demeter, he is unlike the original Dionysus*. The image of Iacchus was crowned with myrtle, and he held a torch as he was borne in the famous procession from Athens to Eleusis to preside over the mysteries.

IC   See Letters Symbolizing Jesus Christ.

Icarus (ik'a-rus)   In Greek legend, the son of Daedalus*, who escaped on feathered wings with his father from the labyrinth* in Crete, built by Daedalus for King Minos*. Flying over the Aegean sea, Icarus disregarded his father's advice, and flew too near the sun. The wax, with which the wings were attached to his body, melted, and he fell into the sea and was drowned. Daedalus rescued the body from the sea and then buried it on the island now known as Icaria in the Icarian Sea.

Ichthus (ik'thus)   The Greek word for fish, used as a symbol for Christ in early Christianity, because the word is formed by the letters *J*(esous) *Ch*(ristos) *Th*(eou) *U*(ios) *S*(oter)—Jesus Christ, Son of God, Savior. See Letters Symbolizing Jesus Christ.

Ida (ī'da)   In Greek mythology, one of the nymphs who took care of the infant god Zeus*, when his mother hid him in a cave on the island of Crete, to save him from being devoured by his father Cronus*. Ida is also a mountain in Crete, and one legend says the baby Zeus was cared for on Mt. Ida by the goat-nymph Amalthea*.

St. Ignatius of Antioch (ig-nā'shus)   In Christian tradition, St. Ignatius was the little child whom Christ set in the middle of his disciples as an example of humility (Matthew 18:1-6). He was a convert of St. John the Evangelist*, and was consecrated bishop of Antioch by St. Peter*. He is said to have been thrown to the lions in the amphitheater by Trajan, about 107. Throughout his tortures, he never ceased to invoke the name of Jesus Christ. When asked why, he said the name was written in his heart. After he was dead, they took out his heart and cut it up; within it was written the sacred name in golden letters. The scene is sometimes shown in art. In reference to his martyrdom, he is represented accompanied by lions, or chained and exposed to them. Feast day: February 1.

St. Ignatius of Loyola (1491-1556)   This influential saint was the youngest son of the Spanish ducal house of Loyola, the founder of the Society of Jesus, or Jesuits. As a young soldier, he was wounded in battle and consequently left the army and dedicated himself to the religious life. In 1531, he began the order of the Jesuits, which grew from ten members to a thousand, before his death, spreading from country to country. From the first, the order was active in the mission field, and, in 1547, began its work of education in schools and universities. Ignatius was, above all, a man of prayer, who received deep religious illumination. In art, he is shown with the sacred monogram IHS (see Letters Symbolizing Jesus Christ) on his breast, his head and body surrounded by the luminous light called "glory*," in allusion to his assertion that understanding of the Trinity* had been miraculously given to him.

IHC and IHS   See Letters Symbolizing Jesus Christ.

St. Ildefonso   The patron saint of Toledo, Spain, where he was born and died (606-667). He was the abbot of a monastery and then made archbishop of Toledo in 657. He was highly praised for his ability and virtue, but only lived to serve for nine years. He was a musician and writer, the first Spaniard to write a treatise on the Virgin Mary*. Painting: *St. Ildefonso*, El Greco, National Gallery, Washington.

Ilex   See Holly.

Iliad (il'i-ad)   The story of the siege of Troy (Ilium), an epic poem attributed to Homer, written sometime before the eighth century B.C. (see Trojan war)

Immaculate Conception   The Roman Catholic doctrine that the Virgin Mary* was, from the moment of conception, free from any stain of original sin (the sin of disobedience committed by Adam* and Eve* in the Garden of Eden*, developed into the idea that the flesh lusts against the spirit). The doctrine was declared an article of faith in 1854 (see Mary the Virgin—Immaculate Conception).

Immanuel   See Emmanuel.

Incarnation   The Latin word means to "take on flesh," and refers to the dogma of the Christian church that the Word of God took on human form and nature in the person of Jesus Christ*, the son of God.

Incense   A compound of sweet gums and spices which were burned in ritual in the Tabernacle and Temple of the Hebrews in Biblical times. It was condemned by certain prophets in the Old Testament, because of its association with idolatrous rites. It has been used in the Christian church since earliest times and symbolizes the ascent of prayer to God.

St. Inez or Ines   The Spanish name for St. Agnes*. Painting: *St. Ines and St. Tecla with the Virgin*, El Greco, National Gallery, Washington.

Inferno   The infernal regions of Hades* or Hell*, the underworld where punitive measures were enforced on the dead souls who were confined there. The subject is frequently illustrated in art.

Innocents, Massacre of   The wholesale execution of all male infants under the age of two in the area of Jerusalem, just after the birth of Jesus*; an order given by Herod the Great*. (See Jesus Christ—Life Events.)

INRI   See Letters Symbolizing Jesus Christ.

Inquisition   A court instituted to inquire into the offenses against the Roman Catholic religion, established in 1229 by Gregory IX, and generally administered by the Dominicans (see St. Dominic). Torture was allowed as a means of extracting evidence, and those found guilty were handed over to the secular courts to be dealt with. It was most active in southern Europe, where it flourished until 1820.

Invention of the Cross   See St. Helena.

Io (ī'ō)   In Greek mythology, the beautiful daughter of the river god Inachus, a priestess of the goddess Hera*, at Argos. When she was seduced by the god Zeus*, she was transformed into a heifer, either by Hera to separate her from her husband Zeus, or by Zeus to protect her from Hera's jealousy. Hera appointed Argus*, a fabulous man with a hundred eyes scattered about his body, to watch over Io. Inachus, looking everywhere for his daughter, at length came upon Argus and the heifer. She ran to him, licked his hand, and finally spelled out her name in the dust with her hoof, but Inachus was helpless. Finally the messenger god Hermes*, at the command of Zeus, lulled Argus to sleep with stories and songs until all of his eyes were closed, and then cut off his head. Hera then sent a gadfly to pursue Io, and she wandered all over the world, persecuted by it, until she reached Egypt. Here she was restored to her human form, and bore Zeus a son named Epaphos. Io is sometimes identified with the Egyptian moon goddess Isis*.

Iobates   See Bellerophon.

Iolaus (i-ō-lā'us)   In Greek legend, the son of Iphicles*, who was the half-brother of Heracles*. Iolaus became the faithful companion and charioteer of Heracles, and for his devoted help, Heracles transferred to him his first wife, Megara. Iolaus was the companion who helped Heracles kill the Lernaean hydra*, the second labor for Eurystheus*. Iolaus extended his friendship to the children of Heracles and defended them against Eurystheus. He was worshipped as a comrade of Heracles in Thebes where the gymnasium was named after him.

Iphicles (if'i-klēz)   In Greek legend, the twin brother of Heracles*, but the son of the mortals Amphitryon* and Alcmene*, while Heracles was the son of the god Zeus* and Alcmene. He took part in several of the adventures of Heracles, among them the Calydonian Boar hunt, and was killed in the fighting when Heracles attacked and killed Augeas, king of Elis, after Augeas refused to hand over the cattle he had promised for the cleaning of his stables (see Heracles—Sixth Labor).

Iphigenia (if-i-jē-nī'a)   In Greek legend, the daughter of Clytemnestra* and Agamemnon*, and sister of Electra*, Chrysothemis*, and Orestes*. In some legends, she is the daughter of Helen* and Theseus*, and was brought up by her aunt Clytemnestra*. When Agamemnon's ships were becalmed at Aulis, enroute to Troy, Agamemnon, under great pressure, undertook to sacrifice Iphigenia to the goddess Artemis*, because the goddess was angry with him for killing one of her sacred stags and was causing the calm. He sent to Clytemnestra, pretending he was giving Iphigenia to the great hero Achilles* in marriage, but when she arrived she was placed on the altar. Artemis, as the sacrifice was made, spirited Iphigenia away in a cloud, and took her to Tauris. Here Iphigenia became a priestess for Artemis, in whose temple all shipwrecked strangers were offered in sacrifice. Years later, Orestes came to Tauris to capture the image of Artemis, and take it back to Attica. Iphigenia, discovering who he was, saved him from sacrifice, and escaped with him to Greece, taking the sacred image with her. In some legends, Iphigenia dies in Aulis. Painting: *Sacrifice of Iphigenia*, Giovanni Francisco Romanelli, Metropolitan, New York.

IR   See Letters Symbolizing Jesus Christ.

St. Irene   Irene was martyred at Salonika with her sisters Agape and Chiona. They were brought before the governor of Macedonia for refusing to eat the food offered in sacrifice to pagan gods. Agape and Chiona were burned alive. The governor examined Irene again when he heard she possessed Christian books, and after he issued a decree against the books, she fled to the mountains. Later the governor found her again, and had her sent naked to a brothel, but she was unmolested. Finally she was sentenced to death in 304, and her books were publicly burned. Feast day: April 3.

Iris (i'ris)   In Greek mythology, the goddess of the rainbow, the arc that touches the earth and sky. She was the daughter of one of the Oceanides, Electra, and of Thaumus; her sisters were the harpies*. She was the messenger of the Olympian gods, and could go to the ends of the earth or the underworld with her golden wings, travelling along the rainbow. As a messenger of the gods, she resembles their other messenger Hermes*, and like him carries the herald's staff called the caduceus*.

Iris (Sword Lily)   In Christian iconography, the iris flower is a symbol of the Virgin Mary, an allusion to her suffering at the crucifixion* of Christ (see Jesus Christ—Life Events). In Spain, the iris is a symbol of the Immaculate Conception*. Iris leaves are shaped like a sword.

IS   See Letters Symbolizing Jesus Christ.

Isaac (i-sak)   In the Old Testament, the only son of Abraham's* beloved wife Sarah*, conceived as an act of God when Abraham* was said to be a hundred and Sarah ninety-one years of age. As a supreme act of faith, Abraham, at the Lord's bidding, offered the

Sacrifice
of Isaac

Marriage

Move to
Gerar

King Abim-
lech dis-
covers
Rebekah's
marriage
status

Blessing of
Jacob

precious Isaac as a sacrifice to God, when Isaac was still young. The deed was then prevented by divine intervention through the angel of the Lord, who provided a ram for the burnt offering instead. At the age of forty, Isaac married Rebekah, a kinswoman from his father's birthland. She had been found for him at her father's well by a well trusted servant, whom Abraham had sent into Mesopotamia for this purpose. Rebekah bore Isaac two sons Esau* and Jacob. In the time of famine, Isaac moved to Gerar, and was able to make arrangements for a stay with the Philistine king Abimelech. It was here that Isaac pretended, as his father had done before him, that the fair Rebekah was his sister and not his wife, lest he be killed by those who might covet her. One day King Abimelech looked out of his window and caught Isaac "sporting with Rebekah." The king called him and said, "What have you done to us? Someone might have been guilty of lying with her." And he quickly charged his people to leave this man and woman alone. Isaac grew rich in land and possessions, and lived a long, uneventful life. Just before his death, Rebekah helped her son Jacob receive the chief inheritance and blessing from Isaac, which should have gone to the elder son Esau, and this brought about bitter family enmity. Painting: *Isaac Blessing Jacob*, Gebrandt Van den Eeckhout, Metropolitan, New York.

Isaiah (i-zā'ia)   In the Old Testament, Isaiah is generally regarded as the greatest of the Hebrew prophets, and the book of his name is the longest one. He devoted his whole life trying to save the state, believing that his tribe of Judah was chosen by God. Pursuing his convictions, he did not hesitate to defy kings while watching the wars and entanglements of the Assyrians and Babylonians, and he foretold the destruction of Israel and Damascus within a lifetime. He maintained that Assyria was a real danger, and things turned out as he said. At the last, when the Assyrian king Sennacherib had conquered all cities but Jerusalem, Isaiah advised King Hezekiah to hang on. Sennacherib's army was decimated by an avenging angel, the plague, and he retreated to Assyria where he was murdered by his sons. Miraculously the tribe of Judah had survived. Isaiah is the evangelical prophet, a man of intellect with a literary style of great sweep. Isaiah is shown in a painting: *The Nativity*, Duccio di Buonisegna, National Gallery, Washington.

Ishmael (ish'ma-el)   In the Old Testament, the son of Abraham* and his Egyptian concubine Hagar*, who was the handmaiden of Abraham's beloved wife Sarah*. Jealousy between Hagar and Sarah led to the departure of Ishmael and his mother from the family home, but an angel of the Lord appeared to Hagar and advised her to return to her mistress, promising her a long line of descendants through Ishmael. Later Ishmael mocked and teased Isaac, the favorite small son of Abraham and Sarah, whereupon he and his mother were permanently cast out by Abraham. They went to the desert of the Egyptian border, where the timely discovery of a well saved their lives. Hagar picked out an Egyptian wife for Ishmael, and as the angel had promised, many descendants came of this union. The narrative is really a tribal story.

Ishtar (ish'tar)   In ancient religion, the chief female deity of the Assyrian and Babylonian gods. In her role of goddess who travels to the underworld to restore her youthful husband Tamuz, the god of vegetation, she plays a role parallel to that of the Greek goddess Aphrodite* seeking Adonis*.

Isis (i'sis)   The principal goddess of ancient Egypt, sister and wife of Osiris*. She was identified with the moon, and the cow was sacred to her, its horns representing the crescent moon. In late times, she was worshipped as a nature goddess. She is identified with the Greek Io* and with Aphrodite*; also with the Roman Selene*, Ceres*, Juno*, and Venus*. Her cult persisted into A.D. 6th century. In art, she is given human form, sometimes with a woman's head, sometimes with a cow's, or with a cow's horns above the human head. In late art, she holds her infant son Horus.

Ismene (is-mē'ne)   In Greek legend, the daughter of Oedipus* and Jocasta*, the sister of Antigone*, Eteocles*, and Polynices*. Antigone was to be buried alive by order of her uncle King Creon*, because she had defied his wishes and had carried out the funeral rites for her brother Polynices*, slain in battle by Eteocles*. Ismene, who had been afraid to defy Creon's orders, now declared that she had helped her sister, and asked to share the punishment. Antigone disdained this late show of feeling, and told Ismene she must live.

Israel (iz'rā-el)   The name given Jacob* by an angel, after he had wrestled with it at the ford of the river Jabbok. The event took place the evening before he was reunited with his brother Esau* (Genesis 32:28). The name was also given to him by the Lord at Bethel (Genesis 35:10). The twelve sons of Jacob became the twelve heads of the tribes of Israel, and the name was applied to the clan and nation descended from them.

St. Ives or Yves (also St. Ivo Helory)   A Breton lawyer and priest, ordained in 1284, a zealous protector of the poor, noted

163

for justice and kindliness. He was advocate for the bishop of Rennes and became the patron saint of lawyers. Painting: *St. Ives,* Jacob Jordaens, Metropolitan, New York.

Ivy   In Christian iconography, a symbol of immortality and fidelity, because it is always green.

Ixion (ik′si-on)   In Greek legend, a king of the Lapithae* who tried to seduce the goddess Hera*. Zeus* forestalled him by sending a cloud in the form of Hera, and from this cloud Ixion fathered the centaurs. As a punishment for his audacity, he was bound eternally to a revolving wheel of fire in the infernal regions of Hades (underworld).

IXθYC   See Letters Symbolizing Jesus Christ; also ICHTHUS.

J

Jacob (ja'kup) In the Old Testament, Jacob is the third Hebrew Patriarch, the younger of Isaac* and Rebekah's* twin sons, and Rebekah's favorite. Jacob was an agriculturalist, Esau* a hunter, and once when Esau had been long without game, he came to Jacob for food. Jacob used the request to coerce Esau into selling his birthright for "a mess of pottage" (lentils). Jacob did not forget the agreement, and when Isaac was a blind, old man, he acted upon it. With the help of his mother and an animal skin, he passed himself off for the hairy Esau, and thus obtained the blessing and chief inheritance which was Esau's right, despite their bargain, and intended for him by Isaac. Esau was so enraged, Jacob was forced to flee to his uncle in Haran. On the journey (at Bethel) he had a dream of angels ascending and descending the ladder of heaven, above which stood the Lord who blessed him and all his descendants. When Jacob arrived at Haran he met Laban's* beautiful daughter Rachel* coming to water the sheep. Jacob rolled away the stone from the well, watered the sheep, kissed Rachel, and told her who he was. Then he bonded himself to his crafty uncle Laban for seven years, in return for which Laban promised to give him Rachel in marriage. When the seven years were up, Laban tricked Jacob and put Leah, Rachel's older sister, in the marriage bed in her stead. Jacob then had to serve another seven years for Rachel. Leah conceived many times but Rachel remained barren. Finally she bore a son whom they called Joseph. Now Jacob, having lived for twenty years with Laban, and having set aside cattle and riches, decided to go back to Hebron, the home of his father. He gathered his wives and children together, eluded Laban, and set off for a new life. Laban pursued the group, but decided to make a covenant of peace with Jacob, and set up a pillar and a heap of stones as witness to the

Jacob obtains Esau's birth- right

Dream of Ladder

Rachel at the well

Service to Laban

Birth of Joseph

agreement. Approaching Seir, where Esuu resided, Jacob sent messengers and many animals ahead to his brother, fearing reprisal. That night, at the river Jabbok, he found himself wrestling violently with a man. As the day broke, the man, who was an angel, blessed him and renamed him Israel. The next day a meeting of reconciliation between Jacob and Esau followed, and they continued the trek together. As they progressed a second child, Benjamin*, was born to Rachel but she died giving him birth. When the group finally reached Hebron, they found Isaac on his deathbed, but the sons had arrived in time to bury him. Esau decided he would live at Mt. Seir; Jacob stayed on the land of his father in Canaan with his twelve sons. These sons were the ancestors of the twelve tribes of Israel. Jacob soon lost his favorite son Joseph* because his ten older brothers sold him into slavery, and he was taken to Egypt. Late in life the family migrated to Egypt and Jacob was united with Joseph, and it was in this foreign land that he ended his days. A painting: *Isaac Blessing Jacob*, Gerbrandt van den Eeckhout, Metropolitan, New York.

Wrestles with angel

Birth of Benjamin

Joseph sold by his brothers

Last days in Egypt

Jael (jā'el) A woman of the Kenite tribe, friendly to the Israelites and Canaanites. When Barak and Deborah* defeated Sisera of Canaan, the defeated general found refuge with Jael. According to the laws of hospitality, he should have been safe, but she violated the code and murdered him as he slept.

Jairus' Daughter See Jesus Christ—Miracles.

James, the Brother of Jesus This James is fabled to have been the eldest of the three brothers of Jesus, all of them opposed to his mission. He was won to the faith after the Resurrection* (see Jesus Christ—After Life Events) by a special vision of the risen Christ (1 Corinthians 15:7), and later presided over the Christian community at Jerusalem, its first bishop, known as "The Just." He was martyred by Scribes and Pharisees in A.D. 52, some say stoned to death. Another account says he was hurled from the pinnacle of the Temple, after which he was beaten to death by a mob with a club. The Epistle of St. James in the New Testament is commonly attributed to him. In art, he is seen with the club of his martyrdom. He is often identified with James the Less. Feast day: May 1.

James the Great or Major In the New Testament, one of the twelve disciples of Jesus, the elder brother of John* with whom his name is always paired. Salome*, who witnessed the crucifixion*, was probably their mother. Zeberdee*, their father, was a fisherman of Galilee. James forsook the fishing trade to follow Jesus. James, his brother John*, and Peter* were always on terms of special intimacy with Jesus; present at his transfiguration and his agony at Gethsemane*. James became the military patron of Spain, where he is called Santiago, and is said to have established Christianity at Compostella, a place of miracles and one of the greatest centers of pilgrimage in Christendom. One legend says that after martyrdom in Jerusalem, his body was put in a sailboat which reached Compostella the next day. Another legend says that the relics of St. James were seen by a knight as they arrived in port on a marble ship. The knight's horse jumped into the sea in terror. When the knight boarded the boat he found himself covered with scallop shells, the attribute-shell of pilgrims. It is also said that the body of St. James was discovered in 840 by Bishop Theodomirus through divine revelation. In Spanish art, Santiago is represented on horseback, bearing a banner, symbolizing his liberation of Spain from the Moors. In Italy he is portrayed with a pilgrim's staff and the scallop shell, or, gourd, of pilgrims. As an apostle he bears a scroll, as witness of the incarnation of Christ. He was the first disciple to be martyred, and his death in Jerusalem (beheading with a sword), was ordered by Agrippa I in 44. An early story relates that his accuser suddenly repented, declared himself Christian, and was beheaded with him. Feast day: July 25.

James the Less or Minor In the New Testament, a disciple of Jesus* who was the son of Cleophas* and the Mary* who was present at the Crucifixion* (see Jesus Christ—Life Events), and who tried to minister to Jesus at the sepulcher (Mark 15:40; 16:1). He had a brother Joses and tradition also makes him a brother of the disciple Matthew*. The entire, remarkable family seems to have been converted to Christianity. The attributes of this James are a fuller's pole and a saw, because he is said to have been martyred with them. Painting: *James the Less* by the Master of St. Francis, National Gallery, Washington.

Janus (jā′nus) In Roman mythology, an ancient god who in earliest times was a god of light and sun; he opened the gates of heaven as he went forth in the morning and closed them upon his return at night. He became the god of doorways, and was generally represented as a keeper with two bearded faces, back to back, looking in opposite directions, a key and a staff or scepter in his hands. He was the god of beginnings and was saluted at the break of day, at the beginning of each month, at birth, etc. His temple doors were open in time of war and closed when peace was declared. In late times, he was represented with one face bearded and one shaven, carrying, instead of key and staff, the number 300 (Roman *CCC*) in one hand and in the other the remaining days of the year. His feast, The Agonalia, was celebrated January 9.

Jason (jā'son)   In Greek legend, the son of King Aeson of Thessaly, brought up in secret by the centaur Chiron* because his uncle Pelias had seized the throne from his father. When Jason reached manhood, he returned to Thessaly to claim the kingdom. He arrived wearing only one sandal, having lost the other helping an old hag over a river (the goddess Hera* disguised). Pelias had been cautioned to look out for a one-sandled man, but when Jason stated his case, he pretended he would gladly abdicate. He asked Jason to fetch the celebrated Golden Fleece* first, which was still in the distant kingdom of Aeëtes at Colchis. As the voyage was long and perilous and King Aeëtes hostile, Pelias hoped Jason would never return. Jason had the largest ship built, naming it *Argo* after its builder. Many heroes joined the expedition and became known as Argonauts*. After they set sail, they had many adventures and finally reached Colchis. Jason found the fleece fastened to a sacred oak, guarded by an unsleeping dragon, and King Aeëtes unwilling to part with it. The goddess Athena* and the goddess Aphrodite then came to Jason's aid, and caused Medea*, the daughter of King Aeëtes, to fall so passionately in love with Jason, she decided to betray her father. As a sorceress, skilled in magic, Medea charmed the dragon to sleep, and Jason took the fleece from the tree. Medea fled with Jason, taking her young brother Apsyrtus with her, and they all escaped on the ship *Argo*. When Aeëtes and the Colchians pursued them in another vessel, Medea cut her young brother in pieces and flung them into the sea, knowing her father would be stopped, collecting the fragments for burial. The journey home was beset by ills until they stopped at the island of the sorceress Circe* (aunt of Medea), and she purified them of the murder of Apsyrtus, sprinkling pig's blood on their hands. When the Colchians began to catch up with them, Jason quickly made Medea his wife, and so frustrated the Colchian's plan to take her back to her father. Finally they reached the kingdom of Pelias, and the Golden Fleece was taken to Orchomenus and hung in the temple of the god Zeus. Finding that Pelias had murdered Jason's younger brother, Medea, by magic means, did away with Pelias. Jason resigned from the throne in favor of the son of Pelias, and established his own kingdom in Corinth with King Creon. After ten years of marriage, Jason decided to abandon Medea for Creon's daughter Creusa (or Glauce). Medea, in fury, sent a magic robe to Creusa which burned her to ashes. She then killed her two children by Jason and fled in a winged chariot to Athens where she married Aegeus*, father of Theseus*. Jason, because of his faithless behavior, was forced into exile. He is said to have been killed by the keel of his old ship *Argo*, when lying under it on the Isthmus of Corinth. Painting: *Jason Winning the Golden Fleece*,

Jason claims his father's throne

Sent to fetch Golden Fleece

Medea falls in love with Jason and helps him

Escape with Fleece

Circe purifies them

Jason marries Medea

Medea does away with Pelias

Jason abandons Medea and her revenge

Death

on a redfigured Greek vase (5th century), Metropolitan, New York. (see Medea.)

Javelin   In Greek mythology, the javelin is an attribute of the goddess Artemis*, as the goddess of the hunt.

Jehovah or **Yahweh (Je-hō'va—ya'we)**   The name commonly used for God by the prophets in the Old Testament. Jehovah is the Anglicized form of Yahweh. The sacred tetragrammaton JHVH was too holy to use so the scribes added vowels, indicating that the reader was to say, "Adonai" ("my Lord") instead of JHVH. In the Renaissance, these vowels became part of the name itself.

Jericho (jer'i-kō)   A town of Palestine, five miles north of the Dead Sea, lying in fertile, subtropical country, 825 feet below the Mediterranean sea level. In the Old Testament it was the first Canaanite city taken by Joshua*, and was completely destroyed. It was also the site of Herod's great palace, built and burned in the time of Jesus (See Blind Beggar of Jericho under Jesus Christ—Miracles).

St. Jerome (jer'ōm)   (340-420) Jerome is considered to be one of the four Latin Fathers of the Western Church, the translator of the Old Testament into Latin, known as the Vulgate (common language). He was born of Christian parents in Dalmatia. In 374, he moved to Antioch, Syria, to pursue diversified, scholarly studies. Here, a vision of Christ, reproving him for reading pagan literature, caused him to flee to the desert where he lived as a hermit studying Hebrew. In 378, he returned to Antioch and was ordained a priest. Later he lived for a time in Rome but his critical attitude toward the clergy led him to return to Bethlehem where he established a monastery. He was greatly aided by the patronage of a rich lady and her daughter, later to become saints Eustochium and Paula*. It was here that he finished the Vulgate. Legend tells that while at the monastery a limping lion appeared. The monks fled, but Jerome examined the paw and removed a deeply imbedded thorn. The lion became tame, and was made keeper of the monastery's working ass. One day the lion slept and the ass was stolen by some passing merchants. The lion returned to the monastery alone and the monks thought he had eaten it. St. Jerome ordered him to take over the work of the ass to make amends. The lion obeyed but one day the merchants passed by again. The lion recognized the ass immediately, and with a roar brought the whole caravan into the monastery, proving his innocence. In art, Jerome is always accompanied by a lion. He is

St. Jerome in his study. Van Eyck and Petrus Christus. Courtesy of the Detroit Institute of Arts.

shown as an old man, sometimes in the red hat and robes of a cardinal, although they were unknown in his day. He is often shown in his study, also as a hermit in the desert, beating his breast with a stone, symbolizing mortification of the flesh. When shown with a crucifix, and a skull and an owl close by, the attributes symbolize solitude and his meditation upon eternal life after death. Feast day: September 30. Paintings: *St. Jerome in the Wilderness*, Paolo Veronese, Andrea Mantegna, and Pietro Perugino, National Gallery, Washington.

Jerusalem   The chief city of Palestine, 33 miles from the Mediterranean Sea and 15 miles from the Dead Sea, the Holy City of the Jews, and Christians, and later one of the Moslem holy cities too. In the Old Testament, King David* made it his capital. King Solomon* built the Hebrew Temple in Jerusalem, Thus making it a national shrine, and it was still the religious center in the time of Jesus. It was destroyed in warfare and rebuilt many times. See Jesus Christ—Life Events—Entry into Jerusalem.

Jesse (je′se)   In the Old Testament, the prosperous farmer with eight sons, whose youngest son David* was chosen by the prophet Samuel* to be the second Hebrew king and the successor of Saul*. As the progenitor of the religious house of David, the genealogical tree of the family is often shown in art, known as "the Tree of Jesse."

Jesus Christ   The Messiah who, through his teachings, created the Christian religion out of his Jewish background and upbringing. The primary sources for the life of Jesus come from the four Gospels of the New Testament, Matthew, Mark, Luke, and John. Jesus was the son of Mary* the Virgin, wife of Joseph*, a carpenter of Nazareth, Galilee. The Christian era is computed to begin with his birth. The Gospels relate that his birth in Bethlehem was a miraculous one, which was foretold to Mary by the angel Gabriel*. A tremendous star and angels guided shepherds and kings (magi*) to the manger where the baby was born, since there was no room for his mother at the inn. From his infancy until his baptism by his cousin John the Baptist*, nothing is told of Jesus save one incident of his being lost in the Temple of Jerusalem. Then he appears in the Gospels as a man of destiny, and from then until, according to the Gospel, the temple establishment had this successful rival crucified a few years later, he spoke and performed deeds which gathered followers to him. Of these followers, twelve were chosen disciples to carry on his cause. The heart of his teachings was, "The Kingdom of God is within you." He came to believe that this would not be understood unless he suffered death for the sins of man, from which

171

death he would be resurrected by God, a co-act of Father and Son in the drama of human redemption. As a baby and child, Jesus usually appears in art with his mother, often holding symbolic fruit, birds, etc.; always he is the symbol of Incarnation. The years of his ministry generally show him as a young man with flowing hair, parted in the middle, and a beard, the center figure of some event. In after-life, after his ascension*, he is shown as younger than God the Father, sitting on his right hand, judging the living and the dead. Christ may be symbolized as a lamb, "the lamb of God," holding a cross, sometimes as a fish in early Christian symbol, and sometimes as a lion. He is also shown as a fisherman of human souls, as the good shepherd of the flocks, as the teacher making the gesture of blessing, and as the suffering Christ. As the interceder for man against the wrath of God, he is seen showing the wounds of his crucifixion* (sometimes the Virgin Mary with him, showing the breast on which he suckled), and he is shown with his Sacred Heart flaming on his breast, or with rays emerging from an incision next to his heart.

His attributes are the cross, the stigmata (the five wounds from his crucifixion on the cross), a halo* that has a cross within the circle, or three rays of light symbolizing a halo, and a book, upon which is written an inscription. For letters symbolizing Christ, see Letters. The Events in Christ's life are listed alphabetically below, followed by the After-Life Events, which include his Apparitions and After-Life in Christian Belief. The Miracles and Parables are listed last.

LIFE EVENTS

Adoration of the Magi (Kings or Wisemen)   Three eminent men led by a star, journeyed from the East and brought gifts to the Christ Child in the manger (Matthew 2:1-12). Tradition calls them Melchior (king of light), Gaspar (the white one), and Balthazar (lord of treasures). Melchior offered gold, the emblem of royalty, Gaspar frankincense, in token of divinity, and Balthazar myrrh, in prophetic allusion to the persecution and death which awaited him. (Among ancient Medes and Persians, the magi were members of a priestly caste with occult powers.) Painting: *Adoration of the Shepherds*, Hieronymus Bosch, Philadelphia Museum of Art.

Adoration of the Shepherds   After the birth of the Christ Child, the angel Gabriel* appeared to shepherds in the countryside, watching their flocks at night in the fields. Gabriel disclosed to them the birth of the savior and they, greatly amazed, hastened to Bethlehem and "found Mary* and Joseph*, and the babe lying in a manger" (Luke 2:8-16). And they fell on their knees in awe before the child. Paintings: *The Adoration of the Magi*, Mantegna and El Greco, Metropolitan, New York.

Agony in the Garden   See Garden at Gethsemane, below. Painting: *Garden at Gethsemane*, Benvenuto di Giovanni, National Gallery, Washington.

Annunciation to the Shepherds   See Adoration of the Shepherds, above.

Baptism of Christ   About the age of thirty, Jesus came to Galilee from Jordan, and persuaded his cousin John the Baptist* that it was appropriate for him to follow the law's demands and, in all righteousness, baptize him. When Jesus rose from the water the Spirit of God descended on him like a dove, and a voice from heaven cried out, "This is my beloved Son, in whom I am well pleased" (Matthew 3:13-17; Mark 1:9-11; Luke 3:21-22). Paintings: *The Baptism of Christ*, Paris Bordone and Alessandro Magnasco, National Gallery, Washington.

Bearing the Cross   On the way to Golgotha* for his crucifixion, Christ for awhile bore his own cross (see Road to Golgotha, below).

Betrayal   As Jesus left the garden at Gethsemane, he was met by a band of officers, priests, and Pharisees*, accompanied by his disciple Judas Iscariot*. Judas drew near to kiss him and Jesus said, "Judas, betrayest thou the Son of man with a kiss?" And he said to the men assembled, "Whom seek ye?" and they said, "Jesus of Nazareth." Jesus answered, "I am he." Then Simon Peter, drawing his sword, smote off the right ear of Malchus, the priest's servant, and Jesus said, "Put up thy sword . . . they that take the sword shall perish with the sword." And Jesus touched the ear and it was healed. Then the captains and officers bound him and took him away (Luke 22:47-53; John 18:2-12). Scene: *The Betrayal*, on a 15th-Century enamel plaque, Metropolitan, New York.

Birth of Christ   See Nativity, below.

Blessing Little Children   Contrary to the wishes of the disciples who were trying to spare Jesus from the crowds, many children were brought to him that he might touch and bless them. Jesus said, "Suffer little children to come unto me and forbid them not: for of such is the kingdom of God"

173

(Matthew 19:13-15; Luke 18:15-16). Painting: *Christ Blessing the Children*, Pacecco de Rosa, Metropolitan, New York.

Burial   See Entombment, below.

The Calling of the Fishermen or Apostles   Jesus found Simon called Peter* and his brother Andrew* (and later James* and John*), mending their nets on the shores of the sea of Galilee. He called to these fishermen and they abandoned the nets and joined him, as disciples, to become fishers of men (Matthew 4:18-22; Mark 1:16-22; Luke 5:1-11). Painting: *The Calling of Andrew and Peter*, Ducio di Buoninsegna, National Gallery, Washington.

Calvary   See Crucifixion, and Road to Golgotha, below.

Christ Among the Doctors   (The Dispute in the Temple) At the age of twelve, the boy Jesus went to Jerusalem with his parents for the yearly Passover* pilgrimage. Jesus disappeared in the crowd and after three days' search, was found by Joseph* and Mary* in the Temple, sitting in the midst of the doctors (theologians), both listening and asking of them questions. Everyone that heard him was "astonished at his understanding and his answers." (Luke 2:41-50). Painting: *Christ Among the Doctors*, Bernaert Van Orley, National Gallery, Washington.

Circumcision   Eight days after the birth of Christ, the time came for circumcising the child, and he was named Jesus, which was the name given him by the angel Gabriel before his conception. Painting: *The Circumcision*, Rembrandt, National Gallery, Washington.

Cleansing of the Temple   Jesus entered Jerusalem on a Sunday. The next day, he went to the Temple and found merchants and money changers carrying on business within the Temple area. He made a scourge of small cords, overthrew the tables and seats, poured out the money, and drove away the men with their sheep, oxen, and doves crying, "My house shall be called the house of prayer: but ye have made it a den of thieves" (Matthew 21:12-13). Painting: *The Cleansing of the Temple*, El Greco, National Gallery, Washington.

Crowning with Thorns   When the Roman governor, Pontius Pilate, assented to the mob demand that Jesus be crucified, he had him flogged, as was the custom. The soldiers plaited a crown of thorns and put it on his head (see Salvator Mundi

174

Jesus Christ healing the sick. Rembrandt print. New York Public Library.

below), and they put on him a purple robe "... and they bowed the knee before him and mocked him saying, Hail, King of Jews!" Pilate said, "I bring him forth to you. Behold the man." In Latin, this is *Ecce Homo,* and the scene is often so titled in art (Matthew 27:26-29; Mark 15:16-20; John 19:1-5). Painting: *The Crowning with Thorns,* Antonetto da Messina, Metropolitan, New York.

Crucifixion　The events leading up to the Crucifixion are often called, and shown in art as, *The Passion of Christ,* meaning the suffering and death of Christ. They are:

Entry into Jerusalem
The Last Supper
The Washing of the Disciples Feet

The Agony in the Garden
The Betrayal
The Trial before the High Priests, Caiphas and Annas
The Denial of Peter
The Trial before Pilate
The Flagellation
The Mocking or Derobing of Christ
"Ecce Homo"
The Road to Golgotha (Calvary)

A predella with *The Passion of Our Lord*, Benvenuto di Giovanni, National Gallery, Washington; painting: *Christ and Symbols of the Passion*, Birmingham Museum of Art, Alabama.

The final events of the Crucifixion are often divided into fourteen scenes, and are known, and shown, as *The Stations of the Cross*. They are:

1. Jesus condemned to death
2. Jesus receiving his cross
3. Jesus falling with the cross
4. Jesus meets Mary, his mother
5. Simon of Cyrene helps carry the cross
6. Veronica wipes the face of Jesus
7. Jesus falls with the cross again
8. Jesus speaks to a woman of Jerusalem
9. Jesus falls a third time with the cross
10. Jesus is stripped of his garments
11. Jesus is nailed on the cross
12. Jesus dies on the cross
13. Jesus is taken down from the cross
14. Jesus is placed in the sepulcher

Jesus was crucified at a place called Calvary (Golgotha, in Hebrew), meaning "the place of the skull," between two thieves. When the soldiers had nailed him to the cross, they put a placard over his head on which was written, "Jesus of Nazareth, King of the Jews." Jesus said, "Father forgive them: for they know not what they do." Mary*, the mother of Jesus, and the disciple John* whom he loved, were beneath the cross and Jesus said to Mary, "Behold thy son," and to John, "Behold thy Mother," placing her in his care. From the sixth to the ninth hour, it grew dark. Jesus said. "I thirst," and at the ninth hour he cried, "My god, why hast thou forsaken me?" and someone put vinegar on a sponge and gave it to him to drink. At the end, Jesus cried out with a loud voice, "Father, into thy hands I commend my spirit," and gave up the ghost. Longinus*, the centurion, pierced his side; the sun was darkened and the veil of the Temple was rent in two, and Longinus cried, "Surely this man was the son of God." The crucifixion in art usually includes the figures of Mary, the mother of Christ, Mary Magdalene*, John the Evangelist, Mary Cleophas*, sometimes John* the Baptist, Salome*, the wife of Zebedee, and Longinus (Matthew 27:33-56; Mark 15:22-41; Luke 23:32-49; John 19:17-30).

The sequel events to the Crucifixion are:

The Deposition or Descent from the Cross
The Pietà
The Entombment

Paintings: *The Crucifixion*, Roger Van Der Weyden, Philadelphia Museum of Art; Fra Angelico, Fogg Art Museum, Cambridge, Mass.

Denial of Peter Jesus told the disciple Peter* that he would deny that he had any connection with him when put to the test. Peter protested but the denial occurred when Peter was standing in the forecourt of the high priest before whom Jesus was summoned. His first denial was to the maid servant at the door. Warming himself before the coals he denied it a second time. When a servent persisted again, he made a third denial, and immediately a cock crew. Then Peter remembered the words of Jesus, "Before the cock crow thou shalt deny me thrice." And he thought thereon and wept (Matthew 26:69-75; Mark 14:66-72; Luke 22:55-62; John 18:15-18, 25-27).

Deposition or Descent from the Cross After the crucifixion of Jesus, Joseph of Arimathea* went to the Roman governor, Pontius Pilate,* and asked for the body of Christ. Pilate gave him leave, and he took the body down from the cross in the presence of Mary*, the mother of Jesus, Mary Magdalene*, Mary*, mother of James the Less*, and Salome*, wife of Zebedee. With the help of Nicodemus*, who brought a mixture of myrrh and aloes, they wrapped the body with the spices in linen and laid it in a sepulcher. The three Marys are usually seen in the pictures of the Deposition. When Jesus lies on his mother's lap the scene is known as *the Pieta*. Painting: *The Descent from the Cross*, Rembrandt, National Gallery, Washington. (Matthew 27:57-60; Mark 15:42-47; Luke 23: 50-55; John 19:38-42).

Derobing of Christ When the Roman governor Pontius Pilate had delivered Jesus to be crucified, he was taken by a band of soldiers, "and they stripped him and put on him a scarlet robe. . . . and they spit up on him, and took the reed, and smote him on the head (Matthew 27:26-31).

Descent from the Cross   See Deposition, above.

Dispute in the Temple   See Christ among the Doctors.

Driving Money Changers from the Temple   See Cleansing of the Temple.

Ecce Homo   Latin for "Behold the Man." See Crowning with Thorns, above.

Entombment   After Joseph of Arimathea* had taken the body of Jesus down from the cross, and placed it in a new sepulcher, said to be his own, in the Gospel of Matthew (see Deposition, above), he closed the door with a great stone. He was accompanied by Mary Magdalene and Mary, the mother of James and Joses (Matthew 27:59-61; Mark 15:46-47; Luke 25:53-56; John 19:39-42). Painting: *The Entombment*, attributed to Fra Angelico, National Gallery, Washington.

Entry into Jerusalem   Shortly before the Passover, Jesus came to Jerusalem, riding a young ass (as had been foretold in the Old Testament), The people came out to meet him, carrying branches of palms, and they spread garments in the way crying, "Hosanna to the son of David." (Matthew 21:1-11; Mark 11:1-11; Luke 19:29-44; John 12:12-19). Scene: *The Entry into Jerusalem*, on an Italian ivory plaque (about A.D. 1000), Metropolitan, New York.

Flagellation of Christ   When the Roman governor Pontius Pilate* saw that the mob was determined to crucify Jesus, he scourged (whipped) him, as was the custom, and handed him over to the soldiers (Matthew 27:26; Mark 15:15). Painting: *The Flagellation of Christ*, of the Umbian School of Raphael, National Gallery, Washington.

Flight into Egypt   The sudden journey of Joseph*, Mary*, and the Christ Child from Bethlehem to Egypt, because of a dream which came to Joseph in which he was warned by the angel Gabriel* that King Herod* would seek to destroy the child. The scene is usually shown with Mary holding the baby, riding on an ass which is led by Joseph. The return from Egypt is also so depicted, Jesus now a larger child. Painting: *The Rest* *on the Flight into Egypt,* Gerard David, National Gallery, Washington.

Garden at Gethsemane   After the Last Supper (see below), with his disciples, Jesus went to a garden in a place called Gethsemane, with Peter, James, and John. He asked them to stay with him saying, "Pray that ye enter not into temptation," and he withdrew to one side in great agony, praying that this hour of anxiety might pass and that he would have the strength to meet the coming ordeal. When he returned, he found the three disciples asleep and he said, "Couldest not thou watch one hour?" And he went to pray a second and a third time, and always they slept. Then he woke them saying, "Rise up ... he that betrayeth me is at hand" (Matthew 26:36-46; Mark 14:32-42; Luke 22:39-46). Painting: *The Agony in the Garden,* Raphael, Metropolitan, New York.

Guarded Tomb   The Roman governor Pontius Pilate was persuaded by the priests to seal Christ's tomb and set a watch over it, lest the body be stolen, thus to prevent a disciple's claim that Christ had risen from the dead (Matthew 27:63-66).

Joseph's Dream of the Incarnation   When Joseph* was betrothed to Mary* of Nazareth, he found that she was with child. He did not break the betrothal, because he had a dream in which the angel Gabriel* appeared to him and disclosed that the child was conceived of the Holy Ghost* and that, according to prophecy, he was to name the child Jesus (Matthew 1:18-25).

Journey of the Magi   When Jesus was born in Bethlehem, there came magi (wise men—kings) from the East saying, "Where is he that is born King of the Jews? for we have seen his star in the East and are come to worship him." Herod, king of Jerusalem, hearing this, was troubled, but he pretended that he too would worship the child, and sent the magi on to Bethlehem. The star of the East went before them and stood over the place where the young child lay (Matthew 2:1-9). Painting: *Journey of the Magi,* Sasetta, Metropolitan New York.

Last Supper or Lord's Supper   Jesus observed the ceremony of the Passover* supper with his twelve disciples. As they were eating he said that one among them would betray him. They all asked, even the disciple lying on his breast whom he loved most, "Is it I?" In the Gospel of St. Mark, Jesus answers Judas

179

Iscariot, "Thou hast said." In the other Gospels, he says that it is one of the twelve dipping his hand in the dish of food with him, after which he gives a sop of bread to Judas. Then he broke the bread and blessed it, saying, "Eat, this is my body." And he took a cup of wine, saying, "Drink, for this is the blood of the New Testament which is shed for many for the remission of sins." The ceremony is incorporated in the Holy Communion service of the Christian church, known as the Eucharist (Matthew 26:20-29; Mark 14:17-25; Luke 22:14-39; John 13:21-30). Painting: *The Last Supper*, Philippe de Champaigne, Detroit Institute of Fine Arts.

Marriage at Cana   See under Miracles, below.

Massacre of the Innocents   When the magi (see Journey of the Magi and Adoration of the Magi, above) did not report to Herod* the whereabouts of the child Jesus, he saw that he was "mocked of the wise men." He was "exceeding wroth, and sent forth and slew all the children in Bethlehem, and all the coasts thereof, from two years and under." (Matthew 2:16)

Nativity   When the emperor Caesar Augustus put a tax on all the people of the Roman Empire, Joseph* took Mary, his spouse, and went from Nazareth to Bethlehem to pay the tax. While they were there, "she brought forth her firstborn son, and wrapped him in swaddling clothes, and laid him in a manger: because there was no room for them in the inn" (Luke 2:1-7). Painting: *The Nativity*, Fra Angelico, Metropolitan, New York.

Passion of Christ   See Crucifixion, above.

Pietà   See Deposition, above.

Presentation in the Temple   Following the religious laws of Moses, the baby Jesus was presented to the Lord in the Temple at Jerusalem. The ceremony included the sacrifice of two turtle doves or young pigeons. During the ceremony, an old man called Simeon* experienced the revelation of the personage of Christ, and taking the baby in his arms, blessed him. Anna*, an ancient prophetess, joined with him in giving thanks (Luke 2:22-38). Painting: *The Presentation in the Temple*, Giovanni di Paolo, Metropolitan, New York.

Return from Egypt   See Flight into Egypt, above.

Road to Calvary   See Road to Golgotha.

Road to Emmaus   See Emmaus under Apparitions, below.

Road to Golgotha or Calvary   When the soldiers took Christ, bearing his own cross, to be crucified, they caught hold of a man of Cyrene named Simon, and they forced him to carry the cross also. When they came to Golgotha, they gave Jesus vinegar, mixed with myrrh, which he would not drink (Matthew 27:32-34; Mark 15:21-23; Luke 23:26-27; John 19:17). Flemish painting: *Christ Bearing His Cross*, Metropolitan, New York.

Salvator Mundi   Latin words for Saviour of the World, used as a title for paintings of Christ crowned with thorns. (See Crowning With Thorns, above.)

Sermon on the Mount   This sermon was delivered by Jesus to the disciples, within the hearing of the "multitudes." It dealt with the ideal life of the real disciple. The Beatitudes*, the "Golden Rule," and the Lord's Prayer are part of the sermon (Matthew 5:1—7:29; Luke 6:20-38).

Stations of the Cross   See Crucifixion, above.

Supper at Bethany   Six days before the Passover, Jesus was at supper with Lazarus* whom he had saved from the dead (see Miracles below) and his sisters, Martha* and Mary*. Martha served the meal. Mary took a pound of ointment and anointed the feet of Jesus, wiping them with her hair. Judas Iscariot was present and complained that the ointment, worth 300 pence, should have been sold for the poor. Jesus replied, "Let her alone. . . . for the poor always ye have with you; but me ye have not always" (John 12:1-8). The story is told also in Luke of an unknown, sinful woman who anointed the feet of Jesus at the house of the Pharisee Simon. This woman came to be regarded as Mary Magdalene* (Luke 7:37-39).

Supper in the House of Levi   Jesus was eating at the house of Levi, and many tax collectors (publicans) and sinners came and sat at the table with him. The scribes and Pharisees asked him why he sat with people of such ill repute. Jesus replied, "I came not to call the righteous, but sinners to repentance" (Mark 2:17).

Supper in the House of Simon   This is another version of the Supper at Bethany, and is laid in the house of Simon the Leper. A woman came with an alabaster box of ointment, broke the box, and poured the ointment over the head of

Jesus. Indignation is expressed, since the ointment could have been sold for the benefit of the poor. Jesus reprimanded the critical people as he did at Bethany (Mark 14:3-9). See also Debtors under Parables, below.

Taking of Christ   See Betrayal, above.

Temptation in the Wilderness   After Jesus was baptized by John the Baptist, he departed into the wilderness where he fasted for forty days and nights. During this period, he was tested by God in the person of Satan who tried him with every kind of temptation, hoping to spoil his personality at the beginning of his mission. Satan commanded him to perform a miracle and turn a desert stone into bread; he tried to persuade him to hurl himself from the pinnacle of a temple; he offered him the world in exchange for homage to himself. Jesus cried, "Get thee hence, Satan," and the devil left, and angels came to help him (Matthew 4:1-11; Mark 1:12-13, Luke 4:1-12). Painting: *The Temptation of Christ*, Duccio, Frick Gallery, New York.

Three Marys at the Tomb   See Apparitions, below.

Transfiguration   Six days after Christ had told his disciples about his imminent death and resurrection, he took the disciples Peter*, James*, and his brother John* onto a high mountain. There he was transformed before them; his face shone "as the sun, and his raiment was white as light," and they saw the Old Testament leader Moses* and the prophet Elijah* talking with Jesus. (In the Gospel of Luke, the disciples are overcome for awhile by sleep.) A heavy cloud appeared and a voice was heard saying, "This is my beloved son; hear ye him." And the disciples looked again and saw no man save Jesus (Matthew 17:1-8; Mark 9:2-8; Luke 9:28-36).

Trial before the High Priests Annas and Caiphas   When Jesus was arrested by the soldiers, he was taken before the priest Annas to whom he said, "Why question me? Ask them which have heard me." Then one of the officers struck him. When he came before the priest Caiphas, he was asked if he were the son of God. Jesus answered, ". . . hereafter shall ye see the Son of Man sitting on the right hand of power and coming in the clouds of heaven." Then they condemned him to death (Matthew 26:57-67; Mark 14:53-65; Luke 22:66-71; John 18:13-28).

Trial before Pontius Pilate   When the accusing multitude brought Jesus before the Roman governor Pontius Pilate, Pilate asked, "Art thou the King of the Jews?" Jesus answered, "Thou sayest it." Then Pilate said, "I find no fault with this man." According to custom at Passover, one prisoner was released to the people. Pilate offered to release Jesus, for he knew the priests had condemned him out of envy. But the priests aroused the people and they clamored for the prisoner Barabbas instead. "What will ye I do?" Pilate asked. "Crucify him," they cried. Then Pilate took water, washed his hands before the multitude, and said, "I am innocent of the blood of this just person, see ye to it. I find no fault in him" (Matthew 27:15-24). Painting: *Pilate Washing his Hands*, Rembrandt, Metropolitan, New York.

Tribute Money or the Half-Shekel Tax   The tax collectors came to Jesus and his disciples at Capernum, asking for tribute. Jesus pointed out to his disciple Peter* that rulers do not take money from their own children, but he did not wish to anger the tax collectors so he sent Peter to catch a fish, telling him that he would find the money in its mouth (Matthew 17:24-27).

Washing of the Disciples Feet   Jesus washed the feet of his disciples at the Last Supper, to show them that "the servant is not greater than the lord; neither is he that is sent greater than he that sent him" (John 13:1-20).

Woman Taken in Adultery   The Pharisees* tried to trap Jesus into making false pronouncements. They brought an adulterous woman before him and asked him whether she should not be stoned, this being the law of Moses*. Jesus said, "He that is without sin among you, let him cast the first stone." The Pharisees and scribes drifted quietly away. Jesus turned to the woman, asking, "Hath no man condemned thee?" She answered, "No man, Lord." Jesus said, "Neither do I condemn thee: go, sin no more" (John 8:3-11).

Woman of Samaria   Jesus was in the city of Samaria near a well. He asked a local woman to draw him some water. She said, "How is it that, being a Jew, you ask me, a woman of Samaria, to draw you water?" Jesus answered, "If you had asked it of me, I would have given you living water and you would never thirst again." And as he spoke more with her, the woman realized that he was the Messiah Christ, and she went and gathered the people from the city. Jesus stayed two days with them and converted many to belief in him. Painting: *Christ and the Woman of Samaria*, Rembrandt, Metropolitan, New York (John 4:5-42).

AFTER-LIFE EVENTS—APPARITIONS AFTER THE EN-TOMBMENT

Ascension Christ, after appearing to his disciples in Jerusalem, led them to Bethany. Here he lifted up his hands and blessed them and "was parted from them and carried up to heaven" (Luke 24:50-51). In the Acts of the Apostles (1:2-12), Jesus showed himself to the apostles during forty days. They were gathered on Mt. Olivet when "they beheld, he was taken up; and a cloud received him out of their sight. . . . behold, two men stood by them in white apparel;" and they said, "This same Jesus, which is taken up from you into heaven, shall so come in like manner as ye have seen him go into heaven." Painting: *The Ascension*, Perugino, Metropolitan, New York.

Doubting Thomas When Christ appeared to his disciples at Jerusalem, Thomas* was not with the eleven. When they told him that they had seen the Lord, Thomas did not believe them. Eight days later, Christ appeared to them, and said to Thomas, "Reach hither thy finger, and behold my hand; and reach hither thy hand and thrust it into my side: and be not faithless but believing." And Thomas answered, "My Lord, my God" (John 20:24-29). Legend continues the doubting role of Thomas in the story of the Virgin Mary's Assumption. Rhemish ivory plaque: (12th century) *Doubting Thomas*, Metropolitan, New York.

Emmaus On the Sunday afternoon after the Crucifixion, Cleophas and another disciple were walking from Jerusalem to Emmaus. On the road, they met the risen Christ, whom they did not recognize. As they continued on the walk together, they related to Jesus his own crucifixion and his disappearance from the tomb. Jesus did not reveal his identity until they reached Emmaus and sat over a meal together. Then he broke and blessed the bread and they realized who he was (Luke 24:13-32). Painting: *The Supper at Emmaus*, Diego Velasquez, Metropolitan, New York.

At Jerusalem In the late afternoon on the Sunday after the Crucifixion, Jesus appeared to his disciples in Jerusalem, and they were terrified. He showed them his wounded hands, feet, and side so that they would believe it was truly he, and he ate fish and honey with them and "opened their understanding" (see Doubting Thomas, above).

To Mary Magdalene at the Tomb   Early in the morning on the Sunday after the Crucifixion, Mary Magdalene* went to Christ's tomb and found it open and empty. She ran quickly to the disciples Peter* and John*, and told them what had happened, and they came to the tomb to see for themselves. Mary remained at the tomb alone, weeping, and two angels within the sepulcher asked her why she wept. She turned away and thought she saw a man who was the gardener, but when he said her name, she recognized him and answered, "Master." Jesus said, "Touch me not: for I am not yet ascended to my Father" (John 20:1-17). This scene is often shown with the Latin title, *Nole Me Tangere.*

The Marys at the Tomb   On the Sunday after the crucifixion of Jesus, Mary Magdalene and Mary Cleophas (sometimes Mary Salome and Joanna are named) brought spices to the tomb, with which to anoint the body of Jesus, and they found the stone of the sepulcher rolled away. (In the Gospel of St. Matthew, an earthquake causes an angel to come before them and roll the stone away.) A young man clothed in white stood in the sepulcher, who said, "Fear ye not, . . . he is not here; for he is risen, as he said; . . . tell his disciples and Peter that he goeth before you into Galilee." In the Gospel of St. Luke, there are two angels in this scene (Matthew 28:1-8; Mark 16:1-8; Luke 24:1-12).

On the Mountain in Galilee   Jesus appeared to eleven of the disciples in Galilee, and told them to teach his doctrine to all nations. (Matthew 28:11-20). Painting: *The Apparition of Christ*, Bramantino, National Gallery, Washington.

Nole Me Tangere   See Mary Magdalene at the Tomb, above.

The Sea of Tiberias   Jesus, unrecognized, appeared to Peter*, Thomas*, Nathaniel*, James*, John*, and two others by the Sea of Tiberias. They were fishing, and he encouraged them to cast their net. When it became so full of fish they could not pull it out of the water, John realized who he was. Then they all gathered over a fire on the shore and broke bread together, and Jesus tested their understanding as he talked to them (John 21:1-23). In art, this scene is easily confused with the miracle of Christ walking on the Sea of Galilee. See Miracles, below.

The Deposition, with the veil of St. Veronica in the background. Aquatint from the Miserere series by Georges Rouault. Collection Museum of Modern Art.

Descent into Hell   According to Christian belief, Christ descended into hell after his resurrection, before ascending to heaven. Hell is vividly shown in art as a place crowded with human beings, sometimes under the feet of Christ, with the devil hovering on one side. Christ is a shining figure, carrying the banner of Resurrection, as a symbol of victory. Often Adam*, Eve*, David*, Moses*, and John* the Baptist are present.

Last Judgment   In Christian belief, this is the time when Christ shall return to judge the living and the dead, and sin will be followed by loss, and goodness will reap reward. In art, Christ is shown presiding on his throne of glory, angels above him; sometimes he bears the wounds of the crucifixion*. He may be shown dividing the nations, separating the sheep* from the goats*, or raising the elect to heaven and casting the damned down to hell. The Virgin Mary* and John the Baptist* are often shown on his right and left. St. Peter* stands nearby; the archangel Michael* balances good and evil on his scales. Sometimes heaven and hell are shown as separate pictures. Painting: *The Last Judgement*, Joos Van Cleve, Metropolitan, New York.

Resurrection   This is the Christian belief that Christ rose from the dead on the third day after his crucifixion. The great miracle is the proof of his divinity, commemorated on Easter Sunday. In art, Christ is shown in radiant garments, sometimes with the Resurrection banner of victory. His tomb is often seen behind him, guarded by sleeping soldiers. Painting: *The Resurrection*, Perugino, Metropolitan, New York.

MIRACLES
Miracles and parables are often shown as a series in art, particularly in early medieval art.

The Blind

BLIND BEGGAR OF JERICHO   Once when Jesus was surrounded by great crowds, a beggar called out to him to restore his sight saying, "Jesus, thou son of David, have mercy on me." The crowd told him to hold his peace, but Jesus commanded the blind man over to him. "Receive thy sight, thy faith hath saved thee," he said, and the man regained his vision. In the Gospel of Matthew, there are two beggars whose eyes are touched by Jesus, and sight is restored (Matthew 20:29-34; Mark 10:46-52; Luke 18:35-43).

BORN BLIND   Jesus healed this man by anointing his eyes with a clay mixture of his own spit with earth. Then he told the man to wash in the pool of Siloam. The man followed the directions and was cured (John 9:1-8).

Dead Restored to Life

JAIRUS' DAUGHTER   Jairus, a ruler of the synagogue, begged Jesus to restore his young daughter to life. Jesus went to the man's house which was surrounded by wailing people. Jesus said, "Weep not, she is sleeping," but they laughed, scornfully. So Jesus put everyone out of the house. He took the girl by the hand, just as she lay, and she rose to her feet and walked, and the unbelievers were amazed (Matthew 9:18, 23-25; Mark 5:22-24, 35-42; Luke 8:41-42, 49-56).

LAZARUS RAISED FROM THE DEAD   Lazarus, the brother of Mary* and Martha* of Bethany, fell ill and died. He lay four days in the grave, a cave with a stone over the opening. Mary and Martha sent for Jesus, and Martha went to meet him, believing he would help. Mary followed and they all went to the cave. Martha was fearful that Lazarus had been dead too long. Jesus chided her for lack of faith, and had the stone of the burial cave removed. He called to Lazarus in a loud voice to come out, and Lazarus came forth, bound still in his grave clothes but alive. (John 11:1-44). Painting: *The Raising of Lazarus*, Benozzo Gozzoli, National Gallery, Washington.

Decapolis Deaf Mute   Jesus passed along the shores of Decapolis, and they brought him a deaf mute, and besought his help. Jesus took him aside, put his fingers in his ears, and spit, and touched his tongue. He looked up to heaven and said, "Be opened," and the man regained his hearing and speech (Mark 7:31-37).

Devils (madness) Cast Out

CAPERNAUM MAN POSSESSED OF THE DEVIL   Jesus found a man in the synagogue of Capernaum, crazed with an unclean devil. It cried out, "What have we to do with Jesus of Nazareth? . . . Art thou come to destroy us?" Jesus rebuked and called out the devil, saying, "Hold thy peace and come out of him," and the man was made well (Luke 4:31-35).

DUMB MAN POSSESSED OF THE DEVIL "They brought to him a dumb man possessed with a devil. And when the devil was cast out, the dumb man spoke: and the multitude marvelled, saying, It was never so in Israel" (Matthew 9:32-33).

GADARENE DEMONIAC Jesus and the disciples were in the Gadarene country, and met a mad man called Legion, because of the many devils within him (described as two men in the Gospel of Matthew). Jesus transferred the unclean devils to a heard of swine, and the herd ran violently to a cliff and jumped off into the sea (Matthew 8:28-34; Mark 5:1-13; Luke 8:26-33).

MULTITUDES POSSESSED OF DEVILS AND SICKNESS "When the even was come, they brought many unto him that were possessed with devils: and he cast out the spirits with his words, . . . and he suffered not the devils to speak, because they knew him. And he laid hands on every one of them with diverse diseases, and healed them" (Matthew 8:16; Mark 1:32-34; Luke 4:40).

SYROPHOENICIAN WOMAN'S DAUGHTER A Greek Syrophoenician woman besought Jesus to cast the devil out of her daughter. Jesus said, "It is not meet to take the children's bread and cast it unto the dogs." She answered, "Yes, Lord, yet the dogs under the table eat the children's crumbs." Jesus said, "O woman, great is thy faith, be it unto thee as thou wilt." And when she came to her house, she found the devil gone out and her daughter laid upon her bed. (Matthew 15:22-28; Mark 7:25-30).

Dishonest Land Agent   *See Unjust Steward, below.*

Epileptic Boy Healed   A man brought Jesus his epileptic son, who fell on the ground before him wallowing and foaming. The man said, "Lord, have mercy on my son, for he is a lunatic and sore vexed, for oft times he falls into the fire and oft into the water." Jesus said, "If thou canst believe, all things are possible to him that believeth." The father answered with tears, "Lord, I believe, help thou mine unbelief." Then Jesus rebuked the foul spirit and healed the boy and delivered him again to his father (Matthew 17:14-18; Mark 9:17-29; Luke 9:38-43).

Galilee   See Sea of Galilee

Hemorrhaging Woman   A certain woman had been suffering

from a hemorrhage condition for twelve years, and the physicians had only made her worse. When she heard of Jesus, she came in the crowd to see him and touched his garment as he passed, and straightway was healed of this plague. Jesus immediately sensed the cure, and asked who had touched his clothes. The woman, in fear, fell down before him and told him the truth. Jesus said, "Thy faith hath made thee whole. Go in peace" (Matthew 9:20-23; Mark 5:25-34).

Loaves and Fishes　After the death of John the Baptist*, Jesus went into a desert place, and multitudes followed him. He preached into the evening, and the disciples suggested that he dismiss the people since there was nothing to eat but five loaves of bread and two fishes. Jesus sent for the food, ordered the people to sit down, blessed the fish and the bread which he broke, and gave these to his disciples. The multitudes were filled and twelve baskets of food remained and were collected (Matthew 14:13-21; Mark 6:35-44; Luke 9:11-17; John 6:1-13). This same miracle is repeated with seven loaves of bread and a few fishes in Matthew 15:32-39 and Mark 8:1-9.

Marriage at Cana　There was a wedding in Cana, and Jesus and his mother Mary* and the disciples attended the wedding feast. When the guests called for more wine, Mary said to Jesus, "They have no wine." Jesus rebuked her, and Mary told the servants to do anything he asked. Jesus instructed them to fill the water jugs to the brim and take them to the governor. When the governor tasted the wine out of the jug, he called the bridegroom saying, "Most people serve the good wine first while the guests are still sober, but you have kept the best wine until now." This was the first miracle performed by Jesus. Painting: *Marriage at Cana*, Master of the Retable of the Reyes Catolicos, National Gallery, Washington (John 2:1-11).

Mother-in-law of Simon Called Peter　Jesus came into Peter's* house and saw his wife's mother sick with a fever. He touched her hand and the fever left her, and she rose and attended to them (Matthew 8:14-15; Mark 1:30-31; Luke 4:38-39).

Paralytic Sick with Palsy　A paralytic was brought to Jesus, and because the crowd was great, those carrying him climbed onto the house top, and let the man down on his couch through the roof tiling. Jesus seeing their faith said, "Son, thy sins are forgiven." Observing the skeptical scribes about him, he said to the paralytic, "Arise, and take thy bed and go into thine house." The paralytic arose, and the scribes were amazed and filled with fear (Matthew 9:1-8).

Sea of Galilee   After feeding the multitudes (see Loaves and Fishes, above), Jesus sent his disciples off in the ship to Capernaum. In the middle of the night, seeing them row with difficulty in the wind, Jesus walked across the water to join them. The disciples were terrified, but Jesus reassured them. Then Peter* tried to join him on the water, but he did not have faith, and started to sink. "Lord, save me," he cried, and Jesus gave him his hand, they came to the ship together, and the wind ceased (Matthew 14:25-33; Mark 6:45-56; John 6:15-24). Painting: *Christ at the Sea of Galilee*, Tintoretto, National Gallery, Washington.

Stilling the Tempest   Jesus was crossing the sea in a ship with his disciples. He had fallen asleep when a great storm arose and flooded the ship. The terrified disciples woke him saying, "Lord, save us, we perish!" Jesus asked them, "Why are ye fearful, O ye of little faith?" Then he rebuked the raging wind and water, and there was a great calm (Matthew 8:23-27; Luke 8:22-25; Mark 4:36-41). Painting: *Christ Stilling the Tempest*, Rembrandt, Gardner Museum, Boston.

Walking on the Sea of Galilee   See Sea of Galilee, above.

PARABLES
Jesus used parables as a means of challenging the minds of his casual listeners, hoping that as they pondered the story, they might see the spiritual message. More particularly, they disclosed the truth of his dogma to his inner circle of disciples. They are often confusing and remain challenging.

Barren Fig Tree (Luke 13:6-9)   A man had a fig tree which, for three years, bore no fruit. He ordered his gardener to cut it down. The gardener persuaded the owner that he should be allowed to fertilize the tree before destroying it, giving it another chance to bear fruit.

Candle Under a Bushel ((Matthew 5:15-16; Mark 4:21; Luke 8:16)   No man puts candles under bushel baskets or beds. He places them in candlesticks that they may give light to everyone in the house.

Debtors (Luke 7:36-50)   Christ was eating at the table of the Pharisee Simon. A sinful, weeping woman entered the place and washed his feet with her tears, and anointed them with

191

ointment. Simon was astonished that Jesus would let this type of woman near him. Jesus said; If a creditor was owed 500 pence by one man and 50 by another, and forgave both debtors equally, which of them would be most grateful to him. Simon replied, The one to whom he forgave the most. Jesus said, Just so. This woman gave me more than you have given me. She kissed and anointed my feet with great love. Her sins are many and forgiven, for she loves much. Those to whom little is forgiven, love little.

Drag Net (Matthew 13:47-48)   "The kingdom of heaven is like unto a net that was cast into the sea and gathered of every kind: which, when it was full, they drew to shore ... and gathered the good into vessels and cast the bad away."

Father and Sons (Matthew 21:28-32)   There was a man who had two sons whom he asked to work in his vineyard. the first son refused but afterward went to work. The second son acquiesced, but afterward did not work. Which did his father's will? Not the first, as you think, Jesus said to the questioning priests in the Temple. The harlots and the tax collectors understand righteousness better than you do. They believed in John the Baptist when he first appeared, but you priests did not repent and acknowledge him even afterward, when you knew he was a man of God.

Fig Tree (Matthew 24:32-33; Mark 13:28-30; Luke 21:29-30)   (See also Barren Fig Tree, above.) "Behold the fig tree and all the trees; when they shoot forth, ye see and know of your own selves that summer is night at hand. So ... when you see these things ... know ye that the kingdom of God is nigh at hand."

Friend at Midnight (Luke 11:5-8)   If a man goes to a friend at midnight and asks for bread, because he has nothing in his house to offer an unexpected guest, the friend may answer, "Leave me alone, I'm in bed with my children." He will rise, however, if the man is insistent, although he may not do so out of friendship.

Goats and Sheep   See Sheep.

Good Samaritan (Luke 10:30-37)   A man was robbed near Jericho, stripped of his clothes, and left half dead. A passing priest crossed to the other side of the road; a Levite also looked at him and passed on, but a Samaritan traveller stopped, bound up his wounds, put him on his own horse, and brought him to an inn where he cared for him. On the following day, he left money with the innkeeper to give the man further care. Painting: *The Good Samaritan*, Domenico Fetti, Metropolitan, New York.

Great Supper   See Marriage of King's Son.

Growth of Seed (Mark 4:26-29)   When a man plants a seed in the ground, it springs up and produces fruit which the man can reap, yet its growth is a mystery beyond his understanding.

Hidden Treasure (Matthew 13:44)   The kingdom of heaven is like some hidden treasure in a field, "the which when a man hath found, he hideth, and for joy thereof goeth and selleth all that he hath and buyeth that field."

House Built on Rock and Sand (Matthew 7:24-25; Luke 6:48-49)   Whosoever builds his life on the teaching of Christ is like a wise man who lays the foundations of his house on rock instead of sand; for this house cannot be shaken by rain, floods, or winds.

Household Watching (Mark 13:34-36; Luke 12:35-40)   The Christ is like a man who, when he leaves home, commands his servants to watch for his return at all times; for he might come suddenly when the household is asleep, even as a thief might break into an unguarded house.

Importunate Widow (Luke 18:1-8)   A widow, in trouble, sought help from a selfish, ungodly judge who would not bother with her case. The woman pleaded with him continuously and finally the judge gave in, that he might rid himself of her.

Laborers in the Vineyard (Matthew 20:1-17)   A landowner hired laborers in the marketplace to work at a penny a day. He continued throughout the entire day to hire idle men, assuring them that he would pay what was right. In the evening, the laborers came for their wages and every man received a penny. Those who had worked all day protested, seeing that those who had worked only one hour, received the same recompense as themselves. The landowner replied that he paid them what he had agreed to pay, and that he chose to pay the last ones hired the same amount. "So the last shall be first and the first last: for many are called but few are chosen."

Leaven (Matthew 13:33-34; Luke 13:20-21) "The kingdom of heaven is like unto leaven (yeast) which a woman took and hid in three measures of meal until the whole leavened."

Lost Piece of Money (Luke 15:8-10) If a woman had ten silver coins and should lose one, wouldn't she search the whole house to find it? And when she found it, wouldn't she call in her neighbors to rejoice with her?

Lost Sheep See Sheep.

Marriage of the King's Son (Matthew 22:1-14) A king was arranging for his son's wedding and prepared a marriage feast. He sent his servants out to summon the invited guests but they would not come. He sent his servants once more to explain that the feast was ready, but the invited guests gave excuses and even slew the servants. When the king heard of this, he sent forth his army and destroyed the murderers and burned their city. Then he said to the servants, "those who were invited were not worthy, go into the highways and find guests." So the servants went and collected as many people as they could find. When the king came in to see the guests, he found one who was not in wedding garments. He said, "Friend, why did you come in ordinary clothes?" The man had no reply, so the king had him bound hand and foot and cast into the darkness. ". . . there shall be weeping and gnashing of teeth. For many are called but few are chosen."

Master and Servant (Luke 17:7-10) If a servant has ploughed and has fed his master's cattle, the master does not thank him when he returns from the fields and offer him food. Rather the master will say, you may serve me my food and afterward you may eat. So each man should follow what he is ordered to do, knowing it is his duty.

Mustard Seed (Matthew 13:31-32; Mark 4:30-32; Luke 13:18-19) The kingdom of heaven is like a grain of the humble mustard seed which, if cast into a garden, will grow into a great tree so that birds may lodge in its branches.

New Cloth and Old Garments (Matthew 9:16; Mark 2:21, Luke 5:36) No one takes a piece from a new cloth to patch an old garment, for the piece which is taken to fill the hole ruins the new piece and does not match the old.

New Wine and Old Bottles (Matthew 9:17; Mark 2:22; Luke 5:37) Put new wine in old bottles and the bottles burst. Put new wine into new bottles and both are preserved.

Pearl of Great Price (Matthew 13:45-46)   "The kingdom of heaven is like unto a merchantman seeking goodly pearls: who, when he had found one pearl of great price, went and sold all he had and bought it."

Pharisee and Publican (Luke 18:9-14)   A Pharisee* and a publican (tax collector) were both worshipping in a temple. The Pharisee thanked God that he was such a righteous man, superior to others. The tax collector smote his breast declaring himself a sinner. Christ declared that the tax collector was the righteous one for, "he that exalteth himself shall be abased and he that humbleth himself shall be exalted."

Pounds or Talents (Matthew 25:14-29; Luke 19:12-27)   An austere and much disliked nobleman went into a far country to receive a kingdom. In his absence, he gave each of his servants a pound. When he returned he called his servants, wishing to know how they had profited by the money. The first said he had gained ten pounds. The nobleman commended him and said he would give him authority over ten cities. The second said he had gained five pounds, and to him the nobleman gave authority over five cities. The third said, "Here is your pound which I feared to spend and hid in a napkin, for you are a hard man and reap where you have not sown." The nobleman answered, "I will judge you by your own words. You should have put the money with the money exchangers and let me collect the interest." And he gave the third servant's pound to the first servant who had already made ten. Christ explained, "Unto everyone that hath shall be given . . . but from him that hath not shall be taken away."

Prodigal Son (Luke 15:11-32)   A man had two sons, the younger of which asked for his inheritance, so the father divided his living between the two. The younger son departed to a far country, and wasted his money in riotous living. A famine spread through the land and this son, hired out as a swineherd, barely survived. He thought of his father's well nourished servants, and repenting his folly returned home, declaring himself a sinner and an unworthy son. His father saw him coming a great way off, and ran and fell on his neck. He called to his servants to bring the best garment for his son and to kill the fatted calf. When the elder son saw the feast and merrymaking, he was angry and would not join in the welcome, protesting that he had never been given a feast to make merry with his friends. The father answered, "Son, thou art ever with me, and all that I have is thine. It was meet that we should make merry and be glad: for this thy brother was dead, and is alive again; was lost and is found." Painting: *Return of Prodigal Son*, Murillo, National Gallery, Washington.

Rich Fool (Luke 12:16-21)   A rich farmer had such successful crops he had no room to store them, and planned to pull down his barns and build bigger ones, thinking he could then rest easily for years. But God asked, For whom is he providing? This night this fool shall die; he lays treasures up for himself but not for God.

Rich Man (Dives) and Lazarus (Luke 16:19-31)   Lazarus, a beggar covered with sores, was laid before a rich man's door, hoping he would be fed some crumbs. He was ignored, died, and went to heaven. The rich man also died and went to hell. In hell's fire, he lifted up his eyes and saw Lazarus in Abraham's* bosom. He cried out to Abraham, asking that Lazarus cool his tongue with water. Abraham replied that he had done nothing for Lazarus on earth, and besides there was a great gulf between heaven and hell. The rich man begged Abraham to send Lazarus back to his kinsfolk on earth so that he might explain sin to them. Abraham replied that since his kinsfolk had been unable to hear the prophets, they would be unable to hear a dead man. (The rich man is sometimes given the name Dives.) Painting: *The Parable of Dives and Lazarus*, Domenico Fetti, National Gallery, Washington.

Servant Unmerciful   See Household Watching, above.

Sheep and Goats (Matthew 25:31-46)   When all the nations shall come before Christ in heaven, he will separate them as a shepherd separates the sheep from the goats: for those who have taken in the poor, the hungry, and the unfortunate have taken in the Christ, and are righteous and deserving of life eternal; but those who have turned their backs on the unfortunate shall go to everlasting punishment (see Last Judgement under After-Life in Christian Belief, above). Relief on a 4th-century sarcophagus: *Separating Sheep from Goats*, Metropolitan, New York.

Sheep Lost (Matthew 13:3-8; Mark 4:3-8; Luke 8:5-8)   If a man has a hundred sheep and one goes astray, he leaves the other ninety-nine and seeks the lost one. And if he finds it, "he rejoiceth more of that sheep than of the ninety-nine which went not astray."

Sower of Seeds (Matthew 13:3-8; Mark 4:3-8; Luke 8:5-8)   A sower scattered some seeds; some fell by the wayside, some on stony places, some among thorns, and some on good ground. The first was eaten by fowl, the second sprang up but were scorched by the sun, the third were choked by the thorns, and the fourth brought forth fruit a hundredfold.

Steward on Trial (Luke 12:42-48)   The steward whom the master finds serving in his absence as though he were there will be rewarded with further responsibility. The servant who takes advantage of his master's absence, eating and drinking, and beating the other servants, will be severely punished, for much is required of those to whom responsibility is given.

Steward Unjust (Luke 16:1-13)   A rich lord accused his steward of wasting his goods. The steward, at a loss, decided to put his lord's debtors in a position of indebtedness to him. So he called them and reduced their debts twenty to fifty percent. The lord, learning of this, commended the steward's astute act. It is right, Christ said of this parable, to make friends of even the unrighteous, in case you fail and need their help. "He that is faithful in that which is least is faithful also in much: and he that is unjust in the least is unjust also in much. . . . No servant can serve two masters: for either he will hate the one, and love the other; or else he will hold to the one, and despise the other. Ye cannot serve God and mammon [material wealth]."

Talents   See Pounds.

Tares (Matthew 13:24-30)   A man sowed good seed in his field, but his enemy came at night and sowed tares (weeds) among the wheat. As the wheat ripened, the tares also sprang up, and the servants reported this to their master and asked if they should pull out the tares. The master was afraid the wheat would be uprooted so he said, Let them grow together, and at harvest pull the tares and burn them and gather wheat for my barn.

Vineyard and Husbandman (Matthew 21:33-41; Mark 12:1-9)   A man planted a vineyard, built a wine vat and a watchtower, and leased it to a husbandman (farmer). When it came time for the harvest, he sent a servant to collect the fruit. The farmer beat the servant and sent him away. The owner sent a second and a third servant, each of whom was also beaten. Then the man sent his own son, thinking the farmer would have respect for him; but the farmer killed the son, believing he could gain his inheritance. So the owner's only recourse was to come and destroy the farmer, and give the vineyard to another who would render him the fruit in season.

Wine   See New Wine, above.

Wise and Foolish Virgins (Matthew 25:1-13)   The kingdom of heaven is like ten maidens who took their lamps to bed with them while waiting for the bridegroom. The five wise ones filled their lamps with oil; the foolish ones took no oil with them. At midnight, the bridegroom arrived. The maidens rose and trimmed their lamps. Then the foolish ones, as their lamps started to go out, begged oil from the wise ones. The wise ones had no oil to spare, and sent the others to get oil for themselves. When the bridegroom came, they went in with him to the marriage and shut the door. When the foolish maidens arrived at the door, asking to be let in, the lord answered that he knew them not. Painting: *The Wise and Foolish Virgins*, William Blake, Metropolitan, New York.

Jethro (jeth′rō)   A Midian shepherd-priest to whom Moses* escaped from Egypt, after he had slain an Egyptian, and whose daughter Zipporah became Moses' wife. After forty years of service with Jethro near Mt. Horeb, Moses was summoned by God to lead the Hebrews out of Egypt from bondage.

Jezebel (jez′e-bel)   A princess from Tyre who became the wife of King Ahab* of Israel. She was a worshipper of the pagan gods Baal and Astarte, and she led Ahab and the Israelites into the gross immoralities of this religion. She brought hundreds of priests of this cult from her Phoenician homeland and persecuted the prophets of Israel's god, among them Elijah* whom she forced at one time to flee into the wilderness. When Naboth, a citizen of Jezreel, would not sell his vineyard which adjoined the property of King Ahab, Jezebel cleverly had him accused of blasphemy and stoned to death. Elijah prophesied she would have a horrible death, and when the conquering Jehu came to Jezreel, he had Jezebel thrown out of her house and trampled under the conquering rider's horses. When Jehu's men came to bury this king's daughter, they found she had been devoured beyond recognition by dogs, the death Elijah had foretold (2 Kings 9:30-37).

Joab (jō′ab)   King David's* nephew, a courageous and ruthless soldier who became commander of David's army. He carried out David's order to send Uriah* to his death in the front line of battle, making it possible for David to marry Uriah's wife Bathsheba*, whom he coveted. During Absalom's* rebellion, he remained loyal to David, trying to mediate between the two, but he finally killed Absalom when convinced of his treachery. In

David's old age, Joab supported the wrong claimant to the successorship. This later cost him his life.

Joab King of Israel See Elisha.

Joachim (jō'a-kim) Father of the Virgin Mary* and husband of Anne*, the Virgin's mother. He is generally represented in art as an old man carrying two turtle doves in a basket, in allusion to an offering made for the purification of his daughter. According to Apocryphal* writings, Joachim was a rich and devout man, but he was childless. Rebuked for offering gifts at the altar because "he had begotten no offspring for Israel," Joachim went into the desert to fast and pray, leaving his desolate wife behind. Angels appeared to him there, telling him to leave his solitude and rejoin his wife who had been divinely blessed. Anne waited for him at the gate of the city (Golden Gate) and when he came with his flocks, she hung on his neck and gave thanks to God. A 16th-century wooden relief: *St. Joachim & St. Anne*, Metropolitan, New York.

St. Joan of Arc (1412-1431) An illiterate and highly intelligent peasant girl from Domrémy, in Lorraine, France. At the age of thirteen, she experienced inner "voices," urging her to save France from the English and Burgundian aggressors. In 1429, she obtained an audience with the dauphin, whom she won over and persuaded to be crowned at Rheims. She was provided with a suit of armor, joined the army, and routed the English at Orleans, followed by victories at Patay and Troyes. In 1430, she went to relieve the beleaguered town of Compeigne. She was captured by the Burgundians and sold to the English. After nine months of brutal confinement, she was arraigned before the court on charges of witchcraft, and heresy*, found guilty, and burned in the marketplace of Rouen, less than twenty years old. In art, she is usually shown wearing armor, carrying a banner on which lies the French fleur de lys.

Job (jōb) Job is the subject of one of the great books of the Old Testament, whose theme is the problem of innocent suffering. It tells the story of a man, blameless before God and man alike, who lost everything but his integrity. He tries, through dialogue with God and three friends, to find God's meaning for his many troubles, and finally accepts the humbling revelation of God's interest in him, and finds a kind of peace.

Jocasta (jō-kas'ta) The wife of Laius*, king of Thebes and sister of Creon*. When her son Oedipus* was born, Laius had the baby's feet pierced and bound, and ordered him exposed on Mt. Cithaeron because an oracle had foretold that his son would slay him and marry his mother. His orders miscarried and Oedipus was brought up by Polybus in Corinth. When Oedipus was grown he killed his father, unaware of the relationship, and married the newly widowed Jocasta. She bore him two sons, Eteocles* and Polynices*, and two daughters, Antigone* and Ismene*. After many years, a terrible plague ravaged Thebes and the Oracle at Delphi* stated that the plague would not be lifted until the murderer of Laius was found. Hints arose that Oedipus might be the assassin; Jocasta reassured Oedipus, but the pieces of his story fell into place, a ghastly truth. When Jocasta realized that Oedipus was her son, the father of her children, and his father's murderer, she hanged herself.

St. John, Apostle and Evangelist   The youngest of the twelve apostles, known as the disciple "whom Jesus loved." He was the son of Zebedee*, a prosperous Galilean fisherman, and possibly Salome*, who may have been a sister of the Virgin Mary*. He was early called to follow Jesus while he and his brother James (the Great)* were mending nets. He is always mentioned among the first three disciples and was with Jesus at his Transfiguration*, and at the scene of his Agony in the Garden of Gethsemane*. At the Last Supper*, he is the disciple who leaned on the breast of Jesus. At the Crucifixion*, he alone was faithful and was entrusted with the care of the mother of Jesus. It was he who ran before Peter* on the morning of the Resurrection*, and seeing the tomb empty believed in the event; it was he who first recognized the risen Lord by the Sea of Tiberius (see Jesus Christ—Life Events and After-Life Events). John is said to have founded seven churches in Asia Minor and to have retired to Ephesus, where he endured persecution at the hand of the emperor Domitian. Legend says that the emperor ordered him to drink a cup of poisoned wine, but when John took the cup, the poison departed in the form of a snake. He was thrown into a cauldron of boiling oil, but emerged unhurt. In art, as apostle or evangelist, his principal attributes are the eagle, symbol of highest inspiration, and the book, although his authorship of the epistles and Gospel bearing his name is uncertain. He is also shown with the cup and the snake, or with the cauldron of oil. Sometimes he is symbolized by the eagle, together with the symbols of the three other evangelists*. Feast day: November 24.

John the Baptist   The son of the aged priest Zacharias* and Elisabeth*, and kin to Jesus*. His early religious training led him to lead an austere desert life, preparing himself for a ministry which made him the forerunner of the promised savior. The

Jordan river was the main scene for his distinctive baptism of immersion. Jesus insisted that his own baptism be performed by John as part of his messianic mission. John's career was cut short by Herod Antipas*, who brought about his arrest. John had publicly denounced Herod's marriage to his niece Herodias*, the divorced wife of his half-brother. When Salome*, the daughter of Herodias, danced for Herod, Herodias directed her to ask for the head of John the Baptist, as her promised gift. The executioner brought John's head on a platter and presented it to Salome, who gave it to her mother. When the disciples of Jesus heard of the execution, they came and took John and laid him in a tomb. In art, John the Baptist is often shown in desert garb of camel's hair, carrying a staff, or a crude, wooden cross with a pennant bearing the words, *Ecce Agnus Dei* (Behold the lamb of God). Sometimes he is holding a book on which a lamb is lying, or holds a lamb in his hand and has a banner or a reed cross. If he is seen with Christ in heaven, he wears more sumptuous clothes. He may be shown with a halo*; he is very frequently seen as a child with a lamb and a cross in scenes of the Holy Family*. His feast day is June 24. Paintings: *John the Baptist in the Desert*, Domenico Veneziano; *St. John (as a Child)*, Jacobo del Sellaio, both at National Gallery, Washington.

St. John Chrysostom   The greatest of the Greek Fathers of the Church. He was bishop of Constantinople from 398 until he was deposed in 403 by the empress Eudoxia and Bishop Theophilus of Alexandria, with whom he was in conflict because of his reform efforts. An opportune earthquake, combined with popular demand, forced his reinstatement, but he was soon exiled to the Black Sea where, in a weakened condition, he either died or was killed. He was the most eloquent preacher of the early church, hence his name Chrysostom, or Golden-mouthed. Legend makes him one of the saints who in babyhood, had a swarm of bees settle on his mouth, symbolizing honeyed words. Feast day: December 27.

St. John Climacus   This John was a monk who died at Mt. Sinai in 649, a famed holy man. His second name came from the Greek "ladder," because of the book he wrote, *Ladder to Paradise*, translated into English as *The Ladder of Divine Ascent*. It treats with the attainment of moral perfection, to be reached by the thirty "rungs" into which the book is divided. The ladder is frequently seen in Byzantine iconography, as the ladder of heaven.

St. John of the Cross (1542-1591)   A Spaniard born of good family, St. John of the Cross was one of the greatest mystics the church has ever known, who wrote from the depths of his own experience. He was the founder of the Reformed Carmelite Order with St. Theresa*, and labored outstandingly to spread reform. In 1557, he was imprisoned at Toledo by order of the prior general of the Carmelite order, and was subjected to brutal treatment. During this period, he started his mystical writings and his first poems. After nine months, he escaped, but when disagreement emerged in reformist ranks, John sided with the moderates. He was removed from office by the extremists and from then on was either ill or badly treated. He was canonized in 1726. Feast day: November 24.

Jonah (jō'na)   In the Old Testament, a minor prophet of Israel, best known, in the book of his name, for his adventure in the belly of a whale. The subject is a favorite in art. Jonah was sent on a mission by the Lord to reform wicked people in Nineveh. He was apprehensive about the task and sailed to Tarshish to avoid the undertaking. On the voyage, the Lord stirred up a terrible storm, and Jonah, confessing that it must be caused by the Lord's anger against him, consented to be thrown overboard. The Lord prepared a great fish to swallow Jonah, and Jonah, after praying in its belly for three days and nights, was vomited onto shore. Now he willingly went to Nineveh, convinced the inhabitants of their wickedness, and predicted that the city would be overthrown in forty days. The king and his people repented quickly, put on sackcloth and ashes, and God forgave Nineveh and removed the doom Jonah had foretold. Jonah was angry with the Lord for upsetting his prophecy but the Lord showed him that mercy was necessary. This he did by making a great gourd grow which shaded Jonah, sitting in the sun. Then he caused it to wither and pointed out to the angry Jonah that although he had not made the gourd grow or die, he had been sorry to lose it, and should show the same pity for the ignorant people of Nineveh.

Jonathan   In the Old Testament son of King Saul* who was not destined to succeed to the throne of Israel. A brave and able soldier, he is one of the most winning and modest characters of the Old Testament, worthy of the great friendship accorded him by David*. Even when aware that David would occupy the throne, it made no difference to this friendship, which is one of the greatest in history. He risked his father's anger to restore David to favor, and when King Saul suggested Jonathan kill David, he warned David to hide, using arrows in the open field as signal between them. The people loved him, his father trusted him, and constantly sought his advice. He met his death with his father and two brothers at Mt. Gilboa, in one of the battles against the Philistines, and his body was affixed to the walls of

202

Bethshan. His body was brought back by David and buried in the Sepulcher of Kish.

Jordan   The chief river of Palestine, and the boundary between East and West Palestine.

Joseph   A patriarch of the Old Testament, the son of Jacob* and Rachel*, born in their old age; a first child of the long-barren Rachel, who died giving birth to her second son Benjamin*. Joseph was much spoiled by his father, given a coat of many colors (a holiday garment), and allowed to roam and daydream. This caused resentment among his ten half-brothers, and they decided to kill him. But Reuben, the eldest, persuaded the others to throw him into a pit, and when Ishmaelite slavers went by on their way to Egypt, Joseph was pulled out and sold into slavery. In Egypt, he was bought by Potiphar*, the captain to the Pharaoh's* guard. Potiphar's wife made advances to the young man, and when he resisted them, she accused him, before Potiphar, of assault. Joseph was then thrown into prison, but he gained a reputation there for interpreting dreams. The Pharaoh* had been troubled by curious dreams: seven fat cattle ate seven lean cattle, seven good ears of corn were eaten by seven poor ones. Joseph was sent for. Listening to the Pharaoh, he predicted seven good years of harvest and seven years of famine, and having impressed the Pharaoh with his ability, he offered to manage the economy in the years ahead. The Pharaoh agreed and Joseph was successful. He set aside grain in the good years so that Egypt, when the famine came, was able to provide food for hungry neighbors as well as for her own population. The elderly Jacob, in Canaan, sent Joseph's half-brothers down to Egypt to buy corn. When they came to Joseph they failed to recognize the great administrator, although Joseph knew them. He was now married to an Egyptian, with children of his own, and had no hard feelings left toward his brothers. Still, he cleverly planned to get back at them and insisted that they bring his young brother Benjamin on their next trip to Egypt. When Benjamin turned up, Joseph gave the brothers a fine feast. He slyly concealed a cup in Benjamin's sack and then accused the brothers of theft. This gave him a dramatic opportunity to reveal his identity, accompanied by an emotional reunion. Soon after he sent for his incredulous, old father, and the whole clan came to settle in Egypt. Joseph died there at the age of 110. Painting: *Joseph Accused by Potiphar's Wife*, Rembrandt, National Gallery, Washington.

Joseph of Arimathea   In the New Testament, wealthy, pious Israelite, a member of the court of justice, who was a secret disciple of Jesus. He took no part in the condemnation of Jesus*, nor did he do anything to prevent it. At the Crucifixion*, perhaps shame for his neglect of duty gave way to courage, for he petitioned Pilate* for the body of Jesus, so that it could be buried before the Sabbath. Pilate granted the request. Near Calvary (Golgotha*), there was a newly hewn sepulcher, meant for Joseph's own use. Joseph provided a linen shroud, and in this Jesus was entombed. Joseph rolled a great stone across the entrance. This garden and tomb are supposed to have been discovered by St. Helena* early in A.D. 4th century and may be the present site for the Holy Sepulcher. Legend says that Joseph of Arimathea also collected some of Christ's blood in a chalice, and took it to England where it was guarded by knights on a mountain top. It was known as the Holy Grail*, and is the center of Arthurian legend. Joseph of Arimathea is in the painting of the *Pietà*, Fillipino Lippi, National Gallery, Washington.

St. Joseph of Nazareth The husband of the Virgin Mary*. Joseph was of the house of David, in Bethlehem, and had migrated to Nazareth where he followed the trade of carpenter. Tradition makes him much Mary's senior, a just, self-effacing man. In the Apocryphal* writings, he is supposed to be a widower, whose role is that of guardian, and the brothers of Jesus* are supposed to be his sons by a former marriage. His betrothal to Mary was supervised by the high priest Zacharias and guided by the Lord. Zacharias summoned Joseph and other widowers as suitors. Each man was asked to bring a rod, and when the Lord gave a sign, the bridegroom would be known. Joseph's rod blossomed, and a dove flew onto his head. The betrothal was consummated in a wedding performed by Zacharias. In the Gospels, Joseph is kindly and chivalrous when he discovers his betrothed is with child. He is aided by a dream in which an angel tells him there is nothing to fear, for Mary will bear a son, the Messiah who is to save the people from their sins, whom Joseph must call Jesus. Joseph therefore accepted Mary as his wife, and took her with him to Bethlehem for the census-taking, which saved her from slanderous gossip. After the birth at Bethlehem, he was warned from heaven by another dream: first to flee with Mary and the child to Egypt, in order to escape a massacre of young children by Herod the Great*, and afterward, when Herod was dead, to return to Israel. Joseph took Jesus when he was twelve to the Passover* at Jerusalem and searched faithfully for him when he disappeared. It is presumed that he died before Jesus began his ministry, which would explain why Jesus waited until his thirtieth year. As eldest son of the carpenter, if one does not follow the Apocryphal version which makes Christ's brothers sons of Joseph by his previous marriage, Jesus probably supported Mary and the younger children. In art,

Joseph is represented as an aged man with a budding rod in his hand, in reference to the betrothal story. He also has the attributes of a carpenter's saw, plane, and hatchet, and sometimes a lily. Feast day: March 19. Painting: *Joseph's Dream*, Andrea del Sarto, Metropolitan, New York; painting: *Marriage of the Virgin*, Bernart Van Orly, National Gallery, Washington.

Joshua (josh'ū-a)   In the Old Testament, the efficient soldier who succeeded Moses* in command of Israel. As soon as Moses had died, Joshua gave Israel three days to get ready for invasion. He sent out spies and moved camp up to the river Jordan. In one assault after another, he reduced the fortified towns on the opposite banks, the first of which was Jericho*. Guided by the Lord, Joshua marched his army around the walls for six days, bearing the Ark of the Covenant*. On the seventh day, they circled seven times, the priests blew their trumpets, and Joshua ordered the people to shout. As the shout went up, the walls fell down, and the army went in and took the city. Joshua apportioned the conquered area among his troops, asking little for himself. In another battle, as the enemy was escaping to the dark woods, Joshua ordered the sun to stand still, so that the fighting could continue in the daylight. When the enemy was destroyed, the sun continued on its course. Before his death, Joshua appealed to the Israelites to remain loyal to God.

Journey of the Magi   See Jesus Christ—Life Events.

Judas Iscariot   The disciple in the New Testament who betrayed Jesus. He was the son of Simon Iscariot, and probably came from Kerioth, not Galilee, like most of the disciples. As a stranger, he may have always felt he was an outsider among the others. It was his assignment to handle the financial problems of the busy disciples and if he had a worldly view of Christ's mission, he was probably disappointed that Jesus failed to usher in an earthly kingdom. He resented the rebuke of Jesus at Bethany when he criticized Mary* for wasting all her ointment on the feet of Jesus (see Jesus Christ—Life Events—Supper at Bethany). Judas reasoned that the ointment could have been sold for the benefit of the poor. At the Last Supper*, Jesus indicated to Judas that he was to be his betrayer, adding, "That thou doest, do quickly" (John 13:21-28). Whatever the reasons, Judas went to the chief priests and accepted thirty pieces of silver (the price of a slave) in return for revealing Christ's presence in the Garden of Gethsemane*. When Judas encountered Jesus, he betrayed him with a kiss. Judas may have believed that Jesus would save himself, but as the trial proceeded, he realized what he had brought about and tried to call off the plot by returning the money. When he was scoffed at by the priests and elders, he threw the silver on the Temple floor and went out and hanged himself with a rope. His attributes are a bag, as keeper of money, and a rope, the instrument of his hanging. Scene: *Betrayal of Christ* on a 15-century enamel plaque, Metropolitan, New York.

Judas Maccabeus In the Old Testament, the great Jewish military leader who led a resistance group of six thousand soldiers, known as the Maccabees, against the Seleucid king Antiochus. They took Jerusalem, and freed the city. The rebellion came about because Antiochus was trying to force Hellenic culture on the Jews, and in 168 B.C., he defiled the Temple at Jerusalem by sacrificing swine there to the god Zeus* on a Greek altar, erected over the Jewish one. After conquering Jerusalem, the Temple was purified and restored to the worship of Jehovah*.

Jude See Thadeus St.

Judgement Day or The Last Judgement In the Old Testament, the time when sin will be followed by loss, and penalty and goodness followed by promised reward. By the end of the second century B.C. this belief had acquired a highly developed angelology and demonology (fallen angels). The New Testament carries over much of the old, apocalyptic, colorful teaching, exemplified in the book of Revelation, making the Last Judgement the end of one age and the beginning of another. This world will come to an end, the dead will be raised in general resurrection, and Jesus will come in glory to judge the living and the dead. The sinners will be cast into hell, and the righteous shall live forever in heaven (see Jesus Christ—After-Life in Christian Belief). Painting: *The Last Judgement*, Herbert Van Eyck, Metropolitan, New York.

Judgement of Paris See Apple of Discord.

Judith The heroine of the Old Testament Apocryphal book of that name. King Nebuchadnezzar* of Babylon ordered his army captain Holofernes to invade Israel, because the Jews had not bowed to his commands. The Israelites prepared as best they could in citadels. Holofernes besieged the city of Bethulia by cutting off its water supply. Judith, a beautiful widow of this city, persuaded its governors to allow her to save the city in her own way. First she prayed to God clothed in sackcloth, with ashes on her head. Then she put on her finest raiment and went from the citadel to the camp of the Babylonians. She gained an audience with Holofernes by saying she knew how to take the city of Bethulia, and impressed him with her intelligence. For three days she visited the camp and was always welcomed. On the fourth evening, she attended a banquet at which Holofernes was overcome with wine. When Judith was alone with him in his tent, she grasped his sword and smote off his head. Then she concealed it in a bag she was accustomed to carry, quietly left the camp, and returned to Bethulia. The next morning the Babylonians were so dismayed and unorganized, they were easily defeated by the Israelites. In art, Judith is usually portrayed with the severed head of Holofernes in her hands. Painting: *Judith with the Head of Holofernes*, Andrea Mantegna, National Gallery, Washington.

St. Julian   The patron saint of travellers, minstrels, ferrymen, and hospitality. Legend tells that he was a huntsman and one day as he brought a stag to bay, it spoke to him and told him he would kill his parents. Fearful that the prophecy might come true, he fled to a foreign land where he married. Julian's parents, overcome with grief at his disappearance, set out in search of him and discovered his castle while he was away on a journey. His wife, however, received them with joy, and gave them her bed to rest in while she went to church. Julian returning unexpectedly, found what he thought was his wife and her lover in bed together. He drew his sword and slew them. In penitance, Julian and his wife founded a hospice for the poor near a dangerous river, where Julian became the ferryman. One stormy night he saw a leper freezing on the other side. He crossed the raging water and brought him to the hospice, placing him in his own bed. Soon the leper was transformed into an angel who told Julian that the Lord had accepted his repentance. In art, Julian is usually shown as a huntsman with a stag by his side; sometimes a river and a boat are shown in the background. Feast day: February 12.

Juno (jū'no)   In Roman mythology, the ox-eyed queen of heaven, the highest deity next to the god Jupiter*, identified with the Greek Hera*. As queen of womanhood, Juno was representative of women in general and every woman sacrificed to her and swore by her. As the foundress of marriage, she was the goddess of birth, and in Rome, pieces of gold were placed in her sanctuary at the birth of every male child. At her feast, the Matronalia, the goddess was represented veiled, with a flower in her right hand and an infant in swaddling clothes in her left. She was worshipped by the Sabines* as a war goddess, and when she is so represented she wears a goatskin mantle, bears a shield, and carries a spear, and like Minerva*, the goddess of war, is accompanied by a serpent. Domestic geese were sacred to her in her role as protectress of citadels. In the Aeneid*, Juno was the implacable enemy of Aeneas* because she feared the Trojans would destroy her favorite city Carthage. She also hated the Trojans because of the Judgement of Paris* (see Apple of Discord), and she resented

Ganymede* for taking the place of her daughter Hebe* on Mt. Olympus. Painting: *Juno and Selene**, Giovanni Battiste Tiepolo, Metropolitan, New York. (See Hera.)

Jupiter or **Jove (jū'pi-ter—jōve)**   The supreme deity of Roman mythology who became the representative of the pagan world in general, corresponding to the Greek god Zeus*. He was married to Juno and ruled with her over all. The central seat of his cult was the Capitoline Hill at Rome, where as god of state, he had the title of Optimus Maximus, and presided over festivals and games held in honor of him. He is predominantly a sky god, the bringer of light, and cause of day, as well as the full moon at night; he controls all weather, including lightning and thunder storms. He was worshipped with Juno at the commencement of harvest and honored as the giver of wine. He watches over justice and truth, and is the most important god of oaths. His prophecies were all carried out, and he saw to it that Aeneas* succeeded in founding the Latin race in Italy, erasing the Trojan name, so despised by Juno. The color white was sacred to him; hence white animals were offered in sacrifice to him. On the Ides of the month (the 13th and 15th), he was offered a white lamb. His priests wore white caps, his four chariot horses were white, the consuls wore white when sacrificing to him. In art, he was shown seated on a throne, holding a scepter in his left hand and thunderbolts in his right. Heated thunderbolts were thought to be discharged from thunderclouds by Jupiter. The eagle was sacred to him. His temple in Rome was filled with treasures from offerings. The last temple erected to him in A.D. 82 continued to stand until the ninth century. (See Zeus.)

St. Katherine of Alexandria   See Catherine of Alexandria.

Katherine of Siena   See Catherine of Siena.

Keys   In Christian iconography, they are a symbol for St. Peter*, as the guardian of the gate of heaven. Martha of Bethany* is often shown with keys, in her capacity as housekeeper. St. Genevieve* carries the keys of Paris.

Kings   See Magi.

Kitchen Utensils   An attribute of Martha of Bethany*.

Knife   In Christian iconography, a knife and a cross are attributes of St. Edward Martyr*, murdered at fifteen. The knife is also an emblem of the martyrdom of saints Peter Martyr* and Bartholomew*. St. Bartholomew sometimes has human skin over one arm, a reference to his being flayed alive.

Knights of the Round Table   The knights of Arthurian legend, the ideal of medieval knighthood and chivalry, who met around a circular table so that questions of precedence might not arise. King Arthur's court was at Camelot. He was an illegitimate son of King Uther Pendragon, and as a boy showed his royal blood by drawing a sword from a stone. The Lady of the Lake presented him his famous sword Excalibur. He was married to Queen Guinevere who was unfaithful to him in her love for Sir Launcelot, and it was through this love that a war resulted which disrupted the Round Table and caused the death of King Arthur. Launcelot was the father of Sir Galahad* by Elaine, the daughter of King Pelles. He represents fidelity, bravery, frailty in love, and repentance because he retired to a monastery. Sir Galahad represents chastity; Sir Gawain, who was Arthur's nephew, knightly courtesy; Sir Kay, rude boastfulness; and Sir Modred, treachery. The legends of Tristan and Isolde and Parsifal were developed in Germany. Mural paintings: *The Quest of the Holy Grail*, Edwin Austin Abbey, Public Library, Boston.

Knossos or Cnossos   In ancient geography, the capital of Crete and the site of the fabulous Minoan palaces.

Kore (ko're)   The word means maiden, and was the Attic cult name given to Persephone*, the daughter of Demeter*. (see Persephone.)

Kronus   See Cronus.

Labyrinth (lab'i-rinth)   A maze, a construction so complicated it is difficult to find one's way through it. The famous Cretan labyrinth, which had a thousand turnings, was built by Daedalus* for King Minos* who needed it to guard the Minotaur*, a monster which was the son of his wife Pasiphae* by the Cretan Bull*.

Ladder   In Christian iconography, a symbol of Christ's descent from the cross (see Deposition). It refers to Jacob's dream in the Old Testament, in which Jacob* sees a ladder reaching from heaven to earth, on which angels were ascending and descending (Genesis 28:12). It is also an attribute of St. Benedict* who had a vision of his Benedictine brethren ascending a ladder to heaven. The Ladder of Ascent symbolizes the perfection of virtures (see St. John Climacus).

Ladle   In Christian iconography, an attribute of Martha*, the housekeeper sister of Mary* and Lazarus*.

Lamb   In Christian iconography, the lamb is often a symbol of Christ*, manifesting purity. The lamb of God is shown with a halo (nimbus), standing on a hill, the hill being the mountain of God's church. From it flows four streams which symbolize the four Gospels. Sometimes the lamb represents the sinner whom Christ, the Good Shepherd, rescues. Young John the Baptist* points to a lamb, indicating his recognition of Christ as the Lamb of God, in scenes of the Holy Family*. The lamb is also an attribute of St. Joachim*, the father of the Virgin Mary, who was a shepherd, and of St. Clement* who was guided to water by a lamb. A lamb on a book is an attribute of St. Agnes* who was martyred because she declared herself to be the bride of Christ. It

211

is an attribute of St. Genevieve*, because she guarded her father's sheep, and is often shown with St. Francis*.

Lamp   In Christian iconography, a symbol of wisdom and piety. It is an attribute of St. Lucy* to whom St. Agatha* appeared in a vision saying, "Thou art a light."

Lance   In Greek mythology, the lance is an attribute of Athena*, as goddess of war. In Christian iconography, it is a symbol of the Passion* because the body of Christ was pierced by the Roman centurian Longinus*. It is an attribute of St. Thomas*, as a symbol of his martyrdom and is usually shown with St. George* of Cappadocia, who ran a dragon through with a lance.

Lantern   In Christian iconography, an attribute of St. Christopher*, as the patron of travellers. He is often shown carrying a lantern as he wades across a raging river.

Laius   In Greek legend, the husband of Jocasta* and father of Oedipus*.

Laocoon (lā-ok′ō-on)   In Greek mythology, Laocoon was a priest of the god Apollo* at Troy. He offended the god by marrying, and by profaning his image. At the end of the Trojan war*, when the Greek wooden horse was brought by night to the beach before Troy, Laocoon hurled his spear against it and warned his countrymen not to accept it. While he was sacrificing to the god Poseiden* for the Trojans because they had slain one of Poseiden's priests, Apollo took his revenge on Laocoon and sent a great serpent out of the sea. The serpent seized him and his two sons violently, and crushed them to death. The Trojans thought this was punishment for Laocoon's doubt about the horse. They hauled it into the city, and fell into the Greek trap. Painting: *Laocoon*, El Greco, National Gallery, Washington.

Lapithae or Lapiths (la′pi-thē or la′piths)   In Greek legend, a Thessalian, fully human tribe who were cousins of the centaurs, a wild tribe, half-men half-horse who inhabited the Thessalian mountains. King Pirithous* of the Lapithae*, on the occasion of his marriage to Hippodamia*, daughter of Adrastus*, invited the centaurs to the wedding feast. The centaurs became excited by the wine and attempted to carry off the bride and other women guests. A fierce fight ensued in which the Lapiths were finally victorious. The subject is a favorite in Greek art and exemplifies the triumph of civilization over barbarism. Theseus* is often shown as one of the guests fighting the centaurs. Scene: *Lapiths*

The Laocoon. El Greco. National Gallery of Art.

and Centaurs, on a red-figured Greek bowl (5th century B.C.), Metropolitan, New York.

Lash   In Christian iconography, an attribute of St. Ambrose in reference to his violent expulsion of Arians (heretics) from Italy.

Last Judgement   See Judgement Day.

Last Supper   See Jesus Christ—Life Events.

Latona   See Leto.

Sir Launcelot   See Knights of the Round Table.

Laurel   In Greek mythology, a symbol of expiation, sacred to the god Apollo*, commemorating his adventure with Daphne*.

Laurel was used to crown victors at the Delphic games, held in honor of Apollo. In Roman religion, laurel was consecrated to the Roman Vestal Virgins*. In Christian iconography, it is a symbol of eternity because it is an evergreen and does not wilt. It is also a symbol of triumph, associated with its use as an award in Classical times, and a symbol of virtue, because it was consecrated to the Vestal Virgins, in Rome.

St. Laurence   Fourth-century martyr, born at Huesca, Spain. Laurence, as a very young man, became deacon in Rome to Pope Sixtus I, and was put in charge of the treasure of the church. When Sixtus was condemned to death by the prefect of Rome for his religion, he instructed Laurence to distribute the wealth of the church to the poor. Laurence did this in three days. When the prefect asked for the church treasures, Laurence pointed to the sick and the poor around the church saying, "These are the treasures." The enraged prefect had Laurence roasted on a gridiron. In the midst of the torment, the defiant Laurence shouted, "I am roasted on one side, now turn me over and eat me!" St. Laurence is known as the courteous Spaniard, because it is said that 400 years after his burial at Rome, his tomb was opened to receive the body of St. Stephen*. St. Laurence moved to one side and offered his hand to St. Stephen. In art, Laurence is shown in the dress of a deacon, bearing a palm, the symbol of triumph over death, and often the gridiron, the instrument of his martyrdom. Sometimes he holds gold or treasures in allusion to his distribution of the church's wealth. Occasionally he is dressed in a tunic covered with flames, sometimes he carries a cross or a censor*. Painting: *St. Laurence Giving the Treasures of the Church to the Poor*, Bernardo Strozzi, Portland Art Museum, Oregon.

Lazarus (la'za-rus)   In the New Testament, the brother of the Martha* and Mary* who entertained Jesus at Bethany, just outside of Jerusalem. Lazarus was taken seriously ill and died. The sisters summoned Jesus but he could not come immediately. When he did arrive after four days, he used the situation to perform a great miracle, restoring Lazarus to life in the presence of many witnesses (John 11). See Jesus Christ—Miracles.

Leah (lē'ah)   In the Old Testament, the eldest daughter of Laban, married through trickery to Jacob* after he had served seven years for her younger sister Rachel*. Leah bore Jacob many sons and a daughter (Genesis 29). She was buried in the family cave at Hebron before Jacob, in his old age, joined Joseph* in Egypt.

Leander (lē-an'der)   See Hero.

Leda (lē'da)   In Greek mythology, the wife of Tyndareus of Sparta. The god Zeus* fell in love with her, transformed himself into a swan, and seduced her. Subsequently she bore an egg from which Helen* and Polydeuces* were born. By her husband, she bore Clytemnestra* and Castor*, who was always spoken of as the twin of Polydeuces. In another legend, there were two eggs, and Zeus fathered all four children. Statue: *Leda and the Swan*, Michel Anguier, Metropolitan, New York.

Leek   In Christian iconography, the leek is an attribute of St. David* of Wales.

Leg of a Horse   In Christian iconography, an attribute of St. Eloi*.

Leg Shorter than the Other   In Classical representation, the god Hephaestus* and Roman Vulcan* are shown with one leg shorter than the other, to indicate lameness.

Lemon   In Christian iconography, a lemon is a symbol of fidelity in love.

Leo I, the Great   Italian Pope from 440-461 and one of the greatest pontiffs of early times. He was not only a man of great ability but unswerving in religious duty, typifying the best in Roman character. He waged a firm campaign against schism and heresy*, and succeeded in gaining the authority of the pope over his bishops. He wrote the famous tome which defined the two natures and one person of Christ. He courageously went in person to Atilla the Hun, and persuaded him, for a consideration, to keep his invading army out of Rome. His feast day was April 11.

St. Leonard   According to legend, Leonard was a Frank at the court of King Clovis of France in the 6th century, who was converted to Christianity. He spent much time visiting prisoners, and persuaded King Clovis to give him permission to release those prisoners whom he visited. He lived at Limoges as a hermit, after establishing a monastery there, and died within its walls in 546. Many miracles were attributed to him, and as patron saint of prisoners, he was a popular saint with crusaders. He is represented in art holding chains and fetters in his hand, or with prisoners kneeling at his feet. Feast day: November 6.

Leopard   In Classical representation, the leopard skin was an attribute of the god Pan*. In Christian iconography, the leopard became a symbol of sin and the devil. Sometimes it indicates Christ's Incarnation*, an imperative that he rescue the world from sin.

Leto (lē'tō)   In Greek mythology, the mother, by the god Zeus*, of Apollo* and his twin sister Artemis*. When Zeus pursued her, he transformed both himself and Leto into quails before he embraced her. His wife, the goddess Hera*, wild with jealousy, sent a python to pursue Leto. She was saved and borne either by the south wind or a dolphin to the island of Ortygia, near Delos, where she bore the goddess Artemis. Artemis then helped Leto to Delos where she bore the god Apollo. Some legends say that Ortygia turned into Delos, and that both children were born there. Hera continued to pursue Leto and she was forced to leave Delos and take up a wandering life. Once when she was going by a lake, she tried to quench her thirst, but some peasants tried to prevent her by muddying the water. Leto, as a revenge, turned them into frogs. At last, Apollo killed the pursuing python, and Leto, as the mother of two Olympic gods, went to live on Mt. Olympus*. Artemis and Apollo were devoted children, and when Niobe* boasted that she and her many beautiful children should be worshipped, rather than Leto, they took instant revenge. Leto was worshipped in conjunction with Apollo and Artemis. Painting: *Leto Mounting her Chariot with Apollo Standing By*, on a black-figured Greek vase (6th century B.C.), Worcester Museum of Art, Massachusetts.

Letter in the Hand of a Prone Man   Representation of St. Alexis*.

Letters Symbolizing Jesus Christ

IC	These are the first letters of the name *J*esus *C*hrist, in Latin.
IHC and IHS	These letters stand for the first three letters of the name JESus, in Greek—IHCYC or IHSYS. The letter "C", normally not seen in Greek, is a variant of the letter sigma "S". Sometimes IHS represents the first letters of the Latin phrase *J*esus *H*ominum *S*alvator (Jesus Saviour of Men). They are an attribute of St. Ignatius Loyola*, and of St. Bernardino of Siena* who is often shown in art carrying the monogram, inscribed on a sun.
INRI	These are the first four Latin letters for *J*esus *N*azarenus *R*ex *J*udaeorum (Jesus of Nazareth, King of the Jews). This was the sign placed on the cross of Jesus when he was crucified by Pontius Pilate.
IR	These letters stand for *J*esus the *R*edeemer, in Latin.

IS These letters stand for *Jesus Salvator* (Saviour), in Latin.

IXθYC The Greek letters for "fish," read as an acrostic, for Jesus Christ, Son of God (see Icthus).

XC These letters stand for the first and last letters of the Greek word Χριστοσ (or Christos).

XP The Greek letters Chi and Rho are the first two letters of the Greek word ΧΡιστοσ. They are often made into a monogram.

NIKA This is the Greek word for victory and is often used in the monogram IC XC NIKA (see above for IC and XC).

Levi See Jesus Christ—Life Events—Supper at the House of Levi.

Leviathan (le-vī'a-than) In the Old Testament, the name given to a mystical, many-headed sea monster, capable of devouring on a large scale, or conversely, furnishing food for a large company.

Liber and Libera (li'ber and lib'er-a) In Roman mythology, the god and goddess of the vine, worshipped as fertility gods. Liber became identified with the Greek Dionysus*, Libera with Persephone*. Their festival was celebrated March 17.

Light Rays In Christian art, light rays symbolize the Holy Ghost*.

Lightning In Greek mythology, the god Zeus*, whose name means bright sky, was the maker of lightning, hence lightning is one of his attributes.

Lilith (lil'ith) A Semitic demon, probably Babylonian in origin, supposed to haunt children and pregnant women. In the Talmud (the book of Jewish law), Lilith is the name given to a wife that Adam* is fabled to have had before Eve*. Since she refused to submit to him, she left Paradise* for a region of the air, and still haunts the night.

Lily There is a tradition that the lily sprang from the repentant tears of Eve*, as she went forth from Paradise*. In Christian iconography, it is a symbol of immortality and of the purity of the Virgin Mary*. A lily surrounded by thorns is a symbol of the Immaculate Conception*, since Mary was conceived without original sin and bore the Christ child in like manner. The angel

217

Gabriel* is often shown with a lily in scenes of the Annunciation*, and it is one of his attributes. When shown with the infant Jesus* and with saints, it is a symbol of chastity, related to the idea of original sin* (see Fleur de Lys).

Lily of the Valley   In Christian iconography, the lily of the valley symbolizes the birth of Christ. It is also an attribute of the Virgin Mary*, derived from the Song of Solomon (2:1): "I am the rose of Sharon, and the lily of the valleys," referring to the dogma of the Immaculate Conception*.

Limbo   The half-way house between heaven and earth, where those righteous people, and unbaptized children who died before the coming of Christ, await the Last Day, when they will be received into heaven. It is sometimes conceived of as the "hell" into which Christ descended after his crucifixion*, before his ascent into heaven (see Judgement Day).

Lion   In Greek mythology, the lion is an attribute of the god Dionysus*, who became a lion in spring festivals, as one of his manifestations. It was sacred to Cybele*, as goddess of wild mountains. Cybele turned Atalanta* and Hippomenes* into lions, because they violated her temple, and then used them to draw her chariot. The lion skin was worn by Heracles*, which was the skin of either the Cithaerean lion which he killed with a club, or the Nemean lion*, which he strangled for his first labor for Eurystheus*. The lion skin is also worn by Theseus* and the hunter Orion*. In the Old Testament, the lion is the emblem of the tribe of Judah, and Christ is called the "lion of the tribe of Judah." The lion appears metaphorically in the New Testament, paired with the lamb*, forming a symbol of peace. Legend recounts that young lions are born dead, and come alive three days after birth when breathed on by their sire. They are therefore a symbol of resurrection* and the Christ. It is an attribute of St. Jerome*, who removed a painful thorn from a lion's paw, and it became his friend; also of St. Gerasimus* and Androcles*, who performed the same deed. It is an attribute of the desert saint Mary of Egypt*, of St. Euphemia*, of St. Paul the Hermit* who is said to have been buried by two lions, and of St. Ignatius*, in allusion to his martyrdom. The winged lion is an attribute of St. Mark* the Evangelist, proclaiming the resurrection* of Christ, and is an emblem of Venice.

Lizard   In Christian iconography, the lizard represents old age.

Loaves and Fishes   See Jesus Christ—Miracles.

Locusts Migratory grasshoppers which frequently plagued Egypt and Palestine in Biblical literature. In the Old Testament, they were sent to plague the Pharoah* who had hardened his heart against the Lord; hence, in Christian iconography, they symbolize both the plague and those who do not worship Christ.

St. Longinus The Roman centurion at the crucifixion of Christ (see Jesus Christ—Life Events), who is said to have pierced the side of Christ with his spear and who cried out at Christ's death, "Truly this man was the son of God" (Mark 15:39). Legend continues that he was subsequently baptized by the apostles, and that he converted many people. A blind Roman governor condemned him to death for his faith. Longinus, unshaken, told the governor that his sight would be restored after the governor had executed him. Longinus was beheaded, the governor's sight came back, and he too was converted. Longinus is frequently shown in pictures of the Crucifixion*, either afoot, with a lance in his hand, or on horseback, clad as a Roman soldier, holding his helmet in his hands. Painting: *Crucifixion with Longinus*, Lucas Cranach, the elder, National Gallery, Washington.

Lot In the Old Testament, the nephew of the patriarch Abraham* with whom he migrated to Haran from Ur in Mesopotamia, and then accompanied to and fro from Egypt, and like him, prospered. When Abraham decided that the two households should settle on separate land, Lot chose the fertile valley of Sodom, but the people in Sodom turned out to be wicked, *Sodom* sexual sinners. When King Chedorlaomer warred with the kings of Sodom and Gomorrah for rule over their lands, Lot was carried off as a prisoner, and Abraham had to fight Chedorlaomer to rescue him. Melchizedek, one of the rulers of Sodom, gratefully *Melchiz-* bestowed gifts on Abraham, in recognition for his help, but *edek* Abraham distributed the gifts among the soldiers. Lot, a good man, returned to Sodom to live. One night, two angels visited him *Angels'* and warned him to flee from the destruction God had planned for *visit* the evil city. The next day they forced him to leave with his wife and two daughters, forbidding them to look back when they heard the destruction. God rained fire and brimstone from heaven onto Sodom, Gomorrah, and the plains. Lot's wife, unable to *Lot's* resist the sound, looked back and was turned into a pillar of salt. *wife* In the mountains, Lot was made drunk by his daughters whose husbands had stayed in Sodom. The daughters lay with their bemused father, from which unions the Moabites and Ammonites were the descendants. Painting: *The Destruction of Sodom*, Jean Baptiste Corot, Metropolitan, New York.

Lot's Wife See Lot.

St. Louis of France (1214-1270) Louis IX became king of France at the age of twelve, and seven years later married Margaret of Provence by whom he had eleven children. He was an ideal monarch, sincerely religious, impartial and merciful in administering justice, a man of peace and an efficient soldier. He was a crusader, and led his first crusade in 1248, from which he returned with what was believed to be Christ's crown of thorns, and part of the True Cross (see St. Helena). On his second crusade in 1270, he contracted dysentery and died. He is shown in art with his attributes; the crown of thorns, the cross, the sword, royal crown, fleur de lys, and sometimes a pilgrim's staff. Feast day: August 25.

St. Louis of Toulouse Nephew of St. Louis of France* and St. Elizabeth of Hungary*, who was kept as a hostage for his father from the age of fourteen to twenty-one with the King of Aragon. When he was released, he was offered the throne of Naples, but he refused it to dedicate himself to the order of St. Francis*. He was made bishop of Toulouse and served his diocese with ardor and dedication, but died in 1297 at the age of twenty-four. In art, he is represented as a beardless, gentle youth, in the costume of a bishop, the fleur de lis embroidered on his cape, symbol of French royalty. The crown and scepter he renounced are at his feet. Painting: *St. Louis of Toulouse with St. Augustine*, Fra Filippo Lippi, Metropolitan, New York.

Lucifer (lū'si-fer) The name was applied to the king of Babylon, when fallen from high estate. In Christian religion, it was applied to Satan* by St. Jerome* and other Fathers of the Church who regarded it as the name of Satan before his fall from heaven. It is also the name given to the planet Venus, when it is the morning "daystar."

Lucretia (lūkrē'sha) or Lucrece In Roman legend, the wife of Tarquinias Collatinus, famed for her beauty and for her virtues. She was violated by Tarquinias Sextus, a kinsman, and upon her husband's return, she persuaded him and his friends to avenge her. Having told of the deed, she killed herself, and Junius Brutus organized a subsequent uprising in revenge. The Tarquins were expelled from Rome and a republic was established, about 510 B.C. Painting: *Lucretia*, Rembrandt, National Gallery, Washington.

St. Lucretia A Spanish saint, born into the Mohammedan faith, who was converted to Christianity. For this she was martyred, and bears the palm of martyrdom in art. Portrait: *St. Lucretia*, Dosso Dossi, National Gallery, Washington.

St. Lucy. Francesco del Cossa. National Gallery of Art.

St. Lucy   Lucy is the patron of eye afflictions. She is supposed to have lived in Syracuse, Sicily, and to have suffered martyrdom for her faith about 303. Legend relates that a nobleman wanted to marry her for the beauty of her eyes, so she tore them out and sent them to him on a dish saying, "Now, let me live for God." The remorseful young man became a Christian. One legend adds that Christ gave Lucy new eyes, more beautiful than before. St. Agatha* is said to have appeared to her and said, "Thou art Light." When she was martyred, she was dragged through the streets by oxen, then placed on a burning pyre where the flames did not touch her, and finally was stabbed to death with a dagger. In art, she is represented with her eyes on a dish, or in her hand. Sometimes she is seen with a dagger and a wounded neck, sometimes with a lamp to suggest light and wisdom. Feast day: December 13. Paintings: *St. Lucy*, Andrea Mantegna, Francesco del Cosa, and Paolo Veronese, National Gallery, Washington.

St. Luke the Evangelist   Luke was born in Antioch, Syria, and is known as the author of the New Testament Gospel of his name, and for the Acts of the Apostles. He became the constant companion of the disciple Peter*, was a missionary with him, and recorded his life. He is called the "beloved physician," from the greeting given to him with that title in Colossians (4:14), and is therefore supposed to have been of that profession. He is the patron saint of painters because of the legend that he painted several portraits of the Virgin Mary*. In art, Luke is represented with the winged ox, symbol of sacrifice, because of his emphasis on the sacrificial aspects of Christ's suffering to redeem mankind. He often holds the Gospel book in one hand; he may be shown painting a picture of the Virgin or the Virgin and Child, sometimes just with painting materials. Feast day: October 18. Painting: *St. Luke the Evangelist*, Giovanni di Paolo, Seattle Art Museum, Washington.

Lute   In Greek mythology, the lute is an attribute of the Muse Euterpe*. It is also carried by Orpheus*, the great musician and poet of Greek legend.

Lynx   In Greek mythology, the lynx is an attribute of the god Dionysus*, a skin which is said to have been presented to him by the mother-goddess Rhea*.

Lyre   In Greek mythology, an attribute of Apollo*, as god of music, poetry, and dance. The god Hermes* was the inventor of the lyre and exchanged it for cattle with Apollo. Terpsichore*, as muse of dance and choral dance, carries a lyre; also Erato*, as muse of lyric poetry. Orpheus* was given the lyre by Apollo, who may have been his father, and the nymphs taught him to play on it. In Christian iconography, it is an attribute of St. Cecelia*, the patroness of music.

Madonna (ma-don'na)   The word means "my lady" in Italian, and is a name given to representations of the Virgin Mary in art, particularly when she is seen with the Christ child, and when she is given idealized representation. Painting: *Madonna and Child*, Carlo Crivelli, Metropolitan, New York.

Maenads (mē'nadz)   The female followers of the god Dionysus*, the priestesses of his cult who roamed the world with him, also called Bacchae* and Thyiades. They celebrated festivals with wild songs and boisterous orgies, donning faun skins, chewing laurel leaves, and carrying the pine-tipped thyrsus of Dionysus. Relief: *Dancing Maenad*, Roman copy of a Greek original (5th century B.C.), Metropolitan, New York.

Magi (mā'jī)   Known also as kings and wise men. The magi were a sacred caste of Medeans, sages who received and imparted truths. In the New Testament, they are the Three Wise Men who came from the East, bringing gifts to the infant Jesus* (see Jesus Christ—Life Events—Adoration of the Magi). Legend says that the skulls of these three wise men were discovered by Queen Helena, and were taken to Cologne (Germany), whose cathedral claims they are deposited in one of its chapels. Painting: *Adoration of the Magi*, Boticelli, National Gallery, Washington.

Magnificat   The words expressed by the Virgin Mary* at the home of her cousin Elisabeth, after she had been greeted by her. The greeting scene in art is known as The Visitation* (Luke 1:46-55).

The Journey of the Magi. Sasetta. The Metropolitan Museum of Art. Bequest of Maitland F. Griggs.

Mammon (mam'an) The false god of riches and avarice. The word is often used in the New Testament to designate the evil spirit.

Mandorla The Italian word for almond. In Christian iconography, it is an aureole*, which is in an almond-shaped frame. This field of radiance is shown surrounding Christ in scenes of the Last Judgement (see Judgement Day) and in scenes of the Assumption* of the Virgin Mary*.

Manna In the Old Testament, the food miraculously supplied to the Israelites on their trek from Egypt to Canaan (Exodus 16:14-15). See Moses. A painting: *The Gathering of Manna*, Bacchiacca, National Gallery, Washington.

Man's Face with Wings Attached In Christian iconography, this representation symbolizes St. Matthew as Evangelist*, expressing the mystery of the Incarnation* and the virtue of reason. St. Matthew is also seen as a winged man.

Marathonian Bull   See Cretan Bull.

St. Margaret   Margaret was the Christian daughter of a pagan priest who lived in Antioch, Asia Minor, during the reign of the Roman emperor Diocletian. The governor of the city was so captured by her beauty, he wished to marry her, but Margaret decided that she was dedicated to Jesus. She was then denounced as a Christian, and cast into a dungeon where the devil visited her in the form of a dragon. Margaret held the cross before him, or made the sign of the cross, and the dragon fled. Another version of the legend says that the dragon swallowed her, whereupon the cross swelled to such proportions, the dragon was split in two. The governor, frustrated by this miracle, had her executed. The populace, having witnessed her courage and constancy, were converted to Christianity. In art, Margaret is shown with a dragon, which she tramples under her feet; she holds a cross and the palm leaf of martyrdom. She is prayed to against the pains of childbirth, her helpful power symbolized by her escape from the gripping pain of the jaws of the dragon. Painting: *St. Margaret of Antioch*, Girolamo di Benvenuto, New Orleans Museum of Art, Louisiana.

St. Mark the Evangelist   The author of the second, and probably the earliest, Gospel of the New Testament. He was a travelling companion of the apostles Peter* and Barnabas* on their early missionary journeys. Tradition says he went to Rome as a helper and secretary to Paul* and Peter*, and that he wrote his Gospel there from material given him by Peter. According to legend, he was preaching along the shores of the Adriatic sea when his ship was driven by a great storm into a lagoon. An angel appeared to him saying, "On this site a great city will arise in your honor." Four hundred years later, Venice was founded in this area. St. Mark is believed to have gone to Libya, and to have established the Christian church in Alexandria. In 832 his body is supposed to have been taken from Alexandria to Venice by Venetian merchants. He was made the patron saint of the'city, which also took over the winged lion as its emblem. The lion is winged because the Gospel of Mark emphasizes the mystery of the Resurrection* (see Jesus Christ—After-Life Events) and the virtue of courage. In art, Mark is shown with the winged lion, and in his character of Evangelist, he is given a pen and the book of his Gospel. Gothic statuette (German): *St. Mark*, Metropolitan, New York.

Mars   In Roman mythology the god of war, identified with the Greek Ares*. According to legend, Mars was the father of Romulus* and Remus, the founders of Rome, and thus the ancestor of the Roman nation. He was probably an ancient Italian god of fertility, and in the ten-month Roman calendar, March is the first month of the year. As god of war, Mars not only aided in battle, but protected the agricultural fields of these fighting people. As with the Greek god Ares, he was a lover of Venus*, the greek Aphrodite, and is frequently shown with her and their son Cupid*, in art. He is represented as a handsome, well built man, usually wearing armor. His attributes were the sword, spear, and shield, and the wolf and woodpecker were sacred to him. Bellona, the Roman goddess of war, was his charioteer wife, sister, or daughter. Painting: *Mars and Venus United by Cupid*, Paolo Veronese, Metropolitan, New York. (See Ares.)

Marsyas (mar'si-us)   In Greek mythology, a Phrygian peasant or satyr, a follower of the Phrygian goddess Cybele* who, according to Greek legend, picked up a flute which the goddess Athena* had invented, and then discarded because it distorted the features of the player. Marsyas became so skillful a flutist, he challenged the god Apollo* to a contest with his lyre. The contest was so close the Muses, who were acting as judges, could not decide for Apollo until he turned his lyre upside down and continued to make sweet music upon it. Apollo now flayed the vanquished Marsyas alive for his audacity. King Midas*, who had sided with Marsyas, was given the ears of an ass by Apollo as punishment. (This same tale is told about the god Pan*.) The subject is a favorite one in ancient art. Painting: *The Torture of Marsyas*, Conservatori, Metropolitan, New York.

Martha and Mary of Bethany   In the New Testament, the sisters of Lazarus* (see Jesus Christ—Miracles) and the friends of Jesus, who entertained him at their house in Bethany. The Gospels represent Martha as domestic and efficient, while Mary preferred to sit at the feet of Jesus, seeking spiritual instruction. Martha complained that Mary left her to do all the work, and this drew rebuke from Jesus (Luke 10:38-42), but Martha was an admirable woman of faith and action. When her brother sickened, she summoned Jesus, and went to meet him, sure of his ability to help and heal. Jesus said then, "I am the resurrection and the life: he that believeth in me, though he were dead, yet shall he live" (John 11:25-26). Mary is the one who, at the supper in Bethany, anointed the feet of Jesus with ointment, for which act Judas Iscariot scolded her (see Jesus Christ—Life Events—Supper at Bethany). Since the scene also occurs at the house of Simon,

227

Mary is sometimes confused with Mary Magdalene*, who is identified with the woman of that story. One legend asserts that Martha converted Mary Magdalene to Christ's doctrine. Another legend says that Martha, after the death of Christ, was driven out of Palestine with other persons (sometimes Mary Magdalene and Lazarus), and came by open boat to Marseilles, France. She proceeded to evangelize Provence, and saved the people of Aix from a fearful dragon by sprinkling him with Holy Water from an asperges*. Martha is usually shown in art with a kitchen utensil in her hand, household keys on her belt, or with a dragon at her feet. Painting: *St. Martha with Saints Peter*, *Mary Magdalene*, *and Leonard*, Coreggio, Metropolitan, New York.

St. Martianus and St. Processus   According to Christian tradition, the two men were the prison guards of St. Peter* in Rome. They were converted and baptized by him, and later martyred in the presence of their parents. Their relics are preserved in St. Peter's, under the altar dedicated to them.

St. Martin   Martin was a soldier's son, born in Hungary about 315, who ran away as a boy to a monastery. Later his father forced him to take up the profession of soldier. One cold, winter day, while stationed in France, he saw a poor beggar in rags. Cutting his officer's coat in two with his sword, he gave half of it to the beggar. That night Christ appeared to him, and soon after, he left the army, saying, "I am Christ's soldier and not allowed to fight." For awhile, he lived on a secluded island; later he founded the first monastery in Gaul, near Poitiers. His tastes were simple, and when he learned that he was appointed bishop of Tours, he hid from the emissaries, preferring to stay in the monastery. Unfortunately a quacking goose revealed his presence, and he was forced to accept the honor. He is often shown in art in military attire, dividing his cloak with the beggar, or in bishop's habit with a goose. He is the patron of beggars, drunkards, and innkeepers. Feast day: November 11. Painting: *St. Martin and the Beggar*, El Greco, National Gallery, Washington.

Mary of Bethany   See Martha.

Mary of Egypt   According to legend, this Mary was a harlot at Alexandria. She was suddenly converted to Christianity, while on a trip to Jerusalem. Leaving Jerusalem, she crossed the river Jordan with only three loaves of bread, and lived a solitary life of penitence in the wilderness for the rest of her days. After many years, she was discovered across the river by a priest named Zosimus. Mary, wishing him to give her Holy Communion, passed miraculously over the water to him, dry. The following year, the aged Zosimus came again to give her the sacrament and found her dead. While trying to bury her, a lion appeared and helped to dig the grave with his paws. Mary is usually represented in art as a very old woman with long, white hair and three loaves of bread. Sometimes a lion stands beside her. Feast day: April 2.

Mary Cleophas, Mother of James and Joses   In the New Testament, this Mary followed Jesus from Galilee, witnessed the crucifixion (see Jesus Christ—Life Events), watched the burial, and visited the sepulcher with Mary Magdalene* and Mary Salome on the morning of Christ's resurrection. Painting: *St. Mary Cleophas and her Family*, Bernhard Strigel, National Gallery, Washington.

Mary Magdalene   In the New Testament, Jesus healed this Mary of seven devils (Luke 8:1-2), and she followed him in gratitude. She may have been a harlot, and, as such, has become the great example of the penitent sinner. She is also identified with the unnamed sinner at the house of the Pharisee, Simon (see Jesus Christ—Life Events) who, after washing the feet of Jesus with her tears, anointed them with ointment from her alabaster box, with which she is usually shown in art (Luke 7:37-50). She accompanied Jesus to Calvary*, and stood weeping at the foot of the cross. She watched the burial of Jesus by Joseph of Arimathea, and came early to the sepulcher with Mary Cleophas to anoint the body of Jesus with spices. They discovered the stone of the sepulcher had been rolled away, and the tomb empty. It was to this weeping Mary, outside the tomb, that the risen Christ first appeared and gave comfort, saying to her, "Touch me not" (Noli Me Tangere), but to bring the news to the disciples, that he was ascending to God (see Jesus Christ—After-Life Events—Apparitions). She is also identified with the Mary who accompanied Martha to Marseilles. In this legend, she retired to the desert where she subsisted on celestial food. In art, she is shown in scenes of the Crucifixion*, at the tomb, and anointing the feet of Jesus. She is often represented with flowing hair, a symbol of penitence, which covers her body as she is carried to heaven by angels. French polychromed statue: *Mary Magdalene*, Cloisters, Metropolitan, New York.

Marys, the Three   When three Marys are shown in art, they are Mary Magdalene*, Mary Cleophas*, and Mary Salome*.

Mary Salome   In the New Testament, Mary Salome, or just Salome, is the wife of Zebedee. She witnessed the crucifixion of Jesus, and visited the tomb with ointments for the anointing of his body.

The Three Marys and the Angel on Christ's Tomb and *Christ Meeting the Three Marys*. 14th century Italian illuminated letter on parchment. The Metropolitan Museum of Art

Mary, the Virgin   The daughter of Joachim* and Anna*, the wife of Joseph of Nazareth*, and the mother of Jesus Christ*. Her birth by divine intervention is connected with the concept of Immaculate Conception*, making her worthy to be the mother of the Saviour. Very little is told in the Bible about Mary. Legend concerning her was written by the Apocryphal* writers between the 2nd and 6th centuries, out of the need of early Christians to render honor to her. The title Virgin grew to mean that Mary was ever virgin, before, during, and after the birth of Christ, a miracle that occurred by the will of God. Mary is also known as the mother of God, as the Blessed Virgin, as Our Lady, and as the Madonna. In the Roman Catholic church, she is considered to be the most influential intercessor before the Tribunal of God (God the Father, God the Son, and God the Holy Ghost*). Mary is represented more frequently in Christian art than any other figure but Christ. The attributes seen with her are listed first below; then the scenes of representation, including those of idealized imagery. All are listed alphabetically.

ATTRIBUTES OF THE VIRGIN MARY

Book—in scenes of the Annunciation.

Book Sealed—taken from Psalm 139:16 "... in thy book all my members were written."

Fountain Sealed, Garden Enclosed—taken from the Song of Solomon 4:12: "A garden inclosed is my sister, my spouse, a spring shut up, a fountain sealed."

Gate Closed—a symbol of Mary's virginity.

Girdle—see Virgin's Girdle in representations, below.

Lily—a symbol of purity.

Lily Among Thorns—a symbol of Immaculate Conception.

Mirror, Spotless—a symbol of virginity.

Moon—see Sun, Moon, and Stars, below.

Rose Without Thorns—a symbol of the Virgin without sin.

Sun, Moon, Stars—taken from Revelation 12:1 "... a woman clothed with the sun and the moon under her feet, upon her head a crown of twelve stars." Attributes for Mary Queen of Heaven and for the Virgin of the Immaculate Conception. The star of Bethlehem on the shoulder of the Virgin refers to her Hebrew name, Miriam.

Tree of Jesse—the tree with the Virgin holding the Christ Child represents the genealogy of the house of David. The tree with the Virgin at its top is a symbol of Immaculate Conception*.

REPRESENTATIONS OF THE VIRGIN

Annunciation   The angel Gabriel* announces to the Virgin that she is blessed among women, and will give birth to the Saviour. Mary is usually shown in contemplation or reading, sometimes in prayer. Symbols shown are a well or fountain, the Holy Ghost* in the form of a dove. The angel Gabriel has large wings and may carry a lily or a scepter, as the herald of God. Painting: *The Annunciation*, Jan Van Eyck, National Gallery, Washington.

Assumption   After the apostles had gathered around Mary's death bed (see Dormition, below), the house was filled with sound, and Jesus appeared with a host of angels. Mary's soul left her body and was received into the arms of Jesus, who carried it up to heaven. The disciples then took her body to the sepulcher. Three days later, Mary's body was transported to heaven to join her soul (see Virgin Enthroned, below, and St. Thomas). Painting: *The Assumption*, El Greco, Art Institute of Chicago.

Birth of the Virgin   Anna*, the mother of the Virgin, is seen in bed, usually in prosperous surroundings, while the baby is being washed in the foreground by servants, and visitors call with congratulations. Painting: *The Birth of the Virgin*, Andrea di Bartolo, National Gallery, Washington.

Coronation of the Virgin   The Virgin is received into heaven by Jesus, and he places a crown on her head, as queen of heaven (see Queen of Heaven, below). The Dormition and scenes of the tomb and the apostles are often depicted around the main scene of the coronation. Painting: *The Coronation of the Virgin*, Paolo Veneziano, National Gallery, Washington.

Dormition or Death of the Virgin   Legend says that the Virgin lived until her death, supposedly at Ephesus, with the apostle John, in whose care Jesus had placed her. In old age, she prayed for death, and an angel appeared, granting her request, presenting her with a palm. Mary then asked that the apostles gather at her deathbed, and in art, they are usually so shown (see Assumption, above). Gothic sculpture (16th century): *The Dormition*, Metropolitan, New York.

Flight into Egypt   See Jesus Christ—Life Events.

Immaculate Conception   See Virgin of Immaculate Conception, below.

Madonna and Child   Mary may hold the child in her lap for the world to worship, or she may kneel before the baby in prayer and reverence. Painting: *Madonna and Child*, Fra Filippo Lippi, National Gallery, Washington; painting: *The Madonna and Child*, Pietro Lorenzi, Philadelphia Museum of Art.

Madonna Enthroned or in Majesty   Mary is shown enthroned in heaven, surrounded by angels. The Madonna may also be seen enthroned with the Christ Child. Painting: *Madonna Enthroned with Saints*, Master of the Fabriano Altarpiece, National Gallery, Washington; two paintings: *Enthoned Madonna and Child*, Byzantine School (13th century), National Gallery.

Madonna of Humility   Mary sits humbly on the ground with the child. Painting: *The Madonna of Humility*, Fra Angelico, National Gallery, Washington.

Madonna of Mercy (Misericordia)   Mary stands before kneeling worshippers, whom she protects with her cloak.

Madonna of the Plague (Peste)   Mary is shown with saints, who are invoked against plague; sometimes she appears over a plague-stricken town.

Madonna of Succor (Soccorso)   Mary as the protector of children. She chases the devil away with a club.

Madonna of Victory (Vittoria)   Mary is shown in the air, with fighting armies below her, or enthroned, with military leaders paying homage to her.

Marriage of the Virgin   Mary was dedicated to the service of God by her parents, and from early childhood until the age of fourteen, she remained in the Temple. The priests then told her that the time had come for her to marry and they chose widowers as suitors. Each suitor was asked to leave his staff at the Temple overnight, awaiting a sign from the Lord. In the morning, the staff belonging to Joseph, the carpenter of Nazareth, had blossomed. As he was chosen to be Mary's husband, a dove flew onto his head. The marriage ceremony is a frequent subject in art, sometimes in front of the Temple, with guests attending. Their hands are joined by the priest, Joseph may place a ring on Mary's finger. Painting: *The Marriage of the Virgin*, Bernaert Van Orly, National Gallery, Washington.

Mother of Sorrow (Mater Dolorosa)   Mary in sorrow weeps for the suffering of her son. Often she wears a crown of thorns. Painting: *The Mourning Madonna*, Master of the Franciscan Crucifixes, National Gallery, Washington.

Nativity of Jesus   The birth of Jesus is usually shown in a stable, because there was no room available at the inn. An ox and an ass are in the background, referring to the prophecy of Isaiah (1:3) "The ox knoweth its owner, and the ass his master's crib." The Virgin kneels before the baby, and Joseph* stands in awe. Painting: *The Nativity with the Prophets Isaiah* and Ezekiel**, Duccio di Buonensegna, National Gallery, Washington.

Nativity of the Virgin   See Birth of the Virgin, above.

Pentecost   When the disciples were celebrating the festival of Pentecost after Christ's ascension, Mary was with them. As described in Acts 2:2-4 of the New Testament, it was a miraculous event. "Suddenly there came a sound from heaven as of a rushing mighty wind, ... And there appeared unto them cloven tongues like as of fire, ... And they were all filled with the Holy Ghost*, and began to speak with other tongues." In paintings of this scene, rays of light express the Holy Ghost, and there are often stylized tongues of fire on the heads of the disciples.

Presentation of the Virgin   When Mary was three or four years old, she was taken by her parents to the Temple to be dedicated to the service of the Lord. Legend says that she danced with her feet before the altar, so that "all rejoiced with her, and loved her." Painting: *Presentation of the Virgin*, Hans Memling, National Gallery, Washington.

Purification of the Virgin   Israel's religious law code specified that a woman must pass through a 33-day period of purification, after bringing forth a male child. Not until then could she go to the Temple, but after the purification had been observed, Mary took the child to the Temple, and presented him to the Lord (see Jesus Christ—Life Events—Presentation in the Temple).

Queen of Heaven   In this idealization, Mary stands on the crescent moon, usually crowned with twelve stars (see Attributes, above). Painting: *Mary Queen of Heaven*, Master of the St. Lucy Legend, National Gallery, Washington.

Seven Joys and Sorrows of the Virgin   See after Visitation, below.

Virgin's Girdle   The disciple Thomas* was absent when the Virgin's soul and body were transported to heaven (see Assumption, above). Doubting the Virgin's assumption, Thomas insisted that her grave be opened. When he saw it was empty, he looked upward and saw the Virgin rising toward heaven. In her hand, she held her girdle which she dropped into his hands to prove that her body was rising to the kingdom of God. Painting: *Assumption of the Virgin*, Girolamo da Carpi, National Gallery, Washington.

Virgin of the Immaculate Conception　Mary is shown with her attributes (see above), often crowned with the twelve stars, surrounded in space by cherubs (putti). She may be seen with the symbols of the Trinity* (Father, Son, and Holy Ghost), or with her father and mother. Painting: *Virgin of the Immaculate Conception*, Guido Reni, Metropolitan, New York.

Virgin of the Rosary　This scene is the legend that the Virgin appeared to St. Dominic* and gave him a rosary (prayer beads). He then instituted the devotion of the rosary in his order of monks.

Visitation　After the Annunciation (see above), the Virgin went to visit her kinswoman Elisabeth*, who had also been miraculously blessed by God, and was to give birth to the child who became John the Baptist*. The two women met with emotion, each aware of the magnitude of the Virgin's role. In art, the Virgin is shown much younger than Elisabeth, who usually embraces her or makes a gesture of welcome. Painting: *The Visitation*, Piero di Cosima, National Gallery, Washington.

SEVEN JOYS AND SORROWS OF THE VIRGIN
These are often depicted in sequence, and are as follows:

Joys　The Annunciation, Visitation, Nativity of Christ, Epiphany (or baptism of Christ), Jesus found in the Temple, Resurrection, and Assumption.

Sorrows　Simeon's prophecy concerning Jesus when he was presented at the temple as a baby, the flight into Egypt, Jesus lost in Jerusalem, the Meeting of Jesus on the road to Calvary, Crucifixion, Descent from the Cross, Entombment (see Jesus Christ—Life Events and After-Life Events).

Mask　In Greek mythology, an attribute of Dionysus*, as the god of drama. Melpomene, the muse of tragedy, carries the tragic mask. Thalia*, the muse of comedy, carries the comic mask.

Massacre of the Innocents　Herod the Great*, ruling at the time of the birth of Jesus, heard the rumor that a child was born who would become "king of the Jews." In order to destroy the child,

235

he gave the command that all male children of Bethlehem under the age of two should be slaughtered. Joseph*, Mary*, and the baby Jesus* left for Egypt to escape the horrible massacre (Matthew 2:16).

St. Matthew the Evangelist One of the twelve disciples of Jesus*, and according to tradition the Evangelist who wrote the Gospel of that name in the New Testament. He was called to discipleship by Jesus (Matthew 9:9), and may have been the brother of James the Less*, and son of Alphaeus. Legend says that after the Ascension (see Jesus Christ—After-Life Events), Matthew preached 15 years in Judea, and then carried the gospel to Ethiopia, where he was martyred. As an Evangelist, he is represented symbolically in art as a winged man, or a man's face with wings; sometimes as a cherub, recording the genealogy of Jesus. As a Gospel writer, he is shown as an old man with a long beard, pen and scroll in hand, often accompanied by an angel, dictating the Gospel to him. As an apostle, he carries a purse, referring to his early life as a tax collector, or an axe, the instrument of his martyrdom. Feast day: September 21. Painting: *St. Matthew*, Simone Martini, National Gallery, Washington.

Matthias (muth-ī′as) In the New Testament (Acts 1:23-26), Matthias becomes the successor of Judas Iscariot*, and is chosen to take his place as the twelfth disciple by the other eleven. After prayer, he was chosen by lot. His attribute, like St. Matthew's, is an axe, said to be the instrument of his martyrdom likewise, and an open Bible, as an emblem of his missionary work.

Maurus, Brother See St. Benedict.

Medea (me-dē′a) In Greek mythology, the daughter of King Aeëtes of Colchis, skilled in witchcraft, whom the goddess Aphrodite* induced to fall in love with Jason*, so that she would betray her father, and help Jason to steal the Golden Fleece*. She escaped with Jason to Greece, becoming his wife. When they reached Thessaly, Jason found that his uncle Pelias had murdered his younger brother and that his father was dead. Medea decided to avenge the murder with her magic arts. She went to the daughters of Pelias and told them she was able to make him young again. This she demonstrated to them by cutting up an old goat which she boiled before their eyes in a large cauldron. After a while she brought out a young lamb. The daughters were then persuaded to cut up Pelias in his sleep, and place him in a boiling cauldron. But as Medea did not use her magic herbs, Pelias did not revive. Jason then seized the throne, which was rightfully his, but resigned it to Acastus, a son of Pelias, and went to live with

King Creon* in Corinth instead. Medea had ten happy years of wedlock with Jason. Then he decided to abandon her for Creon's daughter Creusa (or Glauce). After much pleading with Jason, Medea sent Creusa a magnificent robe, which burned her to ashes as soon as she put it on. Then she killed her own sons by Jason, and escaped to Athens in a chariot drawn by serpents, which were sent to her by her grandfather Helius*. (Some legends say the Corinthian populace stoned her children to death.) In Athens, Medea married King Aegeus*, the father of Theseus*, and by Aegeus had one son. When Theseus came to his father's court, unidentified, Medea, recognizing him, tried to poison him. When the plot failed, she had to flee again, and taking her son Medeus, whom the Greeks regarded as the ancestor of the Medes, she returned to Colchis once more, and reinstated her father on the throne, which had been usurped by his brother. At Corinth, Medea was thought to be immortal, and was regarded as a benefactress of the city, because she had delivered it from famine. Black-figured vase (6th century B.C.): *Medea Boiling Up Pelias*, Boston Museum of Fine Arts. (see Jason.)

Medusa (me-dū′za) In Greek mythology, one of the three Gorgons*, the only one that was mortal. Originally a beautiful maiden, she was turned into a winged monster with snaky locks by the goddess Athena* because she had violated one of the temples of the goddess with the god Poseiden*. Her face became so terrible that all who looked on it were turned to stone. Eventually her head, which had been severed by Perseus, was given to Athena, who placed it on her Aegis* (shield). The head of Medusa was a favorite subject in Greek art. Statue: *Perseus Carrying the Head of Medusa*, Antonio Canova, Metropolitan, New York.

Melchizedek See Lot.

Meleager (mel-ē-ā′jer) In Greek legend, a celebrated hero, the son of Oenus* and Althaea* of Calydonia, and sister of Deianira* who became the wife of the hero Heracles*. When he was a baby, the Fates* announced to his mother that he would die when a log of wood, then on the hearth, was consumed by flame. Althaea seized the log and hid it in a chest. Meleager grew to manhood, and was one of the heroes to join with the Argonauts. He brought about the celebrated chase of the Calydonian Boar*, which was ravaging his father's territory. The most renowned heroes of the time joined in the chase and the huntress Atalanta* was the first to wound the boar. Meleager killed it, and then awarded the tusks to Atalanta. When his two uncles objected to the award, Meleager, in sudden fury, killed them. Althaea, distraught at this violent act to her brothers, fetched the half-burned log she had concealed for so long, and threw it on the fire. When the log was entirely burned, Meleager suddenly died. Althaea, learning of the death, hanged herself in anguish. Meleager was seen by Heracles in Hades* (the underworld), and it was there that Heracles promised to marry Deianira. Bronze statuette: *Meleager*, Italian (16th century), Metropolitan, New York.

Melpomene (mel-pom'e-nē) In Greek mythology, one of the nine daughters of the god Zeus* with Mnemosyne* (memory), called the muses*. Melpomene was the muse of tragedy. She is generally represented as a young woman, bearing the tragic mask of the theatre. She may have the club of Heracles*, as an attribute of violent tragedy. The vine wreath on her head is a symbol of her connection with the god of drama Dionysus*. Fresco transferred to canvas: *Melpomene*, Giulio Romano, Metropolitan, New York.

Menelaus (men-e-lā'us) In Greek legend, the son of King Atreus* and Queen Aërope of Mycenae, the younger brother of King Agamemnon*, with whom he was exiled after the murder of his father by his cousin Aegisthus*. Fleeing to Sparta, he married the daughter of Tyndareus, the famous beauty Helen, and inherited the throne after the death of Helen's twin brothers, Castor* and Polydeuces*. When Trojan Paris* ran off with Helen and much treasure, Menelaus, accompanied by Odysseus*, went to Troy with just claims, which were refused. Accordingly he formed an expedition with his brother Agamemnon, and waged war for ten years against the Trojans. He distinguished himself in battle, and would have won the war in single combat against Paris (this method of deciding the outcome of the war having been accepted by the combatants), if the goddess Aphrodite* had not rescued Paris and carried him off. When the Greeks were finally victorious, Menelaus, having recovered Helen, spent eight arduous years trying to sail home. He finally reached Sparta again, and lived out his life quietly with Helen. Their only child was Hermione*, who married Neoptolemus*, the son of Achilles*.

Mephistopheles (mef-is-tof'e-lez) A manufactured name for the devil, which first appears in the German legend of Faust.

Mercury In Roman mythology, the equivalent of the Greek god Hermes*, the son of Maia, a fertility goddess, and the god Jupiter*, for whom he acted as messenger. He was the god of science and commerce, the patron of travellers, rogues, vagabonds, and thieves. It was he who guided the dead souls to the underworld. He is represented in art as a young man with a flat, winged hat or cap, bearing the staff intertwined with snakes, called the caduceus, and sometimes a purse. Posts with marble heads of Mercury were erected where two or more roads met to point the way. Terracotta statuette: *Mercury*, Jean-Baptiste Pigalle, Metropolitan, New York. (See Hermes.)

Messiah (me-si'a)   Hebrew for anointed one. It was the title of the expected leader of the Jews who was to deliver the nation from enemies, to reign eternally in peace. Equivalent to the Greek word Christ, it is applied by Christians to Jesus.

Methusalah (me-thū'ze-la)   In the Old Testament, a man who lived to the incredible age of 969 years, having begotten many sons and daughters.

Metis (mē'tis)   In Greek mythology, a Titaness*, the daughter of Oceanus* and Tethys. According to some legends, she was the first wife of the god Zeus*, and it was she who gave Zeus the potion which forced his father Cronus* to disgorge his brothers and sisters, whom he had swallowed at birth. An oracle predicted that Metis would bear a son mightier than Zeus. Zeus, learning of this, swallowed Metis. Some time later he had a violent headache, and the smith god Hephaestus* was summoned by the god Hermes*. Taking an axe, Hephaestus struck Zeus on the forehead, and the goddess Athena* sprang forth, fully armed.

Michael, Archangel   In the Old Testament, the great prince and leader of the celestial armies, the protector of the Jewish nation, who became the protector of the Church Militant in Christendom, and the guardian of the redeemed. It is he who receives the spirits of the dead and weighs their souls against the Day of Judgement*, and he will sound the last trumpet at this general resurrection. In the Old Testament, it is Michael who is sent with a ram to save Isaac* from sacrifice (see Abraham); he is present at the scene of the burning bush* (see Moses), he is at Jericho with Joshua. In the New Testament, he is the angel who answers the prayers of the Virgin Mary for death (see Mary, the Virgin—Dormition). In art, he is shown as a beautiful, winged young man, clad in armor, often in a coat of mail, carrying a sword, spear, and shield, with which he combats Satan in the form of a dragon. In scenes of the Last Judgement, he is shown as the weigher of the risen dead souls. Painting: *Archangel Michael*, Domenico Ghirlandaio, Portland Art Museum, Oregon.

Midas (mi'das)   In Greek mythology, king of Phrygia, who was the son of the goddess Cybele* and a satyr*. Once the forest god Silenus* fell into his hands, and after enjoying his fantastic tales,

St. Michael. Ghirlandaio. Courtesy of the Portland Art Museum.

Midas returned him to the god Dionysus*, since he was one of his followers. In return for this favor, Dionysus told him he could choose any reward. Midas said that he would like everything he touched to turn to gold. His request was granted, but when even his food turned to gold, he prayed to Dionysus to take back the gift. In one legend, his little daughter leaped into his arms and became gold. Dionysus took pity on him, and told him to bathe in the neighboring river Pactolus. As he bathed, the gift passed from him into the sands of the river bed. Midas then promoted the worship of Dionysus, and was the first foreigner to send gifts to the shrine at Delphi*. He had further trouble, however, when attending a musical contest between the god Apollo* and Pan (or Marsyas). The judges gave the victory to Apollo, but Midas cast his vote for Pan. The indignant Apollo changed the ears of Midas into those of an ass. Midas hid them under a Phrygian cap, and swore his barber to secrecy. The barber could not resist telling about the ears just once, and whispered the story into a hole which he dug in the ground and then covered up. Reeds growing on the spot, whispered the secret to the winds, and soon it was known far and wide. Midas had the barber killed, and then drank bull's blood which caused him to die. Drawing: *Midas Bathing in the Pactolus River*, Nicolas Poussin, Metropolitan, New York.

Millstone   In Christian iconography, the millstone is an attribute of Sts. Florian* and Vincent*, each of whom suffered martyrdom by being thrown into the water with a millstone tied to his neck.

Minerva (mi-ner'va)   In Roman mythology, the goddess of wisdom, and patron of arts and trades, identified with the Greek goddess Athena*, and as goddess of intelligence, the patroness of schoolmasters and school children. She is fabled, like Athena, to have sprung fully armed from the head of the god Jupiter with a tremendous battle cry, and as war goddess, was honored in association with the war god Mars* during the spring equinoxes. She is one of the three chief deities with Jupiter* and Juno*, and the seat of their cult was on the Capitoline Hill at Rome. In art, she is represented as grave and majestic, wearing a coat of mail over full drapery, bearing the aegis* on her breast and a helmet on her head. Her festival was March 19. Statuette: *Minerva*, 16th-century Italian, Metropolitan, New York. (See Athena.)

Minos (mī'nos)   In Greek mythology, a king of Crete, the son of the god Zeus* and Europa*, who seized the throne in consequence of a quarrel with his brothers. He was supported in this victory by the god Poseiden*, to whom he prayed for a bull worthy of sacrifice to him. Poseiden responded by sending him a snow-white bull that was so magnificent, Minos sacrificed another animal in its place. Poseiden retaliated by inspiring Pasiphae*, the wife of Minos, with an unnatural love for the bull. From her union with this creature, a monster was born, known as the Minotaur*. The bull escaped from the herds of Minos, and ravaged the land until subdued by Heracles*, as his seventh labor. The Minotaur was kept in a labyrinth*, built by the mastersmith Daedalus*. When the son of Minos, Androgeus, was killed on a visit to Greece, Minos vowed revenge, and with the help of his father Zeus, all Greece was shaken by earthquakes. The Athenians, on the advice of the Delphic oracle*, submitted to the demands of Minos, who asked that seven youths and seven maidens be sent to Crete as tribute every nine years to be fed to the Minotaur. Theseus* succeeded in killing the monster; Daedalus, who had helped him, was himself confined to the Labyrinth with his son Icarus, but they escaped on wings of feathers. He was pursued by Minos who caught up with him in Sicily at the court of King Cocalus. The daughters of Cocalus scalded Minos to death in a bath of boiling water, so that Daedalus could remain with their father. The body of Minos was sent to his followers, and given a fine burial in Sicily. He was the greatest ruler of his time, considered to be the founder of naval supremacy for Crete, before the era of the Trojan war*. His great palace is said to have been at Knossos. As a son of Zeus, he was made a judge in the underworld and assigned the spirits to their final homes in Hades*.

Minotaur (min′a-tor) In Greek mythology, the monstrous offspring of Queen Pasiphae*, wife of King Minos* of Crete, resulting from her unnatural passion and union with the Cretan bull*. He had a human body and the head of a bull, and was fed on human flesh. He was confined in the labyrinth at Knossos, the famous maze with a thousand turnings, built for him by the architect Daedalus*. The Minotaur was killed by Theseus* who came to Crete with Greek youths and maidens from Athens as "tribute" for Minos to feed the Minotaur. Painted scene: *Theseus Slaying the Minotaur*, on a black-figured Greek vase (6th century B.C.), Boston Museum of Fine Arts.

Miracles of Christ See Jesus Christ—Miracles.

Miriam The Hebrew name for Mary. In the Old Testament, Miriam is the sister of Aaron* and Moses*, the sister who suggested to the Egyptian princess who adopted Moses that she use his own mother for a wet nurse. After the Exodus* across the Red Sea (Sea of Reeds), she led the ceremonial dance of grateful Hebrew women. When she was critical of Moses' marriage with an

Ethiopian, she was afflicted by temporary leprosy from which she was cured by the intercession of Moses.

Mirror   In Christian iconography, a spotless mirror is a symbol of the Immaculate Conception* of the Virgin Mary*.

Miter or Mitre   The headdress of a bishop or pope. Three miters, at the feet of a saint, represent the bishoprics he has refused. Sts. Bernard* and Bernardino* are said to have refused this recognition.

Mithras or Mithra (mith'ras)   In Persian religion, the god of created light and all earthly wisdom, identified with the sun god who conquers the demons of the darkness. Bulls and bulls' blood are sacrificed to him. His cult was brought to Rome by merchants and soldiers in the first century B.C., and by A.D. the second century, Mithraism was more common than Christianity. In art, Mithras is represented as a young man in oriental dress, often stabbing an overthrown bull with his dagger.

Mnemosyne (ne-mos'i-nē)   In Greek mythology a Titaness*, the daughter of Gaea* (earth) and Uranus* (heaven). She was the goddess of memory and the mother, by the God Zeus*, of the nine muses*. Fresco, transferred to canvas: *Mnemosyne with Four Muses*, Giulio Romano, Metropolitan, New York.

Moerae   See Fates.

Money   In Christian iconography, a money bag is an attribute of St. Matthew*, in reference to his early career as a tax collector. Money on a platter is an attribute of St. Laurence✝, who distributed the treasure of the church to the poor. Two hands filled with money indicate the betrayal of Christ by Judas Iscariot* (see Jesus Christ—Life Events—Betrayal). Three money bags (often shown as three balls) are an attribute of St. Nicholas* of Bari.

Monstrance   In Christian religion, a receptacle in which the consecrated Host (bread) is shown for adoration. The word comes from the Latin *monstro*, to show. It is an attribute of St. Clare* (see ampula).

Moon   In Greek mythology, the crescent moon is a symbol of Artemis* as goddess of the moon. In Christian iconography, it is a symbol of the Virgin Mary from The New Testament book of Revelation (12:1): "... the moon under her feet." See Mary the Virgin—Attributes.

Mordecai (mor'de-kī)   In the Old Testament, the cousin and foster father of Esther*, who, when sent by Mordecai before King Ahasuerus (the Persian Xerxes) with many other young maidens, found such favor in his eyes, she became his queen. Mordecai, who was the king's gatekeeper, saved the life of the king by informing Esther of a plot to kill him. Later, however, a jealous courtier, named Haman, tried to have him executed for refusing to bow before him. This was also a plot to do away with the Jews. Mordecai put on sackcloth, thus making known his plight to Queen Esther. The king remembered Mordecai's great service to him, and Queen Esther cleverly helped him to expose Haman and his plots. Haman was executed in Mordecai's stead, and Mordecai was made grand vizier (see Esther).

Morpheus   In Classical myth, the son of Hypnos* the god of dreams, identified with the Roman Somnus. Painting: *Morpheus,* Jean Honore Fragonard, Cleveland Museum of Art.

Mortar and Pestle   In Christian iconography, these are the symbol for the mixing of drugs, and are an attribute of the physician saints Cosmos* and Damian.

Moses (mō'zez)   The great Hebrew statesman and lawgiver, who led the people of Israel from slavery in Egypt to freedom. Moses *Birth* was born in northeast Egypt of humble Hebrew parents, at a time when Pharaoh* commanded that all male Hebrew children be drowned in the Nile. Moses might have perished, but for the resourcefulness of his mother and sister Miriam*, who placed and *Cradle in* guarded his bulrush cradle among the Nile reeds. He was found by *bulrushes* a childless Egyptian princess, who then hired his mother to be his wet nurse. This led to his adoption and a superior upbringing in the court. As a young man he saw an Egyptian strike a Hebrew. In anger, he killed the Egyptian, and since he had been observed, he fled to the Midian shepherds. He served the shepherd-priest *God speaks* Jethro for many years, and married his daughter by whom he had *to Moses* two sons. It was here in the Sinai Peninsula that he heard the *from burn-* voice of God issuing from a burning bush*, commanding him to *ing bush* lead Israel out of Egypt. Pharaoh dismissed all pleas of Moses to let the Jews leave the country, until the Lord miraculously *Pleas to* induced a series of plagues, which Moses and his brother Aaron* *Pharaoh to* effected through the use of their divining rods (symbols of *leave Egypt* prayer). Pharaoh was finally convinced of the displeasure of the God whom Moses had invoked, and gave his reluctant permission. Moses then led his people across the Red Sea (Sea of Reeds). The Old Testament passage in the book of Exodus describes Moses *Exit across* stretching his hand out over the water and the sea dwindled, *Red Sea* allowing the people of Israel to cross over. The Pharaoh, regretting his decision, sent his army in hot pursuit, but Moses stretched out his hand again, and the sea covered over Pharaoh's chariots and horsemen. Moses treked for forty years with his people. In lean times, he sustained them with manna* (a wild, sweet edible), with quails, and once he brought forth water by striking a rock with his rod of authority. After the third month of wandering, he went up on a high peak of Mt. Sinai and received from God two tablets, on which were written Ten Commandments. The tablets were preserved in the Ark* of the Covenant. Moses died at Mt. Pisgah, having passed his leadership on to Joshua*. He himself had not reached the "Promised Land," but his followers were launched as a people. In art, Moses is shown as an imposing man with a beard, often carrying the rod of authority. Sometimes he is shown with horns on his forehead, symbolizing God's gift to him of power and prosperity. One legend of his childhood tells of his sitting on the Pharaoh's lap. He threw a crown, decorated with an idol to the ground. The wise men of the court said this indicated that Moses would overthrow the throne, and suggested that he be killed. To put the child to the test, two platters were put before him, one heaped with coals and one with cherries; if he chose the hot embers, he would be saved. Moses seized the coals, and screaming, put his hands in his mouth. This caused him speech difficulties throughout his life. Painting: *The Finding of Moses*, Sebastian Bourdon, De Young Memorial Museum, San Francisco; painting: *Moses Before the Burning Bush*, Dirk Bouts, Philadelphia Museum of Art. (see Ten Commandments.)

Trek in wilderness

Ten Commandments given to Moses on Mt. Sinai

Childhood legend

Mount of Olives or Olivet   The Mount of Olives is the most conspicuous, landmark of Jerusalem, separated from the plateau of the city by the Kedron Valley. Its associations in the Old Testament include the barefoot flight of the weeping King David* over it, when his son Absalom* revolted against him (2 Samuel 15:30), the vision of Ezekiel there, and Zechariah who saw God standing on its summit. In the New Testament, Jesus travelled often to it. Here the crowd welcomed him with hosannas; Gethsemane* was to the west of the hill. Painting: *On the Mount of Olives*, Bartolommeo Tomaso di Foligno, Metropolitan, New York.

Mouse   In Greek symbology, an attribute of the god Apollo*, as an emblem of healing, associated with disease and cure.

Muses (mū′zez)   In Greek mythology, the nine daughters of the god Zeus* and Mnemosyne* (memory). They are the inspiring goddesses of the arts, and are frequently shown as beautiful, young women with long, flowing garments. As nymphs identified with springs, they were early connected with the god Dionysus*. Apollo*, the god of poets, was looked upon as their leader. They are listed, with their attributes, below:

Calliope, Chief of the Muses, and Muse of Epic Poetry—a tablet or stylus.

Clio, Muse of History—a scroll, a wreath on her head, or a trumpet.

Euterpe, Muse of Music—a double flute.

Thalia, Muse of Comedy—ivy wreath, comic mask, shepherd's staff.

Melpomene, Muse of Tragedy—tragic mask, ivy wreath, club, or sword.

Terpsichore, Muse of Choral Dance and Song—lyre.

Erato, Muse of Lyric, Amorous Poetry—small lyre.

Polyhymnia, Muse of Sacred Song and Religious Dance—veil.

Urania, Muse of Astronomy—celestial globe.

Mussels   In Greek mythology, mussels are an attribute of Aphrodite*, as the sea goddess, born from sea foam.

Myrmidons (mer′mi-dons)   In Greek mythology, a warlike tribe from Thessaly, who originated on the island of Aegina. Legend recounts that the Myrmidons were led by Achilles* in the Trojan war*, and were as tireless and faithful as the ants they were named for (see Aeacus).

Myrrh (mur)   A fragrant, gum resin exuded from the shrubs of Arabia and eastern Africa, used in making incense, perfume, and medicine. In Solomon's time, his fleet carried myrrh to the Fertile Crescent (Palestine to Baghdad). Myrrh was scarce and in demand at the time of the birth of the Christ Child, its worth ranked with gold, and was therefore considered a suitable gift for the Magi* to bring as an offering. Myrrh is another name for the Greek word *Chrism*, meaning "to anoint," and is supposed to have been instituted as a sacrament after the washing of the feet of the disciples at the Last Supper* (see Jesus Christ—Life Events). See Myrrha.

Myrrha (mir′a)   In Greek mythology, the daughter of King Cinyrus, whose wife declared that her daughter was more beautiful than the goddess Aphrodite*. In revenge, Aphrodite inflicted upon Myrrha an incestuous love for her father. Myrrha tried to hang herself, but she was saved by her nurse, who took her to her father disguised as a stranger. When Cinyrus discovered the truth, he tried to kill the girl, but as she fled, the gods turned her into a twisted tree from which bitter tears of resin weep. When Adonis*, her son of this union, was ready for birth, her trunk split open, and the child was cared for by the nymphs.

Myrtle (mer'tl) In Greek mythology, a tree sacred to the goddess Aphrodite*. Myrtle nymphs cared for the beekeeper Aristaeus, and taught him the art of keeping bees. Myrtle was given by the god Dionysus* to the queen of the underworld Persephone*, to persuade her to release his mother Semele* from the shades; hence, a symbol of death. Myrtle is said to have dropped blood, when it was torn up by Aeneas*. Its leaves are also said to have been pierced by Phaedra*, while whiling away the time waiting for Hippolytus*.

Mysteries The name given by the Greeks, and later by the Romans, to various kinds of secret worships. These rested on the belief that, besides the general manner of honoring gods, there was another mode, revealed only to the select few. The most famous of the mysteries was the worship held at Eleusis (see Eleusinian Mysteries).

Naiads (nā'adz or nē'adz) In Classical mythology, female spirits, light hearted, musical, and beneficient, who presided over springs, rivers, and fountains. They were represented as young and beautiful, their heads crowned with flowers.

Nails In Christian iconography, nails are a symbol of the Crucifixion (see Jesus Christ—Life Events), usually shown in a group of three, referring to the nails used for either hand and for the feet. Nails are also seen with St. Helena*, who believed she found the nails with Christ's cross, in A.D. the 4th century.

Narcissus (nar-sis'us) In Greek mythology, the beautiful son of the river god Cephissus. He rejected the love of the nymph Echo*, and the goddess Aphrodite* punished him for this frigidity by inspiring him with a passion for his own reflection, which he saw in the surface of a pool. Each time he reached for it, it disappeared, and he pined away in desire. A lovely flower with yellow and white petals took his place and name. The flower became a symbol of death and the ephemeral, sacred to the god of the underworld, Hades*. Persephone* is said to have gathered a Narcissus when she was abducted by Hades. In Christian iconography, the narcissus became a symbol of selfishness and self-love, derived from the Greek legend.

Nativity, the In Christian reference, the Nativity is the designation given to the birth of Jesus Christ (see Jesus Christ—Life Events).

Nausicaa (naw-sik'ā-a) The daughter of Alcinous*, king of the Phaeacians, described by Homer in his narrative, The Odyssey*.

Odysseus* was wrecked on the shores of King Alcinous, and found Nausicaa playing ball with her maidens beside the sea. Pitying his naked plight, she gave him clothes and food, and directed him to her father's palace where he was entertained. Alcinous would have been happy to have him as a son-in-law, but when Odysseus insisted on continuing home to Ithaca, Alcinous provided him with passage on his own Phaeacian ships, laden down with presents.

Nazarene (naz'ar-ēn) One of the names applied to early Christians, derived from the town of Nazareth, where Jesus* was raised as a child, and where he lived until its citizens reacted violently against his teaching.

Nebuchadnezzar (neb'ū-kad-nez-er) The greatest king of Assyria who reigned from 604-561 B.C. He was at war for the better part of his 43-year reign, ruthlessly subduing his neighbors and looting their treasures. He rebuilt Babylon, restored the temple of the pagan god Bel, and probably built the celebrated Hanging Gardens of Babylon*. He is the center of many legends, and supposedly went mad at the height of his achievements, as described in the Old Testament (Daniel 4:33): he "did eat grass as oxen . . . his hairs were grown like eagles' feathers, and his nails like birds' claws" (see Daniel and Three Holy Children). Scenes: *Life of Nebuchadnezzar*, 15th-century Umbrian cassone panel, Metropolitan, New York.

Nectar In Greek mythology, the drink of the Olympian gods*, reputed to have life-giving properties, and to preserve all who drank it from decay and corruption.

Nemean Lion ('ne-mē'an) In Greek mythology, a terrible lion, which kept the townspeople of Nemea in constant alarm. The first of the twelve labors of Heracles* was to slay it. He tried initially with his arrows, sword, and club, but they had no effect on the beast. When the lion retreated to his cave, Heracles blocked it up and then strangled the lion with his arms. Scene: *Heracles Strangling the Nemean Lion*, on a black-figured vase (6th century B.C.), Museum of Fine Arts, Boston.

Nemesis (nem'e-sis) In Greek mythology, a daughter of Nyx* (night) and Erebus (darkness). She was a goddess of chastisement and vengeance, as well as a goddess of proportion, who stood for moderation and restored the normal order of things. She allotted to men their share of good or bad fortune. In one legend, the god Zeus* visited Nemesis in the form of a swan, instead of Leda*, but Nemesis gave the egg, resulting from the union, to Leda, who then claimed the children born from it as her own. In art, Nemesis is represented as a thoughtful maiden with a measuring rod, a bridle, and a yoke, all symbols of measurement and control. Her sword and scourge are symbols of punishment, and her wings, wheels, and chariot, drawn by griffins, symbolize swiftness. In Rome, she was worshipped by victorious generals.

Neoptolemus (ne-op-tol'e-mus) Also known as Pyrrhus. In Greek legend, the son of Achilles* and Deidamia*, who was raised by his grandfather, King Lycomedes of Scyros. After the death of Achilles*, Neoptolemus was taken to Troy by Odysseus*, despite the protests of his mother, in order to fulfill the prophecy that the city of Troy could not be taken by the Greeks without the aid of a descendant of Aeacus, his great grandfather on his father's side. Like his father, Neoptolemus distinguished himself in battle and was one of the heroes in the Trojan horse*. He is also the one who cruelly killed the aged Priam*, king of Troy, and the one who hurled Hector's* small son Astyanax* from the walls of the city. After the fall of Troy, he took Hector's wife Andromache* as concubine, and finally, after many adventures, returned to Greece. He went to Delphi*, and upbraided Apollo for the death of his father, plundering, and burning the shrine. He continued to Sparta and wed Hermione*, the daughter of Menelaus* and Helen*. Andromache had given Neoptolemus sons, but Hermione was barren. Neoptolemus, therefore, returned to Delphi with offerings. Here he was slain, probably by the priests of the god Apollo*, as judgement for the murder of Priam and his previous destruction of the shrine.

Neptune (nep'tūn) The Italian god of the sea, taken over by the Romans and later identified with the Greek god Poseiden. He was originally a rain god and water giver, associated with vegetation. In Rome, he was worshipped as a patron of horses and horsemen. In the Aeneid*, he calms the storms for Aeneas*, and lifts a sunken ship and its sailors from the deep, taking for himself the life of the steersman, Palinurus. In art, Neptune is represented as an elderly, bearded man of stately presence, carrying a trident*, and sometimes riding a dolphin or seahorse. His wife Amphitrite* is frequently shown with him, as they ride the seas in a chariot drawn by dolphins and Tritons*. Painting: *Neptune Calming the Tempest*, Rubens, Fogg Art Museum, Cambridge, Massachusetts; painting: *The Triumph of Neptune and Amphitrite*, Nicholas Poussin, Philadelphia Museum of Art. (See Poseiden.)

Nereid (ner'ē-id) In Greek mythology, the fifty sea-nymph daughters of Nereus* and Doris. The most famous were

Amphitrite* and Thetis*. They were beautiful maidens, helpful to travellers on the sea, and were female followers of the god Poseiden*. In art, they are represented in waving draperies, posed as though they were waves, and often ride fanciful creatures.

Nereus (ner'ūs or ner'ē-us)   In Greek mythology, the father of the nereids*, a god who could transform himself into any form he chose and, like all sea gods, had the gift of prophecy. When Heracles* wished to learn the whereabouts of the Golden Apples of the Hesperides*, he seized Nereus, and held him firmly through all his transformations until he gave him directions (see Heracles—Eleventh Labor).

Nero, C. Claudius   The depraved and infamous Roman emperor from A.D. 54 to 68. Legend says he set fire to Rome to see "what Troy would have looked like when it was in flames." As Rome was burning, he is said to have fiddled, or played on his lyre. Christian persecution* was initiated during his reign.

Nessus (nes'us)   In Greek legend, a centaur who was a ferryman. Once he ferried Deianira*, the wife of Heracles*, across the river, and attempted to carry her off. Heracles shot him with one of his poisonous arrows. As he was dying, Nessus in revenge, gave Deianira some of his poisoned blood, deceitfully telling her that it would preserve her husband's love if she gave it to him. Once when Deianira suspected that the affections of Heracles might be straying, she sent him a tunic, smeared with the blood, which consumed him as soon as he wore it. Painting: *The Rape of Dejanira* (Deianira), Antonio Pollaiuolo, Yale University Gallery, New Haven, Connecticut.

Nestor (nes'tor)   In Greek legend, one of the twelve sons of Neleus and Chloris, and ruler of Pylos and Messinia. When Heracles* came to Pylos to ask Neleus to purify him for the murder of Iphitus (a seizure of madness), Nestor was the only son to plead his cause. Later, when Heracles attacked Pylos, he spared Nestor while killing all his brothers. Nestor married Anaxibia (Homer calls her Eurydice), by whom he had seven sons and two daughters. In his youth he performed many valorous deeds against neighboring enemies, was a member of the Calydonian Hunt*, and fought in the battle between the Centaurs and the Lapithae*. When the Trojan expedition was organized, Nestor was ruling over a third generation of his countrymen. Nevertheless, he joined forces with Agamemnon* and was his greatest councilor, known for his wisdom, justice, and benign character. He was one of the few warriors to have a prosperous trip home to Greece from Troy, after the war was over. Ten years later, Telemachus*, the son of Odysseus*, seeking advice from him, found him enjoying a prosperous, old age.

St. Nicholas of Bari or Myra Nicholas is one of the most popular, legendary saints in Christendom, reputed to have been bishop of Myra, in southwestern Asia Minor in the 4th century. He is the patron of Russia and Aberdeen in Scotland, of clerks, mariners, scholars, little boys, fire, and also pawnbrokers, whose three golden balls symbolize three purses of gold. The legend says that Nicholas once discovered the three daughters of an impoverished nobleman trying to earn their dowry money through disreputable living. Nicholas quietly threw three bags of gold through the nobleman's window one night, and saved the girls. Another legend tells that the devil once disguised himself as a woman and joined some pilgrims, travelling on a ship to visit St. Nicholas. The woman gave them oil with which to anoint the house of St. Nicholas. Instantly an image of St. Nicholas appeared to them, saying, "That was the foul Diana [pagan goddess]; cast this oil on the water." The pilgrims did so, and the sea burst into flames. St. Nicholas is the patron of mariners, because he rebuked the waves in a heavy storm, on his way to the Holy Land. He became bishop of Myra, because he was the first priest to enter the church the day the bishop was to be elected. He was the patron of little boys, because he discovered an innkeeper had stolen three little boys, cut them up, and pickled them in a salting tub for bacon. St. Nicholas made the sign of the cross, and restored the boys to life. From this story, St. Nicholas became the bringer of toys to children, which turned him later into Santa Claus. In art, he is represented in bishop's clothes with either three purses of gold, three gold balls, three small boys, or sometimes an anchor or ship in the background. Feast day: December 6. Painting: *St. Nicholas Leaving the Three Dowries*, Florentine School, Columbia Museum of Art, Columbia, South Carolina; painting: *St. Nicholas Resuscitating Three Youths*, Bicci di Lorenzo, Metropolitan, New York.

St. Nicholas of Tolentino A 13th-century Augustinian friar, born in Fermo, Italy, who was stationed most of his life at nearby Tolentino. His life was passed in tireless, pastoral work, and in effective preaching. Legend says that a star flashed across the horizon from Fermo to Tolentino at the time of his birth. His fame was largely due to the miracles attributed to him, influenced by the legends about his namesake, St. Nicholas of Bari. In art, he wears the black, Augustinian robe, and is often painted with a star on his breast, referring to the legend about his birth, and a lily-twined crucifix. Painting: *St. Nicholas of Tolentino During a Storm at Sea*, Giovanni di Paolo, Philadelphia Museum of Art.

Nicippe (nĭ-sip'ē)   In Greek legend, the mother of Eurystheus* who gave early birth to this son through the influence of the goddess Hera*, which made Eurystheus king of Mycenae, instead of Heracles*.

Nike (nē'kā)   In Greek mythology, a daughter of the nymph Styx. Nike was brought to the god Zeus* by her mother, to assist him in his struggle against the Titans*. After the successful outcome of the battle, Nike remained on Mt. Olympus*, as the goddess of victory. She was identified often with the goddess Athena*, with whom she is seen, as well as with Zeus. The Romans identified her with their goddess, Victoria*. In art, she is generally winged, and wears or carries a wreath, and holds a palm branch. As the herald of victory, she carries the wand of the god Hermes*, known as the caduceus. Painting: *Victory Sacrificing at the Altar*, on a red-figured vase (5th century B.C.), Fogg Art Museum, Cambridge, Massachusetts.

Nimbus   In Christian religion, a symbol of holiness, the Latin word for cloud. The symbol is also called a halo (see halo).

Nimrod (nim'rod)   In the Old Testament, an ancient, legendary character who had a fabulous reputation as a hunter, builder, and founder of kingdoms. Babylon was the area where he performed his great feats (Genesis 10:8-9).

Nine   The number, nine, in Christian religion is the number referring to the nine choirs of angels, spoken of in the Bible.

Niobe (nĭ'ō-bē)   In Greek mythology, the daughter of Tantalus*, and the wife of Amphion, king of Thebes, the mother of six sons and six daughters. In maternal pride, she dared to compare herself to Leto*, suggesting that she had more reason to be worshipped than Leto, who had only two children, the god and goddess Apollo* and Artemis*. Apollo and Artemis took instant revenge, and slew all of Niobe's children for this presumption. Niobe, inconsolable, wept herself to death, and was changed into a marble statue whose face was constantly covered with tears.

Niobids (nĭ-ō-bidz)   The name for the children of Niobe*.

Noah (nō'a)   In the Old Testament, the son of Lamech, a tenth-generation descendant of Adam*. Noah was the first grower of the vine, but he is primarily the hero of the Great Deluge* and the builder of the ark*, or houseboat, in which he saved a male and female of every living species, during the long flood that God

Top left: *The Building of Noah's Ark.* Top right: *The Flood.* Lower left: *Leaving the Ark.* Lower right: *The Sacrifice of Noah.* Illumination from The Pierpont Morgan Library Collection.

254

occasioned when he determined to destroy man for his wickedness. Noah was entrusted with this divine mission by God, as the head of the only family worth saving, and when the rains descended, all the evil inhabitants of the world were destroyed. When the waters finally began to subside, the ark rested on Mt. Ararat, and Noah dispatched a raven and a dove to determine the degree of their recession. The dove returned with a bit of an olive branch, which showed that the water had abated, and gave the assurance that God had made peace with man. At last, the earth was again dry, and God directed Noah to disembark with everything in the ark. Noah erected an altar, and made a sacrifice to God, and God blessed Noah and his sons and generations to come. Painting: *Noah's Sacrifice*, Bernardo Cavallino, Museum of Fine Arts, Houston, Texas; Painting: *The Animals Entering the Ark*, Edward Hicks, Philadelphia Museum of Art.

Noli Me Tangere   Latin for Touch Me Not, used in the New Testament by Jesus*, when he spoke to Mary Magdalene* beside his tomb, after his resurrection* (John 20:17). The words are often used as the title for paintings of this scene (see Jesus Christ—After-Life Events).

Nymphs   In Greek mythology, young maidens who were inferior divinities of nature, dwelling in forests, caves, springs, streams, and sometimes on islands, as did Calypso* and Circe*. They were usually benevolent spirits, and led a life of liberty, sometimes weaving, sometimes dancing and singing, or hunting with the goddess Artemis*, revelling with the god of wine Dionysus*, with the god Hermes*, or Pan*. They were believed to have the gift of prophecy and poetical inspiration. Places sacred to them received offerings.

Nyx (niks)   In Greek mythology, the daughter of Chaos. She was the goddess of night, and was a force for both good and evil. She rode a chariot, accompanied by stars, and led forth sleep and death at the close of day. She was revered for her oracular powers, which were pronounced from a cave.

O

Oak   In Greek symbology, the oak is sacred to the god Zeus*, its rustling leaves revealing his will; also an attribute of Cybele*, goddess of wild forests. In Christian iconography, a symbol of endurance against adversity. It is one of several species of wood, thought to be that from which Christ's cross was made.

Oceanus (o-sē-a'nus)   In Greek mythology, the ancient river flowing around the world. According to Homer, the Greek author (8th century B.C.), Oceanus is the beginning of all things, including the gods. He lived with his wife Tethys in the far west, away from the world's affairs. The 8th-century author Hesiod describes Oceanus and Tethys as Titans*, children of Uranus* (heaven) and Gaea* (earth), and parents to 6000 children. Oceanus is represented in art as a venerable, old man with a long beard. As a river god, he sometimes has bull's horns on his head. As a sea god, he has crab's claws, and is surrounded by creatures of the ocean.

Octagonal Forms   See Eight.

Octavius Augustus (ok-tā'vi-us)   In history, the first Roman emperor, a grandson of the sister of Julius Caesar*, whom Caesar named as his heir. He gradually defeated his opponents, and became master of all Roman territories in 30 B.C. He reformed the city of Rome and the government of the provinces, and fostered colonization throughout the empire. His most noted opponent was Mark Antony* who became his brother-in-law, and with whom he was allied for many years prior to their final falling-out. He was munificent in the arts and beautified Rome. He is frequently shown as a fine-featured, clean-shaven young man, usually with a laurel crown on his head.

Odysseus (ō-dis'ūs or ō-dis'sē-us) (Ro. Ulysses or Ulixes)   In Greek legend, king of Ithaca, the grandson of Autolycus*, son of Laertes, husband of Penelope*, and father of Telemachus*. While Telemachus was still an infant, Odysseus was asked by Menelaus* and Agamemnon* to join the expedition to Troy to fetch Helen*, the abducted wife of Menelaus. Odysseus tried to escape this duty by feigning madness, and yoked a horse and a cow together to *Feigned* plough a field, but he betrayed himself when his baby *madness* Telemachus was placed in one of the furrows by Palamedes*, a lieutenant of Agamemnon. He was now compelled to join the Greeks, and became one of the leading heroes of the Trojan war*, famed in legend for his craft, strategy, and ingenuity, combining courage and determination with eloquence. He was first sent to Troy with Menelaus to demand, with just claims, the surrender of Helen. When this failed, he was sent to find Achilles*, who was *Unmasking of* hidden among the girls at the court of King Lycomedes. He was *Achilles* the messenger who tried to reconcile Achilles* with Agamemnon, when they quarreled over the captive girl Briseis*, and he was sent to get the bow and arrows of Heracles*, which had been left in the hands of Philoctetes*, without which, an oracle had *Philoctetes* declared, the war could not be won. With Diomedes*, he stole the Palladium* from the city of Troy, and it is said that it was he *Palladium* who devised the strategy of the Trojan Horse*, which brought *Trojan Horse* about the destruction of Troy. His return from Troy to Ithaca is described below, under Odyssey.

Odyssey, The (od'i-see)   Homer's epic poem describing the wandering journey of Odysseus*, on his way home from the Trojan war*. After the sack of Troy, Odysseus departed with his ships for his kingdom on the island of Ithaca. He was driven immediately to Thrace, where he plundered the city of Cicones, losing 72 men. As he continued, and tried to round the Peloponnesus, a storm carried him to North Africa, where he encountered lotus eaters, and had to drag his companions away *Lotus eaters* by force, to prevent them from forgetting their homes. Next he came to the country of the Cyclops*, and was shut up in a cavern with twelve of his men, six of whom the Cyclops Polyphemus *Polyphemus* devoured. Odysseus escaped by intoxicating Polyphemus, and then depriving him of his one eye. His remaining companions sneaked from the cave by clinging to the underbellies of sheep, as they exited to the open. He spent some time at the island of the sorceress Circe*, and on the island of Calypso* who kept him *Circe* with her for eight years. When he finally left her, he was shipwrecked again, but reached the island of the Phaecians alone and naked, the sole survivor. He was discovered on the shore by Nausicaa*, the daughter of King Alcinous, and after receiving the *Nausicaa* hospitality of Alcinous was taken on one of his ships to Ithaca.

Twenty years had elapsed since the departure of Odysseus, and during this prolonged absence, a hundred suitors had appeared asking for the hand of his wife Penelope. She, however, had remained faithful to Odysseus. The suitors then persecuted his son Telemachus*, now growing to manhood, so Penelope promised she would make a decision when she had finished weaving a shroud for her father-in-law. This weaving she secretly unravelled every night, but the ruse was discovered, and she had to say she would marry the man, who, using the bow of Odysseus hanging on the wall, should win in a shooting match. On the eve

of this event, Odysseus arrived at Ithaca, disguised as a beggar by the goddess Athena*. He hid in the cabin of Eumaeus*, a faithful shepherd, and was joined there by his son Telemachus, returning from a trip to Nestor's palace. Together they plotted the overthrow of the suitors, and Odysseus entered the palace, still dressed as a beggar. The nurse, Eureclea*, washing his feet, recognized him by a scar on his leg, but he swore her to secrecy. He entered the shooting contest of the suitors, and since he was the only man who could bend his own bow, he won the contest with a master shot. Then, with the aid of Telemachus and Eumaeus, he shot down the suitors, made himself known to Penelope, and with the help of Athena, was reconciled with the relatives of the slain suitors. Odysseus is described as red-haired, bearded, and is so shown in art, sometimes with a semi-oval sailor's cap. Painting: *Odysseus Rescuing his Companions from Circe*, and a scene: *Odysseus Making Himself Known to Telemachus*, on red-figured Greek vases (5th century B.C.); plaque (5th century B.C.): *The Homecoming of Odysseus*, all at Metropolitan, New York.

Oedipus (ed'i-pus or ēd'i-pus)   In Greek mythology, the epic hero who killed his father and married his mother. A descendant of Cadmus*, his parents were Laius* and Jocasta*, king and queen of Thebes. An oracle foretold that Laius would die by the hand of his son, so the baby Oedipus was exposed on Mt. Cithaeron, with his feet pierced. He was saved by a Corinthian shepherd, and taken to the childless king and queen of Corinth who adopted him. When Oedipus was grown, he also learned from an oracle that he was fated to kill his father and marry his mother. Not knowing that he was adopted, he fled from Corinth and set out for Thebes. At the crossroads he met Laius, his real father, who was on his way to Delphi* to question the god Apollo* concerning the devastation of his lands by a neighboring Sphinx*. As Oedipus would not move aside for Laius, a quarrel ensued, and in the heat of the moment, he killed his father and all but one attendant. He then proceeded to Thebes, and liberated the city by answering the riddle of the Sphinx. As a reward, he received the king's widow Jocasta* (his mother) for his wife, thus fulfilling the prophecy. After many years, Oedipus learned the truth while endeavoring to find the murderer of Laius, which the oracle had said was necessary, if a terrible plague was to be lifted from Thebes. In horror, he put out his eyes and Jocasta hanged herself in despair. Creon*, Jocasta's brother, took the throne, and Oedipus was banished, accompanied by his daughter Antigone*. Pursued by the Furies*, Oedipus finally came to Colonus, and here found peace in death. He was buried by Antigone and Theseus*. Painting: *Oedipus and the Sphinx*, Gustave Moreau, Metropolitan, New York. (see Sphinx.)

Oeneus (ē'nus)   In Greek legend, the king of Calydon in Aetolia, married to Althaea*, and by her, the father of Meleager* and Deianira*. Dionysus*, the god of wine, gave him the vine plant, and he is supposed to be the first to cultivate grapes. Once he forgot to offer first fruits to the goddess Artemis* when he made other offerings, so she sent a savage boar to ravage his land. Meleager organized a large hunt to kill the beast, and many heroes took part (see Calydonian Boar Hunt).

Oenomaus (ē-nō-mā'us)   In Greek legend, a son of the god Ares* and a nymph. He was the king of Pisa, in Elis, and the father of Hippodamia*.

Oil   In Christian religion, oil is a symbol of consecration.

Olive   In Greek symbology, the olive branch is sacred to the goddess Athena*, because she gave the olive tree to Athens. Heracles*, who founded the Olympic games*, decreed that the olive wreath should be the award for the victors. The goddess Eirene* carries the olive branch, as goddess of peace. The god Zeus* wears an olive wreath on his head. In Christian iconography, the olive branch is a symbol of peace, derived from the story of the dove sent forth by Noah* from the ark. An olive branch carried by a dove indicates the peaceful departure of the dead. It is carried by the angel Gabriel*, in scenes of the Annunciation* (see Mount Olive or Olivet).

Olympia (ō-lim'pi-a)   The site of the celebrated sanctuaries of the Greek god and goddess Zeus* and Hera*, and of the Olympic games of Classical antiquity, situated in Elis, in the valley of the Alpheus river. The games were held every four years, in July. They started with sacrifices, and included all sorts of athletic contests, ending on the fifth day with banquets, processions, and awards to the winners, who were garlanded with olive leaves. Tradition held that the Olympic games were initiated by the hero Heracles*, and that the olive wreath was decreed by him.

Olympians (ō-lim'pi-anz)   In Greek mythology, the twelve great gods who lived on Mt. Olympus. They were Zeus*, the chief and greatest of the gods; Hera*, his wife and sister, the greatest feminine deity; Hestia*, another sister, the oldest of the virgin goddesses; Poseiden*, his brother and lord of the sea; Athena*, Artemis*, Aphrodite*, and Hebe*, all daughters of Zeus, the first two being virgin goddesses; and Ares*, Apollo*, Hermes*, and Hephaestus*, all sons of Zeus. Demeter* and Dionysus* are sometimes added to the twelve, and also Heracles*.

St. Olympias (366-408)   A faithful follower of St. John Chrysostom*. She married at eighteen, was widowed at twenty, and determined to remain single, devoting herself and her considerable wealth to charity. In 391, she was made deaconess of the church of Constantinople. When St. John Chrysostom was deported to Armenia, she suffered persecution with other deaconesses, and was charged with conspiring to burn down the cathedral. She was fined heavily, and harried from then until her death. A number of letters to her from Chrysostom are extant.

Olympic Games   See Olympia and Heracles.

Olympus (ō-lim'pus)   The mountain in Thessaly regarded as the abode of the Olympian gods. The clouds below it are the gates to the celestial region. On the highest peak, the god Zeus* had his throne, and it was there that he summoned assemblies of the gods.

Omega (o-mē'ga)   The last letter of the Greek alphabet. See Alpha.

Omphale (om'fal-ē)   In Greek legend, the queen of Lydia, for whom Heracles* performed many services to expiate his sin of the murder of Iphitus, which deed he had done in a fit of madness. Fresco transferred to canvas: *Heracles and Omphale*, Pinturicchio, Metropolitan, New York.

Omphalos (om'fal-los)   A sacred stone in the temple of the god Apollo* at Delphi*, Greece. The ancient Greeks believed it marked the "navel" or exact centerpoint of the earth. Legend said this point was located by the god Zeus*, who released two eagles in opposite directions. They flew until they met at Delphi, and thus determined the center. The stone was also said to be the one Rhea* gave to Cronus*, to swallow in place of the baby Zeus, and which he later disgorged with the brothers and sisters of Zeus.

One In Christian religion, the number one is a symbol of unity.

Oracle In Greek religion, the answer of the god, or an inspired priest, to a human inquiry respecting the future; also, the place where the deity could be consulted. In ancient Greece, oracles were numerous, and for centuries had a strong influence on the course of human affairs. In most of the temples, women sat on a tripod and made the responses, many of which were either ambiguous or so obscure as to be misleading. Famous sites of oracles in Greece and the Grecian world were those of Dodona, Epirus, Trophonius, and Delphi.

Orange Tree and Blossom In Christian iconography, a symbol of purity and chastity as well as generosity; it has therefore become the blossom for brides. It may be an attribute of the Virgin Mary*. The orange tree is sometimes seen in the Garden of Eden* in place of the apple tree, referring to the fall of man* and his atonement.

Orcus (or'kus) In Roman mythology, a god of the underworld, who carried the dead to the lower regions, and kept them imprisoned there. He was later identified with the Greek god Hades*, the god and the region Hades* becoming, eventually, synonymous.

Orestes (ō-res'tez) In Greek legend, the only son of Agamemnon* and Clytemnestra*, the brother of Electra*, Iphigenia†, and Chrysothemis*. When he was a child, his father was murdered by his mother and her lover Aegisthus*. Fearing revenge, his sister Electra sent the boy to the court of Strophius of Phocis, but when he grew to manhood, he returned with Pylades*, the son of Strophius, and his great friend. He revealed himself to Electra, and with her help, avenged their father's murder by killing his mother and her lover. In consequence of this matricide, he was pursued by the Erinyes* or Furies, and wandered in madness around the country until he reached Athens, where he stood trial before the Areopagus (the Athenian court). The god Apollo* was his counsel; the chief of the Furies was the prosecutor. The opinion of the jury was evenly divided, so the goddess Athena*, as impartial judge, decided in favor of Orestes, and thus lifted the curse from the house of Atreus*. To win full purification for his crime, Orestes went to Taurus to bring back an image of the goddess Artemis*. In the temple, he found his lost sister Iphigenia, acting as priestess for Artemis. With the help of Athena, they escaped to Greece, carrying the sacred image with them. Orestes returned to the kingdom of Mycenae, rightfully his, slew Aletes, the son of Clytemnestra and Aegisthus who had seized the throne, and became the ruler. Some legends claim he married Hermione*, the daughter of Menelaus and the famous Helen* of Troy.

Organ In Christian iconography, the organ is an attribute of St. Cecelia*, who is said to have invented the organ.

Original Sin In Christian dogma, this is the fall of man* from original goodness and God's grace, through the sin of disobedience, committed in the Garden of Eden*. The thesis is that the consequences of Adam's sin have been transmitted to everyman through natural generation, and thus Adam's sin, in effect, is the original sin of every individual (see also Immaculate Conception and Seven Deadly Sins).

Orion (ō-rī'on) In Greek mythology, a gigantic hunter of great beauty, who was able to walk on the sea as well as on land; in some legends, the son of the god Poseiden*. He visited the island of Chios, and fell in love with Merope, the daughter of King Oenopion. The king, however, kept delaying the marriage, and in a fit of intoxication, Orion violated Merope. Oenopion blinded him, in revenge, but his eyes were healed by the rays of the sun. Later he joined the goddess Artemis* in hunting exploits. The god Apollo*, fearful for his virgin sister, sent a giant scorpion to attack Orion, and Orion leaped into the sea for safety. When his head was a distant speck, Apollo tricked Artemis into transfixing it with an arrow. Stricken with grief, Artemis placed his image with the scorpion in the heavens, the great hunter with the sword, club, and lion's skin.

Orpheus (or-fē'us) In Greek legend, a son of the god Apollo* and the muse Calliope*. He was a poet and musician of such talent, he was said not only to charm the creatures of the woods but to affect inanimate things with his music. Apollo gave him his lyre, and the muses taught him his art. He was initiated into the mysteries* of Samothrace and Egypt, while journeying through them, and in imitation of these, he instituted the mysteries of Dionysus* in Thrace. He accompanied the Argonauts* to Colchis, soothing disturbances with his music. He sang the marriage song for Jason* and Medea* on the return trip of the Argonauts, and when he reached Greece he married the lovely Eurydice*. One day she stepped on a serpent in the fields, was bitten, and died. Orpheus was inconsolable, and descended to Hades*, and with his music charmed Charon*, the ferryman, Cerberus*, the watch dog, and the god of the underworld himself. Eurydice was released on condition that Orpheus would not look back at her, as she followed him, until they had reached the light of the upperworld. When they had almost arrived, Orpheus could not refrain from seeing whether she was behind him, and as he turned, Eurydice vanished forever. After this second loss, Orpheus retreated to Thrace where his prolonged grief so enraged the Thracian women whom he ignored, they tore him to pieces in a Bacchanalian* orgy. His body was collected by the muses, and buried at the foot of Mt. Olympus*, but his head and lyre, which had been thrown into the river Hebrus, floated out to sea, still singing, until they reached the island of Lesbos, where they were buried separately. In art, the journey from the underworld often shows the god Hermes* accompanying Orpheus and Eurydice, as the intermediary between the world of the living and the dead. Marble group: *Orpheus and Eurydice*, Auguste Rodin, Metropolitan, New York.

Orthrus (orth'rus) In Greek mythology, a two-headed dog who guarded the cattle of Geryon*. He was the father of the Theban Sphinx* by his mother Echidna, and father of the Nemean lion* by the Chimaera*. He was killed with a club by the hero Heracles*, when Heracles came to fetch Geryon's cattle, as his tenth labor for Eurystheus*.

Osiris (o-si'rus) In Egyptian mythology, the god of the dead and the underworld. He became identified with all forces that made fertility and the arts of civilization, and with many gods in other religions, among them the Greek god Dionysus*. In art, he is shown as a bearded, human figure, swathed in mummy wraps, wearing a crown of Upper Egypt, a dome-shaped hat with a papyrus tuft. In his hands, protruding from the swathing, he holds a shepherd's crook and a threshing flail, attributes of agriculture.

Owl In Greek mythology, a symbol of wisdom, sacred to the goddess Athena*. In Christian iconography, it is seen with hermits, and is a symbol of solitude. In scenes of the crucifixion* of Christ, it symbolizes the giving of light to those who sit in darkness. As its habit is to remain in the dark, it may also symbolize Satan*, the prince of darkness.

Ox In Renaissance art, the ox may symbolize the Jews, since it was one of their sacrificial animals. In scenes of the Nativity*, the ox represents patience and strength (see Ass). A winged ox is an attribute of St. Luke* the Evangelist because, in his Gospel, he emphasized the sacrificial aspects of Christ's suffering to redeem mankind. The ox is also an attribute of St. Thomas Aquinas*, because he was nicknamed "dumb ox" as a boy. In Greek religion, the ox is an animal of sacrifice to the god Dionysus*. In some cults, Dionysus was worshipped as a horned animal or horned man, in reference to the fact that he was the first to yoke oxen, or because he was sacrificed in the form of a yearling bull, cut into nine pieces, during festivals in honor of his mother Semele*. This worship occurs in some of his other epiphanies.

Painting of the Virgin or **Painting Materials**   In Christian iconography, these are attributes of St. Luke* with whom they are shown, in reference to the legend that Luke painted the Virgin's portrait.

Palamedes (pal-a-mē′dez)   In Greek legend, one of King Agamemnon* of Mycenae's chief lieutenants in the Trojan war*. It was he who detected the assumed madness of Odysseus*, by placing his infant son in a furrow in front of his plow, thus gaining the services of Odysseus for the Trojan expedition. Odysseus never forgave him for this act, and when the Greeks encamped before Troy, he contrived to make Palamedes look guilty of bribery. The Greeks, on this false evidence, stoned Palamedes to death. He was reputed to have invented measures, weights, lighthouses, the discus, and to have added four letters to the alphabet.

Palladium of Troy (pa-lā′di-um)   In Greek legend, a wooden image of a maiden about five feet high, which the god Zeus* caused to fall down to Troy from heaven. The prosperity of the city depended on it, since the Trojans had been promised that Troy would not fall, if it was kept in the city (see Pallas). When Diomedes* stole the image with the help of Odysseus*, Troy fell. In Roman legend, Aeneas* rescued the image from burning Troy, and took it to Rome. Many Greek and Roman cities claimed to own it, and it was an attribute of Vesta*.

Pallas (pal′as)   In Greek mythology, a daughter of Triton*. She was a youthful playmate of the goddess Athena*, who accidentally killed her while wrestling. Athena, much grieved, put the name of Pallas in front of her own name, and made a wooden image of Pallas. This image was flung from heaven before the tent of Ibes, founder of Troy, and became the Palladium (see above).

Pallas Athena   See Pallas and Athena.

Palm   In Greek mythology, the palm was an attribute of the god Apollo*, because he was said to have been born under a palm tree at Delos. The date palm is an attribute of the goddess Artemis*, when she is worshipped as an orgiastic nymph. In Christian iconography, the palm is a symbol of martyrs and their triumph over death, derived from Christ's triumphant entry into Jerusalem and his victory over sin and death. A dress of palm leaves is seen on St. Paul the Hermit*, who lived all his life in the desert; the palm tree is also his attribute. The palm staff is seen with St. Christopher*, patron of travellers, who used it while ferrying the Christ Child across a river. To the Romans, its frond was used as an emblem of victory, and it is often seen in representations of military success.

Pan (Ro. Faunus)   In Greek mythology, the god of pastures, forests, flocks, and herds, a deity of creation pervading all things, and a follower of the god Dionysus*. He had the legs and tail of a goat, and the upper body of a man, finished off with goat horns and a beard. His lustful nature symbolized the spermatic principle of the world; the leopard skin he wore indicated the variety of created things. He was born in Arcadia, said to be a son of the god Hermes*, and his days were spent in idleness, cavorting with the nymphs, while in the evening he played the syrinx* or panpipes. Sudden terror, without cause, was attributed to his influence. He was a god of prophecy, and is reputed to have taught the art to the god Apollo*. He considered himself a fine musician, and even challenged Apollo (see Midas). Legend says that when the veil of the Temple was rent in twain, at the time of Christ's crucifixion (see Jesus Christ—Life Events), a cry swept across the ocean, "Great Pan is dead," and from then on, the responses of the oracles ceased forever. (see Oracle). The pine tree and tortoise were sacred to Pan and his attributes were the syrinx, a shepherd's crook, and pine leaves or twigs. Fresco transferred to canvas: *Pan, Bacchus, and Silenus,* Pinturicchio, Metropolitan, New York.

Panathenaea (pan-ath-a ne′a)   In ancient Greek religion, the greatest festival celebrated annually in honor of the goddess Athena* at Athens. It was held in July and August, and every fourth year with greater festivities. There were games, musical contests; above all, a procession from the Agora (market place) to the Acropolis (citadel), in which women carried a newly woven and embroidered garment to adorn a statue of the goddess Athena, animals were led up for sacrifice, and there were chariots and riders on horseback.

St. Pancras A patron saint of children, martyred under the Diocletian persecution* at the age of fourteen, about 304. He is usually represented in art as a boy with a sword in one hand and a palm branch in the other, the symbols of his martyrdom.

Pandora (pan-dō'ra) In Greek mythology, the maiden created by the god Hephaestus*. She was given a dowry box of all the evils in the world, and sent by Zeus to Epimetheus*. Sketch: *Pandora Opening Her Box*, John Flaxman, Metropolitan, New York. (see Epimetheus.)

Panther Skin In Greek symbology, an attribute of Dionysus*. In one of his epiphanies he was said to have been born a panther in winter.

Parables told by Christ A parable is a short story from which a moral may be drawn, sometimes an allegory (see Jesus Christ— Parables).

Paradise A Persian word meaning "garden" originally, brought into English by transliteration as "paradise," and used this way in the New Testament. It was not thought of as the abode of God until later in Christian dogmatic thinking.

Parcae See Fates.

Paris In Greek legend, the second son of King Priam* and Queen Hecuba* of Troy. Before his birth, his mother dreamed she would bring forth a fire brand, which would set Troy afire. King Priam, therefore, had the baby exposed at birth on Mt. Ida, but a bear suckled him for five days, and he was then found by a shepherd who reared him with his own children. As a youth, he married the nymph Oenone, and was living as a shepherd when the god Hermes*, sent by the god Zeus* called upon him, to decide the strife between the goddesses Hera*, Athena*, and Aphrodite*, over the Apple of Discord*. Paris awarded the apple to Aphrodite, and gained her protection, but he also won the eternal hatred of Athena and Hera against all the Trojans. About this time, King Priam held funeral games in memory of this lost son. Paris took part in the contests, and vanquished everyone. His prophetess sister Cassandra* divined who he was, and he was joyfully received by his parents. Spurred on now by Aphrodite,

Left: *Athena, Hera and Aphrodite vie for the Apple of Discord.* Right: *The Judgement of Paris.* The Paris Master. Fogg Art Museum, Harvard University.

Paris set out for Sparta in Greece, and carried off Helen*, the fairest woman in the world, who was the wife of Menelaus*. This act precipitated the Trojan war*. Paris was an active warrior, but he had the reputation of being a coward. After ten years of the war, he and Menelaus* fought in single combat as a means of settling the war's outcome, and he was defeated by Menelaus, but Aphrodite, unfairly, spirited him away at the last moment. Paris, however, was the one to shoot an arrow into the vulnerable heel of Achilles* and kill him. His own death came from one of the poisonous arrows of Heracles*, aimed at him by Philoctetes*. He was unmourned by anyone but his first wife Oenone, who in final remorse, leaped into the flames of his funeral pyre, and was consumed in his arms. In art, Paris is shown as a beautiful youth, sometimes with the high, pointed Phrygian cap. Painting: *The Judgement of Paris*, Nicolo dell Abate and Denys Calvaert, National Gallery, Washington.

Parnassus (par-nas'us) A mountain near Delphi in Greece, northwest of Athens. In Greek mythology, it was consecrated to the god Apollo, the muses* and the god Dionysus*, and was regarded as the seat of music and poetry. On its slopes was located the famous oracle* of Apollo* at Delphi. The mountain was a favorite place for the orgies of Dionysus.

Parthenos (par'the-nos)   A Greek epithet meaning virgin, given to several Greek goddesses.

Partridges   In ancient religion, partridges were sacred to the "Great Mother" in the spring dances of the equinox. In Christian religion, the partridge is a symbol of two opposites: the truth of the church, on the one hand, and deceit, theft, and the devil, on the other.

Pasiphae (pa-sif'a-ē)   In Greek legend, the wife of King Minos* of Crete, and the mother by him of Ariadne* and Phaedra*. At the request of Minos, the god Poseiden* sent a magnificent white bull for sacrifice to himself, but Minos, not wishing to sacrifice so fine a creature, sacrificed another bull in its place. In revenge, Poseiden caused Pasiphae to fall in love with the bull. Pasiphae confessed her passion to the builder Daedalus*, who made a great wooden cave for her in which she could consort with the bull. From this union, she produced the unsightly Minotaur*, with the body of a man and the head of a bull. Daedalus then built a labyrinth* to hide the monster. When Minos heard of the part Daedalus played in the affair, he locked him in the labyrinth as well, but Daedalus escaped on wings with his son Icarus*.

Pasithea (pa-sith'ē-a)   In Greek mythology, one of the Graces*, a daughter of the god Zeus* and the ocean nymph Eurynome. Pasithea was given to Hypnos* (sleep) by the goddess Hera*, in return for his putting Zeus to sleep. This was to prevent Zeus from helping the Trojans during the Trojan war*.

Passion, the   The title used for the sufferings of Jesus Christ*, from the time of his entry into Jerusalem until their culmination, in his death on the cross (see Jesus Christ—Life Events—Crucifixion). Painting: *The Passion*, Benvenuto di Giovanni, National Gallery, Washington.

Passover   The Jewish festival commemorating the deliverance of the Israelites. As described in Exodus 12:12-14, the angel of death slew the firstborn of the Egyptians, "passed over" the Hebrew houses, and spared all those who had followed the commands of Moses. In the time of Jesus, every male Hebrew over the age of thirteen was expected to celebrate the feast in Jerusalem.

St. Patrick   Patron saint of Ireland. He was the son of a Roman official, born at Dumbarton, England, about 373. He was captured in a raid, as a boy of sixteen, and was sold as a slave in Ireland. Here he first became interested in prayer, and when he escaped to Gaul, about the age of twenty, he studied under St. Martin* at Tours. Soon he had a supernatural call to preach to the heathen in Ireland, and returned with zeal. He met with much resistance at first, but later founded many churches, and a cathedral, and monastery at Armagh in 444. In Meath, it is said, he confronted the high king on Easter eve, kindled the light of the paschal fire on the hill of Slane, silenced the druids, and gained a hearing for himself as a man of power. Many legends are told of his miraculous healing ability. A famous legend tells how a serpent resisted him. Patrick made a box and invited the serpent to enter it, but the serpent thought it was too small. After a long argument, the serpent got in to prove it was too small. Patrick slammed the lid down, and threw the box into the sea. Tradition also says that he rid Ireland of vermin. Patrick is usually shown with a serpent and a shamrock leaf, the shamrock in allusion to the fact that he used it to explain the Trinity* to the heathen. Feast Day: March 17.

Patroclus (pa-trō′klus)   In Greek legend, the bosom friend of the hero Achilles*, who accompanied him, with the Myrmidons*, to the Trojan war. When Achilles withdrew his ships in the tenth year of the war, because of his feud with King Agamemnon of Mycenae*, over his captive girl Briseis*, Nestor*, Agamemnon's councilor, appealed to Patroclus to persuade Achilles to return to the aid of the Greeks. Achilles refused, but loaned Patroclus his armor. In a fight with Trojan prince Hector*, Patroclus lost his helmet, and Hector dealt him his death blow. Hector then donned the armor, and a struggle broke out for the body of Patroclus. The Greeks succeeded in capturing it, and carried it back to their camp. Achilles was wild with grief, and his goddess mother Thetis* preserved the body, which Achilles then refused to bury. Patroclus, however, appeared to him in a dream, asking for burial, and requesting that his ashes be put in the same urn as that which would eventually hold those of Achilles.

St. Paul the Apostle   The great 1st-century apostle of Jesus, known chiefly through the New Testament book The Acts, and his epistles. He was born in Tarsus, in Asia Minor, of Jewish Pharisee* parents who were Roman citizens, and was called Saul, but was usually known by his Roman name Paul. He was well educated in law at Jerusalem and knew Arabic, Hebrew, and Greek. As a student, he succumbed to student fanaticism against Christians, and aided those who stoned St. Stephen, the first deacon of the church in Jerusalem. He became a leader, and was on his way to Damascus, where he was being sent by the high priest to suppress Christianity, when he was suddenly struck blind by a great light from heaven, and heard a voice ask, "Saul, Saul, why persecutest thou me?" Paul was led into the city, and was

The Conversion of St. Paul. Jacopo Tintoretto. National Gallery of Art.

visited by the disciple Ananais, who laid his hands on him saying, "The Lord ... hath sent me, that thou mightest receive thy sight, ... and he received sight forthwith" and "straightway he preached Christ in the synagogues" (Acts 9). St. Paul and St. Peter were founders of the Christian church, and Paul made journeys through Asia Minor and Greece, carrying the word, chiefly to the Gentiles*. Defiant Jews attacked him in Jerusalem, and he was taken into custody by the military police. Rather than face local trial, Paul, as a Roman citizen, appealed for a hearing before Emperor Nero*. He was sent to Rome, and imprisoned there for several years, before he was probably, as a Roman citizen, beheaded with a sword. In art, he is shown with a sword as the symbol of his martyrdom, and an open book, indicating his epistles to the Gentiles. He is usually short of stature, with a bald head and a bushy beard. Legend relates that when he was executed in A.D. 66, milk flowed from his veins, instead of blood, indicating he had converted one of Nero's concubines. Feast day: June 29. Painting: *St. Paul the Apostle*, Vincenzo Foppa, Isaac Delgado Museum of Art, New Orleans, Louisiana; painting: *The Conversion of St. Paul*, Jacopo Tintoretto, National Gallery, Washington.

271

St. Paul the Hermit   This Paul is traditionally regarded as the first Christian hermit to go to the Egyptian desert, where, as a young man, he sought refuge from Thebes and from persecution under the rule of Emperor Decius. Legend relates that he spent 98 years in a cave. A raven brought him half a loaf of bread daily, and he had a date tree and a well. He was discovered here by St. Anthony Abbot*, and the two old men lived together until Paul's death, about 347, when Anthony buried him with the help of two lions. In art, he is shown as a very old man with long, white hair and a beard, sometimes clothed in palm leaves. The lions, who helped bury him, are seen with him, and the raven bringing bread. Feast day: January 15. Painting: *The Death of St. Paul the Hermit*, Sebastiano Ricci, University of Kansas, Lawrence.

St. Paula (347-404)   Paula was a Roman matron from a distinguished, wealthy family, who was left a widow at thirty-three, with five children. She devoted herself to religious study, influenced by St. Jerome*, and in 385 decided to join him, near Bethlehem, with her daughter Eustochium. They both learned Greek and Hebrew, and managed the affairs of Jerome, building communal houses for his followers and hospices for pilgrims. Paula's fortune was spent at her death, and she left St. Eustochium with a large debt. She was buried beneath the Church of the Nativity in Bethlehem. Painting: *St. Jerome, St. Paula, and St. Eustochium*, Francisco Zurban, National Gallery, Washington.

Pax   See Eirene.

Peach   In Christian iconography, the peach, like the apple, symbolizes salvation. It may also symbolize the virtue of the silent tongue and a virtuous heart, because of the pit within its pit.

Peacock   In Greek mythology, the peacock is an attribute of the goddess Hera*, sacred to her because she set the "all-seeing," one hundred eyes of Argus* in the peacock's tail. In Christian iconography, it is a symbol of immortality, because legend relates that the peacock's body does not molder. The hundred eyes of its tail are the "all-seeing" church. Peacock feathers are seen with St. Barbara*, in allusion to the fact that she was born in north Africa.

Pear   In Greek mythology, the pear tree is an attribute of the goddess Hera, as prime goddess of the Peloponnesus. In Christian iconography, it is shown with the "living" Christ, alluding to his love of man.

Pegasus (peg'a-sus)   In Greek mythology, the immortal, winged horse, born from the blood of Medusa*, when she was slain by Perseus*. Athena presented Pegasus to the muses; with the print of his hoof, he created the spring of Hippocrene, which gave the gift of song to all who drank from it. Bellerophon* captured Pegasus with the aid of a golden bridle, given to him by the goddess Athena*, while Pegasus was drinking from the spring of Pirene, at Corinth. He threw the bridle over the horse's neck, and tamed him. Then, seated on the back of the flying Pegasus, he was able to kill the fire-breathing Chimaera*. After the death of Bellerophon, the image of Pegasus was placed among the stars as a constellation.   Scene: *Bellerophon on Pegasus, Killing the Chimaera*, on a vase from South Italy (4th century B.C.); design, *Pegasus*, on a Steuben glass vase, Sidney Waugh, Metropolitan, New York.

Peleus (pē'lē-us)   In Greek mythology, the king of the Myrmidons*, the son of Aeacus*, husband of Thetis*, and the father of Achilles*. He took part in the Calydonian Hunt*, he went with the hero Heracles* to fetch the girdle of the Amazon queen Hippolyta*, and was one of the Argonauts*. He won the sea goddess Thetis for his bride by taking the advice of the centaur Chiron*, and at her noonday sleep, he seized her and manfully held her, as she attempted to escape him, changing herself into fire, water, a lion, and a serpent. At last, she yielded and they were married near Chiron's cave, with all the gods and nymphs attending. The only goddess who had been forgotten was the goddess of discord, Eris*, who in fury threw her Apple of Discord* among the wedding guests. This led to the Judgement of Paris, and ultimately the Trojan war*. Thetis bore Peleus seven sons; the first six she made immortal, Achilles was immortal except for his heel.   Scene: *Peleus Wrestling with Thetis*, on a red-figured Greek vase (5th century B.C.), Metropolitan, New York.

Pelias (pē'li-as)   See Jason, Medea.

Pelican   Legend says the pelican pierces its breast to feed its young. In Christian iconography, it has therefore come to represent Christ's sacrifice on the cross, through his love for man. It is sometimes shown on top of the cross.

Pelopia (pe-lō-pi'a)   See Aegisthus.

Pelops (pē'lops)   In Greek mythology, the son of Tantalus* and Atlas's* daughter Dione. When he was a child, his father slew him and served him up at a feast of the gods to test whether a god would recognize the taste of human flesh. The gods did not touch the meal, with the exception of Demeter*, who, grieving for her daughter Persephone*, ate of his shoulder bone, inadvertently. When the god Hermes* reassembled Pelops and restored him to life, Demeter replaced the shoulder with one of ivory. When Pelops grew to manhood, he won the hand of Hippodamia* in a chariot race against her father Oenomaus*. The defeat was accomplished by bribing the charioteer of Oenomaus to remove the axle pin of his chariot just before the contest. After the victory, Pelops did not pay the charioteer his promised reward, and drowned him instead. The dying charioteer cursed the house of Pelops, causing the misfortune that continued in the house of Atreus*. Pelops succeeded to the throne of Oenomaus, and the Peloponnesus was named after him. A sanctuary containing his bones was dedicated to him at Olympia.

Pen   In Christian iconography, a pen, usually shown with an inkwell, is an attribute of the Evangelists, and other writers of the Christian faith.

Penelope (pe-nel'ō-pē)   In Greek legend, the daughter of Icarius of Sparta, the wife of Odysseus*, and a model of domestic virtues. Her hand was won by Odysseus in a footrace, after which he took her to his island kingdom Ithaca. Before Odysseus left for the Trojan war*, she had one son by him, Telemachus*. Odysseus was away for twenty years, and was presumed by many to be dead. Penelope was pursued by over a hundred suitors who made themselves at home in the palace, eating and drinking her food and wine. She still hoped for the return of Odysseus and put the suitors off, saying she must finish weaving her father-in-law's shroud, secretly unravelling each night what she had woven during the day. When this statagem was discovered, she promised the enraged suitors to marry the man who could bend the bow of Odysseus in a shooting contest. Young Telemachus was not strong enough to expel the suitors, and went to Nestor's* palace for advice. The suitors planned to ambush him on his return, but he was aided by the goddess Athena*, and she brought him safely back to Ithaca, just as his father returned, disguised as a beggar. Penelope was drawn to the beggar and confided in him, but when he and Telemachus killed off all the suitors, and he revealed himself to her, she suspected him of being an imposter. To test him, she gave orders to have his old bed moved. Odysseus told her the bed could not be moved as he himself had carved it out of a living oak tree, growing through the palace. With this proof, Penelope was satisfied, having waited with nobility and fortitude for over twenty years. Terracotta plaque: *Homecoming of Odysseus* (5th century B.C.), Metropolitan, New York.

Pentagram   This form symbolizes, in Christian iconography, the five wounds received by Christ on the cross.

Pentecost (pen'ta-kost)   The festival held by the Jews on the fiftieth day after the second day of Passover*, a harvest and "First Fruits" (the earliest fruits of the crop) celebration. On the Pentecost after the resurrection* of Jesus, his disciples were gathered together with the Virgin Mary*. Suddenly there came a sound from heaven like a rushing wind, and cloven tongues appeared to them like fire, and they were filled with the spirit of the Holy Ghost*, and were able to speak diverse languages. This event is described in Acts 2:2-4. In Christian religion, the feast of Pentecost commemorates the event, and is observed as the birthday of the Christian church and the feast of the Holy Ghost*. Pentecost falls on the seventh Sunday after Easter in Christian calendars.

Penthesilea (pen'the-si-lē-a)   In Greek legend, an Amazon* queen of great beauty, who came to fight for the Trojans* after Achilles* had slain Hector*. With twelve Amazon princesses, she sped into battle, causing the Greeks to flee in terror, until she came against Achilles. Her lance broke on his shield, and he transfixed her and her horse with his spear. When he removed her helmet and saw her beauty, he fell madly in love with her and was filled with remorse. He restored her body to King Priam* of Troy, and she was given full funeral honors by the Trojans.

Persecutions   The first three centuries of the Christian church were spent in torture and suffering, and are called the Period of Persecutions. These tortures were started by the Jews, and continued by the Romans; the first under Emperor Nero* was in 64, and the last, under Diocletian, was in 303.

Persephone or Kore (per-sef'o-nē or kō're) (Ro. Proserpina)   In Greek mythology, the daughter of the god Zeus* and the goddess Demeter*. The god of the underworld Pluto wished to marry her, but her parents would not consent. One day while Persephone was gathering flowers, Pluto suddenly appeared in a chariot, drawn by four black horses, seized the girl, and as the earth opened, disappeared with her in the chariot. Demeter was wild with grief, and withdrew fertility from the earth. Zeus then sent his messenger, the god Hermes* to restore Persephone to her mother, on condition that she had eaten nothing in the underworld. Pluto had tricked her into eating a few pomegranate seeds, however, and for that reason she was compelled to spend the equivalent number of months every year in his kingdom. As his wife and queen, she had great powers. As goddess of fertility, she personified the birth and death of vegetation, and new, young growth, in contrast to Demeter, as goddess of the ripened harvest. Under the name of Kore (maiden), she appeared with Demeter and Dionysus in the Eleusinian Mysteries*, the virgin daughter of Demeter. In art, she is represented as a beautiful maiden, frequently with her mother. Her attributes are the horn of plenty (cornucopia), a sheaf of wheat, and a cock, the emblem of her early rising in spring. As the severe queen of the underworld, she holds a torch and a pomegranate, symbolizing rebirth after death. She was especially worshipped in Sicily with Demeter. Two woodcuts, one from Paris (1539) and one from Venice (1501): *Abduction of Persephone*, from Ovid's *Metamorphoses*, Metropolitan, New York.

Perseus (per'sē-ūs)   In Greek mythology, the son of the god Zeus* and Danaë, and grandson of Acrisius. When Perseus was a child, his grandfather was warned by an oracle that his grandson would kill him. Fearful, he placed Perseus and his mother in a wooden box, and cast it into the sea. The waves carried it to the island of Seriphus, where it was caught in the net of the fisherman Dictys. He brought it to land and befriended Danaë and her son. After a number of years, Polydectes, king of the island, fell in love with Danaë. Perseus, growing to manhood, was in the king's way, so Polydectes sent him to fetch the head of the snaky-haired Gorgon, Medusa*, thinking he would die in the attempt. But the god's favored Perseus, and the god Hermes* was sent to join him on his journey. Hermes took him to the Graeae*, sisters of the Gorgons, who shared one eye between them. Under the guidance of Hermes, Perseus stole the one eye, and did not give it back until the Graeae directed him to the nymphs of the north. These nymphs equipped him with winged sandals, a wallet, and a cap of invisibility, and directed him to the clawed, staring-eyed Gorgons*. Hermes added a sickle-shaped sword to his equipment and the goddess Athena* a shield so bright, it enabled him to see the Gorgon's reflection in it. Thus armed, Perseus could avoid looking directly at the monsters, whose glance turned the beholder to stone. He found the Gorgons asleep, and with his face averted toward the shield, and hovering on his winged sandals, he smote off Medusa's head from the air. Then he thrust the head, whose powers remained active, into the wallet and flew off, pursued by the other two Gorgons, who could not find him in his invisible state. When he passed the giant Atlas*, he stopped and asked for shelter. Atlas refused, so Perseus exposed Medusa's head and turned him into the stone mountains of that name. As he flew on, he saw Andromeda* chained to a rock by the sea, awaiting her end from the sea monster that was ravaging her father's land. Perseus slew the monster from the air with one blow, and Andromeda became his bride. At the wedding feast, Perseus was attacked by a former suitor, who claimed the bride was his. Perseus was forced to expose the head of Medusa to save himself, and the suitor and all his followers were turned to stone. Returning next to his mother with Andromeda, he found Danaë had been forced to go into hiding to avoid the king's attentions. Perseus went to the palace where Polydectes was holding a banquet. As he entered the hall, all eyes turned to him. He held up Medusa's head, and the king and all his company were turned to stone. Perseus put Dictys on the throne in Polydectes' place, and then gave his magic armaments back to Hermes, who returned them to their owners. He gave the head of Medusa to Athena, who set it in the middle of her shield, or Aegis*. Then he returned to Argos with his mother and his wife. At Argos, while competing in a discus contest, at funeral games, he accidentally killed his grandfather, thus fulfilling the prophecy. Statue: *Perseus with the Head of Medusa*, Antonio Canova, Metropolitan, New York.

St. Peter   In the New Testament, Simon, called Peter, was one of the leading apostles, and one of the three favorites of Jesus*. He and his brother Andrew* were fishermen, sons of Jonas in Bethsaida, Galilee, and were called to be followers at the same time. Jesus* recognized Peter's powers of leadership early, and he became spokesman for the disciples. It was to Peter that Jesus said, "Thou art Peter, and upon this rock I will build my church; ... And I will give unto thee the keys of the kingdom of heaven" (Matthew 16:18-19). Peter was also rash and impetuous. When Jesus was arrested at Gethsemane*, he suddenly cut off the ear of the high priest's servant. He vowed loyalty, but when he followed Jesus to the court of the high priest's house, he denied his discipleship three times. When the cock crowed, he remembered that Jesus had foretold these denials, and wept (see Jesus Christ—Betrayal and Denial, under Life Events). After the burial of Jesus, Peter took the lead in investigating the open tomb. It was he who was the leader when the resurrected Christ visited the disciples on the shore of Galilee, and it was he who dared to walk on the sea of Galilee with Jesus (see Jesus Christ—Miracles). Peter carried the message of Christ throughout Asia Minor. From Antioch, he went to Rome and founded its first Christian church. When he was persecuted during Emperor Nero's* rule, he fled from the city, but in a vision met Christ entering it. "Lord, whither goest thou?" he asked. Jesus replied, "I go to Rome to be crucified anew." Peter returned to Rome and suffered crucifixion in A.D. 66, head downward at his own request, since he did not feel he was worthy of the same death as Christ. In art, Peter usually holds the keys of heaven, sometimes a fish, as a fisherman

The Calling of the Apostles Peter and Andrew. Duccio Di Buoninsegna. National Gallery of Art.

of souls, sometimes a cock, in reference to his denial of Jesus. If his mantle is yellow, it symbolizes revealed faith. He is usually shown as a bald, old man with a flowing beard, a book or a scroll in his hand, in reference to his epistles, or a sword, symbolizing his Christian zeal. He is the patron saint of fishermen. Feast day: June 29. Painting: *St. Peter*, Marco Zoppo, National Gallery, Washington.

St. Peter, Martyr A Dominican friar, considered the most important influence in the order after St. Dominic*. He was an

278

excellent preacher, and Pope Gregory IX made him the inquisitor general, an office for the persecution of heresy*. His acts of suppression were so cruel, the people turned against him, and he was assassinated near Milan. In art, he wears the robes of the Dominican order, and is seen with a wounded head, he carries a sword or knife, all references to his martyrdom. Painting: *St. Peter, Martyr,* Vittore Carpaccio, Philbrook Art Center, Tulsa Oklahoma.

St. Petronilla   A virgin saint who did not wish to marry a nobleman, called Flacco. Through constant prayer, she obtained the grace to die, and was buried before his eyes.

Phaedra (fē'dra)   In Greek legend, a daughter of King Minos* and Queen Pasiphae* of Crete, and a sister of Ariadne*. When her father died, she was given in marriage to Theseus*, king of Athens, and bore him two sons. Theseus had a son by his former wife Antiope*, called Hippolytus*. Phaedra conceived a passionate love for this stepson, but Hippolytus rejected her emotions, in horror. Phaedra then slandered the boy to Theseus. Hippolytus was banished by his father, and drove himself to his death in his chariot. Phaedra confessed her guilt and hanged herself in remorse.

Phaëton or **Phaethon (fā'a-tun** or **fā'a-thon)**   In Greek mythology, the son of Helius*, the sun god, who was brought up by his mother, the sea nymph Clymene. When Phaeton was grown, he visited his glorious father and begged, as proof of his paternity, that he be allowed to drive the golden sun chariot through the heavens for one day. Helius, having promised to grant him any wish, was forced to allow this rash plea. Phaeton started out, elated, but was not powerful enough to restrain the spirited horses. The chariot plunged toward earth, parched Libya, and blackened the inhabitants, and would have set the world on fire, had not the god Zeus* transfixed Phaeton with a thunderbolt, and hurled him into the Eridanus river.

Pharaoh (fā'ro)   The title given to the rulers of Egypt, in the early days of the great dynasties.

Pharisees (fa'ri-sēz)   The members of one of the sects of Jewry, noted for their attempts to separate themselves from the mainstreams of life for the purpose of cultivating piety.

Philemon and Baucis (fil-ē'mon & baw'sis)   In Greek legend, an old couple livin in Phrygia who opened their cottage to two strangers, sharing with them their meager meal of bread and wine.

During the repast, the couple noticed that the wine jug was never empty, no matter how many times it was poured. When the strangers noticed their surprise and anxiety, they revealed themselves, and the old couple found they had been entertaining the gods Zeus* and Hermes*. The gods gave their thanks, and promised the hospitable hosts whatever request they would like. Philemon and Baucis asked that they might both die at the same moment, and so it was. One day, in their old age, Baucis quietly became a linden tree and Philemon an oak, their branches intertwining at the top. Painting: *Philemon and Baucis*, Rembrandt, National Gallery, Washington.

St. Philip In the New Testament, one of the twelve apostles of Jesus* who came from Bethsaida in Galilee. He is associated with feeding 5000 people from five barley loaves and two fishes (see Jesus Christ—Miracles—Loaves and Fishes), and was present with the disciples in Jerusalem after the Ascension*. He is supposed to have preached the gospel in Syria. Legend recounts that he found the people of Hierapolis worshipping a serpent. Philip made the serpent disappear with a cross, but it left such a stench many people died, among them the king's son. Philip, again with the aid of the cross, brought the youth back to life. The enraged serpent priests seized Philip, and put him to death. In art, he is usually represented bearing a cross fastened to a staff or reed. The dragon or serpent is often shown, and sometimes loaves of bread, in reference to the miracle of loaves and fishes. Marble relief: *St. Philip*, Andria Bregno, Nelson Gallery of Art, Kansas City, Missouri.

Philistines Members of a non-Semitic people who were continuously at war with the Israelites for control of the country around Palestine from 1200 B.C. on.

Philoctetes (fil-ok-tē′tēz) In Greek mythology, the king of the Malians, to whom Heracles, at his death, gave his bow and poisonous arrows. On the way to the Trojan war, he was bitten by a snake, and left on the desolate island of Lemnos to recuperate. When an oracle declared, after many years of war, that Troy could not be taken without the weapons of Heracles*, Odysseus* and Diomedes* fetched Philoctetes from the island. His unhealed wound was restored to health by Machaon, the son of the great healer Asclepius*. Philoctetes then came to Troy, and was the one to kill Trojan Paris* with one of the famous, poisoned arrows of Heracles. Painting: *Philoctetes*, on a red-figured Greek vase (5th century B.C.), Metropolitan, New York.

Phoebus Apollo (fe′bus) In late Greek mythology, an epithet for the god Apollo*, when viewed as a sun god, and bright, light-bringer.

Phoenix (fē'nix)   In Christian iconography, a fabulous, legendary bird that symbolizes immortality and resurrection, because it was said that it burned itself periodically upon a funeral pyre, and rose from its own ashes, restored to youth. It is often seen in scenes of the Resurrection* and the Crucifixion*.

Phrixus   See Golden Fleece.

Phyleus   See Augeas.

Pick Axe   In Greek mythology, an attribute of Hades*, as god of the underearth fertility and wealth.

Pietà (pē-ā-tà)   Latin for "pity," this name is used for representations of the Virgin Mary* embracing the dead body of her son, after his descent from the cross* (see Jesus Christ—Life Events). Painting: *Pieta*, Filippino Lippi, National Gallery, Washington.

Pig   In Greek mythology, the pig is sacred to Demeter*, as a symbol of productivity. In Christian iconography, the pig represents lust and gluttony, and is shown with St. Anthony Abbot* who was greatly tempted, but overcame these temptations.

Pigeon   In Greek iconography, the pigeon is an attribute of the goddess Demeter*.

Pilate, Pontius   Pontius Pilate was the fifth Roman governor of Judea, from A.D. 26 to 36, whose administration was marked by tactless blunders. His supreme mistake was his cowardly responsibility for the crucifixion of Jesus, whose innocence he admitted publicly in his praetorium (court). Trying to exempt himself from personal responsibility, he literally washed his hands of the whole affair, even though his wife, Claudia Procla*, had warned him to have nothing to do with the righteous man. Pilate was finally brought to trial in Rome for slaughtering Samaritans, and was either killed or committed suicide (see Jesus Christ—Life Events— Trial before Pontius Pilate).

Pillar   In Christian iconography, a pillar is an emblem of the flagellation of Christ*. St. Sebastian* is often shown bound to a pillar, his body pierced with arrows. Pillars are also seen with Samson*, the strong man, in the Old Testament, who died pulling down the pillars of the temple of the Philistines*. The Pillar of

Cloud and Fire, which was cloud by day and fire by night, was believed by the Israelites to be God's torch, leading them on their wilderness trek from Egypt. It is described in the Old Testament, Exodus 13:21-22 (see Jesus Christ—Life Events—Flagellation).

Pillars of Hercules or Heracles The rocks opposite each other at the entrance of the Mediterranean sea are called the Pillars of Hercules. The tale is that they were bound together until torn apart by Hercules*, on his way to Gades (Cadiz), as his tenth labor for Eurystheus*. One legend says the way between the continents was much wider, and Hercules narrowed it to keep the monsters out from the great sea beyond.

Pincers or Shears In Christian iconography, pincers are a symbol of the martyrdom of St. Agatha*, who had her breasts torn off with them, and of St. Apollonia*, who was martyrized by having her teeth pulled with them. St. Dunstan* also seized the devil with a pair of red-hot tongs.

Pine Trees In Greek mythology, the pine tree was sacred to the god Poseiden*. Pine wreaths were used to crown victors at the Isthmian games, initiated by Poseiden. Pine trees are also an attribute of the goddess Cybele*, as the goddess of the wild forests.

Pirithous (pī-rith-ō-us) The king of the Lapithae*, whose bride, Hippodamia*, was attacked at their wedding feast by the Centaurs. He was a friend of Theseus*, and when he persuaded him to join him on an expedition to the underworld, they were both caught there on chairs of forgetfulness.

Placidus, Brother See St. Benedict.

Plague Spot In Christian iconography, St. Roch* is shown with a plague spot on his leg, in reference to his care for the stricken and his own suffering from the disease.

Plane In Christian iconography, a carpenter's plane is an attribute of Joseph of Nazareth*, who was a carpenter by trade.

Pleiades (plē'a-dēz) In Greek mythology, seven daughters of the giant Atlas* and the ocean nymph Pleione. Maia, the most beautiful of the girls, was the mother of the god Hermes* by the god Zeus*. Either because of their grief over the fate of Atlas* or because they were pursued for five years by the giant Orion*, they killed themselves, and Zeus placed them among the constellations. Their rising is the sign of the opening of spring, and their setting the sign of harvest. Painting: *The Pleiades*, Elihu Veddar, Metropolitan, New York.

Pluto (plū′tō) (Ro. Dis)   In Greek mythology, a cult name for Hades*. The name means wealth-giver, and is therefore associated with Plutus*. It is the name commonly used for the abduction myth of Persephone*.

Plutus (plū′tus)   In Greek mythology, the son of the goddess Demeter* and Iasion. (Zeus struck Iasion with lightning, out of jealousy.) Plutus is said to have been born in Crete, and is the god of riches. He is associated with Eirene*, the goddess of peace, who as a Horae* (goddess of the seasons) was also worshipped as the goddess of wealth. Legend says that Plutus was blinded by Zeus, so that his gifts should be equally distributed between the deserving and the less worthy.

Pole   In Christian iconography, a fuller's pole is an attribute of St. James the Less*, who is said to have been martyred with one. (Fulling is a process of shrinking cloth.)

Polydeuces (pol-i-dū′sēz) (Ro. Pollux)   See Dioscuri.

Polydorus (pol-i-dōr-us)   In Greek legend, the youngest son of King Priam* and Queen Hecuba* of Troy, who was sent to Polymnestor* in Thrace for safekeeping during the Trojan war*.

Polyhymnia or **Polymnia (pol-i-him′ni-a or po-lim′ni-a)**   One of the nine muses*, the muse of sublime hymn, pantomime, and religious dance. In art, she is shown in a meditative pose, heavily draped and without attributes.

Polymnestor (pol-im-nes′tor)   In Greek legend, a Thracian king, married to Illone, the oldest daughter of King Priam* of Troy. Her younger brother Polydorus* was sent to Polymnestor for safekeeping during the Trojan war, with much treasure. Polymnestor changed sides and went over to the Greeks; he murdered the boy and took the wealth that had been sent with him. When Queen Hecuba*, the mother of Polydorus, was brought as captive to Thrace, she blinded Polymnestor and killed his two sons.

Polynices or **Polyneices (pol-i-ni′sēz)**   In Greek legend, a son of Oedipus* and Jocasta*, who was driven from Thebes by his brother Eteocles*, with whom he was supposed to be sharing the throne. He fled to King Adrastus* in Argos, and was given his daughter Argia in marriage. She bore him a son, Thersander. An expedition, known as the Seven Against Thebes*, was formed to regain the throne for Polynices. During the battle for the city, Polynices met Eteocles face to face in single combat, and the two brothers killed each other. The body of Polynices was thrown to the birds by his uncle Creon* who took over Thebes, saying Polynices had fought against his own city. It was rescued by his sister Antigone*, who suffered death at the hands of Creon, in consequence.

Polyphemus (pol-i-fē'mus)   In Greek mythology, a one-eyed, giant Cyclops*, the son of the god Poseiden* and the nymph Thoosa. He held Odysseus* prisoner in his cave, and ate six of his companions. Odysseus made him drunk, blinded his one eye with a wooden stake, and escaped with the six remaining companions by clinging to the bellies of the giant's sheep, as they passed out of the cave to graze. Odysseus and his men sailed away, and Polyphemus called on his father Poseiden to avenge him. As a result, it took Odysseus twenty years to reach his home on the island of Ithaca.

Pomegranate   In Greek mythology, the pomegranate was said to have sprouted from the blood of the god Dionysus* when he was torn apart as a child by the Titans*. (The legend continues that he was reconstituted by his grandmother Rhea*.) It is an attribute of the goddess Persephone*, its ripe fruit, when split open like a wound, symbolizing death at the end of the year, and rebirth. This symbol grew out of the legend that Persephone ate pomegranate seeds in the underworld, when she was abducted by Pluto*. When the pomegranate is shown with the goddess Hera*, it is a symbol of fruitfulness. In Christian symbology, the seeds represent the unity of the church's congregation, as they lie unified within the fruit. From the legend of Persephone, the pomegranate also is a symbol of fertility, immortality, and resurrection*.

Pomona (pō-mō'na)   In Roman mythology, the goddess of fruit trees, a wood nymph, devoted to their culture, and particularly honored in the countryside. Vertumnus*, the god of gardens and orchards, finally won her hand by appearing to her as the handsomest of young men. In art, Pomona is shown as a fair maiden with fruits in her bosom and a pruning knife in her hand.

Pontius Pilate   See Pilate.

Poppy   In Greek mythology, the poppy is an attribute of the goddess Demeter*, for it is the flower growing in wheat, with sleeping and death properties.

Poseiden (po-sī'den) or **Poseidon** (Ro. Neptune)   In Greek mythology, one of the twelve Olympian gods*, the son of Cronus* and Rhea*, a brother of the god Zeus* and Hades*, swallowed at birth by Cronus*. When the universe was apportioned, Poseiden became ruler of the sea and its creatures, Zeus became ruler of the sky, and Hades ruler of the underworld. In earliest times, he was also the god of earthquakes. His wife was Amphitrite*, who bore him three children, and he is often shown with her and their son Triton*, driving over the sea in a chariot drawn by swift steeds, while sea creatures play around them. Poseiden was regarded as the inventor and tamer of the horse that he brought out of a rock with one blow. The bull was sacred to him, as a symbol of storm, and the dolphin, as a symbol of calm. He was always trying to increase his realm, and therefore contested with the goddess Athena* for Athens. He lost to her, but in the end, shared the Erechtheum temple with her, on the Acropolis of Athens. He contended with the goddess Hera* for control of the Argolid, but the river gods awarded the land to Hera. He contended with the sun god Helius* for domination over Corinth, but was only awarded the Isthmus by the sea giant Briareus*. Games were held here in his honor, and altars were raised to him. He was an inconstant husband, like Zeus, and had many love affairs. When he seduced the beautiful Medusa* in one of Athena's temples, Athena changed Medusa into a snaky-locked Gorgon. He may have been the father of Theseus*, and carried out the wish of Theseus to kill his son Hippolytus*. In the Trojan war, he was on the side of the Greeks, but after the war, he was the enemy of Odysseus*, who had blinded his son Polyphemus*, and he kept him wandering twenty years on his way home to Ithaca. Poseiden is the god who raises storms, causes shipwrecks or calm, and is worshipped by sailors. Black bulls were sacrificed to him. In art, he is represented as a powerful man, like Zeus, sometimes more compactly built, with thick, curly hair and beard. His powerful body may be nude, or clothed in long robes. His attributes are the trident (three-pronged fork), which he uses to stir up the sea and to bring water forth from the rocks, the dolphin, the horse, the tunny fish, and the pine tree. Painting: *The Triumph of Neptune and Amphitrite*, Nicholas Poussin, Philadelphia Museum of Art.

Potiphar (pot'i-fer)   In the Old Testament, the chief official of the Pharoah*'s bodyguard, who purchased Joseph* from the Midianites and placed him as an overseer in charge of his household. Later, when his wife falsely accused Joseph of assault, he put Joseph in prison (Genesis 39:1-21).

Potiphar's Wife   When Joseph was employed by Potiphar*, his wife fell in love with the attractive young man, and asked him to lie with her. Joseph, true to his master's trust in him, refused her many advances. One day she caught his garment as he fled from her presence. Then she used the garment to declare to her husband that Joseph had assaulted her. Painting: *Joseph Accused by Potiphar's Wife*, Rembrandt, National Gallery, Washington.

Potter's Field   The piece of land near Jerusalem which was bought by the priests with the thirty pieces of silver, cast at their feet by the remorseful Judas Iscariot*. The "blood money" secured what became the "potter's field" in which to bury strangers (Matthew 27:6-7).

Presentation in the Temple   See Jesus Christ—Life Events, and Mary the Virgin—Representations.

Priam (prī'am)   In Greek legend, the last king of Troy, the father of 50 sons and 50 daughters, 31 of them the children of Queen Hecuba*. Ominous signs before the birth of his son Paris* caused Priam to expose the baby on a mountain, but he was saved by a shepherd, and restored to the family as a young man. When Paris set sail for Greece with the adventurous purpose of abducting the fair Helen*, wife of Menelaus*, Priam gave his approval. In his young days, he had been a great warrior, but he was an old man at the outbreak of the Trojan war, and entrusted the command of the Trojans to his noble son Hector*. When the Greek warrior Achilles* killed Hector and barbarously dragged the body to the Greek camp, the aged Priam set out for the tent of Achilles, alone, by night. He found Achilles sleeping and could have murdered him, but with honor and humility he begged for the body of his dead son, and so touched Achilles, he was given not only the body, but time for the burial and funeral games as well. Subsequently, when the Greeks left the Wooden Horse* before the gates of Troy, Priam, over the protests of his prophetess daughter Cassandra, allowed the horse inside the city. The sack of Troy followed, and Priam was killed by Neoptolemus*, the son of Achilles, at the family altar where he had fled with Queen Hecuba.

Priapus (prī-ā'pus) (also known as Ithyphallus)   In Greek mythology, the son of the god Dionysus* and goddess Aphrodite*, identified with the Roman god Mutinuus. He was a god of the fruits of the field, vine growing, beekeeping, fishing, and goat and sheep breeding. Statues were put up to him in gardens, sometimes faun-like, to promote fertility, often of a phallic nature, or with phallic symbols. Sacrifices to him included asses as well as "first fruits" (the earliest produce of crops). His worship came originally from Asia Minor.

St. Processus   See St. Martianus.

St. Procla or **Claudia Procla**   The wife of Pontius Pilate* who besought her husband, saying, "Have thou nothing to do with that righteous man, for I have suffered many things this day in a dream because of him" (Matthew 27:19).

Procris   See Cephalus.

Prodigal Son   See Jesus Christ—Parables.

Proetus   See Bellerophon.

Prometheus (pro-mē'thē-us) (forethought)   In Greek mythology, one of the Titans*, the son of Iapetus and the ocean nymph Clymene, the brother of Epimetheus* (afterthought) and Atlas*, and the father of Deucalion*. The god Zeus* is said to have employed him to fashion men out of mud and water. Prometheus caused men to walk upright, and then gave them the ability to practice the human arts. When Zeus refused men the use of fire, Prometheus stole it from Olympus, and brought it to them in a hollow reed. To offset this blessing, Zeus sent Pandora* to Epimetheus and chained Prometheus, in punishment for the act, to a rock in the Caucasus. Here an eagle preyed on his liver all day, the liver being renewed each night. Prometheus was eventually released by Heracles*, during his eleventh labor for Eurystheus*, as he was travelling to fetch the Golden Apples of the Hesperides*. Heracles shot the liver-eating eagle (sometimes described as a vulture), and freed Prometheus from his chains. Prometheus then took over the immortality of the suffering centaur Chiron*, thus allowing Chiron, who had endured pain from a poisoned arrow of Heracles for years, to die in his stead, and go to the underworld. Zeus agreed to this exchange, and placed the arrow among the stars as the constellation Sagitta. He made Prometheus wear a ring containing a piece of the rock to which he had been chained, showing that he had been a prisoner, and a willow wreath, as a symbol that he had been freed. Prometheus returned to Olympus, and once more became adviser to the gods. Painting: *Prometheus Bound*, Rubens, Philadelphia Museum of Art.

Promised Land   In the Old Testament, the land of Canaan, so called because God had promised Abraham*, Isaac*, and Jacob* that their descendants would possess it.

Prophets   In the Old Testament, prophets were religious leaders of Israel, who from earliest times were studied for their revelations of the future, especially for the glories of Israel and the

Messiah to come. In art, the prophets were the embodiment of a symbol, rather than actual human beings, and were therefore depicted without special attributes or characterizations. Those most frequently seen are Isaiah*, Jeremiah, Daniel*, Ezekiel*, and Jonah*, who has the distinctive attribute of the whale; the others usually carry a book or a scroll.

Proserpina   See Persephone.

Psyche (sī'kē)   In Greek mythology, the personification of the human soul as loved by Eros*, the god of love. Psyche is carried off by the west wind Zephyrus*, for Eros, to a fine castle where she is visited nightly by the god. When she disobeys his order to love him in the dark only and unseen, he vanishes. Psyche then suffers innumerable trials, until she is finally purified and reunited with Eros in Olympus*. Psyche, as the soul, is often personified as a butterfly or a young maiden with butterfly wings. She is often shown pursued by Eros, sometimes united with him, or revenging herself on him (see Cupid). Wallpaper design: *Psyche and the Sleeping Cupid*, Louis LaFitte; woodcut: *Psyche in Her Chamber*, Edward Burne-Jones, both Metropolitan, New York.

Publicans   The name given in the New Testament to the master tax collectors. They supervised the subordinates who squeezed as much public revenue from the people as possible, and were despised by their fellow-Jews, grouped in the current thinking as sinners.

Purgatory   In the teaching of the Roman Catholic church, the state of death in which the soul destined for heaven is purified of taint. The nature and length of the state of purgatory are not defined, but the suffering is different from hell in that punishment is temporary.

Purple   In Christian iconography, a symbol of suffering, passion, and love of the truth. The color is worn by Mary Magdalene* and by the Virgin Mary* in scenes of the Crucifixion*.

Purse   In Christian iconography, an attribute of St. Matthew*, who is said to have been a tax collector (publican) early in life. Three purses are an attribute of St. Nicholas* (often shown as golden balls), because of the three bags of gold he threw into a poor noble's window to save his three daughters from earning their dowries in a disreputable manner. A purse, or bag of money, is also an attribute of Judas Iscariot*, who handled the money for the disciples of Jesus.

Putti   Naked children with wings, often seen in Christian art, are called putti, and are a symbol of innocence. Painting: *Putti*, Francois Boucher, Metropolitan, New York.

Pygmalion (pig-mā'li-on)   In Greek mythology, king of Cyprus who became so enamored of the statue of a maiden that he himself had carved in ivory, he prayed to the goddess Aphrodite* to endow it with life. When the goddess granted the request, he married the maiden, calling her Galatea*, and she bore him a son called Paphus, whose name was sometimes given to the island of Cyprus. Painting: *Pygmalion and Galatea*, Jean Leon Gerome, Metropolitan, New York.

Pylades (pil'a-dēz)   In Greek legend, a son of Strophius of Phocis, and a sister of Agamemnon of Mycenae*. He became the devoted friend of his cousin Orestes*, when Orestes was sent, as a boy, to the court of Strophius for protection from the evil designs of his stepfather Aegisthus*. Pylades accompanied Orestes on his mission of vengeance against Aegisthus and Clytemnestra*, and eventually married Electra*, the sister of Orestes. In some legends, he also accompanied Orestes on his trip to Taurus.

Pyramus and Thisbe (pir'a-mus & thiz'bē)   Two Babylonian lovers, the children of hostile neighbors who would not sanction their marriage. They communicated through a crevice in the wall, common to both houses, and agreed to meet at night near a mulberry tree. Thisbe arrived first, and fleeing from a lion, dropped her veil which the lion besmeared with the blood on his mouth, from a fresh kill. Pyramus, finding the veil, killed himself in despair. Thisbe, returning to the tree, discovered Pyramus, and killed herself with his sword. The fruit of the mulberry tree is said to be colored with their blood. Painting: *Pyramus and Thisbe*, Andries Lens, Metropolitan, New York.

Pyrrha (pi'ra)   In Greek legend, the wife of Deucalion*. The couple were the sole survivors of the deluge* which the god Zeus* sent to destroy the human race. Pyrrha and Deucalion repopulated the world by casting stones behind them, which turned into men.

Python (pī'thon)   In Greek mythology, a monstrous serpent produced by Gaea*, which haunted the caves of Mt. Parnassus*. It was slain by the god Apollo* with his first arrows, in the cave at Delphi*. A ritual drama was enacted there annually, representing the killing of the python.

Pyx   In Christian religion, the container for the Host* (unleavened bread) symbolizing the sacrifice of Christ* on the cross. It is an attribute of St. Clare*, referring to the tale that she placed the Pyx, containing the Host, on her threshold, and with it drove away besieging Saracens.

Q

Quadriga (kwad-rī′ga)   A two-wheeled chariot, drawn by four horses, harnassed abreast.

Quail   In Greek mythology, the quail is an attribute of Artemis*, in her early role as an orgiastic goddess who had the lascivious quail as her sacred bird. Ortygia (quail island), near Delos, was sacred to Artemis, as the island where she was born and where quails found asylum while migrating north.

Rabbit   See Hare.

Rachel   In the Old Testament, the shepherdess daughter of Laban*, and the great love of Jacob's* life, sought by Jacob to be his wife, in the same tradition as his mother Rebekah* had been sought to marry Isaac*, his father. Jacob was in service to his uncle Laban in Haran "twice seven" years for Rachel's hand, accepting, through the deception of Laban, her sister Leah* as a first wife. Leah bore Jacob six sons and a daughter, but Rachel remained barren. In jealous desperation, Rachel sent her hand-maiden Billah to Jacob, and by him Billah bore two sons. Then Leah, matching this gesture, sent her handmaiden to Jacob, and she also bore him two sons. Finally God blessed Rachel, and she gave birth to the beloved boy Joseph*. Jacob, now prosperous, decided to return to Canaan with his wives and children, cattle and goods, but because of Laban's miserly ways, he stole away secretly. Rachel decided to take the "god images" of the family with her, and hid them under her saddle in the tent. Laban, pursuing the family caravan, demanded the return of these images, but Rachel sat upon them calmly, and they were not discovered. Just before the group reached its destination, Rachel died at Eprath, giving birth to a second son called Benjamin*. Jacob erected a pillar over her grave, "the pillar of Rachel's grave unto this day" (Genesis 35:20).

Rainbow   In Greek mythology, the rainbow is the bridge that unites heaven and earth. The goddess Iris*, as messenger of the gods, personifies the rainbow. In Christian symbology, it represents union, because in the story of the Flood*, the rainbow appears as a manifestation of God's reconciliation with Noah*. In art, it may be shown as the throne upon which God, or Christ*, is seated; also, in scenes of the Last Judgement*.

Ram   In Greek mythology, the ram is sacred to the goddess Aphrodite*, as an emblem of fertility. The golden-fleeced, winged ram, sent by the god Hermes*, bore Phrixus* and Helle* through the air to the Hellespont* and Colchis.

St. Raphael (ra'fē-ul)   Meaning "God heals." In the Old Testament, an archangel, one of the principal angels of Jewish angelology. He is the angel, in the book of Tobit, who is the companion of Tobias*, and travels with him to Medea, teaching him both how to drive away the evil spirit pursuing Sara, and how to win her. In Christian tradition, Raphael is considered the guardian angel of all humanity, and is the angel who appeared to the shepherds after the birth of Jesus*, telling them that the saviour was born (Luke 2:10-11). In art, as a guardian angel, he is shown in beautiful raiment, a gold belt over his shoulder, and he carries a sword in one hand. As a pilgrim saint, he is shown with a staff and sandals, sometimes with a pilgrim's gourd or wallet at his belt. He carries a fish, in reference to the fish he helped Tobias to catch, which cured his father's blindness and was used to exorcise the spirit tormenting Sara.

Raven   In Greek mythology, a bird sacred to the god Apollo*, as a symbol of divination. Originally its plumage was white, but one day a raven told Apollo that the nymph Coronis* was faithless to him. Apollo shot the nymph, and turned the raven black for being a telltale. The raven was also an emblem of the goddess Hera*, in her capacity as guardian of citadels. In Jewish legend, the raven was also originally white, but when Noah* sent it from the ark to bring back evidence, it failed to return, and its plumage was therefore turned black. In the Old Testament, Elijah* was fed by a raven in the desert, and was thus kept alive. In Christian iconography, the raven is seen with hermit saints, symbolizing solitude. The raven carrying a loaf of bread is an attribute of St. Anthony Abbot* and St. Paul the Hermit*, to whom it brought bread daily in the desert. It is an attribute of St. Benedict*, who is said to have fed a raven when he was living as a hermit. A raven is said to have guarded the dead body of St. Vincent*. Sometimes the raven is a symbol of the devil, and is shown with St. Benedict in this capacity also, referring to his temptation by the devil in the form of a raven or blackbird. As a bird of ill omen, it is said to foretell death, and bring bad luck (see Crows).

Re (rā) or Ra   The great Egyptian sun god, who was thought of as travelling across the sky and ocean in a boat every day, descending by another boat to the underworld at night. The Pharaohs* (Egyptian rulers) regarded themselves as sons of Re, his living image on earth.

Rebekah (re-be′ka)   In the Old Testament, the daughter of Milcah and Bethuel, a sister of Laban*, and great niece of Abraham*. She was brought from the ancestral country Aram, by Abraham's trusted servant Eliezer, to be the wife of his son Isaac*, lest the youth marry a Canaanite. Eliezer, upon his arrival in Aram, went to the well to water his camels, and there found Rebekah filling her pitcher. Discovering that she was kin to his master Abraham, he asked for lodging. This granted, he made his request to take Rebekah to Canaan for the young Isaac. Rebekah consented, was blessed by her family, and rode off to the Negeb, accompanied by her maids. At the time of her arrival, Isaac was in the fields. When Rebekah learned that the young man in the distance was Isaac, she alighted from her camel and covered herself with her veil (Genesis 24). In middle life, because of famine, Isaac dwelt in King Abimelech's kingdom in Gerar, where he was well received and became prosperous. He pretended that the fair Rebekah was his sister, because he feared he might be killed if the people thought she was married to him. One day King Abimelech looked out of his window and saw Isaac "sporting with Rebekah." He called to Isaac, saying, "Of a surety, she is thy wife: And how saidst thou, She is my sister?" Isaac replied, "Lest I die for her." Abimelech then charged all his people to respect Isaac, saying, "He that toucheth this man or his wife shall surely be put to death." Rebekah bore Isaac two sons, Esau* and Jacob*, and Jacob, the younger, was her favorite. In Isaac's old age, she planned for Jacob a crafty seizure of the traditional birthright and inheritance of the first son, and by dressing Jacob in Esau's clothes and placing goat skins on his arms, so that he appeared like the hairy Esau, they fooled the blind, old Isaac. She then persuaded Jacob to flee from possible revenge, and sent him to her brother Laban* in Haran to seek a wife in the old, family home that she had come from. Jacob agreed, received his father's blessing, and found the girl Rachel*, as his mother had been found, at her father's well. Rebekah died before Jacob's return, and was buried in the cave bought for her mother-in-law, Sarah*, at Machpelah. Painting: *Rebekah at the Well*, Paolo Veronese, National Gallery, Washington.

Red Cross on a White Background   In Christian iconography, an attribute of St. George* of Cappadocia, and the old, national emblem of England.

Red Sea or Sea of Reeds   In the Old Testament, the sea over which the Israelites crossed from Egypt into the Sinai peninsula, dry shod (Exodus 14). A favorable wind and the tide will shallow the area so it is possible to walk over it. The Israelites, being on foot, were able to do so. The Egyptian chariots were bogged down by a shift of wind and a change of tide (see Moses).

Reed   In Christian iconography, a reed is a symbol of the humiliation of greatness, because Christ on the cross was offered a vinegar-soaked sponge on a reed to quench his thirst.

Regulus (reg'ū-lus), Marcus Atilius   Roman general in the First Punic war (264-261 B.C.). At first, he defeated the Carthaginians at sea and was successful on African soil, but was captured in 255. He was sent to Rome with envoys to solicit peace, but advised the senate against accepting the Carthaginian terms. Resisting the advice of Roman friends to break his parole, he returned to Carthage where he was tortured to death. This act made him a famous patriot-martyr. Painting: *The Death of Regulus*, Salvator Rosa, Virginia Museum of Fine Arts, Richmond.

Remus (rē'mus)   See Romulus and Remus.

St. Remy or Remigus (438-533)   Remy was the son of a count of Gaulish descent. A man of great brilliance and knowledge, he was appointed bishop of Rheims, France, at the extraordinary age of twenty-two. The great official act of his life was the crowning of Clovis I, king of the Franks, in 496, after which the king greatly aided his work. Tradition says that Clovis, like Constantine, was converted to Christianity by a turn of battle, which in this case was brought about by the prayers of his Christian wife Clothild. Remy was a zealous evangelist, and was said to have performed many miracles. He is represented, in art, carrying a vessel of holy oil, and is usually in the act of anointing Clovis, who kneels before him, or is seen in the baptismal font. Painting: *Baptism of Clovis*, Master of St. Giles, National Gallery, Washington.

St. Reparata   A Palestinian girl, who was martyred, for her Christian faith, at the age of twelve, in the third century. According to legend, she was tortured and then killed with a sword. Her soul rose from her body in the form of a dove, and ascended to heaven. In art, she is shown with a dove (her soul) flying from her mouth.

The Resurrection. Andrea Del Castagno. Courtesy of the Frick Collection.

Resurrection of Christ   The dogma that Christ rose from the dead on the third day after his crucifixion* (see Jesus Christ—After-Life in Christian Belief).

Reuben (rū′ben)   In the Old Testament, the eldest of the twelve sons of Jacob*, by his wife Leah*. He was kinder to his half-brother Joseph* than his brothers were, and aware of their guilt in selling Joseph to the Midianites. It was Reuben who guaranteed to their aged father, Jacob, the safety of the youngest brother Benjamin*, whom they brought to Egypt at the insistence of Joseph.

Rhea (rē'a)   In Greek mythology, the great mother goddess, a Titaness*, the daughter of Gaea* (earth) and Uranus* (heaven). She was the sister and wife of Cronus, and bore him the Olympian gods Hestia*, Demeter*, Hera*, Hades*, Poseiden*, and Zeus*. Cronus seized and swallowed each child as it was born, afraid that he would be dethroned. When Zeus arrived, Rhea went to Crete and hid him in a cave, presenting to Cronus instead a stone wrapped in swaddling clothes. At Rhea's urging, Zeus, when grown, compelled Cronus to disgorge his brothers and sisters by giving Cronus a strong potion to drink. Rhea was worshipped as a goddess of the powers of nature, as well as the originator of civilization and the founder of cities. After the rape of Persephone*, Rhea persuaded Demeter* to make the earth fruitful again, and induced her son Hades* to let Persephone return to earth for a part of every year. She purified Dionysus* of the murders he committed during madness, and initiated him into her mysteries, associated as she was with the Asian mother goddess Cybele*, and known as Rhea Cybele. She is also identified with the Roman Magna Mater or Ops. The oak, pine, and lion were sacred to her. In art, as Rhea-Cybele, she is usually represented enthroned between two lions, with a small drum in her hand. Sometimes she has a crown of towers, symbolizing her patronage of cities. Small terra-cotta statue: *Rhea Cybele in her Chariot*, Metropolitan, New York.

Rhea Silvea   See Romulus, and Vestal Virgins.

Ring   In Greek mythology, an attribute of Prometheus*, who was the first person to wear a ring. In Christian iconography, it is a symbol of never-ending eternity, and union. Two rings are an emblem of earth and sky, three rings a symbol of the Trinity*. A marriage ring is an attribute of Sts. Catherine of Siena* and Catherine of Alexandria*, because each of them betrothed her soul to Christ*, and became his celestial bride. The pope's ring bears the image of St. Peter* fishing, a cardinal's ring is of sapphire; other simple rings are worn by religious persons, all symbolizing spiritual union with the church.

Robe   A seamless robe is a symbol of the Passion, because Christ's coat "was without seam" (John 19:23). A scarlet or purple robe is also a symbol of the Passion, because the soldiers of Pontius Pilate*, after taking Christ's clothes, gave him a robe of scarlet or purple (see Jesus Christ—Life Events).

St. Roch or Roque (rosh or rok)   Roch was born at Montpellier, France, in the 14th century, with a birthmark shaped like a cross. While on a pilgrimage to Rome, the plague broke out, and Roch

Rhea Cybele, riding in a processional car, drawn by her lions. Roman, 2nd century A.D. The Metropolitan Museum of Art.

went from place to place, healing the victims by supernatural means. When he was himself stricken at Piacenza, he retired to the woods, where a hound brought him food daily. When he recovered, he returned to Montpellier, where he was arrested as a spy and thrown into prison, unrecognized by his relatives. After a few years, he died, and his cell was flooded with heavenly light. Later his body was stolen by the Venetians, and placed in the church of St. Rocco. In art, he is shown in a pilgrim's garb, with cockleshell, wallet, and staff, lifting his robe to display a plague spot on his leg. He is sometimes accompanied by a dog. Statue: *St. Roch*, Cloisters, Metropolitan, New York; painting: *St. Roch*, Lorenzo Costa, National Gallery, Washington.

Rod   In Greek mythology, the rod is an attribute of the goddess Nemesis*, as a symbol of measurement. In Christian iconography, a budding rod is a symbol of prayer (see Aaron, and Joseph of Nazareth).

Romulus and Remus (rom'ū-lus & rē'mus)   In Roman legend, Romulus was the founder of Rome (753 B.C.) and its first king. Romulus and his twin brother Remus were descendants of Aeneas* (the ancestor of the Romans) through the Alban kings, and were sons of the god Mars and the Vestal priestess Rhea Silvea, daughter of the Alban king Numa. Numa's brother Amulius seized the throne. Rhea Silvea as a Vestal Virgin* was condemned to death, and Amulius had the infants put in a chest and cast into the river Tiber. The children were washed up on a bank, and suckled by a she wolf. A shepherd found and reared them as his sons. When they grew to maturity, the twins restored Numa to the throne, and then founded a new city on the Palatine hill, a site Romulus selected from an omen of a flock of birds. Remus disagreed with the choice, and during the laying out of the city, the brothers quarreled, and Romulus killed Remus. The town prospered and grew, but there were no women for the followers of Romulus. One day the neighboring Sabine men were invited to a festival of games. During the celebration, the young Romans raided the Sabine territory, and carried off all the Sabine women they could find. A war ensued, but was settled when the Sabines were brought into the new city on an equal footing. At the end of a successful rule, Romulus was carried to heaven in Jupiter's chariot, and was worshipped there under the name of Quirinus. His wife was carried off to the heavens on a star, and was known as Hora. Painting: *Rape of the Sabine Women*, Rubens, National Gallery, Washington.

Rood   An English term for crucifix. It was often placed above the ornamental screen serving as a partition between the nave and the choir in a church, thus designated as the rood screen.

Rope   In Christian iconography, a rope is a symbol of the betrayal* of Jesus, because he was bound with a rope and led away by the high priest. It is also an attribute of Judas Iscariot* who is said to have hanged himself with a rope (see Jesus Christ—Life Events—Betrayal).

Rosalie or Rosalia, St. (rōz'a-lē or rō-za'li-a)   The patron saint of the city of Palermo, in Sicily, who is said to have been carried by angels to an inaccessible mountain, in the 12th century. Here she lived for many years in a cleft of a rock, which she wore away with her knees in devotion. In art, she is shown in a cave with a cross and skull, or in the act of receiving roses or a rosary from the Virgin Mary*.

Rosary   A string of beads on which prayers are counted as they are repeated. A rosary is an attribute of St. Dominic*, who instituted the devotion of the rosary. It is often seen in the hands of the Virgin Mary*.

Rose   In Roman mythology, the rose is an attribute of the goddess Venus*, and was a symbol of victory and triumphant love. Rose wreaths were worn by triumphing emperors. In Christian iconography, the white rose is a symbol of purity. A garland of roses is an attribute of the Virgin Mary*, referring to her rosary*. Red roses are a symbol of martyrdom. The thorns of a rose are a reminder of man's sins. Roses are shown with St. Elizabeth of Hungary*, in her apron or in her arms. St. Dorothea* is shown with a basket of roses and apples, and they are also an attribute of St. Benedict*.

St. Rose of Lima (1568-1617)   Isabel de Flores y del Oliva, known as Rose, was born of poor Spanish parents in Lima, Peru, and was the first person in the Americas to be canonized as a saint, in 1671. Rose worked hard as a young girl, declining marriage to support her parents. She joined the Dominican order, spending long hours in prayer in the summerhouse of her parent's garden, inflicting on herself cruel penances. Her mystical experiences and the temptations she suffered became the subject of ecclesiastical inquiry. St. Rose bore everything with patience, finding outlet for her zeal in care for the sick Indians and slaves. It is said that she sang songs to the birds during her mystical transports, and they answered her. She is considered the initiator of social services in Peru. Feast day: August 30.

Round Table   See Knights of the Round Table.

Roxana (rok-san'a)   The wife of Alexander the Great*, a Bactrian princess whom he married in 327. When Alexander died, she killed Statira, a rival wife, who was the daughter of Darius III, and then bore the posthumous son of Alexander at Babylon. Cassander, who was made regent for young Alexander IV, soon fought with Roxana, and in 311 had the boy and his mother murdered at the court in Macedonia.

Rudder   In Greek mythology, a rudder is an attribute of the goddess Tyche*, as the guide of man's fate.

Ruler   In Christian iconography, a carpenter's ruler or square is an attribute of St. Thomas*, the apostle, who was supposed to be a builder.

Ruth   The Old Testament book of this name recounts the story

Top left: *Ruth threshes her gleanings and brings the grain to Naomi.* Top right: *Naomi gives counsel to Ruth.* Lower section: *Ruth lies at the side of the sleeping Boaz while his corn is being threshed.* Illumination from The Pierpont Morgan Library Collection.

of the Moabite daughter-in-law of Naomi, a Bethlehemite. Both Ruth's and Naomi's husbands died in an epidemic, while the entire family was living in Moab. When Naomi decided to return to her native Bethlehem, Ruth, devotedly, insisted upon accompanying her. As they tried to settle in the city, Ruth, under Naomi's guidance, sought employment in the fields as a harvester, and found work with Boaz, who was a kinsman of her husband's family. Her industry won her praise and privileges from Boaz, who was also impressed with her devotion to her mother-in-law, and at night she lay quietly at his feet in an open field. Then Boaz decided to marry Ruth, and purchasing the shares of her dead husband's estate, he rescued her from widowhood. The firstborn of this marriage was Obed, the father of Jesse* and grandfather of King David*. The story certainly came into being in order to exalt the genealogy of David.

The Sacraments: Marriage and Extreme Unction. Flemish tapestry. The Metropolitan Museum of Art.

S   In Christian iconography, the letter *S* stands for the Holy Spirit.

Sabine Women   See Romulus.

Sacrament   A religious ceremony, initiated in the belief that divine grace is conveyed to the participant. In the Old Testament, anointing with holy oil, circumcision, and the slaying of the Passover lamb were sacramental acts. Early Christians used the word to signify a "sacred mystery." In the Roman Catholic and Orthodox church, the seven sacraments are: baptism,* confirmation (the confirming of baptism and admission into the church), Holy Communion* (the consecration of bread and wine), penance and confession, orders (the ceremony of ordaining ministers), matrimony, and extreme unction* (the sacrament administered by a priest at death). Protestatism, in general, recognizes only two sacraments baptism and Holy Communion.

Sacred Way   The ancient road in Greece from Athens to Eleusis, starting from the Diplyon gate and traversing the pass of Daphne. It was used for the procession in celebration of the Eleusinian Mysteries*.

Salome (sa-lō'mē or sa'lō-mā)   In the New Testament, the daughter of Herodias*, and niece of Herod Antipas*, who was her mother's second husband. Her dance before Herod on his birthday was rewarded by granting her request for the head of John the Baptist, a request dictated by her mother because John had denounced her marriage to Antipas. King Herod was taken aback, but he had given Salome his oath. John was beheaded, the head was brought on a platter, and presented to the girl, who gave it to her mother (Matthew 14:1-12). The story is often shown in art. Painting: *The Dance of Salome*, Benozzo Gozzoli, National Gallery, Washington.

Salome (Mary Salome)   In the New Testament, the wife of Zebedee. She witnessed the crucifixion* of Jesus, and visited the tomb with ointments for anointing his body. In art, she is often shown in scenes of the three Marys at the tomb. Painting: *St. Mary Salome and Her Family*, Bernhard Strigel, National Gallery, Washington.

Salvator Mundi   The Latin words for "saviour of the world." It is a title used in Christian art for representation of Jesus Christ, crowned with thorns, sometimes holding the globe, sometimes carrying the cross. Painting: *Salvator Mundi*, Coreggio, National Gallery, Washington; Painting: Hans Memling, Metropolitan, New York.

Samaria, Woman of   In the New Testament, a woman of Hellenistic background whom Jesus used as an example to show that it is the spirit of worship that counts rather than inheritance or culture (Jesus Christ—Life Events).

The Dance of Salome. Benozzo Gozzoli. National Gallery of Art.

Samaritan, the Good   See Jesus Christ—Parables.

Samson   In the Old Testament, Samson is listed as one of the judges, but he is primarily a simple man of supernatural strength who performed amazing feats: the rending of a lion with his hands; the slaying of thirty men, single-handed; the killing of a thousand Philistines with the jawbone of an ass; the carrying-off of the Gates of Gaza; and finally the pushing down of the pillars of the temple of Dagon with his bare hands. Samson owed this extraordinary strength to the uncut hair on his head. Throughout his lifetime, the Philistines* were his enemy, and they, suspecting he possessed some special power, persuaded Delilah*, a whore whom he loved, to wheedle his secret from him. Delilah then cut off his hair while he was asleep and destroyed his strength. The Philistines captured, blinded, and chained Samson in the prison of the temple of Dagon. Time passed, Samson's hair grew again, and he regained his might. At a great feast of the Philistines, he was called out of prison that all could make sport of him. Samson stood between the two middle pillars of the great house, and pulling them down, he collapsed the temple, destroying all his enemies and himself (Judges 13-16). Statuette: *Samson Overcoming Philistines with the Jawbone of an Ass*, Daniel de Volterra, Frick Collection, New York.

Samuel   In the Old Testament, the son of Elkanah and Hannah*, who was to become the first of the prophets after Moses* and a great seer. Samuel was born to the childless Hannah after she had vowed to consecrate her firstborn to God. He was consequently taken early to the priest Eli, and while still young, he had a vision of his religious mission. He soon became an outspoken judge and prophet, condemning pagan cults, drunkeness, and immorality. He was greatly concerned with Israel's national independence, and when his own sons demonstrated their lack of moral fiber, he satisfied the demands of the clamoring Israelites for a leader by anointing Saul* king. When Saul tried to take over Samuel's priestly privileges, Samuel secretly anointed David* as successor to Saul, and later, when Saul was suffering from madness, Samuel gave David shelter at his home in Ramah. Samuel was buried at Ramah with all Israel mourning him. He rose to service once more, however, when Saul went for advice to the witch at Endor. Samuel's spirit then appeared and rebuked Saul, informing him of his approaching end. Painting: *Consecration of Young Samuel by the Priest Eli*, Barent Fabritius, Chicago Art Institute.

Sandals   In Greek mythology, sandals with wings attached are an attribute of the god Hermes*. Winged shoes were given to Perseus* by the Graeae, when he was on his mission to kill Medusa*. Jason*, wearing only one sandal, was recognized by this peculiarity as a claimant to the throne by his Uncle Pelias*. In Christian iconography, discarded sandals are a symbol of humility and are often shown in scenes of hermit saints. They are an attribute of the archangel Raphael* in his role of pilgrim.

Sappho (saf'ō)   The greatest poetess of Classical antiquity, a native of Mytilene on the island of Lesbos, who lived in the 6th century B.C. She was married to a man from Andros and was a woman of strict and pure life, but when she gathered a group of young women about her in later years, unwarranted scandal arose. Equally unfounded is the legend that she threw herself in despair into the sea, rejected by the beautiful youth Phaon.

Sarah or Sarai or Sara (sā'ra or sā'rĭ)   In the Old Testament, the wife and half-sister of the patriarch Abraham*, married to him before they left their childhood home at Ur. Sarah's great beauty was twice the cause for Abraham to pass her off as his sister rather than his wife, because he was afraid he might be killed by those who coveted his wife. First, in Egypt, Sarah was taken into the household of the Pharaoh*, and Abraham was treated well for her sake. Then God sent a plague as a punishment to the Pharaoh's household, and the Pharaoh, discovering Abraham's ruse, sent them back to Canaan (Genesis 12:14-17). Abraham repeated the same trick in Gerar, deceiving King Abimelech, who discovered the imposture through a dream sent to him by God. Sarah was barren for many years. Believing she would never bear a child, she persuaded Abraham to take her bondslave Hagar* for a concubine wife, so that she might arrange for an heir. Hagar bore Abraham a son called Ishmael*, but now her haughty attitude to Sarah was a severe trial. Sarah sent them both away into the desert, but an angel of the Lord appeared to Hagar and advised her to return to her mistress. At last, God was gracious to Sarah, and promised her and Abraham that she would now conceive a son who would be heir to the covenant and father of a great nation. The aging Sarah laughed at the announcement, made by three visiting strangers (identifed as the Lord and two angels) to whom she was serving a hastily prepared meal in their tent. But when the word of God came true and the boy Isaac* was born, she changed her name from Sarai to Sarah, the princess. As Isaac grew, Sarah could not accept the mocking attitude of Hagar's son Ishmael toward this younger, precious child. She turned to Abraham, and once more Hagar and Ishmael were cruelly sent from the household, this time by Abraham. Sarah died at the age of one hundred and twenty-seven, deeply mourned by Abraham. She was buried in the cave purchased by Abraham for her resting place, at Machpelah. In Christian art, the three visitors, or angels, symbolize the Trinity*.

Sarpedon   In Greek legend, a Trojan hero who was the son of the god Zeus*, he fell during the Trojan war at the hands of Patroclus*. His great friend Glaucus* fought for the body while the Greeks captured his armor, and the god Apollo* came to the rescue. Taking the body from among the warriors, he cleaned it and erased the battle-marks and gave it to Hypnos* (sleep) and Thanatos* (death) to bring his body back to his kingdom in Lycia.

Satan (sā'tan)   In the Bible, the name given to the evil power that opposes God, but which God always dominates in the end. From the Apocryphal Book of Enoch, expressed also in the New Testament, comes the idea that Satan is the angel who rebelled against God and was cast from heaven to eternal damnation with minor angels called devils. Much of the sin of the world is ascribed to him, his greatest activity being the destruction of souls through temptation. Satan is also known as "the devil" and "the evil one."

Saturn   In Roman mythology, the god identified with the Greek Cronus* who was driven out by the Greek god Zeus* and fled to Italy where he was received by the Italian god Janus*. Saturn brought the arts of agriculture and its blessings with him, establishing the Golden Age. His wife was Ops, identified with the Greek Rhea*. His great festival of the Saturnalia was celebrated from December seventeenth to the twenty-third, and was a time of merriment, facilitating the transition to the Christian festival of Christmas and New Year.

Satyrs (sa'ters)   In Greek mythology, spirits of the woodland, followers of Dionysus. They had puck noses, bristling hair, goat-like ears, and short tails on their otherwise human bodies. They are represented as sly and immoral, fond of women and wine, playing pranks on others. In early art, they are shown with rather bestial faces, and sometimes horns and a horse's tail. Closely connected with Roman worship of the god Bacchus*, the Romans confused them later with fauns and represented them with the lower half of a goat. Painting: *Landscape with Nymph and Satyr*, Claude Lorrain, Toledo Art Museum.

Saul   In the Old Testament, the son of the Benjamite Kish, who became the first king of Israel after the populace demanded a ruler. The judge Samuel* was asked to choose the king, and he
Saul chosen king selected the striking Saul, who stood head and shoulders above his fellows, a man of wealth and religious nature. Saul soon showed his prowess in battle, fighting the invading Ammonites
Break with Samuel and Philistines*, but he fell out with Samuel, trying to take over his priestly functions. Samuel secretly appointed David* to be Saul's successor, and Saul became suspicious of everyone, melancholic and violent by turns. Not even his beloved son
David's help against Philistines Jonathan* escaped his jealousy. David, who had come as a skilled musician and harpist to Saul's court to alleviate his melancholy, married his daughter and developed into a renowned chieftain helping Saul in the border warfare, but after his triumphs, Saul suspected him of treason. First, he tried to kill David with a javelin; then, he drove him out of the kingdom. For many years
Attempts to kill David he continued a clumsy and insane pursuit, knowing David was anointed to rule after him. When he learned that the priest Ahimelech had fed David, he had Ahimelech and all his followers massacred. David had several chances to kill Saul, coming so near the unsuspecting, sleeping man, he was able to cut a piece off his

robe, but he always refrained and revealed himself openly, hoping to reestablish honorable relations. As the Philistines waxed strong, Saul, without David's help, began to lose all that had been gained. Suddenly he decided he must have the help of the dead Samuel, and went to the Witch of Endor to ask her to summon him from the world beyond. In the witches smoky tent, he thought he saw Samuel's form, and the form foretold his death, and that of his sons in the battle to be waged the next day. When Saul was wounded at Mt. Gilboa, his sons were already dead, and when his armor-bearer would not run him through with his sword, Saul fell by his own hand. The Philistines beheaded him and his sons, and nailed the bodies to the walls of Ashtaroth. Later, the bodies were buried under an oak by the men of Jabesh-Gilead. Watercolor: *The Witch of Endor Summoning the Shade of Samuel for Saul*, William Blake, National Gallery, Washington.

Witch of Endor

Death

Savior or Saviour   In the Old Testament, a term used occasionally by God himself, referring to his activity as deliverer of his people. In the New Testament, the term applies to Jesus Christ* to express his meaning for mankind: the man who came into the world with the purpose of saving it from sin, and to bring God and man together in a fellowship of love.

Saw   In Christian iconography, the saw is an attribute of Joseph of Nazareth*, indicating his profession of carpenter. It is also shown with St. Simon*, as the instrument of his martyrdom.

Scales   In Greek mythology, golden scales are an attribute of the god Zeus* and the goddess Themis*, both of whom preside over law and order, and weigh the destinies of men. In Christian iconography, scales are a symbol of justice and are shown with the archangel Michael* who weighs the souls of the departed.

Scallop Shell   In Christian iconography, a symbol of pilgrimage, because it was worn by returning crusaders from the Holy Land. It is an attribute of St. James the Great* because of the many pilgrimages made to his shrine at Santiago del Compostella, in Spain. It is sometimes shown with Edward the Confessor* A scallop shell with drops of water symbolizes Christ's baptism.

Scepter   In Classical mythology, an attribute of the gods Zeus*, Hera*, and Hestia* as a symbol of deity. Perseus* sometimes carries a scepter as a sign of his having achieved his kingdom. In Christian iconography, it is carried by kings and by archangels*, notably Gabriel*, as a symbol of sovereignty.

St. Scholastica (480-543)   The twin sister of St. Benedict* who also dedicated herself to the religious life and founded the Benedictine nuns. She was dedicated to God at an early age, and until she moved near to Monte Cassino, she probably lived at home. The brother and sister used to meet once a year near the monastery. Legend relates that, at their last meeting, Scholastica implored her brother to stay the night, "so that we may go on talking till morning about the joys of heaven." Benedict refused, whereupon Scholastica fell to prayer, and so fierce a storm suddenly arose, his departure was impossible. Three days later she died, and it is said that Benedict had a vision of her soul, in the form of a dove, ascending to heaven. When Benedict died, he was buried in the same grave with his sister so that death should not separate the bodies of the two who were so united in mind. In art, Scholastica is represented with a dove at her feet, pressed to her bosom, or flying toward heaven. She also holds a crucifix* or lily*. Feast day: February 10.

School of Athens   The school of philosophy founded by Plato in Athens in 387 B.C., known as the Academy.

Scissors   See Pincers.

Scorpion   In Greek mythology, Orion* was attacked by a scorpion. In Christian iconography, the scorpion is a symbol of treachery because the bit of its tale is a treacherous one. It is sometimes used as a symbol of Judas Iscariot*.

Scourge   In Greek mythology, the scourge is an attribute of the goddess Nemesis* for ritual flogging. In the Old Testament, a scourge is described as a whip of cords and was used as an instrument of punishment. At the time of the crucifixion of Jesus*, a condemned prisoner was scourged, prior to his crucifixion. In Christian iconography, the whip became a symbol of Christ's Passion* (see Jesus Christ—Life Events). In scenes of the scourging of Jesus, Pontius Pilate* performs the act, before delivering him to the soldiers. In the hands of a saint, a scourge suggests self-inflicted penance. When shown with St. Ambrose*, it is an allusion to his driving the Arian heretics out of Italy. It is an attribute of St. Vincent*, in reference to his martyrdom.

Scroll   In Greek mythology, the scroll is an attribute of the muses Calliope* and Clio*. In Christian representation, scrolls are used to indicate authorship instead of a book, particularly with persons from the Old Testament. It may also be seen with saints and Fathers of the church, usually hanging open with writing on it. The scroll is shown also with the Four Evangelists*. A scroll of music is an attribute of St. Cecelia*, as patroness of musicians, of

St. Ambrose*, who originated a mode of intoning liturgy, and of St. Gregory*, who originated the Gregorian chant.

Scylla   In Classical mythology, a sea nymph with whom the sea god Glaucus* fell in love. When he asked the sorceress Circe* to help him win Scylla's love, Circe fell in love with him herself. She transformed her rival into a monster by throwing magic herbs into her bathing pool. Scylla's upper body was untouched, but her waist was girdled with the necks and heads of six hideous dogs, and her lower limbs became a dolphin's tail. Whenever a ship passed near her cave, the dog heads reached out to grasp the seamen and devour them. Opposite Scylla is the whirlpool of Charybdis*. There is a coin (5th-century B.C.) stamped with *Scylla*, from Agrigentum, Sicily, in the Museum of Fine Arts, Boston.

Scythe   In Christian iconography, an attribute of death, symbolizing the cutting off of life. It is also an attribute of time*, or Father Time.

Sea of Tiberius   See Jesus Christ—Apparitions.

St. Sebastian (3rd century)   Sebastian was a Christian nobleman, born in Gaul, who became an officer of the Imperial guard of Emperor Diocletian. When Diocletian* learned of Sebastian's faith and his refusal to worship Roman gods, he sentenced him to be bound to a stake and shot to death with arrows. The archers left him for dead, but his wounds were healed by a widow of another martyr. When the Emperor discovered Sebastian was still alive, openly testifying to his faith in Jesus, he ordered that he be battered to death with cudgels. His body was thrown into the sewer of Rome but was rescued and buried at the feet of St. Peter* and St. Paul* in the catacombs. Sebastian is always shown in art, transfixed with arrows, usually bound to a stake or pillar. He is the patron of archers and soldiers. Feast day: January 20. Two paintings: *St. Sebastian*, Tanzio Da Varallo, and Amico Aspertini, National Gallery, Washington.

Selene (se-lē′nē)   In Greek mythology, the moon goddess, the daughter of the Titans*, Hyperion and Thea, and sister of Eos* (the dawn) and Helius* (the sun). One night she discovered the beautiful youth Endymion* sleeping on Mt. Latmus. She instantly fell in love with him, visited him nightly, and by him became the mother of fifty daughters. One legend says she caused him to sleep forever so that his beauty would never fade. Selene was a winged maiden and her golden diadem cast a soft light on the earth. Her chariot was drawn by white cows whose horns

St. Sebastion. Tanzio Da Varallo. National Gallery of Art.

symbolize the crescent moon. Later she was identified with Artemis* and the Roman Diana*. Painting: *Selene and Endymion*, Nicholas Poussin, Detroit Institute of Arts.

Semele (sem'e-le)   In Greek mythology, the daughter of Cadmus* and Harmonia*, who was beloved by the god Zeus*. The goddess Hera*, who was jealous of this love, assumed the form of Semele's nurse. She induced Semele to ask Zeus to grant any request. Having gained the promise, she asked him to appear to her in all his divine splendor. Zeus, unwillingly fulfilled the request, and as he showed himself amid thunder and lightning, Semele was burned to ashes. Zeus seized her unborn child and sewed it into his thigh until it was time for its birth. The child was Dionysus*. When Dionysus was made a god, he raised his mother from the underworld and set her in the heavens under the name of Thyone.

Sennacherib   See Isaiah.

Seraph or Seraphim (ser'a-fim)   Like the cherub*, the seraphim is a celestial being, guarding the throne of God. Its origin is uncertain, possibly derived from the serpentine, Assyrian, mythological creatures, or the Egyptian, guarding griffins*. Isaiah, in the Old Testament describes seraphim as six-winged.

Serpent, Snake, or Dragon   A universal symbol. In the Near East, it was a symbol of fertility cults and, so worshipped in Egypt, decorated the Pharaoh's* (ruler) throne. In Greek religion, the serpent was a guardian spirit, one of prophecy and of seasonal death and rebirth. It is an attribute of the god Apollo*, referring to his killing the Delphic Python, acquiring the gift of prophecy. The serpent is an attribute of the goddess Demeter* and her daughter Persephone* as a symbol of seasonal death through the renewal of its skin. The physician god Asclepius* carries the staff entwined with snakes (the caduceus) which is the staff of the god Hermes*, the renewal of its skin symbolizing the art of healing and of life. It was also supposed to have the power of discovering healing herbs. Dionysus* was said to have been born a horned child crowned with serpents. Eurydice was bitten by a snake and was given the chance of resurrection but the attempt failed. Hygeia*, the goddess of health, feeds a serpent water. The infant Heracles* strangled snakes. Medusa* had snake-like hair. Snakes were an attribute of the Roman goddesses Juno* and Minerva*, as war goddesses. In the Old Testament, the cunning of the serpent in the Garden of Eden* is a symbol of Evil (Genesis 3), mentioned by Jesus*, in the New Testament (Matthew 10:16). The rod of Moses* turned into a serpent, as did

Aaron's* before the Pharaoh (Exodus 4:2-4, 7:8-13). The serpent also denoted Assyrian and Babylonian hostility to God's plans. In Christian art, it is an attribute of many saints, among them St. George* and St. Margaret*, who destroyed dragons; saints are shown trampling on a serpent who represents the evil of Satan*. A snake emerging from a glass goblet is seen with St. Benedict* and St. John* the Evangelist, indicating their miraculous escape from poisoning. St. Patrick* is seen with a snake, because he cleared the country of snakes. When the serpent forms a circle, holding its tail in its mouth, it represents eternity.

Seven Against Thebes   In Greek legend, an expedition fabled to have taken place against the city of Thebes before the Trojan war*. When King Oedipus* abdicated his throne, laying a curse upon his two sons, Eteocles* and Polynices*, the sons agreed to reign alternate years. At the end of the first year, Eteocles, the elder brother, refused to give up the throne, whereupon the younger brother Polynices fled to Argos and induced six Argive chiefs to espouse his cause. The seven men with their followers laid seige to Thebes; Eteocles and Polynices slew each other in single combat, and all the heroes perished except Adrastus* who escaped on his winged horse Arion. Subsequently, the seven sons of the seven chiefs resolved to avenge their fathers' deaths. They marched against the city again, took it, and placed Thersander, the son of Polynices, on the throne. This second group was known as the Epigoni* (descendants). Theseus* is said to have rescued the corpses of the heroes who fell in the first expedition.

Seven Deadly Sins or Vices   The seven great offenses against God in the Christian church, known also as the capital sins, are: pride, avarice, wrath, envy, lust, gluttony, and sloth. In the Bible, the sins that deserve vengeance are: wilful murder, the practice of homosexuality, oppression of the poor, and defrauding the laborer of his wages.

Seven Joys and Sorrows of the Virgin Mary   (See Mary the Virgin)

Seven Last Words   The phrases spoken by Jesus while he was dying on the cross. They are:

"Father, forgive them; for they know not what they do." (spoken to God)

"To day shalt thou be with me in Paradise." (to a thief beside him)

"Woman, behold thy son! . . . Behold thy mother! "(To Mary and John)

"Eli, Eli, lama sabachthani? that is to say My God, My God, why hast thou forsaken me?" (to God)

"I thirst."

"It is finished."

"Father, into thy hands I commend my spirit."

Seven Virtues   See Virtues.

Seven Wonders of the Ancient World   These were listed by the ancients as: The pyramids of Egypt, the hanging gardens of Babylon, the tomb of Mausolus, the temple of Artemis at Ephesus, the Colossus of Rhodes, the statue of Zeus by the sculptor Phidias, and the pharos (lighthouse) of Alexandria.

Shadrach (shā'drak)   In the Old Testament, one of the three Hebrew companions of the prophet Daniel*, miraculously delivered from a fiery furnace into which they were all tossed for refusing to bow down to the golden image of Nebuchadnezzar (see Three Holy Children).

Shamrock Leaf or Clover   In Christian iconography, a symbol of the Trinity* and an attribute of St. Patrick*, who is said to have used the leaf to explain the Trinity to the heathens in Ireland.

Shears   See Pincers.

Sheba or Saba, Queen of (shē'ba or sa'ba)   In the Old Testament, a queen from southwest Arabia, famous for her visit to King Solomon* in the tenth century B.C., a journey of twelve hundred miles, which she made with a caravan of camels, laden with rich gifts and spices. Initially she posed riddles to Solomon to test his famous wisdom. When he came up to her expectations, she stayed on to enjoy his brilliant court and its luxury, while working out a trade alliance between her country and his. Tradition says, before she returned home, she became one of Solomon's wives and bore him a son Menelek, who later migrated to Abyssinia, founding its royal house (1 Kings 10:1-13). There is a legend that, during her visit, the queen had a vision of the crucifixion* and warned Solomon that when the Savior should be nailed to a tree, the end of the Jewish homeland would be near.

Sheep   In Christian iconography, twelve sheep, placed in groups of three, in the angles of the cross, symbolize the twelve apostles* (see Lamb).

Shell   See Scallop Shell.

Shepherd with Sheep   In Christian iconography, this representation is a symbol of the loving care of Jesus* for his flock.

Shield   In Greek mythology, the Aegis* of the god Zeus is described as a shield, forged by the god Hephaestus* with tassels of gold, the head of Medusa* placed on its center. This Aegis was also used by the goddess Athena*, who placed the head of Medusa on the shield, and by the god Apollo*. A shield is also an attribute of Ares*, the god of war. Half-moon shields were carried by warrior Amazons* and by the Roman Juno*, as a war goddess. In Christian iconography, the shield is an attribute of Sts. George*, Joan*, and Anskar*.

Ship   In Christian iconography, the ship is a symbol of the church, first used by Noah* when he built his ark (Genesis 6:14-22).

Shoe   In Christian iconography, an emblem of St. Crispin*, who was a shoemaker.

Shower of Gold   In Greek mythology, this was the form in which the god Zeus* appeared to Danae* in order to seduce her.

Sibylline Books   A collection of oracles, consulted by the Roman Senate in times of emergency. According to legend, the Cumaean sibyl offered nine books of prophecy to King Tarquin at an exorbitant price. He refused and she burned all but three of them, offering these to him at the same price as for all nine. Tarquin was astonished and bought the three, finding that they contained directions for the worship of the gods. He preserved and buried them in a vault beneath the Capitoline temple of Jupiter in Rome.

Sibyls (sib'ilz)   The name given in ancient mythology to prophetesses. They dwelt near springs or in caves, and under the influence of a frenzy, uttered their prophecies, which were supposed to be inspired by a deity. The Cumaean sibyl directed Aeneas* how to find the Golden Bough*, necessary for him to present to Queen Persephone* in the underworld. Medieval monks "adopted the sibyls" and making twelve of them, gave each a prophecy and an emblem. In art, the emblems are:

>   *the Libyan*—a lighted taper
>   *the Samian*—a rose
>   *the Cumaean*—a cradle
>   *the Cuman* or *Cummerian*—a crown
>   *the Erythrean*—a horn
>   *the Persian*—a dragon

the Tiburtine—a dove
the Delphic—a crown of thorns
the Phrygian—a banner and a cross
the European—a sword
the Agrippine—a whip
the Hellespontic—a T cross

Sickle   In Greek mythology, the god Hermes* gave Perseus* a sickle with which to kill the Gorgon Medusa*. It is an attribute of Cronus* who emasculated his father Uranus* with a sickle (see Scythe).

Sign of the Cross   In the Roman Catholic and Protestant church, the sign of the cross is made with the hand open and the thumb touching the palm. The gesture starts by touching the forehead, then the waist, the left shoulder, and the right shoulder. In the Greek Orthodox church, the thumb and index and middle fingers are joined, and the ring and little fingers are closed on the palm of the hand. The sign is made from the right shoulder to the left shoulder to indicate that Christ sat on the right hand of the Father when he ascended to heaven. The left-to-right gesture of the Roman Catholic sign indicates that, through the death of Christ, man was brought from the left of damnation to the right of salvation.

Silenus (sī-lē′nus)   In Greek mythology, a forest god represented as a shaggy, bearded, old man, sometimes with horse's ears and legs, usually drunk, often riding an ass or on a wine bottle. He was noted for his wisdom, and people often attempted to waylay him. King Midas of Phrygia* once got him drunk, plied him with questions, and was told that it would be better never to be born. In the 6th century, he became associated with Dionysus*, whom he is said to have educated, and with whom he appeared in Dionysian processions. There is a black-figured Greek vase (6th century B.C.) with a scene, *Silenus Ambushed by Followers of King Midas*, Metropolitan, New York.

St. Simeon the Stylite (si′mē-on)   The first of the pillar ascetics, born in Cilicia around 390, the son of a shepherd, who from earliest youth subjected himself to bodily austerities. In 423, he began to live on a pillar, on which he spent the last thirty-six years of his life. Over the years, it increased in height to sixty feet. Simeon adopted this extraordinary way of life, ostensibly to avoid the press of people who flocked to him for his prayers and advice. The contrary resulted and people came from all walks of life for his teaching. Many conversions were made, especially among the Arabs. Feast day: January 5.

317

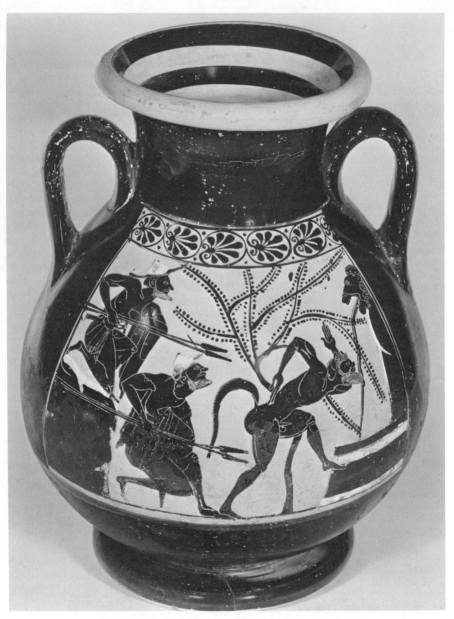

The Ambush of Silenus by henchman of King Midas. Greek 6th century, B.C., attributed to the Achelous Painter. The Metropolitan Museum of Art, Rogers Fund.

St. Simon   Known as the Zealot, Simon was one of the twelve disciples of Jesus* and is supposed to have preached the gospel in Egypt and Persia, where he was martyred with St. Jude*. He is represented in art with a saw in his hand, the instrument of his martyrdom, and sometimes with a fish, in reference to his occupation as a fishmonger, or with a fish on a book because he was a fisher of men through the gospel. Painting: *St. Simon*, Simone Martini, National Gallery, Washington.

Simon   See Jesus Christ—Life Events: Supper in the House of Simon, Parable of Debtors.

Sirens (si'renz)   In Greek mythology, a group of sea nymphs who sang to those sailing by their dwelling place and lured them to their deaths. Half-sea maidens and half-birds, they were once beautiful companions of Persephone*, but when Hades* took her to the underworld, the gods gave them wings to search for her in the sea. When Odysseus* passed the Sirens, he sealed his companions' ears with wax and tied himself to the mast of the ship. The Argonauts* were saved by Orpheus*, who sang even more enchantingly than the Sirens, as they sailed by. Since these mortals were unmoved by their song, legend says the Sirens cast themselves into the sea and became rocks. They were represented in art with great birds' legs, sometimes with wings, and with the upper body and head of a woman. The handle of a bronze Greek vase (5th century B.C.) has the form of a *Siren*, Metropolitan, New York; also, woodcut, *Siren*, Raoul Duffy, Metropolitan, New York.

Sisyphus (sis'i-fus)   In Greek mythology, a legendary king of Corinth, crafty and avaricious, who was possibly the father of Odysseus*, since he seduced Anticlea, the wife of Laertes who passed as the father. He was so deceitful and performed so many crimes, he was sent at death to Tartarus*, the lowest region of the underworld. To pay for his sins he had to roll a huge stone uphill. As soon as it reached the top, it rolled down again, and Sisyphus was doomed to start the toilsome task again throughout eternity.

Skeleton   In Christian iconography, the skeleton is a symbol of death and the brevity of life. It is frequently shown holding a scythe or an hourglass.

Skin over one Arm   An Attribute of St. Bartholomew*.

Skull   In Christian iconography, a symbol of death and an attribute of penitent saints, among them Mary Magdalene*, St. Paul*, St. Jerome*, and St. Francis*. A skull and crossbones, placed beneath a cross, symbolize death overcome by immortality; sometimes they represent Golgotha (Calvary)*, "the place of the skull."

Snake   See Serpent.

Socrates (sok′ra-tēz)   The great Greek philosopher of Athens (470-399 B.C.), one of the teachers of all time, out of whose intellectual school sprang that of Plato and the Dialectic system. He started life as a sculptor, but soon devoted himself to philosophy. During his life time, he served in the Peloponnesian war and was active in Athenian politics. He was married to Xantippe, said to be a shrewish wife, who bore him three sons. At the age of seventy, Socrates was condemned to death, allegedly for corrupting the minds of youth and for impiety (the introduction of new gods). This impiety was his belief in the immortality of the soul. Socrates did not defend himself, nor flee Athens as he easily could have done, but chose to abide by the laws of Athens and to drink poisonous hemlock, when his death sentence took place. He was supposed to be an ugly man and is so shown in art, looking somewhat like a satyr. Painting: *Death of Socrates*, Jacques Louis David, Metropolitan, New York.

Sodom   Sodom was a city that was destroyed by God because of the sexual sinning of its inhabitants. See Lot. Two paintings: *The Destruction of Sodom*, Frans van Oosten and Jean Baptiste Carot, Metropolitan, New York.

Solomon (sol′o-mon) (972-922 B.C.)   The third king of Israel, who was the son of King David* and Bathsheba*, whom David designated as his successor. Solomon was noted for his wisdom, and three thousand observations were credited to him. The most famous story of his judgements concerns two women, both of whom claimed to be the mother of the same child. Solomon called for his sword saying, "Divide the child in two and give each woman half." The true mother instantly cried, "My Lord, give her the living child and do not slay it," while the other woman said, "Divide it." Solomon gave the true mother the child. He was a glamorous personality, surrounded by a luxurious court of pomp and splendor, which was visited by many foreigners, among them the Queen of Sheba*. They were impressed not only with his knowledge, but with his extensive commercial ventures over newly opened caravan routes, and his vast building programs, including the first Hebrew temple in Jerusalem. Painting: *King Solomon and the Queen of Sheba*, Workshop of Sano di Pietra, Metropolitan, New York.

Solon (sō'lon) (640-599 B.C.)   The famous Athenian lawgiver who was also greatly esteemed as a writer of lyric poetry. His noble patriotism and wisdom found expression in his poems, intended to teach principles of humanity. His elegies are said to have amounted to five thousand lines. In art, he is often seen with the virtue Prudence (see Virtues).

Somnus   See Hypnos.

Sparrow   In Greek mythology, the sparrow is sacred to the goddess Aphrodite*. In Christian religion, it is a symbol of the lowly and is an attribute of St. Dominic*.

Spear   In Greek mythology, the spear is an attribute of Ares, as god of war, and of Athena, as goddess of war. Roman Juno is also a goddess of war and the spear is seen in her hand. Many warring heroes carry spears including the Amazons*. In Christian iconography, the spear is carried by St. Michael* and St. George*, as a symbol of spiritual warfare.

Sponge   In Christian iconography, a symbol of the Passion* (see Reed).

Sphinx (sfinks)   In Greek mythology, a creature borrowed from Egyptian symbolism. It had the head of a woman, the body of a lion, the tail of a serpent, and eagle's wings. According to the 8th-century B.C. writer Hesiod, Sphinx was a daughter of the Chimaera* and Orthus*. She frequented a high rock near Thebes and waylaid travelers with the riddle, "What walks on four legs in the morning, on two at noon, and on three in the evening?" Those who failed to give the right answer were hurled to their death from the rock. When Oedipus* came to Thebes, he answered the riddle correctly, "Man" in infancy, prime of life, and old age. The Sphinx, thus defeated, hurled herself from the rock. In Egyptian religion, the sphinx is represented as a wingless lion, with the head and breast of a man, or as a lion in front, a human behind, and bird's claws and wings. There is a marble sphinx (6th century B.C.) from the top of a stele, Metropolitan, New York.

Square   The four-sided square is an emblem of the earth and earthly things, as opposed to the circle, which is the symbol of eternity.

Stabat Mater (sta'bat ma'ter)   Latin for "the mother was standing." It is the Latin hymn, reciting the Seven Sorrows of the Virgin Mary*.

Sphinx. Greek, 6th century B.C. The Metropolitan Museum of Art.

Staff   In Greek mythology, the staff is an attribute of the goddess Hestia*. A staff with wings and a serpent curling around it is the attribute of the god Hermes* and is called the caduceus. Thalia*, the muse* of comedy, carries a shepherd's staff or crook. In Christian religion, the staff is a symbol of pilgrims and hermits. A staff with a white banner and red cross is carried by St. Ursula*. The archangel Raphael* carries a staff in his role of pilgrim. St. Philip carries a staff with a cross at its top. The palm tree staff is seen with St. Christopher* (see also rod and crosier).

Stag   In Greek mythology, the stag is an attribute of the goddess Artemis*, when she is worshipped as an orgiastic nymph. Actaeon* was turned into a stag by Artemis and then torn to pieces by his own hounds. In Christian iconography, the stag is a symbol of solitude and religious aspiration. A stag with a crucifix between its antlers is an attribute of Sts. Eustace* and Hubert*. It is also an attribute of St. Julian*.

Star   In Greek representation, a star on an egg-shaped cap is worn by the Dioscuri*. In Christian religion, the star is a symbol of divine guidance. The five-pointed star is shown as the one that guided the magi* to Bethlehem. It therefore symbolizes the Nativity* and is a sign of Christ. The six pointed star is the star of creation and is known to the Jews as the star of David. Twelve stars symbolized the twelve tribes of Israel and were adopted by the twelve apostles* of Jesus*. The Virgin Mary* is crowned with twelve stars in representations as the Queen of Heaven*, and as the Virgin of the Immaculate Conception*. One star is an emblem for the Virgin Mary as Star of the Sea. St. Dominic* is shown with a star on his forehead; St. Nicholas of Tolentino* is shown with a star on his breast, in allusion to the star that flashed through the sky when he was born.

St. Stephen   The first Christian martyr for the "faith," accused of blasphemy, and stoned to death in the presence of Saul who was to become St. Paul*. As he died, Stephen cried, "Lord, lay not this sin to their charge" (Acts 7:57-60). Legend states that Stephen's burial place was revealed in a vision to a Palestinian priest four hundred years later. The relics were taken to Rome and placed in a tomb with St. Lawrence*. St. Lawrence, "the courteous Spaniard," is said to have moved to one side in the grave and given his hand to Stephen. In art, Stephen is represented as a young man dressed as a deacon, bearing the palm of martyrdom. Stones are shown (sometimes on his head and shoulder) referring to his persecution. He is often seen with St. Lawrence. Painting: *St. Stephen*, Vittore Carpaccio, Philbrook Art Center, Tulsa, Oklahoma.

Stigmata (stig'mata) The marks developed on the bodies of highly religious persons, believed to be supernaturally impressed, which correspond to some or all of the five wounds received by Christ* on the cross. They are frequently seen on the praying St. Francis* and on Catherine of Siena*.

Stones In Greek mythology, the earth was repeopled by stones thrown over the backs of Deucalion* and his wife Pyrrha*. In Christian iconography, they are seen in the hands of saints, symbolizing mortification of the flesh. St. Jerome* and St. Barnabas* are often so shown. Stones are an attribute of St. Stephen*.

Stork In Christian iconography, the stork is a symbol of prudence, vigilence, chastity, and piety, associated with the Annunciation*, as the stork announces the coming of Spring.

Strawberry In Christian iconography, the strawberry is an emblem of perfect righteousness and good works. The strawberry trefoil symbolizes the Trinity*.

Stylus In Greek mythology, an attribute of Calliope*, the muse of epic poetry.

Styx (stiks) In Greek mythology, one of the five rivers surrounding Hades*, over which the souls of the dead had to pass. The river was so sacred that gods and men swore by it.

Sun In Christian symbology, the sun represents Jesus Christ*. The sun and the moon together are symbols of the Virgin Mary*, taken from the words in Revelation 12:1, "a woman clothed with the sun, and the moon under her feet." St. Thomas Aquinas* is shown with a sun on his breast.

Supper at Bethany and **Supper in the House of Simon** See Jesus Christ—Life Events.

Surgical Instruments In Christian iconography, surgical instruments are attributes of St. Cosmos* and St. Damian*, as physicians.

Susanna and the Elders A story from the Apocrypha* of the Bible. Susanna was the beautiful wife of a Babylonian merchant. Two elders of the community lustfully fell in love with her. Together, they hid in a closed garden when she was about to bathe, and sprang out of hiding, demanding that she give herself to them. Susanna repulsed them violently, even though they threatened to bring false witness against her and to accuse her in public of adultery with some youth. When they carried out the threat, Susanna was condemned to death in the place of judgement. Fortunately the young prophet Daniel* cried out, insisting she had not been given a fair trial. The trial was resumed and Daniel separated the accusers. These elders then gave conflicting evidence, proving that they were lying. Susanna was exonerated and the two elders suffered her intended fate. Painting: *Susanna and the Elders*, Tintoretto, National Gallery, Washington.

Swaddling   The practice in the Bible of washing a newborn child, rubbing it with salt and laying it on a square cloth, his head in one corner, his feet diagonally opposite. The cloth was folded over his sides, up over his feet, and swaddling bands were then bound around the bundle.

Swallow   In Greek mythology, the swallow was sacred to the goddess Aphrodite*. In Christian iconography, the swallow is a symbol of the incarnation* and resurrection* of Christ because it was thought to hibernate in winter, emerging from this state in spring. As a symbol of incarnation, it is shown in scenes of the Annunciation* and the Nativity*.

Swans   In Greek mythology, the swan is sacred to the god Apollo*; one legend says his soul passed into a swan. They are sacred to the goddess Aphrodite* because of their white plumage and the V formation of their flight, a female symbol. Leda* was said to have been ravished by the god Zeus*, in the form of a swan. Some legends say it was Nemesis* he seduced in this guise. The bird is fabled to sing beautifully just before it dies, a superstition without foundation but referred to often in literature and art. Another fable says all good poets pass into swans.

St. Swithin   According to legend, St. Swithin, bishop of Winchester who died in 862, wished to be buried in the churchyard, "that the sweet rain of heaven might fall upon the grave." The monks at his canonization a century later thought to honor the saint by moving the body to the choir of the church on a July fifteenth. But, as it rained for forty days thereafter, the monks wisely abandoned the project. Now it is said, if it rains on St. Swithin's day, it will rain for the next forty.

Sword   In Greek mythology, the sword was an attribute of the goddess Nemesis*, a symbol of punishment. It is an emblem of the hunter Orion*, and is sometimes seen with Theseus*, who was recognized by the sword he was carrying when he came to his father's court in Athens. In Christian iconography, the sword is a symbol of spiritual warfare and is carried by the archangel Michael*, St. George of Cappadocia*, and St. Louis of France*. The archangel Raphael* carried a sword as a guardian spirit. Saints Paul*, Euphemia*, Agnes*, Alban*, Peter Martyr*, Catherine of Alexandria*, and Justinia* were all martyred with the sword. When it is carried by a boy, it represents the martyrdom of St. Pancras*. A sword piercing a book is an attribute of St. Boniface*, who carried the gospel to Germany.

Sylvester (sil-ves'ter)   Sylvester became Bishop of Rome in 314, during the reign of the Emperor Constantine*. He is said to have cured Constantine of leprosy (or the leprosy of his sins) by baptism, which caused Constantine to order the worship of Christianity throughout Rome. Sylvester is also fabled to have proved to learned doctors that Christ was the God of Life by restoring a bull to life. In art, he is generally shown in bishop's clothes, holding a bishop's crosier*, and a book. The bull is often shown at his feet, or a dragon, symbolizing the breaking of pagan religion in the Roman Empire.

Syrinx (sē'ringks)   In Greek mythology, a chaste mountain nymph and huntress of Arcadia. She was pursued by the god Pan* and took refuge in the river Ladon, praying to be changed into a reed. The prayer was granted and Pan, hearing its singing sound, cut the reed into uneven lengths, and made his syrinx, or panpipes, with them.

Syrophoenician Woman's Daughter   See Jesus Christ—Miracles.

T As a Greek letter the T stands for Theos, meaning God. It is an attribute of St. Anthony Abbot*, usually shown on his robe at the shoulder.

Tabernacle In the Old Testament, the portable shrine used by the Israelites for worship during their wanderings in the wilderness. In Christian usage, it is the receptacle in which the vessel is placed, holding the consecrated elements of Communion (Eucharist)*.

Tabernacles, Feast of A Jewish festival lasting eight days, beginning on the fifteenth Tisri (end of September), in remembrance of the sojourn in the wilderness.

Tablets In Christian iconography, inscribed tablets symbolize teaching. They also symbolize the Ten Commandments*, which were given to Moses* by the Lord on Mt. Sinai.

Tanagra (tan-a'gra) A general name given to small, terracotta figurines mostly of the 4th and 5th centuries B.C., a great number of which were found at Tanagra, in Boetia, Greece. Originally household ornaments or gods, they were later buried in tombs in Greece, Sicily, southern Italy, and Asia Minor.

Tantalus (tan'ta-lus) In Greek mythology, a prosperous, Lydian king, a son of the god Zeus*, the father of Pelops* and Niobe*. As a favorite of the gods, he was allowed to take part in their deliberations and meals. He fell out of favor by stealing the immortality-bestowing food and drink of Olympus*, ambrosia and nectar, which he then distributed among his friends. He also committed the horrible crime of cutting up his son Pelops and serving him as a repast to the gods, in order to test their omniscience. He is also said to have perjured himself in order to keep a golden dog, which had been stolen for him by Pandareus from the temple of Zeus. As a punishment, he was sent to Tartarus, the lowest region of the underworld, and was condemned forever to stand in water up to his neck, with fruit dangling above him. Every time he stooped to drink, the water receded. When he reached for the fruit, it swayed beyond his reach. A huge stone, hanging above his head, threatened perpetually to crush him. The word "tantalize" comes from this legend.

Tarpeian Rock (tar-p̄e'an) An ancient rock of the Capitoline Hill in Rome, so called from the Vestal Virgin* Tarpeia, who according to legend, agreed to open the gates of Rome to the Sabines*, if they would give her "what they wore on their arms." The Sabines kept the bargain by crushing her with their shields, and hurled her body from the Tarpeian rock.

Tarquinius Sextus (tar-kwin'i-us)   A legendary Roman king (see Lucretia).

Tartarus (tar'tar-us) In Greek mythology, a deep, sunless abyss, situated in the lowest region of the Underworld, in which the wicked were punished.

Teeth In Christian iconography, an attribute of St. Apollonia*, who had her teeth pulled with pincers, as part of her martyrdom.

Teiresias see Tiresias.

Telemachus (tel-em'a-kus) In Greek legend, a son of Odysseus* and Penelope*. He was still an infant when Odysseus left Ithaca for the Trojan war*. When he grew to young manhood, he was unable to rid his father's palace of the unwanted suitors, pursuing his mother Penelope. He left Ithaca, and went to the court of Nestor* in Pylos for advice. In his absence, the suitors planned to ambush and kill him on his return, but he was protected by the goddess Athena*, and came back to Ithaca under her guidance to receive Odysseus, home, after twenty years of wandering. Together they rid the palace of the suitors, and Odysseus was reunited with his family. Some time later, however, Odysseus learned from an oracle that he would be killed by his son, and he banished Telemachus from Ithaca. Telegonus, the son of Odysseus by the sorceress Circe*, carried out the prophecy, unaware of the identity of Odysseus when he attacked him. Telegonus took the body of Odysseus back to Circe, accompanied by Penelope and Telemachus. Circe, through her sorcery, made them all immortal, and married Telemachus.

Tellus Mater   Roman counterpart of the Greek earth goddess Gaea*. When her temple was dedicated in Rome in 286 B.C., an earthquake occurred. Thereafter, she was invoked during earthquakes, and was associated with rites for the dead. She was also invoked in solemn oaths, with the god Jupiter*, and like Ceres*, was a goddess of fruitfulness and marriage. Cows, and cows with unborn calves, were sacrificed to her. The ashes of the calves were kept by the Vestal Virgins* for purposes of purification.

Temptation in the Wilderness   See Jesus Christ—Life Events.

Ten Commandments   According to Biblical record, Moses* ascended Mount Sinai in the third month after the Exodus* from Egypt, and the Ten Commandments were pronounced to him orally by the Lord. After Moses had communed with God on the mount for 40 days, the Lord gave him two tablets, upon which were written the Commandments with the finger of God. Moses returned to the camp of his followers, and found them worshipping a golden calf*. This so angered him, he shattered the tablets. After the congregation had been purged of their bad faith, Moses was again summoned to the mount by God, and bearing two newly hewn tablets, he rewrote the Commandments which God spoke to him. When he descended from the mount and read them to his followers, he covered his face with a veil, so they would not be afraid of his shining face. The tablets were deposited in the Ark of the Covenant*, and finally housed in the Temple of Jerusalem. The Ten Commandments have a permanent place in the ethical system of Judaism and Christianity. (Exodus 20:2-17). They are, as follow (in shortened form):

I am the Lord thy God . . . Thou shalt have no other gods before me.
Thou shalt not make unto thee any graven image.
Thou shalt not take the name of the Lord thy God in vain.
Remember the sabbath day, to keep it holy.
Honour thy father and thy mother: that thy days may be long.
Thou shalt not kill.
Thou shalt not commit adultery.
Thou shalt not steal.
Thou shalt not bear false witness against thy neighbour.
Thou shalt not covet.

Termagant (ter'ma-gant)   The name given, in medieval romances, to an idol or deity that the Saracens were popularly supposed to worship. He was introduced into morality plays as a violent person in Eastern robes, a dress that led to his being thought of as a woman.

Terpsichore (terp-sik'or-ē) In Greek mythology, one of the nine muses*, daughters of the god Zeus* and Mnemosyne* (memory). She was the muse of dance and dramatic chorus, later of lyric poetry. In art, she is usually shown seated, holding a lyre. Fresco transferred to canvas: *Terpsichore*, Giulio Romano, Metropolitan, New York.

St. Thadeus (also known as Jude) Jude is traditionally identified as the brother of James* and of Jesus*, if the Apocryphal virginity of Mary is not accepted; he is the writer of the Epistle of Jude, in the New Testament. He is alleged to have preached the gospel in Persia, where he was martyred with St. Simon*, known as the zealot. Jude is the patron of those in desperate straits. In art, he is represented with a club, or staff, and a carpenter's square, in allusion to his trade. Sometimes he has a halberd (hatchet), in reference to his martyrdom in Persia with this instrument. Feast day: October 28. Painting: *St. Thadeus*, Simone Martini, National Gallery, Washington.

Thais (tha'is) An Athenian courtesan, the mistress of Alexander the Great*, whom she accompanied on his expedition to Asia. She is said to have induced him to set fire to the palace of the Persian kings at Persepolis. After Alexander's death, she became the mistress of Ptolemy, king of Egypt, and bore him two sons.

Thalia (tha'lē-a) In Greek mythology, one of the nine muses*, daughters of the god Zeus* and Mnemosyne* (memory). She is the muse and patroness of comedy, and is also said to supervise planting and farming. In art, she is generally shown holding a comic mask, a shepherd's crook, and a wreath of ivy. Fresco, transferred to canvas: *Thalia*, Giulio Romano, Metropolitan, New York.

Thanatos (than'a-tos) In Greek mythology, a personification of death, the brother of Hypnos* (sleep) and Nyx* (night), sometimes thought of as a killer of pain, and a healer.

St. Thecla or Tecla The first female Christian martyr, a perfect disciple, who was converted to Christianity at St. Paul's* feet, having heard him preach through the open window of her house. When Paul was leaving on a dangerous journey, Thecla asked permission to accompany him, cut her hair short, and put on

330

male attire to do so. She was exposed to many tortures, including flames and wild beasts in the arena. Late in life she was a famous healer, and the jealous, local doctors tried to kidnap her. Thecla fled, and a rock opened to receive her, leaving only a piece of her mantle exposed. In art, she wears a loose mantle and holds the palm of the martyr. Sometimes wild beasts are shown with her. Feast day: September 23. Painting: *The Virgin with St. Thecla and St. Ines*, El Greco, National Gallery, Washington.

Themis (thē'mis) , In Greek mythology, one of the Titans*, the mother of the Moerae* (the fates) and the Horae* (the seasons), the goddess of divine justice. The rites of hospitality were under her protection, as were the oppressed, and she had the power of foretelling the future. In art, she is represented as a commanding woman, holding scales, a symbol of order and justice, and a cornucopia*, as the patroness of hospitality.

St. Theresa or Teresa of Avila (1515-1582) A Spanish Carmelite nun, who came of a noble family. In her early years, she was an uninspired nun, but in 1555, she underwent a "second conversion," after which she experienced inner visions and went far in the path of mysticism. She was interested in reforming the Carmelite order and founded the barefoot rule. She also collaborated with St. John of the Cross*, and helped him to found his monastery of friars. A remarkable woman of brilliance and charm, she combined intense practicality with her rarified spirituality, and inspired not only her associates but a great reform movement across Christendom. She left many writings of great literary worth that are sources of modern mysticism. Painting: *St. Theresa Praying for the Souls in Purgatory*, Rubens Metropolitan, New York.

Theseus (thē'sē-us) In Greek legend, the son of Aegeus*, king of Athens, and of Aethra*. Aethra was seduced by Aegeus while he was on a visit to her father Pittheus, in Troezen. Before his return to Athens, Aegeus laid his sandals and sword, an heirloom from Cecrops*, under a great rock, charging Aethra, if a son was born, to send the boy with these tokens to him, as soon as he was strong enough to lift the rock. Aethra named the son Theseus, and when he raised the rock at the age of sixteen, she sent him on his way to Athens, wearing the sword and sandals. In the years that had passed, Aegeus had married the sorceress Medea*, who bore him a son, Medeus. When Theseus arrived at his father's palace, Medea recognized him before his father did, and tried to poison his cup of wine. As Theseus started to drink, Aegeus noticed the hilt of the sword Theseus was wearing. He dashed the cup to the ground, and overcome with joy, celebrated the arrival

Origins and youth

of Theseus with all Athens. Medea and her child disappeared mysteriously through the air in a chariot drawn by winged serpents. Theseus ingratiated himself with the Athenians by destroying the Marathon bull*, which was terrifying the populace, and sacrificed it to the god Apollo*. Presently the time drew near for the payment of tribute to King Minos of Crete*; seven youths and seven maidens were to be sent from Athens to be fed to the

Cretan Minotaur*. Theseus insisted on joining the group, with the intention of slaying the monster. Aegeus was forced to give his consent, but made Theseus promise to change the ship's black sail for a white one on the return trip, should the mission be successful. Upon his arrival in Crete, Theseus gained the love of Ariadne*, the daughter of Minos. She gave him a ball of thread that had been offered to her by the master inventor Daedalus*, and by means of this thread, Theseus was able to mark his path into the labyrinth* where the Minotaur was kept, slay the monster, and find his way out again. Ariadne escaped on the ship

with Theseus and his companions, but at the island of Naxos, Theseus forsook her, or left her at the command of the gods. Excited by his success, he forgot the signal agreed upon with his father, and did not hoist the white sail as the boat neared the shores of Greece. Aegeus, anxiously scanning the horizon, saw the black sail, and hurled himself from the Acropolis in despair.

Theseus now became king. He induced the Attic communities to recognize Athens as the capital of the country, and thus founded the Attic state. He initiated the Isthmian games, took part in the Calydonian Hunt*; he sailed with the Argonauts*, and fought a war with Heracles against the Amazons (ninth labor of Heracles). He returned to Athens with the Amazon Antiope*, and she bore him a son Hippolytus. Later she was killed, fighting with Theseus against her sister Amazons, who purportedly attacked Athens to rescue her from Theseus. Subsequently Theseus married Phaedra*, who fell madly in love with her stepson Hippolytus, and then killed herself. Theseus next carried off the twelve-year-old beauty from Sparta, who became the famous Helen* of Troy, because he was anxious to make this marital alliance. In this he was aided by Pirithous*, and in turn he helped Pirithous at his wedding, in the battle against the Centaurs*. He then accom-

panied Pirithous to the underworld, because Pirithous wished to bring Queen Persephone* back to the upperworld as a new bride. Unfortunately Theseus was trapped there on a chair of forgetfulness, until Heracles*, on his trip to Hades*, rescued him four

years later. When he came back to the upperworld, all was changed. Helen had been rescued by her brothers, the Dioscuri*, and his mother had been captured with her. In sadness, he went

to the island of Scyros, where King Lycomedes treacherously threw him from a high rock into the sea. Representations of the heroic deeds of Theseus are frequently shown in art, particularly his combat with the Amazons and the battle of the Centaurs. He is generally shown as a powerful, beardless man, of slighter build than Heracles, although he may wear a lion skin and carry a club also, instead of his early emblem, a sword. Painting: *Theseus Fighting the Minotaur*, on a black-figured Attic vase (6th century B.C.), Metropolitan, New York.

Thetis (thē'tis) In Greek mythology, a sea goddess attended by fifty Nereids*. She was the wife of Peleus*, and the mother of the hero Achilles*. When Thetis was pursued by Peleus, she turned herself successively into fire, water, a lion, a serpent, and a fish, but Peleus grasped hold of her firmly, until she consented to marry him. Each son she bore to Peleus she immersed in flames, to burn away their mortal parts, and sent them to Olympus, the home of the gods. Peleus surprised her on the night she was performing the rite on the baby Achilles*, and when Peleus screamed, she dropped the child, fled into the sea, and was never seen again. In the more usual legend, Thetis dipped the baby into the river Styx* and made him invulnerable, except for the heel by which she held him. Thetis performed many services for the gods. She gave Dionysus* refuge under the sea, when King Lycurgus went after him for trying to introduce his worship in Thrace. She hid the god Hephaestus* for nine years, when he was hurled by the goddess Hera out of Olympus*, and it was Hephaestus who made the magnificent armor for her son Achilles. She persuaded the hundred-handed Briareus* to untie the thousand-knot net in which the god Zeus* had been imprisoned by the other gods. She gave safe passage to sea voyagers, among them the Argonauts*, when they went past Charybdis* and Scylla*. At the wedding of Thetis with Peleus, Eris* threw the famous Apple of Discord*.

Thisbe See Pyramus.

St. Thomas A disciple of Jesus, often called "doubting Thomas" because he refused to believe in Christ's resurrection until he touched Christ's wounds with his fingers (John 20:24-29). Similarly, in tradition, he doubted the Assumption of the Virgin Mary*. The Virgin convinced him by lowering her girdle to him from heaven. Thomas is said to have established the church in India, where King Gondoforous gave him money to build a palace. Thomas distributed the money to the poor instead, erecting "a great palace in heaven." Because of this legend, he is patron of masons and architects, and has a builder's or carpenter's rule as his attribute. He may also be seen in art with a lance, the instrument of his martyrdom. Feast day: December 21. Painting: *Assumption of the Virgin*, Girolamo da Carpi, National Gallery, Washington.

St. Thomas Aquinas (1225-1278) , The great medieval theologian, often esteemed to be the greatest. He was one of many children, and was educated in the Benedictine monastery of Monte Cassino, in Italy, but later joined the order of St. Dominic*. He appeared slow-witted and was nicknamed "the dumb ox" by his peers. Thomas, however, was an independant thinker, and quietly became an outstanding theologian and teacher at the University of Naples, basing his Christian doctrine on Aristotle. His major work is the "Summa Theologia." In art, his attributes are the ox, the chalice (sacramental cup) because of his devotion to the sacrament in his writings, a dove, representing the inspiration of the Holy Ghost*, and the sun, which is usually seen on his breast, as an indication of the sorrow of all creation at the death of Christ*. He is usually in monastic robes and sometimes is seen with a star. Painting: *St. Thomas Aquinas, Aided by St. Peter and St. Paul,* Bartolomo digli Erri, Metropolitan, New York.

Three Holy Children A story from the Book of Daniel and the Apocrypha. Shadrach, Meshach, and Abednego, companions of the prophet Daniel*, were bound and cast into a fiery furnace by King Nebuchadnezzar* of Babylonia, because they would not worship his pagan golden image. They were miraculously saved from the flames, which were so hot they killed those who had thrown them into the furnace. Nebuchadnezzar saw the three men walking with the angel of the Lord in the midst of the flames; in astonishment he called them to come forth, and they emerged unharmed. Then Nebuchadnezzar said, "Blessed be the God of Shadrach, Meshach, and Abednego." And he ordered his people to respect the three youths and their god, and he promoted them in the province of Babylon (Daniel 3).

Thorns In Christian iconography, thorns signify grief and sin. Christ's crown of thorns was a parody of the Roman emperor's crown of roses, which was worn on triumphal occasions. When shown with saints, thorns are a symbol of martyrdom.

Three Marys at the Tomb See Jesus Christ—Apparitions.

Thunderbolts In Greek mythology, thunderbolts are an attribute of the god Zeus*, which only he, as king of heaven, might wield.

Thyestes (thī′es′tēz) In Greek legend, a son of Pelops* and Hippodamia*, and a brother of Atreus* with whom he was a rival for the throne of Mycenae. When Thyestes seduced the wife of Atreus, Atreus killed all the children of Thyestes in revenge, and served them up to him at a feast. When Thyestes learned the truth, he pronounced the curse that brought about the terrible misfortune that befell the house of Atreus. A few years later, following the orders of the oracle of Delphi, he seduced his own daughter Pelopia*, the oracle having foretold that a son, born of this union would bring revenge on Atreus. The son, Aegisthus*, grew up to kill Atreus, and Thyestes obtained the throne (see Atreus).

Thyrsus (ther'sus)   In Greek mythology, the thyrsus is carried by the god Dionysus* and his followers, the Maenads*. It is a staff of reeds topped with a pine cone, and is sometimes wrapped in vines.

Tiara   In Christian iconography, the tiara is a three-tiered crown, worn only by the pope. It is an attribute of Sts. Gregory* and Sylvester*.

Tiberias, Sea of   See Jesus Christ—Apparitions.

Tiger   In Greek mythology, the tiger is an attribute of the god Dionysus*, because a tiger helped him build a bridge across the river Tigris on his way to India where he then taught his vine culture.

Time or Father Time   In Renaissance art, time is represented as a nude figure with wings. His attributes are a scythe, an hourglass, a snake or dragon biting its tail, and the Zodiac. Sometimes he walks with crutches to show his age.

Tiresias or Teiresias (tī-rē'si-as)   In Greek legend, the famous, blind soothsayer of Thebes, who lived for seven generations. One legend says he was blinded at the age of seven because he saw the goddess Athena* bathing, and she splashed water in his eyes and destroyed his sight. As retribution, she gave him the gift of prophecy and the power to understand the birds. Another legend says the goddess Hera* blinded him because he decided against her in a dispute she had with the god Zeus*; she maintained that the male derived most pleasure from lovemaking, while Zeus claimed that females did. Tiresias plays an important part in the story of Oedipus* and the wars of Thebes.

Titans (tī'tanz)   The twelve sons and daughters of Uranus* (heaven) and Gaea* (earth), among whom were Cronus* and Rhea* (parents of the Olympian gods)*, Iapetus (father of Atlas*, Prometheus*, and Epimetheus)*, Themis* (mother of the Horae and Moerae)*, and Mnemosyne* (mother of the muses).

Tobias and the Angel. Filippino Lippi. National Gallery of Art.

Gaea incited her children to make war on their father, and made Cronus* ruler in his place. Cronus was dethroned in turn by the Olympian god Zeus*, whereupon half the family, led by Atlas, warred against Zeus and his brothers and sisters, carrying on fierce and lengthy fighting. Zeus finally put them to rout with the aid of the Cyclops*, and hurled all, except Atlas, into Tartarus* in the underworld.

Tobias (to-bī'us) The hero of the Book of Tobit, included in the Apocrypha*. Tobit, a devout Jew of Nineveh, was blinded while sleeping, because sparrows "muted warm dung" into his eyes. He sent his son Tobias on business for him to a distant city in Media. Tobias was accompanied by his dog and the archangel Raphael* disguised as a traveller. At the Tigris river, a fish attacked Tobias. Instructed by Raphael, Tobias, caught the fish, which they ate, and then carefully saved its heart, liver and gall. In the city, they came to the house of Sara, who was possessed of a demon. Her seven husbands had been killed successively on her wedding nights by this demon, called Asmodeus. Tobias, under the guidance of Raphael, exorcised the demon with the heart and the liver of the fish, and then married Sara himself. They all returned to Nineveh, and Tobias cured his father's blindness with the gall of the fish. Raphael went back to heaven, and Tobias praised the Lord. Painting: *Tobias and the Angel*, Filippino Lippi, National Gallery, Washington; *Tobias Cures His Father's Blindness*, Bernado Strozzi, Metropolitan, New York.

Tongs In Christian iconography, an attribute of St. Dunstan*, archbishop of Canterbury, in the 10th century, who was a metal-worker, and used his tongs to good effect against the devil*. In Greek mythology, they are an attribute of the god Hephaestus*, who was a mastersmith.

Torch, Burning In Greek mythology, a burning torch is an attribute of the god Areas*, as a symbol of war; of the goddess Artemis*, who has the power to send sudden death; of the god of love Eros*, as a symbol of sudden passion; of the goddesses Demeter* and Persephone*, symbolizing death and rebirth; of Hymen*, the god of marriage; of Comus*, the Roman god of mirth; and of Vesta*, goddess of the hearth. In Christian iconography, a burning torch is a symbol of Christ, as light of the world. The torch is an attribute of St. Dorothea*, who was burned at the stake. A dog with a flaming torch in his mouth is an attribute of St. Dominic*, symbolizing the spreading of the gospel by his order.

Tortoise In Greek mythology, the tortoise is an attribute of

Aphrodite*, as an earth goddess. Also of the god Pan*, as a woodland god. In Christian iconography, the tortoise is a symbol of reticence and chastity.

Towel with a Pitcher   In Christian iconography, this refers to the act of Pontius Pilate*, when he washed his hands of the guilt of Christ's crucifixion (Matthew 27:24). See Jesus Christ—Life Events—Trial Before Pontius Pilate.

Tower   In Christian iconography, the tower is an attribute of St. Barbara*, who was shut up in a tower by her father.

Transfiguration, the   In the New Testament, a supernatural experience of Jesus* on a high mountain, which he ascended in order to pray with his disciples Peter*, James*, and John*. Before the eyes of the disciples, Christ's garments became glistening white, his face shone, and prophets of the Old Testament, Moses* and Elijah*, appeared and talked with him. The disciples slept briefly; when they awoke a great shadow came over them, and they heard God saying, "This is my beloved Son . . . hear ye him." The disciples fell on their faces, afraid. When Jesus bade them rise they saw no one there but Jesus (Matthew 17:1-9).

Treasure   In Christian iconography, an attribute of St. Lawrence*, who gave away the treasure of the church to the poor.

Tree   The tree of Jesse* is the genealogical tree of Christ's ancestors, which began with Jesse, the father of King David*. A flowering tree is an attribute of St. Zenobius*.

Triangle   In Christian iconography, the triangle is a symbol of the Trinity*.

Trident (tri'dent)   In Greek mythology, the three-pronged spear is an attribute of the god Poseiden*, and is an emblem of his power as sea god.

Trikir   See Dikir.

Trinity   See Holy Trinity.

Tripod (tri'-pod)   In Greek mythology, an attribute of the Pythian god Apollo* at Delphi*, on which the Pythian priestesses gave their oracular responses. It was a bronze altar, resting on three feet, with three rings on top to serve as handles. In art,

Heracles* is often shown trying to steal the tripod of Delphi, because the priestess refused to give him advice. Apollo rushed to protect the priestess, Heracles attacked Apollo, and the god Zeus* sent a thunderbolt to separate the combatants. After this violence, the priestess gave Heracles instructions. Painting: *Heracles and Apollo Fighting Over the Tripod*, on a red-figured Greek vase (6th century B.C.), by the Andokides painter, Metropolitan, New York.

Triptolemus (trip-tol'ē-mus)   In Greek mythology, a son of Celeus of Eleusis, upon whom the goddess Demeter* bestowed the arts of agriculture, and instructed in her worship. Demeter sent Triptolemus around the world in a chariot drawn by winged serpents, so that he might extend the culture of grain to mankind. He is supposed to be the first priest of Eleusis and its mysteries*. Painting: *Triptolemus Going Off in a Winged Chariot to Spread the Knowledge of Grain*, on a Greek vase (5th century B.C.), by the Troilos Painter, Metropolitan, New York.

Trismegistus (triz-ma-jis'tus)   The Egyptian name for the Greek god Hermes*. Many inventions were attributed to him, among them the art of writing hieroglyphics, the creation of harmony, the art of astrology, the invention of the lute and the lyre, and all mysterious sciences.

Tristram (tris'tram)   The hero of a Welsh romance, originally distinct from the Arthurian legends, but early incorporated with them. Tristram, the nephew of King Mark of Cornwall, was sent to Ireland to fetch Isolde (also called Iseult) for the king's bride. During the voyage they unknowingly drank a love potion, and forever loved each other. Discovered by King Mark, Tristram fled to Wales and later to Brittany, where he married Iseult of the White Hands, but did not forget Isolde of Ireland. Later, he sent for her to heal his wounds, but his wife, in jealousy, told him that Isolde refused to help him. Tristram died of grief, and when Isolde heard the news she also died.

Triton (trī'ton) , In Greek mythology, a son of Poseiden* and the sea nymph Amphitrite*, who lived with his parents under the sea in a golden palace. He was represented as a man from the waist up and with the tail of a dolphin from the waist down. His special attribute is a seashell, which he blew to raise or calm storms. In late mythology, many Tritons came into being, sometimes having the forefeet of a horse.

Troilus (troi'lus or tro'i-lus)   In Greek legend, a son of King Priam* and Queen Hecuba* of Troy, who was killed by Achilles* in the siege of Troy, either in the sanctuary of a temple or while he was exercising his horses outside the city. The popular, medieval romance of Troilus and Cressida comes from a 12th-century French story, called *Roman de Troie*. Troilus falls in love with Cressida, daughter of Calchas, but she is faithless to him with Diomed. As in the Greek legend of the Iliad, Troilus is killed by Achilles.

Trojan Horse   See Trojan War.

Trojan War (trō'jun)   This war is the subject of the epic poem, The Iliad, attributed to Homer, and the events are supposed to have taken place about 1200 B.C. The war was waged by a confederation of Greeks who came against the Trojans and their allies from Greece, in consequence of the abduction of the Greek beauty Helen*, wife of Menelaus* of Sparta, by Paris*, the son of King Priam* of Troy (see Apple of Discord). The Greeks, led by King Agamemnon* of Mycenae, besieged the city for more than ten years, and won at last by deceit. Pretending to abandon their camp, they left a large wooden horse outside the gates of Troy, in which warriors were hidden. The Trojans, heedless of the warnings of the prophetess Cassandra* and the priest Laocoön*, carried the horse into the city, as an offering to the goddess Athena*. The hidden warriors left the horse in the dark of night, opened the gates of Troy and admitted the Greek army, which sacked the city. The last year of the siege is the subject of Homer's Iliad. The burning of Troy and the flight of Aeneas* is told by the Roman poet Virgil (1st century B.C.) in the Aeneid. The story of the siege of Troy has historical basis, but its exact date is not established. Scene: *The Trojan Horse and the Fall of Troy*, on a Limoges Enamel, by the French Master of the Aeneid, Metropolitan, New York.

Trojan Women   A tragedy of this name was written by the Greek dramatic poet Euripides, about 415 B.C. It is concerned with a day after the end of the Trojan war*, and powerfully depicts the emptiness of war for victor as well as vanquished. Painting: *The Trojan Women Setting Fire to their Fleet*, Claude Lorrain, Metropolitan, New York.

True Cross   See St. Helena. Painting: *The Finding of the True Cross*, Sebastiano Ricci, National Gallery, Washington.

Trumpet   In Greek mythology, a trumpet is sometimes seen with the muse Clio*, as the muse of history and the proclaimer of fame.

Tub Holding Children   Seen with St. Nicholas*, who saved children from pickling. See also Diogenes.

Tunny Fish   In Greek mythology, an attribute of the god Poseiden*, king of the sea.

Turtle Dove   In Christian iconography, an emblem of purity, and a sign of mourning.

Tusks   In Classical mythology, tusks are seen on the face of the Etruscan Charon*, the ferryman of dead souls to the underworld.

Tyche (tī′kē) (Ro. Fortuna)   In Greek mythology, the goddess of fortune. She ruled over prosperity and good luck; on some, she heaped gifts from a horn of plenty (cornucopia), others she deprived of all they had; her overwhelming aspect was her uncertainty. Like Fortuna*, she is shown, in art, with the cornucopia of plenty and the wheel of fortune. Roman head (A.D. 2nd century); Tyche (or Fortuna), copy of Greek original (4th century B.C.), Metropolitan, New York

Tyndareus   See Leda.

St. Ulrich of Augsburg (890-973)   Ulrich was bishop of Augsburg for fifty years, and was the first saint to be canonized by the decree of a pope, John XV. He is known as the fish-bishop of Augsburg, because one day he was supping with Bishop Wolfgang, and time passed without their noticing that it was already Friday. A messenger appeared from the emperor, and stared aghast at the goose on their table on a fast day. Ulrich cut off a drumstick, and gave it to the messenger as evidence. The latter hastened back to the emperor to explain what he had found St. Ulrich indulging in. He put his hand into his bag to illustrate his point and drew out—a fish! Feast day: July 4.

Ulysses (ū-lis′ēz) (Grk. Odysseus)   In Classical mythology, the king of Ithaca, a small, rocky island of Greece. He was one of the leading chieftains of the Greeks in the epic works of Homer, and the hero of the Odyssey*. Ulysses is represented by Homer as eloquent and full of artifice. He is supposed to have suggested the use of the Trojan Horse* (see Odysseus, Odyssey).

Unicorn (u′ni-korn)   In the Old Testament, the unicorn is a fabulous, wild animal, difficult to catch and domesticate. In medieval times, it is a mythical animal, represented as having the legs of a buck, the tail of a lion, the head and body of a horse, and a single horn set in the middle of its forehead, white at the base, black in the middle, and red at the tip. The body is white, the head sometimes red, the eyes blue. Legend recounts it could only be caught if a young virgin was placed near its haunts as a lure. Another superstition claimed that the unicorn could detect poisoned liquid by dipping in its horn. The unicorn, in Christian iconography, was a symbol of purity and feminine chastity. In

The Hunt of the Unicorn, 15th century. French or Flemish tapestry. The Metropolitan Museum of Art. The Cloisters Collection. Gift of John D. Rockefeller, Jr.

allegory, it represents the Annunciation*, and the Incarnation* of Christ, born of Virgin Mary*. It is an attribute of the Virgin Mary and of the two St. Justinias*, who under great temptation remained pure. Franco-Flemish tapestries: *Hunt of the Unicorn*, Cloisters, Metropolitan, New York.

Urania (ū-rā'ni-a)   In Greek mythology, one of the nine muses*, daughters of the god Zeus* and Mnemosyne* (memory). She is muse of astronomy and fate, and her emblems are a globe and a compass, sometimes a small staff for use as a compass. Fresco transferred to canvas: *Urania*, Giulio Romano, Metropolitan, New York.

Uranus (u-rā′nus)   In Greek mythology, the personification of heaven. He is the son and husband of Gaea* (earth) who bore him the Titans*, the Cyclops*, and the hundred-armed Aegaeus*. He did not allow his children to see the light of day, and hid them in Tartarus, the lowest region of the underworld. Gaea, enraged, set the Titans against him, and they attacked him, led by Cronus*, the youngest of the twelve, whom Gaea armed with a sickle. Cronus emasculated Uranus in his sleep, and from the drops of blood that fell to the earth from the wound, the Erinyes* (furies) were born; some legends say the Giants* also. The dismembered part fell into the sea and, from the foam it created, the goddess Aphrodite* was born, her name meaning "foam born."

Uriel (ū′ri-el)   In the New Testament, one of the four archangels mentioned by name, with the meaning "the light of God." Uriel, in early Christian tradition, was supposed to have appeared to the disciples at Emmaus (see Jesus Christ—After-Life Events). In art, Uriel sometimes carries a book or a scroll, as an arbiter and interpreter.

St. Ursula ,   According to popular legend, Ursula was a virgin martyr of great beauty, who was slaughtered with her 11,000 handmaidens at Cologne. Whether she came from Cornwall or Brittany, she was sought after by many suitors, among them the son of the king of England, Prince Conon. Ursula told the king's ambassadors that she would marry the prince if she could bring her 11,000 maidens with her, adding that, before marriage, she must have three years in which to visit all the shrines of Christian saints, accompanied by her maidens. Further, she insisted that Prince Conon and all his court should become Christians. Prince Conon was so impressed with her demands, he accompanied her on her pilgrimage to Rome. Passing through Cologne on the return journey, they were all slain by Huns who were besieging the city. Ursula is shown in art wearing a crown, holding a pilgrim's staff, from which flows a white banner with a red cross, or with an arrow. Often her many attendants surround her. Painting: *St. Ursula with Angels*, Benozzo Gozzoli, National Gallery, Washington; painting: *St. Ursula with her Maidens*, 15th-century Venetian, Metropolitan, New York.

Saint Ursula with Angels and Donor. Benozzo Gozzoli. National Gallery of Art.

Veil   In Christian iconography, the head of Christ depicted on a veil is an attribute of St. Veronica*, who is said to have dried the face of Jesus on her handkerchief, as he was carrying his cross to Calvary*. The imprint of his face remained miraculously on it. Painting: *The Veil of Veronica*, Dominico Fetti, National Gallery, Washington.

Venus (vē'nus)   In Roman mythology, a goddess of love and grace. Originally a Latin goddess of spring, flower gardens, and vines, she became identified with the Greek goddess Aphrodite*, about 200 B.C. In Rome, as the mythical mother of Aeneas*, she was thought of as the mother of the Romans. In medieval times, she was associated with earthly rather than with spiritual love. A very popular figure in art since Aphrodite was first conceived, she is usually represented nude, often in the company of the Roman god of war Mars*, and their son Cupid*, or Amor. Painting: *Venus with a Lute Player*, Titian, Metropolitan, New York; Painting: *Venus*, Bernardino Luini, National Gallery, Washington. (See Aphrodite.)

Vergil   See Virgil.

St. Veronica (ver-on'ika)   According to apocryphal legend, a pious woman handed her handkerchief to Jesus on his way to Calvary* (Golgotha)* so that he might wipe the perspiration from his brow. He returned it to her, and it was found to bear the imprint of his image, *vera icon*, (true likeness). The woman became St. Veronica. The relic is preserved at St. Peter's in Rome. In art, she is shown with the "veil of St. Veronica," on which is seen the image of Christ, wearing a crown of thorns. She appears often in pictures of Calvary (see Jesus Christ—Life Events).

Saint Veronica. Hans Memling. National Gallery of Art.

Painting on a gold chalice: *St. Veronica*, Hans Memling, National Gallery, Washington.

Vertumnus (ver-tum'nus)   An Italian god of fruits, who presided over the changing seasons, and especially over gardens and orchards. He had the power to change himself into many forms, and, after trying several of these, he finally won the hand of the goddess Pomona* by appearing to her as a glowing youth. In art, he was generally represented as a gardener, bearing fruits and carrying a pruning knife.

Vesta (ves'ta)   In Roman mythology, the goddess of the hearth and its fire, identified with the Greek Hestia*. She was worshipped at Rome in a round temple, not as a statue but as eternal fire. This fire was said to have been brought to Rome by Aeneas* from Troy. It was the duty of the Vestal Virgins*, her priestesses, to keep the fire alight. Vesta was also the goddess worshipped at the end of every sacrificial fire. In later times, she was represented in art, like the Greek Hestia, completely clothed and veiled, with cup, torch, scepter, and Palladium*, the sacred statue from Troy, as her attributes. (See Hestia.)

Vestal Virgins   In ancient Rome, small girls were consecrated to Vesta*, and to the service of watching her eternal fire on the altar of her temple. Their number at first was two, but increased later to six. They entered the service between six and ten years of age, and remained in it for thirty more years. Their persons were inviolable, and any offense against them was punished by death. In the event of their losing their virginity, they were buried alive. Rhea Silvia, the mother of Romulus and Remus, was violated by the god Mars*, and consequently put to death. Claudia Quinta, accused of breaking her vows, proved her innocence by freeing a boat from the mud, which was carrying a statue of the goddess Cybele*. The Vestals were dressed entirely in white, with a coronet-shaped headdress. Laurel was consecrated to them. Painting: *Claudia Quinta*, Nerrocci de Landi, National Gallery, Washington.

Vices   See Seven Deadly Sins.

Victoria   In Roman mythology, the goddess of victory, comparable to the Greek Nike*. She was the goddess of the Roman legions and emperors.

Victory Statue on the Hand   In Greek representation, the statue of Nike*, the goddess of victory, is often carried on the hand of the god Zeus* or the goddess Athena*.

St. Vincent of Saragossa   The deacon, Vincent of Saragossa, Spain, was martyred during the persecution of the emperor Diocletian*, and was put to death at Valencia, in 304. Legend reports that he was cruelly tortured by a proconsul named Dacian, trying to shake his faith. When this was unsuccessful, Dacian tried to undermine him with luxury, and prepared him a fine bed of goose feathers. Vincent lay down upon the bed and, as he prayed to God, he died. Dacian had the body thrown out of the city, but a raven protected it from scavengers. The body was next thrown into the sea with a millstone around Vincent's neck, but the body was washed to shore into a tomb of sand, hollowed out by waves. Later his body was found and buried in Valencia. In art, Vincent is shown as a handsome, young man dressed as a deacon, carrying the palm of martyrdom. His attributes are two crows, said to have accompanied the relics to Lisbon, where they now lie. In another legend, Vincent is said to have been roasted on a grill, like St. Lawrence*, so he is also shown with a grill, as well as with a millstone and a scourge, or whip, all references to his martyrdom. Feast day: January 22. Painting: *St. Vincent*, Frei Carlos, Metropolitan, New York.

St. Vincent De Paul (1576-1660)   A French priest of peasant background, who found himself serving as a chaplain among galley slaves. It altered his whole ouutlook, and from then on he devoted his life to the poor. He established the first organized charity in France to work in rural areas; he initiated the idea of a foundling hospital, and established the Sisters of Charity, with St. Louise da Marillac, to work with the poor in urban areas. A sensitive and inspired man, his influence on Protestants and Catholics alike was enormous. Feast day: July 19.

St. Vincent Ferrer (1350-1419)   Vincent Ferrer had an English father and a Spanish mother. He joined the Dominican friars at the age of seventeen, and soon became known as a powerful preacher, travelling through Europe and converting thousands, including Jews and Moslems. He lived a severe, ascetic life, which his followers imitated, and as he moved from place to place, penitents followed him. Soon many miracles were attributed to him, elaborated upon by his biographers. He died while preaching in Brittany. Feast day: April 5.

Vine and Vine Leaves   In Greek mythology, the vine is sacred to Dionysus*, as god of wine and fertility, as it is, also, to his Roman counterpart, Bacchus. Melpomene*, the tragic muse, who is connected with Dionysus, as god of the drama, wears vine leaves. In Christian iconography, the vine is a symbol of Christ as the "true vine." It may refer to the Christian church, where God is the keeper of the vineyard.

Virgil or Vergil (ver′jil)   The great Roman, epic poet (1st century B.C.). He was a scholar of Latin and Greek poets, and wrote in the tradition of the masters. His most famous works are the Eclogues, poems of pastoral scenes, the Georgics, also celebrating pastoral life, and finally his greatest work, The Aeneid*. This describes the wandering of Aeneas* after the end of the Trojan war*, from Troy to Italy, where he founded the colony the Romans claimed for their origin.

Virgin Birth   In Roman Catholic and Orthodox doctrine, the belief that Christ, being conceived of the Holy Ghost*, his mother Mary* remained virgin, before, during, and after his birth.

Virgin Mary   See Mary the Virgin.

Virtues   The seven virtues shown in Christian art are: faith, hope, charity, prudence, justice, fortitude, and temperance, always represented as women. The first three are called theological virtues; the last four are derived from Plato's cardinal virtues. Religious or historic male personages are associated with them. They are shown as follows:

Hope—with wings, raising her hands to heaven; at her feet is St. James the Great*. Her attribute is an anchor.

Charity—surrounded by children, she holds flames and a heart; at her feet is St. John the Evangelist*.

Faith—with a chalice or cross; at her feet is St. Peter*.

Prudence—she often has two heads and holds a mirror or a serpent; at her feet is Solon*.

Justice—holds scales and a sword, a shield and cross; at her feet is the emperor Trajan.

Fortitude—carries either a sword, club shield, globe, lion's skin, or column, this last in allusion to Samson's destruction of the Philistine temple; at her feet is Samson.

Temperance—holds a sword or two vases; at her feet is Scipio Africanus.

In the Renaissance, many allegorical virtues were added to these seven, such as wisdom, history, truth religion, liberality, strength, usually shown as majestic women, with appropriate attributes. Painting: *The Virtues*, Francesco Pesellino, Nelson Art Gallery, Kansas City, Missouri.

Allegory of Virtue and Vice or The Choice of Hercules. Paolo Veronese. Courtesy of the Frick Collection.

Visitation, the   Title given, in theology, to the visit of the Virgin Mary* to her kinswoman Elisabeth*, before the birth of their sons John the Baptist* and Jesus* (Luke 1:39-40). See Virgin Mary—Representations.

Vulcan (vul'kun)   In Roman mythology, a son of the god and goddess Jupiter* and Juno*. He was the god of fire and the art of smelting, identified with the Greek Hephaestus*. He is also the god who ripens the fruit by his warmth, and is the husband of the goddess Maia, the Italian goddess of spring. Venus* is also regarded as his wife. He is the patron of handicraftsmen. 17th century copy of a painting: *Venus at the Forge of Vulcan*, Breughel, the Elder, Metropolitan, New York. (See Hephaestus.)

Vulture   In Greek mythology, the vulture is sacred to Ares*, as god of war. A vulture is often seen in representations of Prometheus*, eating his liver.

Wafer   In Christian iconography, the wafer is an attribute of St. Barbara* and St. Bonaventura*.

Wallet   In Christian iconography, an attribute of the archangel Raphael*, and St. Roch*, in their role of travellers.

Wand   See Thyrsus.

Wandering Jew   A medieval legend, in which a Jew refused to allow Christ to rest at his door while bearing the cross to Calvary (see Jesus Christ—Life Events—Road to Golgotha). He was condemned, therefore, to wander over the face of the earth until Judgement Day*. Many variations on the story have been told.

Water Thrown on Burning City   In Christian iconography, an attribute of St. Florian*.

St. Wenceslas (907-929)   A Bohemian prince, whose Christian grandfather founded the Bohemian dynasty. His grandmother Ludmilla had great religious and political influence over the boy, until she was murdered by a semi-pagan, rival party of nobles. When Wenceslas took power, he tried to promote Christianity and order, but the opposition, led by his brother Boleslav, resulted in a quarrel between them, in which Wenceslas was killed. He and his grandmother were acclaimed saints, and he is the patron of modern Czechoslovakia. The theme of the Christmas song "Good King Wenceslas" is imaginary. Feast day: September 28.

Whale   In representations of the Old Testament story of Jonah*, the whale is most frequently shown looking like a dolphin. In Christian art, the whale is a symbol of the devil, and his open mouth represents the gates of hell.

Wheat   In Greek mythology, wheat is an attribute of the goddesses Demeter* and Persephone*, and the Roman god Fornax*, as a symbol of productivity. In Christian religion, wheat symbolizes the bread of life, and the Eucharist*.

Wheel   In Classical mythology, the wheel is an attribute of Nemesis* and of the Roman Fortuna*, goddesses who turn the year about and manage chance.

Whip   See Scourge.

St. William of Aquitaine   A soldier of Charlemagne*, who was among those who routed the Saracens from Languedoc. He renounced the world in 808, and died in 812. In art, he is shown as a mailed soldier.

St. William of Norwich   William is said to have been murdered in a wood outside Norwich, at the age of twelve; the local populace claimed it was a ritual murder by Jews. This is the first recorded accusation in the Middle Ages, 1144, of the fanatic belief that Christian children were killed for Jewish ritual purposes. William is shown in art, crowned with thorns, wounded in the side, or holding a hammer and nails, the symbols of Christ's crucifixion*.

Willow Wreath   In Greek mythology, an attribute of Prometheus*, as a symbol of freedom.

Windlass   In Christian iconography, an attribute of St. Erasmus or Elmo*.

Wings   In Classical mythology, wings are worn by Eros* and Cupid*, gods of love, by Iris*, the messenger of the gods, by Nike* and Victoria*, goddesses of victory, by Selene*, the goddess of the moon, Eos* and Aurora*, goddesses of the dawn, Hypnos*, the god of sleep, Tyche* and Fortuna*, goddesses of chance, Hermes* and Mercury*, who wear a winged hat and sandals, as messengers. Wings were used by Daedalus* and Icarus* to escape from the Cretan labyrinth*. The golden-fleeced lamb on which Phrixus* escaped was winged. Pegasus* was a winged horse as was Arion*, owned by Adrastus*. In Christian iconography, wings are a symbol of divine mission, hence emblems of the four Evangelists*, the winged lion of St. Mark*, the winged ox of St. Luke*, the winged face of St. Matthew*, and the winged eagle of

St. John*. (St. Mark is sometimes symbolized as a winged man.) Wings are given to angels*, seraphim* and cherubim*.

St. Winifred   Seventh-century Welsh maiden, who was beheaded by chieftain Caradoc because she refused to marry him, whereupon the earth opened up and swallowed him. A new spring appeared, where Winifred's head fell on the ground, whose waters were healing. In one version of this legend, Winifred's head was restored to her shoulders, and she was brought back to life to live out her days as a nun. She is represented, in art, carrying her head in her hands.

Wisdom   In Christian art, wisdom is sometimes shown as an allegorical figure, characterized as a lady of nobility.

Wise Men   See Magi.

Witch of Endor   See Saul.

Wolf   An attribute of St. Francis of Assisi*, who converted the wolf of Gubbio from a killer into a friend.

Woman Taken in Adultery   See Jesus Christ—Life Events.

Wonders of the World   See Seven Wonders of the World.

Wooden Horse   See Trojan Horse.

Woodpecker   In Roman mythology, an attribute of the god of war Mars*.

Wounds   In Christian representation, wounds on the body of a saint symbolize his martyrdom. Wounds can also signify the wounds of Christ's crucifixion* (see Stigmata).

X A cross which is X-shaped is the cross of St. Andrew*, who is said to have been martyred on such a cross.

X C See Letters.

X P See Letters.

Xanthus and Balius (zan'thus & bā'li-us) In Homeric legend, the two immortal horses given by the god Poseiden* to Peleus*, the father of the hero Achilles*. Achilles took the horses to the Trojan war*, during which time they were endowed with speech by the goddess Hera*. When Achilles loaned the horses to his friend Patroclus*, Patroclus was killed in battle by the Trojan warrior Hector*, and the horses wept.

Xantippe (zan'tip-ē) Wife of the Greek philosoper Socrates*, proverbial for her bad temper.

Xerxes (zerk'sēz) (519-465 B.C.) Persian king, son of Darius the Great, the Ahasuerus of the Old Testament. He invaded Greece by constructing a pontoon bridge across the Hellespont (Dardenelles) from Abydos. The crossing, with his 180,000 men, lasted seven days and nights. As he continued, he cut a canal through the Isthmus of Athos, marched through Thrace and Macedonia, and defeated the Greeks at Thermopylae, in 480 B.C. He then pillaged Athens, but his fleet was destroyed at the great sea battle of Salamis, in the same year. Fearing for his situation at home, Xerxes went back to Persia. His position had been much weakened, he became involved in court intrigues, and was assassinated by the captain of his bodyguard, in 465. He was succeeded by his son Artaxerxes I.

Yahweh (yaw'weh)   The name commonly used for God by the prophets, in the Old Testament. See Jehovah.

Yoke   An attribute of Nemesis, goddess of law and order, as a symbol of control.

Z   The letter Z stands for Zion, the symbolic name for Jerusalem, for the Promised Land, and for heaven.

Zacharius (zak-a-rī'us)   In the New Testament, a priest, married to Elisabeth*, kinswoman of the Virgin Mary*, and father of John the Baptist. While performing his usual duties in the Temple, the aging man had a vision, in which a son was promised to him and his barren wife by the angel Gabriel. When Zacharias was incredulous Gabriel rendered him speechless. Eight days after the child was born, Zacharias went to the Temple with the baby and his family for the circumcision* ceremony. After insisting that the baby should be called John rather than after himself, he suddenly recovered his power of speech (Luke 1:5-25).

Zebedee (zeb'a-dee)   In the New Testament, a fisherman who was the husband of Salome* (Mary Salome*), and the father of the apostles James* and John*.

St. Zeno   Zeno was born in Africa and raised as a fisherman, but he trained early as an orator and became a zealous preacher. In 361, he became bishop of Verona, Italy, which office he kept until his death, in 372. His sermons are the earliest homilies in Latin giving information about Christian worship, and life in the 4th century. Legend recounts that he gave two men three fishes. They stole a fourth but could not cook it because, although in boiling water, it remained alive. In art, he is shown in the vestments of a bishop, with a fish hanging from his crosier (bishop's staff). Feast day: April 11.

Zenobius (zen-ō'bi-us) (1218-1278)   A patron and bishop of the city of Florence, Italy. He was of noble background, and is said to have come to Christianity through the influence of a tutor. The conversion was consecrated when he refused to marry the girl whom his parents had chosen for him, and as soon as he had walked out on her, he was baptized. He then became a priest, and many legends are told about his powers as a healer and his ability to restore the dead to life. Often he is shown, in art, with a dead child or young man in his arms. After his death, he was taken to the cathedral for burial. On the way, his body touched a dead elm tree and the tree burst into leaf. A flowering tree is one of his attributes. Painting: *Three Miracles of St. Zenobius*, Botticelli, Metropolitan, New York.

Zephyrus or Zephir (zef-ir'us or zef'ir)   In Greek mythology, the west wind, identified with the Roman Flavonius. He was the son of Aeolus* and Eos*, and was supposed to be the mildest of the winds. By the Harpy*, Podarge, he was the father of the two wonderful horses, Xanthus* and Balius, which the hero Achilles* took with him to the Trojan war*. When he was spurned by the beautiful youth Hyacinthus, he caused his death by blowing the quoit of his rival, the god Apollo*, against his head. Zephyrus was a messenger of spring, and the lover of the flower goddess Chloris*. In art, he is represented partly clothed, carrying flowers tucked in his robe.

Zeus (zūs)   In Greek mythology, the supreme god, the essence of divine power, identified with the Roman Jupiter*, or Jove. He was the son of the Titans Cronus* and Rhea*, and was hidden by Rhea when he was born, lest his father swallow him, as he had swallowed his brothers and sisters, Hestia*, Demeter*, Hera*, Hades*, and Poseiden*. Rhea presented Cronus with a stone to swallow in place of Zeus, which she had wrapped in swaddling clothes, and took the baby to a cave on Mt. Ida, in Crete, where he was brought up by nymphs, and fed on honey, and the milk of the goat Amalthea*. When Zeus grew to manhood, he obtained a potion from the Titaness Metis*. Disguised as a cupbearer, he gave it to Cronus, who then disgorged the children he had swallowed, as well as the stone, which became the Omphalos* at Delphi*. Zeus then led a successful rebellion, with the help of his brothers and sisters, against Cronus and the Titans*, and when the Cyclops* forged the thunderbolt for him, he hurled them all, except Atlas*, into Tartarus*, the lowest region of the underworld. The universe was then divided between the three brothers;

War against Cronus

Division of universe

359

Zeus took heaven and earth, Poseiden the sea, and Hades the underworld. There was a further battle between the gods and the Giants*, which was won when Zeus, following the advice of an oracle, sent for the aid of the mortal Heracles*, whom Athena* made invulnerable by giving him a magic herb. Zeus married his sister Hera*, who bore him Hephaestus*, Ares*, and Hebe*. He had a series of liaisons with other goddesses, first with Metis* (according to some legends, his first wife). After learning from an Oracle that a son born of this union would overthrow him, Zeus, like his father before him, decided to swallow Metis with the unborn child. Some time later, Zeus suffered from a terrible headache. He summoned his son Hephaestus, who struck his forehead with a double-edged axe. His brow split open and his daughter Athena* sprang forth, fully armed. His next liaisons with Themis*, who bore him the Horae* and the Moerae*; Maia, the mother of Hermes; Eurynome*, who bore him the Graces*; Demeter, mother of Persephone; Mnemosyne*, who bore him the Muses*; and Leto*, the mother of Apollo* and Artemis*. Other of his famous loves were Danae*, Leda*, Alcmene*, Callisto*, Semele*, Thetis*, and Io*. He was also the abductor of Ganymede*, who became his cupbearer. All the loves of Zeus, divine or mortal, were originally rural legends which later became the theme of the mythical stories. He ruled in majesty in his court on Mt. Olympus*, sometimes too harshly, and he was once bound up in a net by the other gods while he was sleeping, and the neried Thetis* had to call Briareus (Aegaeon) to free him. As the father god, he was the symbol of power, rule, law, and enforced morals. In Homeric legend, he weighed the destinies of men on golden scales. He is the destroyer of the wicked (see Deucalian and Pyrrha), the rewarder of the good and the humble (see Philemon and Baucis). Many times he was a mediator (see Heracles, and the Tripod* at Delphi). He was a personification of the powers of nature, his natural attributes being goodness, love, all that is strong, noble, of bodily vigor and valor. He is the giver of victory, the saviour in distress. He announces his counsels to mortals by thunder and lightning, by sky portents, and by birds, especially the eagle. He guards the sanctity of oaths, he is the protector of the household and communal life. The eagle and oak tree were sacred to him. The scepter, lightning, and thunderbolts were his usual attributes. In art he is usually shown as a majestic man with a full beard, the olive wreath of victors on his head. His figure may be draped, partially draped, or nude. Sometimes, like Athena, he bears the goddess of victory on his hand. Bronze statuette: *Zeus*, Roman Imperial period, Metropolitan, New York; marble head: *Zeus*, Greek (5th century B.C.), Museum of Fine Arts, Boston.

War against Giants

Marriage and liaisons

Birth of Athena

Liaisons

Rule and aspects of his power

Zodiac (zō'di-ak)   An attribute, in Christian representation, of Father Time*. It is a round diagram showing the Zodiac signs used in astrology. The Zodiac is an imaginary belt in the heavens, including the paths of the sun and the moon; it is divided into twelve parts, each named for a constellation.

Appendix

Chariots—How Drawn

Cows—usually four, draw the chariot of Selene, the Greek moon goddess.

Dolphins and Tritons*—draw the seashell chariot of Amphitrite and Poseiden, the goddess and god of the sea.

Griffins*—draw the chariot of the Greek goddess Nemesis*.

Hinds—draw the chariot of the Greek goddess Artemis.

Horse-Drawn Chariots—usually a quadriga (four horses).

Achilles* dragged the body of Hector* around the walls of Troy from his chariot.

Eos*, the goddess of dawn (Ro. Aurora), carrying a torch, drives four white horses.

Hades*, the god of the underworld (Ro. Pluto), drives four black horses.

Helius*, the god of the sun (Ro. Sol), drives four white horses. See also Phaëton*.

Hippolytus* drove to his death in his chariot.

Jupiter*, the Roman god, drives four white horses.

Oenomaus* and Pelops* run a chariot race from Olympia to the Isthmus of Corinth.

Lions—draw the chariot of the Phrygian goddess Cybele*.

Man Drawn Chariot—Cleophas* and Biton* draw their mother in a chariot to the temple in Argos.

Panthers—draw the chariot of the god Dionysus*.

Stars—accompany the chariot of Nyx*, goddess of the night.

Winged Serpents—draw the chariot of Medea*, the sorceress.

Winged Serpents—draw the chariot of Triptolemus*, in which the goddess Demeter sent him around the world to spread the arts of agriculture.

Group Combats

Centaurs* and Lapiths* The Centaurs tried to rape the women at the wedding of Pirithous.

Greeks and Amazons* The Amazons attacked the Greeks after Antiope* had been carried off by Theseus*. They fought Heracles* and Theseus*, when they thought their queen, Hippolyta, was in danger. Queen Penthesilea* led her Amazons against the Greeks, in the Trojan war.

Heroes in Single Combat
often shown with spectators looking on

Ajax* and Hector* Fought in single combat, to determine the outcome of the Trojan war.

Diomedes* and Glaucus* fought in single combat, and exchanged armor.

Eteocles* and Polynices* fought in single combat over the throne of Thebes, and killed each other.

Heracles* and Apollo* fought over the Tripod* of Delphi.

Menelaus* and Paris* fought in single combat, to determine the outcome of the Trojan war.

See also the *Twelve Labors of Heracles** for the combats he engages in with lion, boar, bull, etc.

Laurel Daphne* was turned into a laurel tree by her father, the river god Peneus, to save her from the god Apollo.

Myrrh Tree Myrrha* was turned into this twisted tree, to save her from the wrath of her father. Adonis* was born from its trunk, which split open to release him.

Quails The god Zeus transformed himself and Leto* into quails, before seducing her.

Reeds Syrinx* was turned into reeds, to escape from Pan. He cut the reed and made panpipes with them.

Shower of Gold The god Zeus appeared to Danae* in a shower of gold.

Spider Arachne* was turned into a spider by the goddess Athena, for daring to challenge her to a contest of weaving.

Stag Actaeon* was turned into a stag by the goddess Artemis for surprising her in her bathing pool.

Stones Deucalian* and Pyrrha* created a new race of people with stones. The face of Medusa* turned people to stone, when they looked at it.

Swan The god Zeus seduced Leda*, in the form of a swan.

Trees Philemon* and Baucis* were transformed into trees in their old age. Dryope was turned into a poplar tree by the nymph Lotis, because she had picked flowers off the nymph's tree.

Teeth Cadmus* sowed teeth of a dragon in the ground and an army of men sprang up.

Metamorphoses and Acts of Gods

Bears Callisto* was turned into a bear by the goddess Hera, and was placed in the heavens with her son Arcus, by the god Zeus, where they were called the Great and Little Bears.

Bull The god Zeus transformed himself into a bull, so that he might carry off Europa*.

Cow or Heifer Io* was turned into a heifer, either by the goddess Hera or by the god Zeus.

Cuckoo The god Zeus transformed himself into a cuckoo, to win the hand of the goddess Hera.

Fountain Arethusa* was turned into a fountain, to protect her from Alpheus*, by the goddess Artemis.

Murders, Sacrifices and Sudden Violent Deaths

Actaeon was devoured by his own hounds.

Adonis was killed by a wild boar.

Aegeus lept from the Acropolis to his death.

Agamemnon was killed in his bath by his wife Clytemnestra and her lover Aegisthus.

Althea hanged herself for causing the death of her son.

Antigone was buried alive for performing her brother's funeral rites.

Arachne hanged herself after a contest with the goddess Athena.

Astyanax was hurled from the walls of Troy by Neoptolemus at the end of the Trojan war.

365

Atreus was killed by his nephew Aegisthus, who was forced to perform the act by his father Thyestes.

Deianira hanged herself for inadvertently causing the death of her husband Heracles.

Dirce was killed on the horns of a wild bull.

Heracles was burned to death in a poisoned robe.

Iphigenia was sacrificed by her father Agamemnon, to the goddess Artemis.

Laius was killed by his son Oedipus, as a result of a dispute on the road to Thebes.

Laocoön and his sons were killed by an enormous serpent.

Orestes killed his mother Clytemnestra and her lover Aegisthus, to avenge the death of his father Agamemnon.

Pelias was cut up and boiled to death by Medea.

Pleiades killed themselves because they were pursued by Orion.

*See under individual entries.

Supernatural Beings and Monsters

Dog with two heads—*Orthus**

Dog with three heads and a serpent's tail, maybe a mane with serpent heads—*Cerberus**

Dog with nine or more snaky heads—*Hydra**

Eagle with wings for front body, combined with the hindquarters of a lion—*Griffin**

Horse with wings—*Pegasus** (also Arion, the horse of Admetus*)

Lion's body with three heads: one a lion's, breathing fire, one a goat's, and one a serpent's—*Chimaera**

Lion's body with bird wings and a woman's head—*Sphinx**

Man with many arms (100) and hands (50)—*Aegaeon*, also called *Briareus**

Man with three bodies, three heads, and wings—*Geryon**

Man with bull's head—*Minotaur**

Man with dolphin's tail, sometimes the feet of a horse—*Triton**

Man or boy with pointed ears, sometimes goat horns and tail—*Faun**

Man with goat horns and horse's tail—*Satyr**

366

Man with goat horns, beard, goat tail and goat legs—*Pan** or *Faunus**

Man with one eye—*Cyclops* giants*, notably *Polyphemus**

Man with eyes all over his body—*Argus**

Man with two heads back-to-back—*Janus**

Man with three heads, three bodies, sometimes wings—*Geryon**

Man with the body of a horse, from the waist down—*Centaur**

Man with serpent arms and heads around his hips—*Typhon**

Man with serpent's body and tail—*Cecrops**

Man with tusks—Etruscan representation of *Charon**

Woman with bird legs and wings—*Siren**

Woman with cow's head or cow's horns—*Isis**

Woman with dolphin's tail, dog heads around her waist, sometimes twelve arms or feet—*Scylla**

Woman with snaky locks for hair, notably Medusa*, and a girdle of snakes—*Gorgon**

Woman with snaky locks, wings (sometimes dog heads on the body), whip in hand—*Erinye** or *Fury**

Women back-to-back (three of them)—*Hecate**

Women (hags) with one eye and one tooth among them—*The Graeae**